F

FINANCIAL ACCOUNTING
AN IRISH TEXT

Peter J. Clarke

GILL AND MACMILLAN

Published in Ireland by
Gill and Macmillan Ltd
Goldenbridge
Dublin 8
with associated companies in
Auckland, Budapest, Gaborone, Hamburg, Harare, Hong Kong,
Kampala, Kuala Lumpur, Lagos, London, Madras,
Manzini, Melbourne, Mexico City, Nairobi,
New York, Singapore, Sydney, Tokyo, Windhoek
© Peter J. Clarke, 1990
Reprinted 1992
0 7171 1817 7
Print origination by
Seton Music Graphics Ltd, Bantry, Co. Cork
Printed by Colour Books Ltd, Dublin

A catalogue record in available for this book
from the British Library

To Dorothy,
for her understanding and encouragement
and to little Susan and Kevin
who tried to stay quiet
because they wanted to help me with my 'sums'

Contents

Preface

The idea to start this accounting book some years ago was born partly out of the frustration caused by the absence of an Irish-orientated text and partly because available books were either too theoretical or too preoccupied with the 'how' of accounting and not the 'why'.

The book is designed to enable the reader gain a thorough understanding of the important aspects of contemporary financial accounting and the ability to interpret critically what he reads. It is meant primarily for students of introductory financial accounting at third-level institutions in Ireland. However, it is hoped that part of this book may also be appropriate for use on other academic and professional courses and to any individual who wishes to understand the bases on which financial statements are prepared.

The opening chapter sets the framework for financial reporting in Ireland for the 1990s. The basic premise is that accounting should satisfy the information needs of users. However, financial accounting exists within a regulatory environment which includes the effect of Ireland's entry to the European Community, company law changes and the Accounting Standards Board of the accountancy profession. Thereafter the book is divided into three main sections.

The first major section (chapters 2–7) concentrates on the recording and measurement procedures of accounting. This section also provides a discussion on income measurement and asset valuation. The second section (chapters 8–13) deals with financial reporting of limited companies together with some of the more important statements of standard accounting practice (SSAPs), because accounting standards (and company law) now have significant practical effects on published financial statements. It no longer seems possible to cover adequately an introduction to financial accounting without examining this area in some detail. The final section (chapters 14–16) covers the interpretation and analysis of financial statements including different approaches to the valuation of shares.

All chapters contain examples for the reader to work through as he reads the text. There are also end of chapter problems many of which are drawn from professional examinations. Some of these problems are marked (A) in order to indicate that the answer is contained at the end of the book. Answers to the remaining problems are contained in a solutions manual and are indicated (SM). The solutions manual is, however, available only to tutors.

I would like to thank everyone who has made helpful comments and suggestions on the book in draft form. This includes especially the various reviewers and my colleagues in the Department of Accountancy, University College, Dublin who shared their material with me. Therese Dunne provided invaluable assistance with all aspects of the book. I am also grateful to the following professional bodies for permission to use past examination material:

The Institute of Chartered Accountants in Ireland
The Chartered Association of Certified Accountants

I wish to acknowledge the generous financial support received from The Irish Accountancy Educational Trust. However, they are not responsible for any errors or omissions.

Please note that the use of the male annotation throughout this book has been adopted merely for convenience. All references to male persons should be taken to include an equal reference to persons in the female gender.

Finally, and not because it is customary, I thank Dorothy for being herself and little Susan and Kevin whose constant presence reminds me that there are many other things in life than accounting.

Peter J. Clarke
Department of Accountancy
University College, Dublin
Summer 1990

1.

The Purpose and Nature of Accounting

INTRODUCTION

Before we undertake this study it is important to understand what is meant by 'accounting'. Accounting has been defined in many ways during the years but it is now generally recognised among practitioners and educators that the task of accounting is to produce financial information about an economic entity which is considered relevant to different interested parties to allow them assess the performance and financial position of the reporting enterprise. The word 'accounting' describes the subject to be studied. The term 'accountancy' means the work of public practitioners—the accountancy profession.

A number of definitions of accounting are available in the literature. Perhaps the most commonly used definition in these islands is that offered in The Corporate Report, published in 1975, by the Accounting Standards Committee—a committee representing the accountancy profession in the United Kingdom and Ireland. In relation to reporting by companies it stated:

> The fundamental objective of corporate reports is to communicate economic measurements of and information about the resources and performance of the reporting entity useful to those having reasonable rights to such information.

Accounting is, therefore, utilitarian in nature. In other words, the accounting process and ultimately financial statements should help people make economic decisions about a business entity. If accounting is to have any usefulness in the modern world it must be decision-orientated. There are four important questions concerning this definition which need to be asked:

1. Who are the users of accounting information?
2. Are the information needs of managers similar to those of external parties?
3. Who regulates the content and format of financial statements?
4. What desirable qualities should accounting information possess?

USERS OF ACCOUNTING INFORMATION

Users of accounting information may be classified into different 'user groups' and it is the function of the accounting process to satisfy the information needs of such users. The information requirements of each user group can only be identified by undertaking empirical research which would involve asking different users what type of financial information they would like to receive. While this approach is intuitively appealing it is not without its limitations. Since there are different user groups, it is reasonable to assume that each may have information needs. In addition, within each user group there are different levels of sophistication. For example, some shareholders of a company may be highly skilled in interpreting financial statements whereas others may be financially illiterate.

One approach, therefore, to identify the information needs of users is to examine the different decisions made by each user group and to make presumptions about the information needed to make those decisions. However, it is necessary to assume that each decision maker is rational and has sufficient mental ability to process the accounting information.

The different decisions taken by each user group will have an impact on the firm. For example, without shareholders there can be no capital and without employees there can be no workforce. It is now common in the literature of organisation studies to refer to business firms as a coalition of individuals and groups. Coalitions survive by interactive participation and agreement. But each group will always be faced with the alternative to continue as members of the coalition of a particular firm or to seek other opportunities. Thus employees may seek alternative employment and shareholders may seek alternative investment opportunities. These decisions will be made, partly on the basis of accounting information and partly on the basis of non-accounting information. However, this book is concerned only with accounting information. Developing and communicating this information is the role of the business entity's accounting system.

The various user groups and their relationships to each other are highlighted in Exhibit 1.1. In the centre of this diagram are the managers of the business entity. Each user group participates, to some extent, in the enterprise. It is the function of managers to offer inducements to the various groups so that, by participating, the firm can continue and prosper. In addition to each current participant there may be also a potential participant. Thus, the company will have current employees but it may require additional employees in the future.

The main user groups are:

(a) Shareholders—who currently own or are interested in owning shares in a company.

(b) Creditors—who currently provide or are interested in providing finance to the company either by way of supplying goods and services on credit or loans.

(c) Employees (including trade union representatives)—who currently work or may work for the company.

(d) Customers—who currently purchase or may purchase goods and services from the company.

(e) Competitors—who compete with the company in the consumer market.

(f) Government—which assesses taxes and monitors compliance with various regulations.

(g) Managers—who plan and control the activities of the firm.

Exhibit 1.1

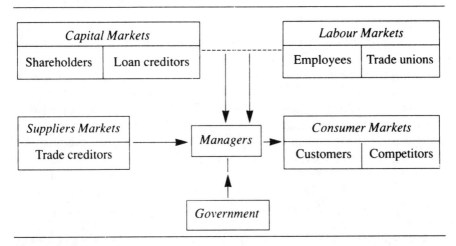

Shareholders

Shareholders, either actual or potential, are primarily interested in the performance of the company and how that performance impacts on their investment. Specifically, they will be interested in the financial benefit that accrues to them and the financial benefit that they perceive will occur in the future.

Decisions to buy and sell shares by shareholders are being taken continuously, and these decisions involve the consideration of many factors and much information. Accounting information is but one kind of information yet it is often basic to this process of evaluation, as shareholders and potential investors will be continuously examining the investment opportunities open to them and reviewing their existing investments.

In evaluating investment opportunities shareholders will be interested in the earnings stream of the company and the portion paid out to them by way of dividend. In addition, they will be concerned with the current and future market value of their shares in the company. They will also be interested in the performance of other companies who are offering greater or lesser returns. Based on past performance shareholders may make estimates of likely future profits of the company and the dividends that can be paid out of such profits. Information on the entity's future cash inflows and future cash payments may also be relevant to shareholders, current or potential. Without cash a company cannot survive in the long term—no matter how skilled the managers and employees are. At the end of the day cash determines a company's fate; cash is the lifeblood of any business entity. In addition, shareholders may be interested in knowing the amount of cash they would receive if the company was dissolved since this provides some indication of the overall security of their investment.

Creditors

Creditors are those individuals or institutions who provide finance to the company. Creditors are divided into those who sell goods and services to the company (trade creditors) and those who provide finance by way of cash loans (loan creditors). Trade creditors are interested in the ability of the company to discharge the amount owing without delay. They do not normally earn interest on the credit advanced to the company and there is no guarantee that they will receive payment. Consequently trade creditors will be interested in the liquidity of the company. Liquidity is evidenced by the excess of cash, or near-cash assets, e.g. debtors, bank deposits, set against the immediate liabilities. They will also be interested in the time taken by the company to pay its bills and whether the credit period is static, increasing or decreasing.

Loan creditors who provide cash to the company, either by way of loan or bank overdraft, require interest and ultimate repayment. Their concern is thus twofold. Firstly, whether the interest payments can be made and secondly, whether the loan can be repaid on maturity. As regards interest payments and eventual repayment of loan, creditors will be concerned with the company's profitability and cash flow, both in the short and in the long term and whether there are any other loans due to be repaid. Profitability will determine the ability of the company to repay the debt when it falls due, either out of the surplus cash flows generated by successful operations, or the company's capacity to borrow new cash funds.

Employees

In recent years there is evidence of an increasing concern by employees that they should be aware of financial data concerning, not only their company, but also other companies. It is natural that employees, and their trade union representatives, should want information about the cost structures, wage relativities and profitability of their companies, together with comparative information about other companies in the same and other industries. This information is, for example, essential to wage negotiation. However, employees are concerned with matters other than monetary gain. They are interested in challenge, reward and recognition. They are also interested in job security and so they would be interested in knowing management plans for the future and the general financial prospects of the company.

Customers

Customers may be interested in the analysis and interpretation of the accounting data produced by companies from whom they are intending to purchase goods or services. Usually their interest will be to establish the ability of the company to supply the goods or services which they are considering and to order the right quality and quantity. They will naturally be anxious to avoid the possibility of selecting a company which either cannot command the resources necessary to complete the order, or whose financial position is such that it will not survive the time necessary to complete the order. It is not always satisfactory to accept the lowest price offered for the goods or services being demanded, because there will be times when a company will quote too low a price in its anxiety to obtain the order. This is neither in the interest of the company nor the potential customer if it creates conditions in which the company will fail. In addition, the lowest price may indicate inferior goods. There will also be times when the potential customer will analyse the accounting data of possible suppliers to establish whether they are likely to overcharge for the goods or services. 'Overcharging' here means that the supplier earns an abnormally high return on its assets employed in providing the goods or services.

It must be acknowledged that many customers will not be interested in looking at a company's financial statements before buying goods. Each week we buy our groceries from the local supermarket and petrol from the local garage—all without reference to financial statements. This fact emphasises the point that within each user group there are different sub-groups, with different levels of sophistication. Although the decision is essentially the same—to buy or not to buy—the monetary amounts involved in purchasing decisions may vary enormously. Thus, the decision to place a contract to build a hospital will be based, partially, on accounting information, whereas the decision to contract for house painting may not.

Competitors

Unless the company is in a monopoly situation it will compete with other companies in the market. Competitors will be interested in ascertaining the profitability, cost structure and capacity utilisation of other companies. Such information could provide clues regarding future plans for expansion as well as price changes. Indeed, it was this dimension that caused some opposition to the provisions of the Companies (Amendment) Act, 1986 which required, inter alia, the publication of financial statements by companies. So sensitive is such information that companies deliberately circumvent the disclosure requirements. One such device is to trade as an unlimited company rather than a limited company. Also Irish subsidiaries of multinational companies do not have to comply with publication requirements provided that the parent company gives certain guarantees—in relation to employees' PRSI contributions, for example.

Government

The use and interpretation of accounting information is necessary for government departments, including local authorities, in order to implement and monitor State policy. Government policy ranges over areas such as taxation to the financial position of insurance companies. There are many other examples, such as, under Irish law, details of any merger or takeover must be notified to the Minister for Industry and Commerce for approval if the assets of each of the companies involved are worth over £5 million, or if the turnover of each of the companies involved is more than £10 million a year. In all these matters, interpretation of accounting information is of major importance.

Another present-day concern of the State is the planning and regulation of the economy. For this purpose there is a large demand by the State for information about existing and proposed activities of companies, in order that forecasts of national economic behaviour can be made and monitored. Tax policy is a major area which is, in turn, dependant on overall corporate profitability, both current and future. The State is also a major customer for goods and services produced in the private sector. Whilst in many cases the price the State pays is determined in normal markets, in other cases this is not so. In these latter cases the analysis and interpretation of companies' accounting data will almost inevitably determine the price for government contracts.

Managers

Managers will analyse and interpret accounting data for the purpose of planning and controlling the performance of the company. The use of accounting data by managers to plan and control the activities of a business comprises the area of Management or Managerial Accounting. The information required for such purposes is, of necessity, very detailed and specific. Information will be reported to managers more frequently and regularly than to any of the other user groups. For example, shareholders may receive information on the profit performance of the company on an annual basis. However, managers would require such information far more frequently.

FINANCIAL AND MANAGEMENT ACCOUNTING

For teaching purposes accounting is usually divided into two parts, namely, financial and management accounting. Financial accounting records the transactions of a business entity and summarises them in accordance with established concepts, accounting standards and company law. For a company the end result is a profit and loss account, balance sheet and a statement of source and application of funds. The company's auditors report on these financial statements and express their opinion that the accounts show (or do not show) a true and fair view. Management accounting on the other hand aims to help managers to plan and control the business.

While this distinction is convenient from a teaching point of view it should not be viewed as dividing the two areas of study into watertight compartments. In many ways it would be preferable if the phrases 'internal' and 'external' accounting were used since management accounting has financial implications and managers have more than a passing interest in financial accounting. The distinction is based mainly on the user groups of accounting information. The first six of the above user groups are mainly *external* to the organisation, in the sense that they take no active part in planning and controlling the enterprise. Conversely, the final user group mentioned above, namely managers, are *internal* to the organisation in the sense that they are responsible for the day-to-day functioning of the company. Not surprisingly, managers will have different information needs from, say, creditors. The information needed by managers is provided by the management accountant and will help managers make decisions such as:

—What product, if any, should be deleted from the product line?
—How does actual performance compare with budget?
—At what level of activity will our costs equal revenues?
—What is the best mix of products to produce?

However, it is important to realise that both financial and management accounting information is derived from the same, single accounting system. Essentially it is the way that the accounting information is presented that distinguishes financial from management accounting. The other major differences between financial and management accounting are summarised in Exhibit 1.2.

THE REGULATORY ENVIRONMENT OF FINANCIAL STATEMENTS

Accounting information can be looked at from a demand/supply perspective as illustrated in Exhibit 1.3. User groups require financial information about a business entity. They represent the *demand* for accounting information; the reporting company represents the source or *supply* of accounting information.

Exhibit 1.2

	Financial	*Management*
Primary users	External	Internal

Type of information	Aggregate/Summarised e.g.
	  Balance sheet
	  Profit and loss
		Very detailed and specific

Frequency and timespan	Usually one year	As required by managers
Time focus	Past orientation (historical)	Future orientation (projections)
Governed by	Companies Acts and accounting standards set by the accountancy profession in Ireland and UK	As required by managers

Exhibit 1.3

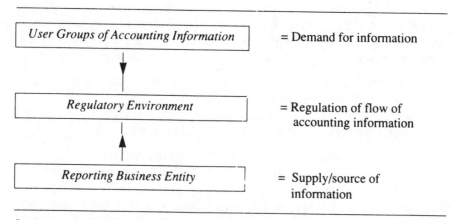

User Groups of Accounting Information	= Demand for information
Regulatory Environment	= Regulation of flow of accounting information
Reporting Business Entity	= Supply/source of information

In an environment where accounting information is unregulated and not subject to the rules of disclosure it is unlikely that the information a company would be willing to supply would satisfy the demand, i.e. user needs. In an attempt to resolve this issue there is an intermediate stage between supply and demand, referred to as the regulatory environment, which influences the content and format of published financial statements. It would be comforting to think that the regulatory agencies would carry out extensive research on the information needs of users and then have sufficient powers to compel companies to disclose such information. However, there are potential problems with this approach. Firstly, the information needs are likely to change over time as the users' understanding of accounting may change, perhaps as a result of the introduction of new concepts in published financial statements. Secondly, in the previous discussion on the information needs of users it was suggested that this information was essentially related to the future, expected performance of the business. Managers do prepare forecasts but these forecasts are subjective, based on numerous assumptions and not easily verified. They can be optimistic, pessimistic, relatively accurate or completely inaccurate. As a result of this, it is difficult to accept that such forecast information provides a useful service to user groups and, indeed, it may be detrimental to the company itself, in that important information is available to competitors.

The financial information that is routinely provided in the financial statements is said to be 'historic'. This is because the financial information reveals the past profit performance (the profit and loss account) and current financial position (balance sheet). The advantage of such information is that it is less subjective than financial forecasts, and also, such information is verifiable. Indeed, the financial statements are audited by a firm of professional accountants who express an opinion that the financial statements show a true and fair view of the profit performance and financial position of the company. Thus users of financial statements must be conscious of the fact that they use historic data in order to make predictions about the future. The content and format of these historic financial statements are subject to a number of influences, the main sources of which are:

(a) Companies Acts and directives of the European Community.

(b) Statements of standard accounting practice (SSAPs) issued by the accountancy profession in Ireland and the UK.

(c) Stock Exchange rules for listed companies.

Companies Acts and EC directives
Company law in Ireland was consolidated by the Companies Act, 1963. There has, however, been important amending legislation in 1983 and 1986 which deals with the different aspects of company law, some of which resulted from directives of the European Community (EC).

The Companies Act, 1963 in Ireland requires a company, once in every calendar year, to present to its members an audited profit and loss account and a balance sheet. These documents are required to be drawn up to give a *true* and *fair* view of the profit or loss for the financial year and the state of affairs at the end of the financial year. The expression 'true and fair' was, until recently, peculiar to Ireland and the UK. It has now been accepted by the European Community. Auditors, who use this phrase when expressing an opinion on a company's financial statements, do not mean that they are guaranteeing that the financial statements are correct. Rather, the auditor is implying that in his *opinion* the financial statements have been drawn up honestly so as to give a balanced view of the performance and position of the company. This balanced view is necessary, bearing in mind that there are several disparate groups or parties interested in a company's performance.

At time of writing the new Companies Bill (which is only a proposal since it has not been enacted in legislation) has been hailed as one of the most important and relevant pieces of commercial legislation in the history of the State. The general purpose of the bill is to strengthen existing provisions of the Companies Act, 1963 and to meet the new circumstances faced by businesses today.

The bill proposes measures to eliminate, deter or penalise specified abuses and malpractices in the management and direction of companies. For example, the bill introduces the concept of 'reckless trading' and covers those cases where directors have operated a company in a way which, while not actually fraudulent, is completely negligent of the interests of its share-holders and of those who have lent money to the company. The application of this concept, if enacted, will put extra demands on the financial statements of companies. In particular, it will ensure that the records of the company have been properly kept and that the directors are aware of the company's precarious financial position.

When Ireland joined the European Community in 1973, a new dimension was added to the needs of financial reporting for Irish companies. Ireland had to conform to a whole series of directives drafted by the European Commission and, where required, incorporate the provisions in national legislation by a stated date. For example, the Companies (Amendment)Act, 1986 implements the fourth EC Council Directive on company law. This act applies to all financial statements of companies for accounting periods commencing after 31 December 1986. The act requires all limited companies incorporated in the Republic of Ireland to publish their financial statements by filing them with the Registrar of Companies in Dublin Castle. Some relief from disclosure is provided to small and medium-sized companies. In addition, prescribed formats for the financial statements are set out. It is likely that more EC Council directives will be issued in future years and member states will be expected to comply with these. Indeed, recent statements coming from the EC Commission indicates a perceived need for further European harmonisation in the area of financial statements.

Statements of standard accounting practice (SSAPs)

The importance of the work of the accountancy profession is, perhaps, that it has been able to respond to the requirements of changing business practices, structures and to the demands of a sophisticated investing community more speedily and with greater flexibility than company legislation. To date, the Accounting Standards Committee (ASC), which was established in 1970 by the various professional accountancy bodies in these islands, has issued in excess of twenty statements of standard accounting practice (SSAPs) with which companies are expected to comply. These accounting standards relate not only to which accounting information must be disclosed but also to how particular transactions must be recorded and measured. For example, until recently a reporting entity had discretion on how to report its expenditure on research. Some companies decided to write-off such expenditure immediately against profits in the accounting period in which the expenditure was incurred. Other companies, notably Rolls Royce, took a less conservative view and considered such expenditure to be in the nature of an investment. Obviously, the reported profits would be affected by either accounting treatment. With the introduction of SSAP 13, such discretion has largely been eliminated, since the standard requires that all research expenditure must be accounted for in a specific way in the financial statements.

Moreover, accounting standards require information to be produced in a company's financial statements over and above the minimum requirements of company law. For example, companies with annual sales of £25,000 must produce a statement of source and application of funds. Such a statement shows the manner in which the operations of a company have been financed and in which its financial resources have been used. This statement is a requirement of the accountancy profession through the ASC but it is not a legal requirement. Likewise a company's earning per share (EPS) must be shown in accordance with good accounting practice but such a disclosure is not required by company law.

Stock Exchange rules

The Stock Exchange places a continuing obligation on companies to report any information necessary to enable holders of the company's listed securities and the public to appraise the position of the company and to avoid the establishment of a false market in its quoted shares. For example, a company must make a public announcement at any time during the financial year when the directors are aware of information that is not public knowledge and which may lead to a substantial movement in the price of its shares. Thus, when the directors are aware of the profit for the year, but the accounts have not been audited, then a preliminary announcement of the profit for the year must be made, stating that it is subject to audit. Annual accounts must be prepared and issued within six months of the end of the financial period to which they relate. The listing agreement requires that these accounts disclose information additional to that required by company law and the accountancy profession. Examples of this additional information are:

(*a*) The name of the principal country in which each subsidiary operates.

(*b*) An analysis of bank and other loans which are repayable in one year or less; between one and two years; between two years and five and in five years or more.

(*c*) Any change in directors' interest in shares between the year end and a date not more than one month prior to the date of the notice of the annual general meeting.

(*d*) They are also required to provide a geographical analysis of profits.

In addition to preparing annual accounts quoted companies are required to prepare a half-yearly report in the form of an abbreviated profit and loss account. These reports must be sent to shareholders or inserted as a paid advertisement in two leading daily newspapers. There are many other requirements imposed on quoted companies in relation to their financial affairs. For example, they must make available for inspection copies of all directors' service contracts of more than one year's duration.

It is clear that the financial reporting environment for companies is heavily regulated but for some companies financial reporting is no longer considered to be purely a regulatory chore. While financial reporting is always governed by regulations, the annual published financial statements provide excellent opportunities for promoting and enhancing the company's image. Companies are now entering their financial statements for Published Accounts Awards, such as that organised annually by the Leinster Society of Chartered Accountants. This award provides for the recognition of companies whose published accounts are meritorious in the opinion of the judging panel and is designed to raise the standard of corporate financial reporting in this country. Previous winners of this award include the Jefferson Smurfit Group and Telecom Eireann, among others. Moreover, there is a special section and award for the published accounts of charities. Charities in Ireland are under no legal obligation to publish their accounts. However, a good annual report can do a very great deal to help the charity, especially in terms of credibility and the cause it exists to promote.

DESIRABLE QUALITIES OF ACCOUNTING INFORMATION

In order for accounting information to influence the decisions of users it must possess certain attributes or desirable qualities. In particular the information must be relevant, understandable, timely, reliable and consistent.

(*a*) *Relevance*. This is determined by the decision being made. Thus, information may be relevant to one particular decision but not to another. Likewise, information may be relevant to one user group but not to another. Relevance is ultimately determined by the user but unfortunately user needs have not, as yet, been empirically determined. As a result it is highly probable that specific user needs are not adequately catered for by the single set of financial statements produced by companies. This in turn raises the interesting issue of how and by whom the content of financial statements should be regulated.

(b) Understandable. If financial statements are not understood by users then they are of little practical use. It is important to present accounting information in such a way that it would be comprehensible to the less informed user of accounts without omitting information which would be of value to the informed user.

(c) Timely. To be useful financial statements should be up to date and published reasonably soon after the end of the period to which they relate to, on the grounds that up-to-date information is of more value to users than stale data.

(d) Reliable. If accounting information is not reliable then misinformed and biased decisions will inevitably result. The reliability of information is enhanced if it is independently verified. Consequently, auditors will check various transactions undertaken by the firm during the accounting period and verify certain items at the end of the year, e.g. cash and stock verification. If the audit is satisfactorily completed, then the auditors will express an opinion on the financial statements. In the majority of cases the auditors will indicate that the financial information gives a true and fair view of the profit (loss) performance and the financial position at the end of the year.

(e) Consistency of preparation. This characteristic has two dimensions, namely the comparability of a company's performance over time and the comparability of the accounts between business entities. If accounting reports are not prepared on a consistent basis, then meaningful comparisons between performance in different time periods and the performances between companies are virtually impossible. The publication of statements of standard accounting practice (SSAPs), with which companies must comply, have helped in this regard, especially when there is a change in accounting methods. In such case, a company will make a note of its results using the new and old accounting methods.

TYPES OF BUSINESS ORGANISATION

In the above discussion we have mentioned the various user groups of financial statements produced by business entities. We now turn our attention to the business entity. Business organisations may take on different forms. In Ireland three types of business structure dominate the private sector, namely, sole traders, partnerships and limited companies.

The *sole trader* is the dominant form of business organisation in Ireland. This type of organisation refers to a business owned by one person. Exact numbers are not available but most small shopkeepers, tradesmen and farmers operate this form of business organisation. Usually the owner is also the manager and such organisations tend to be rather small. The sole trader is totally independent in that he makes all the important decisions by himself.

Sole traders will maintain some financial records. They are obliged, in the majority of cases, to register for value added tax (VAT). Also if they have employees they are required to register for Pay As You Earn (PAYE) purposes. They will be assessed to income tax on the basis of profits earned during the accounting period which is normally a twelve-month period. The lowest rate of income tax is currently 30 per cent and the highest rate is 53 per cent. However, trading profits of limited companies are liable to a flat rate of 40 per cent. So, from a taxation point of view, it may or may not be tax efficient to operate as a sole trader.

There are a number of disadvantages associated with a sole trader type business structure. In the case of the owner's absence or illness some loss of business can and does occur. Also, sole traders may find difficulty in raising finance other than from their own funds, those of relatives and personal borrowing powers. Indeed, their inability to attract external funds is said to be a major inhibiting factor in setting up small businesses in Ireland.

An alternative business structure is that of a *partnership*, which is similar in many respects to that of a sole trader. A partnership is legally defined as an association of persons carrying on a business in common with a view to profit. This form of business structure is common among accountants, solicitors and doctors. Partnerships may be formed by verbal agreement, but it is much more advisable to draft a partnership deed which would include such matters as to how profits are to be shared and the procedures for admitting partners and retirement. For example, without a partnership agreement no new partner can be introduced without the unanimous agreement of all existing partners.

The third form of business structure is that of a *limited liability company* which is a business organisation created by law. Owners (i.e. shareholders) who wish to incorporate their business must register their company with the Registrar of Companies in Dublin Castle, in addition to filing certain documents. Upon incorporation a company becomes a legal entity separate from its owners. However, in contrast with sole traders and partnerships, the shareholders of a limited company have limited liability. This means that the liability of shareholders is limited to the amount they have agreed to pay for their shares. If the shares are fully paid, shareholders cannot be made additionally liable. In other words, if a company is experiencing financial difficulties, those who have lent money to the company can only look to the company's assets for repayment of their claims. Obviously, if the company's assets are negligible very little will be repaid to those who advanced funds to the company. It is not surprising to note that the Companies (Amendment)

Act, 1986 now imposes an obligation on virtually all limited companies in this country to file financial statements in the Companies Office which are available for inspection by the public.

Question 1. 1(A)

(*a*) How could traditional accounting reports be made more useful to those outside the business itself?

(*b*) State *three* classes of people, other than managers and owners, who are likely to need to use financial accounting information. Discuss whether you think their requirements are compatible.

(The Chartered Association of Certified Accountants)

Question 1.2 (SM)

Company financial statements, including profit and loss accounts, balance sheets and statements of source and application of funds are used by a variety of individuals and institutions for a wide variety of persons.

Requirement:

Specify six different types of users of financial statements and explain in each case the aspects of performance or position in which they may be interested.

(The Chartered Association of Certified Accountants)

Question 1.3 (SM)

The accounting function may be divided into two broad classes of activity, first that which is defined as 'financial accounting' and secondly that which is referred to as 'management accounting'. You are required to explain the main differences between these two functions.

(The Chartered Association of Certified Accountants)

Question 1.4 (a)

State *three* different regulatory influences on the preparation of the published accounts of quoted companies and briefly explain the role of each one. Comment briefly on the effectiveness of this regulatory system.

(The Chartered Association of Certified Accountants)

Basic Measurement and Recording Procedures

2.

The Balance Sheet—A Statement of Financial Position

ELEMENTS OF THE BALANCE SHEET

A balance sheet is one of the basic financial statements produced by a business organisation. An alternative term for the balance sheet is a 'Statement of financial position' which is perhaps more descriptive. The latter term is used, for example, in the US.

A balance sheet represents an ordered list, in money terms, of the economic resources owned by a firm and the claims on those resources. The resources possessed by the firm are known as assets. The claims on these resources are represented by capital (owner's equity) and/or liabilities. Owner's capital or owner's equity represents the resources invested in the firm by the owner(s). All other resources supplied to the firm, which must ultimately be repaid, are referred to under the general heading of liabilities. Thus at any point in time a company will possess *assets*, *capital* and *liabilities*.

Assets are economic resources owned and which were acquired at a measurable money cost by a firm and are expected to provide a future benefit. Assets may have a definite physical form such as buildings, machinery or stock. On the other hand, some assets exist not in physical or tangible form, but in the form of valuable legal claims or rights; examples are amounts due from customers or Stock Exchange investments. Assets will be more usually classified as either fixed or current, based on the intention for which they are held. The purpose underlying a classification of assets (and liabilities) is to aid owners, creditors, managers and other interested user groups in understanding the financial position of the business entity. Classification of balance sheet items gives a clearer picture to users of the entity's financial position. In accordance with the Companies (Amendment) Act, 1986 there is no longer any classification for assets which are neither fixed nor current.

Fixed assets are those which have been acquired for use in the business and are used by the firm for many years. They can be formally defined as those assets which are 'intended for use on a continuing basis in the company's activities'. They were originally acquired to facilitate the production and sale of goods and services to customers. Thus fixed assets themselves are not sold in the ordinary course of business. They may however be disposed of (sold) at the end of their useful life. Typical fixed assets are: land and buildings, plant and machinery, furniture and motor vehicles. A more appropriate term for these assets would be long-term assets.

Current assets are those assets which are not fixed assets and are represented by cash or items which are expected to be converted into cash or consumed during the forthcoming year. The three principal current assets of a firm are: (1) stock which represents goods and materials held by the business which are intended for eventual resale or consumption; (2) accounts receivable or debtors which represent amounts due from customers; and (3) bank/cash balances (or short-term investments). Current assets are essentially short term in nature.

Capital, owner's equity or net worth represents the portion of total assets financed by the owner. It typically consists of two items, namely, the original capital invested by the owner plus any profits retained in the business.

Liabilities are financial obligations which must be paid by the company. They may be classified as either long term or current (i.e. short term) based on the time at which payment is expected to be made. Long term represents debts to be paid beyond the next accounting period, usually one year, whereas current liabilities should be discharged within the next twelve months. Long-term liabilities represent long-term loans and debentures. Current liabilities consist mainly of three items: (1) bank overdraft or short-term loans; (2) accounts payable resulting from the purchase of goods or services on credit (which are more commonly known as creditors); and (3) accruals representing expenses incurred at balance sheet date but which have not been paid for. As a result of the Companies (Amendment) Act, 1986 it is proper to refer to current liabilities as 'Creditors (amounts falling due within one year)' and long-term liabilities would be properly described as 'Creditors (amounts falling due after more than one year)'.

Assets, Liabilities and *Capital* are combined to form the balance sheet of a company. It can be looked upon as an accounting equation, prepared for a single moment in time and can be presented in either of the following forms:

(*a*) Total assets = Capital + Total liabilities
(i.e. total assets are financed by capital and liabilities)

c) Fixed Assets + (Current Assets − Current Liabilities)
= Share Cap + Ret. Earnings + Long term
liabilities.

OR

(*b*) Total assets − Total liabilities = Capital
(i.e. net assets represent the amount of owner's equity)

All balance sheets require expansion and some rearrangement of the basic accounting equation. In particular, assets will be subdivided into fixed and current categories; capital in a company will be divided into share capital subscribed and retained profits; liabilities will be classified as either long or short term. Thus:

(*c*) Fixed assets		Share capital		Long-term liabilities
+	=	+	+	+
Current assets		Retained profits		Current liabilities

Basically, all balance sheets have the same headings even though they are presented in different ways. The fundamental message is that it shows the resources owned by the firm and how those resources were financed. However, should the value of the liabilities exceed the assets then a 'deficiency of capital' exists.

There are four essential features of any balance sheet, namely:

(*a*) The name of the business entity for which the balance sheet is being prepared, i.e. the business of J. Brown. Thus, the balance sheet shows, for example, the business assets and not the personal assets of J. Brown. The business is considered to be a separate entity, i.e. distinct from the owner, and this is referred to as the business entity convention. Moreover, in the case of a business trading as a limited company, it is a separate legal entity and is distinct from its owners.

It is part of generally accepted accounting practice that financial statements are prepared on the basis of the business entity principle. Since it is the financial position and performance of the business entity which is the focus of attention, it is important that the financial statements be prepared on the basis that the business is a separate financial entity from that of its owners. If the owners were to intermingle their personal affairs with the transactions of the business, the resulting financial statements would be misleading and would fail to describe clearly the activities of the business.

(*b*) The title of the statement being prepared, i.e. Balance Sheet.

(*c*) The date to which the balance sheet relates e.g. at 31 December 19. . . The Balance sheet is a statement of assets, liabilities and capital, i.e. the financial position at a particular moment in time. It is normally prepared at the end of the entity's chosen accounting period.

(*d*) Assets are classified as either fixed or current and liabilities are classified as either long term or current. As mentioned above, current liabilities will be presented on the balance sheet under the heading 'Creditors' (amounts falling due within one year). Long-term liabilities will be classified under the heading 'Creditors (amounts falling due after more than one year)'. Capital or net worth is also separately shown and divided between original capital subscribed and accumulated retained profits.

A number of years ago most balance sheets were presented in a two-sided format. On one side the assets owned by the company were listed and, on the other side, the claims on those assets in the form of capital and liabilities, as per Exhibit 2.1:

Exhibit 2.1

J. BROWN COMPANY
BALANCE SHEET AT 31 DECEMBER 19 . .

	£		£
Fixed assets	10,000	Capital invested	6,000
		Retained profits	3,000
Current assets	10,000	Long-term liabilities	5,000
		Current liabilities	6,000
	20,000		20,000

A more modern version is that of a vertical presentation (Exhibit 2.2) which shows fixed assets plus *net* current assets financed by share capital and retained profits and long-term liabilities. However, the basic information does not alter:

Exhibit 2.2

J BROWN COMPANY
BALANCE SHEET AT 31 DECEMBER 19 . .

	£	£
Fixed assets		10,000
Current assets	10,000	
Less: current liabilities	6,000	
Net current assets		4,000
		14,000
Financed by:		
Capital invested		6,000
Retained profits		3,000
Long-term liabilities		5,000
		14,000

The main difference between the two formats is a treatment of current assets and current liabilities. In Exhibit 2.2 current liabilities are subtracted from current assets to provide a figure of £4,000, described as net current assets or working capital. Current liabilities provide finance for current assets, hence the logic of deducting current liabilities from current assets. This sum represents the working capital of the business and provides the users of the balance sheet with a guide as to whether or not the current liabilities can be paid. The inability to pay current liabilities as they fall due represents a serious financial problem, and, unless speedily reversed, could lead to the financial collapse of the enterprise.

The important relationship between the major components of current assets and current liabilities is depicted in Exhibit 2.3:

Exhibit 2.3

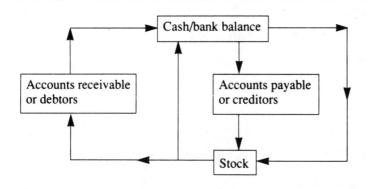

Exhibit 2.3 highlights the flow of cash within the working capital cycle. For example, stock for resale (without which trading profits cannot be generated) can be acquired out of cash resources or purchasing the goods on credit. Regardless of the method used to finance the acquisition of stock the cash position is ultimately affected. However, the stock will be eventually to sold, some on credit (giving rise to accounts receivables) and some for cash. Cash sales have a direct impact on the cash position of the firm. Likewise, sales on credit will eventually affect the cash position when payment is received.

It is useful to stress at this point that although a company may be generating profits from trading it may not be generating an adequate cash flow. Two possible causes may be cited, based on the above diagram, namely (1) too much stock is being held by the firm relative to its sales; and (2) too much credit is being granted to customers (accounts receivable) and/or too little credit is being received from suppliers (accounts payable).

For internal purposes, i.e. for managers, the presentation of the balance sheet is likely to vary from firm to firm. However, for external purposes, i.e. financial accounting purposes, balance sheets of companies must now comply with the provisions of the Companies (Amendment) Act, 1986. These provisions include, inter alia, prescribed formats for published balance sheets. Both horizontal and vertical formats are permitted. The main headings for the vertical format are as follows:

Exhibit 2.4

J. BROWN COMPANY
BALANCE SHEET AT 31 DECEMBER 19 . .

Assets employed	£
Fixed Assets	10,000
Current Assets	10,000
Creditors (amounts falling due within one year)	6,000
Net current assets	4,000
Total assets less current liabilities	14,000
Financed by:	
Creditors (amounts falling due after more than one year)	5,000
Capital and reserves	
Capital	6,000
Profit and loss account	3,000
	9,000
	14,000

Historic cost convention

It has been mentioned in the above discussion that accounting information is recorded in monetary terms. If a transaction or event cannot be measured in monetary terms it is not recorded as part of the accounting process. As a result, certain resources which a business possesses will not be reflected in conventional financial statements. One such example would be a highly skilled and loyal workforce. Although many managers would consider such a workforce as the firm's most valuable 'asset', it will not be reflected on the balance sheet.

The prevailing view in accounting is that all transactions are included at their cost, i.e. the price paid for them. Consequently, assets will be recorded at their historic cost when purchased and will continue to be shown on the balance sheet at cost (less a proportion of cost as they are used up over their useful lives). This policy of accounting for assets at their cost is commonly referred to as the historic cost convention of accounting. The advantage of this convention is its simplicity and objectivity. However, it is important to stress that the historic cost of an asset will rarely (except for cash) exactly equate with the asset's realisable market value. Indeed, if the market price of an asset has risen relative to its cost, the asset may still be shown on the balance sheet at its historic cost.

Historic cost does not therefore equate with 'value' where value is determined by either its realisable value or the income potential of the asset. Indeed, a useful generalisation is that a balance sheet does *not* show 'how much a business is worth'.

EVALUATION OF FINANCIAL POSITION

The balance sheet is a statement of the financial position of a business and there are two important features which can be evaluated from it. These two areas will be investigated in greater detail later (Chapter 14) but it is useful to briefly review them. They are:

(*a*) *Liquidity*—which provides an indication of the ability of the firm to pay off its current liabilities as and when they become due.

(*b*) *Gearing* (leverage)—which provides an indication of the extent to which the firm is relying on borrowings to finance its activities.

Liquidity

Liquidity must be ranked as one of the principal objectives of any enterprise in the short term. Unless a company can pay off its debts as and when they become due, it may be forced by its creditors to stop operations and end its existence. Two ratios are commonly used to assess the liquidity position of the firm. They are the current ratio and the acid-test ratio. The current ratio is calculated as follows:

$$\text{Current ratio} = \frac{\text{Current assets}}{\text{Current liabilities}}$$

This ratio indicates the extent to which current assets are available to meet the current liabilities. Textbooks often quote a ratio of 2:1 as being the norm because stocks, which are included under current assets, may not be easily converted into cash. However, many companies trade quite successfully with ratios considerably less than 2:1 and conversely, firms with ratios of 2 or more may have liquidity problems.

A complementary liquidity ratio is that of the 'acid test' which is computed as follows:

$$\text{Acid-test ratio} = \frac{\text{Current assets less stock}}{\text{Current liabilities}}$$

The acid-test ratio is considered as a somewhat more severe test of liquidity as it excludes the least liquid portion of current assets—stock. Stock is specifically excluded because if the firm sells its stock to pay off its financial obligations then it has no stock to continue trading. In general terms an acid-test ratio of about 1:1 is considered to be the most appropriate for the majority of businesses but, as with the current ratio, it will be found that many firms can survive quite well with ratios considerably less than this and others can have liquidity problems with ratios well in excess of it.

Gearing

Gearing or leverage refers to the extent to which assets have been financed by borrowing. Some borrowing is usually beneficial to a company since interest payments are tax deductible whereas dividends are not. A company is said to be highly geared when it has a high ratio of borrowings to shareholders' funds, where shareholders' funds include capital invested and retained profits. However, excessive 'gearing' or 'leverage' increases the risk to ordinary shareholders. Interest payments must always be made, irrespective of the company's profit level and this could depress future dividend payments. Moreover, all borrowings must be repaid. Should a business be unable to meet the required interest and capital repayments, a lender can appoint a receiver whose express function is to sell off sufficient assets of the company to repay the loan. A commonly used gearing ratio is:

$$\text{Long-term debt/equity ratio} = \frac{\text{Long-term debt}}{\text{Shareholders' funds}} = x\%$$

In contrast with the liquidity ratios there is no commonly accepted desirable percentage. However most financial analysts would be wary if the debt/equity ratio exceeded 100 per cent. This would indicate that long-term financiers have invested more funds than shareholders.

EFFECTS OF BUSINESS TRANSACTIONS ON THE BALANCE SHEET

Capital Invested

All business transactions affect the balance sheet. The first transaction of any business entity is likely to be the investment of capital by the owner.

Assume that A. Smith, a sole trader, deposited £10,000 in a bank account in the business's name 'Smith Traders'. The initial balance sheet of the business would be:

SMITH TRADERS
BALANCE SHEET AT DAY 1

Assets	£	Capital	£
Bank	10,000	Capital invested	10,000

It will be recalled that although capital is frequently used to describe such investment by owners the term equity or owner's equity is also used.

Purchase of an asset for cash

On day 2 Smith acquired buildings for the business. The cost was £8,000 and was paid by cheque. The effect on the balance sheet is twofold; the bank balance has decreased by £8,000 but fixed assets have increased by the same amount. Capital is unaffected. The balance sheet now appears as follows:

SMITH TRADERS
BALANCE SHEET AT DAY 2

Assets	£	Capital	£
Buildings	8,000		
Bank	2,000	Capital invested	10,000

Purchase of an asset on credit

On day 3 Smith acquires furniture, which he purchased on credit for £3,000. Again, the impact of this transaction on the balance sheet is twofold. The business now owns a new fixed asset in the amount of £3,000 but it has also acquired a liability of the same amount in the form of accounts payable (creditors). The balance sheet of the enterprise now appears:

SMITH TRADERS
BALANCE SHEET AT DAY 3

Assets	£	Capital	£
Buildings	8,000	Capital invested	10,000
Furniture	3,000	Liabilities	
Bank	2,000	Accounts payable	3,000
	13,000		13,000

Payment of a liability

On day 4 Smith traders now pays from its bank account the £3,000 which it owes in respect of furniture. Again, there is a dual impact on the balance sheet. The payment causes a decrease in the bank balance (resulting in an overdraft) with an equal decrease in the accounts payable, under the heading of liabilities. The other balance sheet items are unaffected. The resulting balance sheet will be:

SMITH TRADERS
BALANCE SHEET AT DAY 4

Assets	£	Capital	£
Buildings	8,000	Capital invested	10,000
Furniture	3,000	Liabilities	
Bank	Nil	Bank overdraft	1,000
	11,000		11,000

Exchanging one liability for another

On day 5 Smith Traders successfully negotiates a long-term loan in the amount of £2,000 from the bank which is lodged against its overdraft. This transaction results in an additional liability of £2,000 being acquired but there is a corresponding reduction in the bank overdraft. The balance sheet is now:

SMITH TRADERS
BALANCE SHEET AT DAY 5

Assets	£	Capital	£
Buildings	8,000	Capital invested	10,000
Furniture	3,000	Liabilities	
Bank	1,000	Long-term loan	2,000
		Bank overdraft	Nil
	12,000		12,000

The transactions illustrated above were merely preliminary. Formal business trading will commence with the acquisition of stock for resale, incurring operating expenses such as advertising, etc. However, the above transactions illustrate that, from a balance sheet point of view, all transactions have a dual impact. This dual impact in terms of the accounting equation can be summarised to show that there are four basic types of transactions:

Assets	Capital and liabilities
(1) Increase (+)	Increase (+)
(2) Increase (+) and Decrease (-)	----
(3) Decrease (-)	Decrease (-)
(4) ----	Increase (+) and Decrease (-)

QUESTION 2.1 (SM)

Briefly answer the following questions:

(*a*) What is a balance sheet?

(*b*) What is an asset?

(*c*) What is a liability?

(*d*) What is capital?

(*e*) Why does the balance sheet balance?

(*f*) To what extent does that balance sheet value an investment?

(The Chartered Association of Certified Accountants)

QUESTION 2.2 (SM)

The owner of a small business selling and repairing cars which you patronise has just received a copy of his financial statements for the current year.

He is rather confused by some of the items and since he knows that you are studying accounting he has asked you to explain certain points of difficulty to him.

His questions are as follows:

(*a*) 'What is meant by the term "assets"? My mechanical knowledge and skill is an asset to the business but it does not seem to have been included.'

(*b*) 'The house I live in cost £30,000 five years ago and is now worth £60,000, but that is not included either.'

(*c*) 'What is the difference between "fixed assets" and "current assets"?'

(*d*) 'Why do amounts for "vehicles" appear under both fixed asset and current asset headings?'

Requirement:

Write brief replies to each of the above questions.

(The Chartered Association of Certified Accountants)

QUESTION 2.3 (A)

Indicate whether the following items are fixed assets, current assets or long-term liabilities or current liabilities:

(*a*) Motor vehicle for use in the business

(*b*) Cash at bank

(*c*) A loan from a friend repayable in one month

(*d*) Motor vehicle intended for re-sale

(*e*) Stock of goods on hand for sale

(*f*) A bank overdraft

(*g*) A bank loan repayable in five years' time

(*h*) Fixtures and fittings

(*i*) Accounts receivable (debtors)

(*j*) Accounts payable (creditors)
(*k*) Plant and machinery
(*l*) Cash on hands
(*m*) A loan made to a friend repayable in one month.

QUESTION 2.4 (A)

Complete the following tables

	Assets	Liabilities	Capital	Deficiency of Capital
1	295	117	?	?
2	11,961	?	3,215	?
3	?	1,911	2,816	?
4	5,844	9,203	?	?
5	106,412	62,372	?	?
6	?	9,383	?	1,417
7	19,495	12,713	?	?
8	?	14,566	10,862	?

QUESTION 2.5 (SM)

The following information relates to three separate companies at 31 December 19 . . although in companies 2 and 3 one figure is missing, since the accountant was taken ill after eating lunch in the factory canteen.

	Company 1	Company 2	Company 3
	£	£	£
Owners' invested capital	3,000	5,000	?
Plant and machinery	2,000	1,000	6,000
Cash	100	200	Nil
Long-term loan payable	2,000	1,000	Nil
Stock	400	2,000	3,500
Land	2,500	6,000	2,000
Debtors (accounts receivable)	1,300	3,000	1,500
Creditors (accounts payable)	300	1,000	2,000
Bank overdraft	700	Nil	1,500
Retained profits	1,200	?	4,000
Loan receivable (short-term)	900	Nil	2,000

Requirement:

From the above data, construct balance sheets in vertical format. Insert the missing figures and in each case identify:

		Company	
	1	2	3
(a) Current assets			
(b) Current liabilities			
(c) Fixed assets			
(d) Shareholders' funds			
(e) Capital employed			
(f) Net current assets			
(g) Current Ratio			
(h) Acid-test ratio			

QUESTION 2.6 (A)

The accounting equation can be expressed as Assets = Liabilities + Capital. The balances of each item in "Kevin's" accounting equation are given below for 31 August and for each of the next twelve business days.

	Cash	Debtors	Stock	Fixed Assets	Creditors	Capital
	£	£	£	£	£	£
Aug. 31	5,000	10,000	9,000	6,000	6,000	24,000
Sep. 1	7,000	8,000	9,000	6,000	6,000	24,000
2	7,000	8,000	10,000	6,000	7,000	24,000
3	11,000	8,000	10,000	6,000	7,000	28,000
4	13,500	5,500	10,000	6,000	7,000	28,000
5	10,500	5,500	13,000	6,000	7,000	28,000
8	8,500	5,500	13,000	10,000	9,000	28,000
9	6,500	5,500	13,000	12,000	9,000	28,000
10	5,500	5,500	13,000	12,000	8,000	28,000
11	6,500	5,500	13,000	11,000	8,000	28,000
12	6,500	7,500	11,000	11,000	8,000	28,000
15	6,500	7,500	15,000	11,000	12,000	28,000
16	6,500	8,500	15,000	10,000	12,000	28,000

You should assume that only one transaction occurred each day.

Requirement:

(a) State in a single sentence the nature and amount of the transaction which took place on each of the above twelve days.

(b) Compute the current ratio at 16 September, assuming all liabilities are classified as current.

(The Institute of Chartered Accountants in Ireland)

QUESTION 2.7 (SM)

The accounting equation can be expressed as Assets = Liabilities + Capital. The balances of each item in "Susan's" accounting equation are given below for 31 December and for each of the next twelve business days.

	Bank	Debtors	Stock	Fixed Assets	Creditors	Capital
	£	£	£	£	£	£
Dec. 31	9,000	4,000	6,000	10,000	5,000	24,000
Jan 1	15,000	4,000	6,000	10,000	5,000	30,000
2	17,000	4,000	4,000	10,000	5,000	30,000
3	18,000	3,000	4,000	10,000	5,000	30,000
4	15,000	3,000	4,000	10,000	2,000	30,000
5	15,000	3,000	4,000	14,000	6,000	30,000
8	20,000	3,000	4,000	9,000	6,000	30,000
9	20,000	4,000	3,000	9,000	6,000	30,000
10	20,000	4,000	3,000	11,000	6,000	32,000
11	22,000	2,000	3,000	11,000	6,000	32,000
12	22,000	2,000	8,000	11,000	11,000	32,000
15	20,000	2,000	8,000	15,000	13,000	32,000
16	18,000	2,000	8,000	15,000	11,000	32,000

Note: You should assume that only one transaction occurred on each business day.

Requirement:
State in a single sentence the nature and amount of the transaction which took place on each of the above twelve days.
(The Institute of Chartered Accountants in Ireland)

3.

Recording Accounting Transactions

CASH ACCOUNTING AND LEDGER ACCOUNTS

The purpose of any accounting system is to provide financial information about a business entity to various users whose interest in the business will be served by information about its financial position and operating results. The accounting system consists of two inter-related parts, namely the recording of transactions undertaken by the business entity and summarising/reporting the impact of those transactions. The accounting system consists of methods and procedures in order to record its financial activities and to summarise these activities. To achieve these objectives an accounting system may well be maintained manually but increasing use is now being made of computers which are able to store and retrieve accounting data information more quickly. Specific computer software for the accounting function such as 'Take 5' and 'PEGASUS' are commonly used in Ireland. Regardless of whether an accounting system is simple or sophisticated, the financial information must be initially recorded and ultimately summarised.

Accounting is initially concerned with recording economic activity, i.e. transactions and events which have an economic impact on the firm. For example, goods are purchased and resold, cash is received and paid. These transactions are recorded in monetary terms and the recording process will start when the transaction has been made rather than when it is contemplated. This recording function is performed in the ledgers, journals and day books of the organisation. It can also be entered through a computer key-board. It is mainly a mechanical function, based on the 'double-entry' system and is frequently referred to as book-keeping. Not all business events can be objectively measured in monetary terms. Events such as the departure of a key member of staff may have a significant impact on the firm but this event is not part of the formal accounting process since it cannot be objectively measured in monetary terms.

Book-keeping is an integral part of any accounting course. Not only is it important in itself but there are some topics which can be explained more clearly by use of the double-entry technique. This is because of the emphasis it places on the self-balancing mechanisms within accounting based on the accounting equation.

However, it is not sufficient just to record the thousands of individual transactions undertaken by a business entity. To be useful, accounting numbers must generally be summarised. Managers and other users of accounting information are interested in receiving reports containing information such as 'total sales', 'total expenses', or 'net profit'. Thus the second element of accounting is that of periodically summarising and reporting the available accounting information. Reports may be prepared for limited circulation among a specialist group within the organisation, or for circulation to a much wider readership embracing the general public. Reports may differ in form or language, but should be capable of being readily understood by the recipient. Unfortunately the level of comprehension of accounting reports by their recipients is often quite low. Moreover, the accountant is not free to produce the financial statements of a company in the form which the users might be thought to understand. There are, in many cases, legal obligations and constraints imposed on the reporting enterprise which determine the form and content of the financial statements and the measurement process to be adopted in producing them. There are no such restrictions, however, on the presentation to management.

Finally, in order to make decisions it is necessary for users to understand the accounting information and to be able to evaluate and appreciate the 'message' it contains. Thus, the third part of the accounting process involves the interpretation of accounting information, and this element is covered mainly in chapters 14 and 15.

The accounting process commences with the recording of a multitude of transactions engaged in by the firm. It would not be practical to prepare a separate balance sheet after each transaction, apart from the fact that it would be quite unnecessary to do so. Nevertheless the recording stage is most important since inaccuracies will distort subsequent financial statements and perhaps result in incorrect interpretation. The volume of transactions necessitates a system that is simple to operate and yet allows a regular check to be made on the accuracy of the recording function.

All transactions can be recorded in *Ledger Accounts*. A separate ledger account or record is kept for each asset, liability etc. and these are maintained in a book called the ledger. Many businesses use computers for recording accounting transactions. However, an understanding of the accounting process is more easily acquired by references to a manual accounting system. Indeed, the knowledge gained by working with a manual accounting system is readily transferable to a computerised accounting system.

Ledger accounts are also referred to as T-Accounts because they take the form of the capital letter T. Each account has two sides : the left- and right-hand sides. It is unquestionably a source of considerable confusion to beginners in the study of accounting that the left-hand side of an account is referred to as *debit* and the right-hand side as *credit*. So, an account for the asset 'cash' appears as follows:

Cash Account	
Left-hand side or DEBIT	Right-hand side or CREDIT

The terms *debit* and *credit* have been used for over 500 years, since modern book-keeping was first formulated. Debit means one thing and one thing only—the left-hand side of a ledger account. Also, credit means the right-hand side of a ledger account. Even though the terms 'left-hand side' and 'right-hand side' are more appropriate in relation to a ledger account, debit and credit are more commonly used. Debit and credit are usually abbreviated as Dr. and Cr. respectively. Also debit and credit are frequently used as verbs. Thus, if an accountant wishes to record a transaction by way of a left-hand entry to an account, he will use the expression 'debit the account'.

Double-entry book-keeping

In chapter 1 it was mentioned that each transaction has a dual impact on the balance sheet. Since transactions can be recorded in the ledger accounts it follows that at least two ledger accounts will be affected by each transaction. A systematic approach is needed to record this financial impact and the approach has as its foundation the accounting equation which is:

$$\text{Assets} = \text{Capital} + \text{Liabilities}$$

The accounting equation allows us to classify ledger accounts as being either asset accounts or capital/liabilities accounts. The capital account is a special type of liability account since, in the liquidation of the company, it would be repaid to the owner(s). It is now a convention that any transaction which results in an increase of an asset is recorded in the debit side of that account. Not surprisingly, reductions in those assets are recorded on the credit side of the ledger account. Thus the general rule for assets is:

Asset account	
Increases (+) of assets are 'debits'	Decreases (-) of assets are 'credits'

To record any transaction in a ledger properly the following three pieces of information should be shown: (1) date of the transaction; (2) brief details of the transaction; and (3) the monetary amount of the transaction. All transactions are recorded in vertical order so that a typical bank account would appear as follows:

Dr.		Bank account			Cr.
2 Jan.	Issue of capital	10,000	3 Jan.	Purchases (goods)	400
4 Jan.	Sales	900	5 Jan.	Wages	300

The above bank account indicates that on 2 January £10,000 share capital was raised by the company and another cash inflow was received on 4 January in respect of sales. Conversely, on 3 January £400 was paid out in respect of purchase of goods for resale and on 5 January £300 was paid out for wages.

The reverse procedure is adopted to record changes in capital/liabilities. Increases in capital/liabilities are recorded as credit entries in the relevant account and decreases are recorded as debit entries. Thus, the general rule for recording transactions involving liabilities is:

Liability account

Decreases (-) of liabilities are 'debits'	Increases (+) of liabilities are 'credits'

These rules of debit and credit are designed so that equal amounts of debit and credit entries are needed to record every transaction. This is referred to as 'double-entry book-keeping'. Since every transaction or event is recorded by equal amounts of debit and credit entries, it follows that the total of all debit entries must equal the total of all the credit entries. This equality of entries enables one to detect and locate errors made, if any, in the recording process.

In the previous chapter we highlighted a few preliminary transactions of Smith Traders and how they affected the balance sheet. We now look again at those transactions and see how they should be recorded in ledger accounts.

On day 1 A. Smith, a sole trader, deposited £10,000 in a bank account in the name of the business.

On day 2 Smith acquired suitable buildings. This cost was £8,000 which was paid for by cheque.

On day 3 Smith acquires furniture, which he purchased on credit for £3,000.

On day 4 Smith traders now pays from its bank account the £3,000 which it owes in respect of furniture.

On day 5 Smith Traders successfully negotiates a long-term loan in the amount of £2,000 from the bank which is lodged against its overdraft.

Date	Financial Impact	A/c to be debited	A/c to be credited
Day 1	Increase in bank	Bank a/c	
	Increase in capital		Capital a/c
Day 2	Increase buildings	Buildings a/c	
	Decrease bank		Bank a/c
Day 3	Increase furniture	Furniture a/c	
	Increase liabilities		Creditors a/c
Day 4	Decrease bank		Bank a/c
	Decrease creditors	Creditors a/c	
Day 5	Increase bank*	Bank a/c	
	Increase loans		Loans a/c

* Alternatively this transaction can be described as *decreasing* the liability in the form of bank overdraft In which case it will still be a debit entry in the bank account since decreases of liabilities are debit entries.

Bank account

(1)	Capital	10,000	(2)	Buildings	8,000
(5)	Loan	2,000	(4)	Creditors	3,000

Buildings account

(2)	Bank	8,000	

Capital account

			(1)	Bank	10,000

Furniture account

(3)	Creditors	3,000	

Term loan account

			(5)	Bank	2,000

Creditors account

(4)	Bank	3,000	(3)	Furniture	3,000

Balancing an account

At the end of each accounting period it is usual practice to 'balance' each account. The purpose of balancing is to ascertain, for example, the amount of funds in the firm's bank account. The balance on any account is the arithmetical difference between the two sides of the ledger account. In the case of the bank account above, the total debit entries amount to £12,000 compared with total credit entries of £11,000. Thus, the total amount of the debit entries exceed those of the credit side by £1,000 and the account is said to have a debit balance. (If credits exceed debit entries the account has a credit balance.) The balance is formally recorded by inserting on both sides the bigger of the two totals, i.e. £12,000. This is done with underlines so as not to be mistaken for a transaction. The balancing figure of £1,000 is entered on the credit side. Both sides are arithmetically correct but the balance is brought down on the opposite side, below the underlines, to show the starting position for the next accounting period. (The balances should be dated.) The balanced bank account is as follows:

Bank account

(1) Capital	10,000	(2) Buildings	8,000
(5) Loan	2,000	(4) Creditors	3,000
		Balance	1,000
	12,000		12,000
Balance	1,000		

Accounting for stock movements

The transactions illustrated above were preliminary. Formal business trading will commence with the acquisition of stock which will eventually be sold. The purchase of stock represents an increase in the asset stock and so should be recorded on the debit side of the stock account. Conversely, sales of stock represent a decrease of the assets stock and should be recorded as a credit entry in the stock account. However, it would be inappropriate to record both purchases and sales in the same ledger account. Purchases are recorded at their historic cost and sales at their invoiced value. The resulting balance on the stock account would be confusing. It would not represent the profit earned during the period since there will be probably unsold stock on hand. Neither will the balance reflect the amount of closing stock since debit and credit entries reflect cost and selling price respectively. For these reasons it is more appropriate to record purchases and sales in separate ledger accounts. In addition, the separate recording allows for quick determination of the amount of purchases and sales during the period.

The stock account is therefore subdivided into two parts. One part reflects the acquisition (i.e. increase) of stock and is referred to as the purchases account. The other part reflects the disposal (i.e. decrease) of stock and is referred to as the sales account. By using this sub-division it allows us to record sales transactions at their full selling price. (The profit on such sales will therefore be determined at the end of the accounting period and this will be discussed in the next chapter). This sub-division can be illustrated as follows:

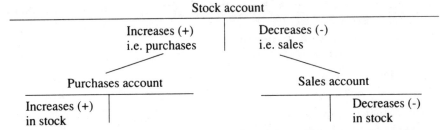

Some businesses will open two further sub-divisions of the stock account. One will record goods previously purchased but subsequently returned (i.e. purchases returns account). The other will record goods previously sold but subsequently returned by customers (i.e. sales returns account). There may well be four sub-divisions of the stock account in operation at any one time. However, the underlying logic remains intact. The increase of stock will always be a debit entry since it represents an increase of the asset stock. The debit entry will be either in the purchases account or the sales returns account. The decrease of stock will always be a credit entry since it reflects a decrease of the asset stock. The credit entry will be recorded in either the sales account or the purchases returns account.

However a stock account will be maintained in the ledger. Its sole purpose is to record any opening or closing balance of stock on hand at the start or end of an accounting period. In many ways the *stock* account is a dormant account; all movements in stock during an accounting period will be recorded in the appropriate subdivisions of the stock account.

ACCOUNTING FOR CREDIT TRANSACTIONS
Accounting for debtors (accounts receivable)

Many trading transactions are carried out on a credit basis—the goods are transferred but cash payment will be made at a subsequent date. Thus goods will be sold on credit with cash being received within, say, sixty days. This indebtedness is recorded in a ledger account entitled *Debtors* or *Accounts Receivable*. The account is an asset account since it represents a future cash inflow.

Example: On 2 January sold goods on credit, £1,000
　　　　　　9 January received payment on account, £600

The credit sale is credited to the sales account as normal reflecting a decrease in the asset stock. The bank account is unaffected by this transaction. Rather, instead of receiving immediate cash the company has been promised that they will be paid in the future. Thus, the debit entry will be to the debtors or accounts receivable account. Therefore, the balance on the debtors account, at any time, indicates the amount of money the firm expects to receive from the specified customer. It is anticipated that all debit entries to the debtors or accounts receivable account shall eventually be cleared by a corresponding credit entry when cash is ultimately received.

When the cash is received from the customer the recording entry is:

> Dr. Cash/Bank account
> Cr. Debtors (Accounts Receivable) account

The debit entry in the bank account indicates an increase in the asset bank. The credit entry in the debtors account reflects a decrease in the asset debtors. In balance sheet terms the firm has received one asset (cash) for another (debtors). The completed entries are:

Debtors account		Sales account	
2/1 Sales 1,000	9/1 Bank 600		2/1 Debtors 1,000

Bank account	
9/1 Debtors 600	

Thus out of £1,000 sales during the period, the company has received £600 with an additional £400 outstanding from debtors at the end of the period. Note that debtors accounts normally have the debit side greater than the credit side thus indicating expected future cash inflows.

Accounting for creditors (accounting for accounts payable)

Normally a firm will purchase goods on credit, giving an undertaking to pay the supplier at a future date. This indebtedness is recorded in the firm's ledger under the heading of *Creditors* or *Accounts Payable*.

Example: 1   February Purchased goods on credit £ 900
      9   February Paid supplier £700 on account

The purchase on credit is recorded by a debit entry in the purchases of stock account, reflecting an increase in the asset stock. The corresponding credit entry is recorded in the creditors (accounts payable) account indicating an increase in the firm's liabilities. The transaction has no direct effect on the firm's bank position. The transaction is summarised as follows:

> Dr. Purchases account
> Cr. Creditors (accounts payable) account

The payment to suppliers represents a decrease in the asset bank, requiring a credit entry in the bank account. Simultaneously, there is a decrease in liabilities (creditors) which is recorded by a debit entry in the creditors account. The payment to suppliers is summarised as follows:

Dr. Creditors (accounts payable)
Cr. Cash/bank account

Creditors account		Purchases account	
9/2 Bank 700	1/2 Purchases 900	1/2 Creditors 900	

Bank account	
	9/2 Creditors 700

Note that creditors accounts will normally have the credit side greater than the debit side, indicating expected, future cash outflows. Thus the balance in a creditors account will represent an amount to be paid by the company at some future date. Amounts owing to creditors at the end of the accounting period will appear on the firm's balance sheet under the heading of current liabilities.

The impact of debtors/creditors on cash resources

It is useful to visualise accounts receivable as representing future cash inflows in the short term and accounts payable as being future cash outflows in the short term. Thus in assessing the liquidity position of an enterprise one should take into consideration the current bank position of the firm together with the level of debtors, creditors and the length of credit given and received. The following exhibit (Exhibit 3.1) depicts the situation:

Exhibit 3.1

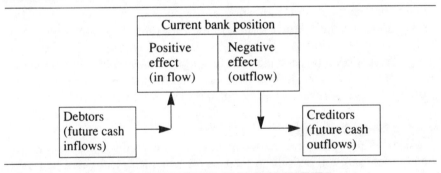

ACCOUNTING FOR EXPENSES AND REVENUES

So far we have discussed transactions in the context of their direct impact on assets, capital and liabilities. There are two other transactions, whose impact on the balance sheet is a little less obvious and we discuss them under the heading of expense and revenue transactions. The recording of these two transactions is important because, as we shall see later, profit is the difference between revenue and expenses.

Expenses are the cost of goods and services used up in the process of generating revenue. Examples include wages and salaries, advertising, rent, rates etc. These are the costs of doing business. Most day-to-day expenses will be paid for by cheque/cash resulting in a credit entry in the firm's bank account. Where is the debit entry recorded to reflect the dual impact? In terms of the accounting equation an expense causes a reduction in owner's capital. Thus, when a firm pays wages to its employees the asset bank is reduced, the liabilities are unchanged and owner's capital declines by the amount of wages paid. Strictly speaking, the debit entry for the payment of wages should be debited to capital account.

However, it would be more informative for each expense to be recorded in a separate ledger account. This makes it easy to ascertain how much has been spent under different expense headings such as wages, advertising etc. It is usual for a separate ledger account to be opened for each type of expense so that ledgers will include a wages account, an advertising account etc. However, some degree of amalgamation may take place and accounts, such as rent and rates, postage and telephone may be maintained. There is no hard and fast rule regarding whether expense headings should be combined or not in an expense account.

Revenue transactions increase owner's capital. For example, the receipt of deposit interest will have a dual impact on the accounting equation. The inflow of, say, cash interest increases the asset bank, liabilities will remain unchanged so that owner's capital increases to match the increase in total assets. Thus, revenue is the gross increase in owner's capital resulting from a business transaction or event. The double-entry for this transaction would be to debit bank account, indicating an increase in the asset bank and to credit capital account. However, there are different sources of revenue so that it would be useful to classify and record each source of revenue separately. Typical revenue accounts will be deposit interest or dividend income received, rent received and discount received. In the context of clubs, the principal source of revenue will be subscription income.

Discounts and bad debts

An inevitable part of conducting business on credit is that some customers (debtors) will default on their payment which results in a bad debt. Likewise, some customers are encouraged to pay their bills early by being offered a discount. For example, if a firm is owed £100 from a customer, it may accept £98 for full and immediate settlement. The £2 difference is described as discount allowed. The principle underlying both bad debts and discount allowed are identical. Both represent a reduction in the total assets of the business. For example, an asset of £100 (debtors) is being exchanged for another asset (cash) in the amount of £98. Alternatively, a debtor is proved worthless and no cash will be received.

In such circumstances the asset debtor is reduced requiring a credit entry, for example, of £2 in the asset debtor account. Simultaneously, owner's capital is reduced by the same amount. However, rather that debiting owner's capital account the debit entry is recorded in an expense account entitled either discount allowed account or bad debts account. Separate ledger accounts for both discount allowed and bad debts provides a quick way of ascertaining the amounts involved under these two headings during an accounting period.

Thus the general rule for these two items is:

Discounts allowed   DR. Discount allowed (expense) account
                     CR. Debtor (asset) account
Bad debts   DR. Bad debts (expense) account
                     CR. Debtor (asset) account

In contrast to discount allowed the firm may obtain discount received from its suppliers. This discount may be an inducement to the firm to settle its account quickly. Thus if a creditor is owed £100 he may accept £97 cash for immediate and full settlement. In terms of the accounting equation discounts received represent an increase in owner's capital. For example, if the above payment of £97 is made, then assets (cash) decrease by £97, but liabilities (creditors) decrease by £100. The £3 difference must be reflected as an increase in owner's capital.

The payment of £97 is debited to the creditor's (liability) account and credited to the bank account. This reflects a corresponding decrease in both the liability and asset account. The £3 discount received is debited to the creditor's account to highlight an additional decrease in that liability and a credit entry could be placed in the owner's capital account. However, for information purposes a separate discount received account will be maintained, and which will be credited with the amount of the discount received.

Discount received   DR. Creditor's (liability) account
                     CR. Discount received (revenue) account

The above discussion can be summarised by saying that expense and revenue accounts are really sub-divisions of the owner's capital account. Revenue transactions increase owner's capital and so are recorded as credit entries in the appropriate revenue accounts (and debited to, say, an asset account). Conversely, expense transactions represent reductions in owner's capital and so are recorded as debit entries in the appropriate expense accounts (and credited to, say, asset account). As we shall see in the next chapter, all expense and revenue transactions are eventually transferred to the owner's capital account via a profit and loss account prepared at the end of the accounting period.

REVIEW OF DOUBLE-ENTRY BOOK-KEEPING

The following example provides an overview of the debit-credit mechanism for recording cash and credit transactions:

Example: Record the following fifteen transactions in the ledger of A. Hill

		£
1.	Introduced capital (lodged to bank)	15,000
2.	Purchased motor vehicle by cheque	4,000
3.	Purchased stock for resale by cheque	9,000
4.	Sold stock for cash (lodged to bank)	5,000
5.	Purchased stock on credit	2,000
6.	Paid wages by cheque	3,000
7.	Credit sales	9,000
8.	Introduced additional capital (lodged to bank)	1,000
9.	Paid light and heat by cheque	1,500
10.	Purchased stock on credit	3,900
11.	Paid accounts payable (creditors) by cheque	2,100
12.	Received from accounts receivable (debtors)	8,000
13.	Credit sales	2,500
14.	Received from accounts receivable (debtors)	1,100
15.	Paid wages by cheque	2,000

Solution to recording transactions – A. Hill

Bank account

(1) Capital	15,000	(2) Vehicle	4,000		
(4) Sales	5,000	(3) Purchases	9,000		
(8) Capital	1,000	(6) Wages	3,000		
(12) Debtors	8,000	(9) Light	1,500		
(14) Debtors	1,100	(11) Creditors	2,100		
		(15) Wages	2,000		
		Bal.	8,500		
	30,100		30,100		
Bal.	8,500				

Capital account

		(1) Bank	15,000	
Bal.	16,000	(8) Bank	1,000	
	16,000		16,000	
		Bal.	16,000	

Motor vehicles account

(2) Bank	4,000		
		Bal.	4,000
Bal.	4,000		4,000

Purchases account

(3) Bank	9,000		
(5) Creditors	2,000		
(10) Creditors	3,900	Bal.	14,900
Bal.	14,900		14,900

Sales account

		(4) Bank	5,000
		(7) Debtors	9,000
Bal.	16,500	(13) Debtors	2,500
	16,500		16,500
		Bal.	16,500

Creditors account

(11) Bank	2,100	(5) Purchases	2,000
Bal.	3,800	(10) Purchases	3,900
	5,900		5,900
		Bal.	3,800

Debtors account						Wages account		
(7) Sales	9,000	(12) Bank	8,000		(6) Bank	3,000		
(13) Sales	2,500	(14) Bank	1,100		(15) Bank	2,000	Bal.	5,000
		Bal.	2,400			5,000		5,000
	11,500		11,500		Bal.	5,000		
Bal.	2,400							

	Light & heat account	
(9) Bank	1,500	
		Bal. 1,500
	1,500	1,500
Bal.	1,500	

When all the transactions of the accounting period have been recorded, the balances can be extracted from the ledger accounts and presented as a Trial Balance (Exhibit 3.2). The trial balance is a listing of all the balances on the accounts in the ledger and checks the arithmetic accuracy of the book-keeping entries. It should not be confused with the balance sheet which is an ordered listing of assets, liabilities and capital only.

Exhibit 3.2

TRIAL BALANCE—
A. HILL

	Debit £	Credit £
Bank account	8,500	
Capital account		16,000
Motor vehicle account	4,000	
Purchases account	14,900	
Sales account		16,500
Creditors account		3,800
Debtors account	2,400	
Wages account	5,000	
Light and heat account	1,500	
	36,300	36,300

The above trial balance indicates that the firm's bank account at the end of the accounting period is in funds (i.e. an asset) in the amount of £8,500. Capital, in the amount of £16,000 has been contributed by the proprietor. In addition, £4,000 has been spent acquiring a motor vehicle, and £5,000 and £1,500 have been spent on wages, light and heat respectively. £2,400 is due to be collected from debtors based on sales of £16,500 and £3,800 is owing to creditors in respect of purchases of £14,900.

Locating errors

It is inevitable that some trial balances will not balance at the first attempt. Obviously there are many possible explanations including incomplete or incorrect entries and incorrect balancing. In such circumstances one potentially useful device to locate possible errors is to divide the trial balance discrepancy by '9' since this will reveal the transposition of figures which is a common error when dealing with accounting numbers. For example, if a balance of £2,147 is recorded in the trial balance as £2,417 the difference in the trial balance will be £270 which is exactly divisible by 9, suggesting a transposition of figures. It will also apply where the last zero has been omitted from or added to a string of figures, for example, £10,000 being recorded as £1,000 or £500 being recorded as £5,000. If the trial balance difference is the transposition of figures then all the entries in the ledger accounts should be systematically checked including opening balances in addition to the balancing of each account and its inclusion in the trial balance. The trial balance is usually the starting point in the preparation of final accounting reports. However, prior to doing this, some additional work may need to be undertaken. Firstly, some of the above figures will be verified by checking the documents and vouchers for the different transactions, e.g. the invoice for the purchase of a motor vehicle. In addition, the accountant will want to ensure that all transactions have been properly recorded in the firm's books and are free from error. Secondly, stocktaking must be done at the end of the accounting period to ascertain the physical volume of closing stock which is then valued in accordance with recognised accounting principles. Having prepared a trial balance and obtained a closing stock valuation the accountant is now in a position to prepare a profit and loss account for the accounting period.

As the next chapter explains, the measurement of revenue and expense is fundamental to profit measurement and determination.

QUESTION 3.1 (A)

Record the following transactions in the ledger accounts of A. Green, and extract a trial balance at 31 March.

		£
Jan. 1	Introduced capital to business	5,000
3	Bought equipment by cheque	2,000
5	Bought fixtures by cheque	1,500
6	Bought stock by cheque	3,000
9	Sold stock (lodged)	4,000
12	Paid wages by cheque	1,000
15	Bought stock by cheque	2,000
18	Purchased stationery by cheque	1,000

21	Sold stock (lodged)	5,000
24	Paid motor expenses by cheque	1,000
16	Bought stock by cheque	2,000
28	Paid wages by cheque	2,000
29	Sold stock (lodged)	3,000
30	Sold equipment (at cost: lodged)	1,000
31	Paid monthly telephone charges	200

QUESTION 3.2 (SM)

The following transactions relate to V. Black who commenced business on 1 February 19 . . .

		£
Feb. 1	Introduced capital (lodged)	5,000
2	Purchased motor vehicle by cheque	4,000
3	Purchased stock for resale by cheque	9,000
4	Sold stock (lodged)	5,000
8	Purchased stock on credit	2,000
9	Purchased motor vehicles on credit	2,000
10	Paid wages by cheque	3,000
11	Sold stock on credit	5,000
12	Sold motor vehicles (at cost: lodged)	2,000
15	Introduced additional capital (lodged)	1,000
16	Paid rent for month by cheque	1,200
17	Paid wages by cheque	2,000
18	Paid light and heat by cheque	1,500
22	Purchased stock on credit	3,900
23	Paid accounts payable (creditors)	2,100
24	Received from accounts receivable (debtors)	4,000
25	Sold stock on credit	2,500
28	Received from accounts receivable (debtors)	1,100

Requirement:

Record the above transactions in the ledger accounts of V. Black and extract a trial balance.

QUESTION 3.3 (A)

The following transactions relate to John Arnold who commenced business on 1 March 19. . .

		£
March 1	Lodged to business bank account for capital	5,000
1	Purchased goods from O'Sullivan on credit	950
2	Purchased furniture on credit from S. Ltd	2,500
2	Sold goods on credit to Bailey	475
3	Cash sales (lodged)	4,512
4	Drew cheque for petty cash	20
5	Paid O'Sullivan by cheque	950

5 Sold goods on credit to Robson Ltd	425
8 Received cheque from Bailey (lodged)	400
9 Paid wages and salaries by cheque	479
10 Paid S. Ltd	2,500
10 Purchased goods by cheque	1,200
11 Sold goods on credit to Stapleton	1,500
12 Purchased goods from O'Sullivan	5,000
12 Paid O'Sullivan on account	2,000
15 Paid rent and rates by cheque	214
16 Paid wages and salaries by cheque	526
16 Sold goods to Bailey on credit	1,300
18 Received cheque from Stapleton (lodged)	1,200
25 Paid advertising by cheque	373
27 Paid wages and salaries by cheque	614
27 Paid sundry expenses from petty cash	12
28 Drew cheque for petty cash	50
29 Received cheque from Bailey	1,000
31 Paid sundry expenses by petty cash	22

Requirement:

Enter the above transactions in the ledger accounts and extract a trial balance at 31 March 19. . .

QUESTION 3.4 (SM)

James Cooke commenced business as a sole trader on 1 January 19. . . His transactions for the month of January 19. . are as follows:

1 Lodges £5,000 to business account for capital
  Draws £100 cash for petty cash
  Purchased premises £8,000, paying by cheque
  Purchased equipment £4,000, paying by cheque
2 Bought goods £2,698, by cheque
  Paid wages £220 by cheque
  Paid advertising £170 by cheque
3 Sold goods for £980 (lodged)
4 Sold goods on credit to Murphy £900
  Bought goods on credit from Coyle £1,642
  Sold goods on credit to O'Sullivan £4,950
  Sold goods on credit to Butler £146
5 Purchased stationery £324 by cheque
7 Paid advertising £400 by cheque
  Received £870 from Murphy (lodged)
14 Bought motor vehicle £1,200 by cheque
  Received loan of £1,000 from Bates and lodged this to bank
  Sold goods on credit to Doyle £5,163

Received from Doyle £500 (lodged)
Bought goods on credit from Coyle £1,100
15 Paid cheque £1,400 to Coyle
Bought goods for resale by cheque £570
Sold goods for cash £916 (lodged)
16 Bought goods on credit from Coyle £845
25 Paid wages £249 by cheque
Paid rent £500 by cheque
Paid £41 motor expenses by cheque
31 Sold goods on credit to Doyle £845.

Requirement:
Enter the above transactions in appropriate ledger accounts and extract a trial balance at 31 January 19. . .

QUESTION 3.5 (A)
The outline ledger accounts which appear below contain all of the transactions of the Harp Sales Company during the month of October (in £'s).
There was no stock on hand at the beginning or end of the month.

Requirement:
Explain in narrative form each transaction (1 to 14):

	Cash in Bank					Capital – James Harp	
(1)	30,000	(3)	1,200			(1)	30,000
(8)	7,344	(5)	15,000			(4)	1,000
(12)	30	(7)	300				
		(9)	3,440			Rent	
		(11)	170	(3)	1,200		
		(13)	720				

	Purchases					Sales	
(2)	8,700	(10)	600			(6)	14,400

	Furniture and Fittings				Salaries	
(4)	1,000		(9)	3,440		
(5)	15,000					

	Advertising				Postage and Telephone	
(7)	300	(12)	30	(11)	170	

	Discount allowed			Travelling Expenses	
(8)	56		(13)	720	

Beta Ltd				George Cranwell and Sons			
(10)	600	(2)	8,700	(6)	14,400	(8)	7,400

(The Institute of Chartered Accountants in Ireland)

QUESTION 3.6 (A)

The accounting equation can be expressed as Assets = Liabilities + Capital. The balances of each item in 'Mary's' accounting equation are given below for 31 December and for each of the next twelve business days.

		Bank £	Debtors £	Stock £	Fixed Assets £	Creditors £	Capital £
Dec.	31	9,000	4,000	6,000	10,000	5,000	24,000
Jan.	1	15,000	4,000	6,000	10,000	5,000	30,000
	2	19,000	4,000	4,000	10,000	5,000	32,000
	3	19,000	3,000	4,000	10,000	5,000	31,000
	4	17,500	3,000	4,000	10,000	2,000	32,500
	5	17,500	3,000	4,000	14,000	6,000	32,500
	8	18,500	3,000	4,000	9,000	6,000	28,500
	9	18,500	3,000	3,000	9,000	6,000	27,500
	10	18,500	3,000	3,000	11,000	6,000	29,500
	11	20,000	1,000	3,000	11,000	6,000	29,000
	12	20,000	1,000	8,000	11,000	11,000	29,000
	15	18,000	1,000	8,000	15,000	13,000	29,000
	16	16,500	1,000	8,000	15,000	11,000	29,500

Note: You should assume that only *one* transaction occurred on each business day.

Requirement:

State in a single sentence the nature and amount of the transaction which took place on each of the above twelve days.

QUESTION 3.7 (SM)

The accounting equation can be expressed as Assets = Liabilities + Capital. The balances of each item in 'Henry's' accounting equation are given below for 31 August and for each of the next twelve business days.

		Cash £	Debtors £	Stock £	Fixed Assets £	Creditors £	Capital £
Aug.	31	5,000	10,000	9,000	6,000	6,000	24,000
Sep.	1	7,000	8,000	9,000	6,000	6,000	24,000
	2	7,000	8,000	10,000	6,000	7,000	24,000
	3	11,000	8,000	10,000	6,000	7,000	28,000

4	13,500	5,000	10,000	6,000	7,000	27,500
5	13,500	5,000	9,000	6,000	7,000	26,500
8	11,500	5,000	9,000	10,000	9,000	26,500
9	9,500	5,000	9,000	12,000	9,000	26,500
10	8,500	5,000	9,000	12,000	7,500	27,000
11	10,500	5,500	9,000	11,000	7,500	28,500
12	13,000	6,000	7,000	11,000	7,500	29,500
15	13,000	6,000	7,000	10,000	7,500	28,500
16	13,500	6,500	7,000	8,000	7,500	27,500

You should assume that only *one* transaction occurred each day.

Requirement:

(a) State in a single sentence the nature and amount of the transaction which took place on each of the above twelve days.

(b) Compute the current and acid-test ratios at 16 September.

QUESTION 3.8 (SM)

L. Ryan had the following assets and liabilities at the start of an accounting period:

	£
Bank overdraft	470
Debtors	1,100
Creditors	900
Stock	2,000
Loan receivable from Mr Rodgers	1,500
Capital	?

Requirement:

From the above information compute opening capital, and enter the above balances in the appropriate ledger accounts. Record the following transactions therein and extract a trial balance.

(a) Received a cheque for £700 from debtors
(b) Sold stock for cheque £1,500 (lodged)
(c) Paid creditors £650 by cheque
(d) Rodgers repaid his loan, £1,500 (lodged)
(e) Bought stock on credit £800
(f) Sold goods on credit £915
(g) Bought goods by cheque £645
(h) Returned goods, previously purchased on credit £150
(i) Received cheque from debtors £500, on account (lodged)
(j) Sold goods on credit, £1,200
(k) Received cheque from debtors, £1,000 on account (lodged)

(*l*) Paid creditors, £500, on account

(*m*) Goods were returned, valued at £100, previously being sold by L. Ryan on credit

QUESTION 3.9 (SM)

The assets and liabilities of A. Wood on 1 January were as follows:

	£
Balance at Bank	1,800
Stock	8,000
Plant and Machinery	8,750
Loan payable—Mr Devlin	600
Motor Vans	2,000
Capital	??

Requirement:

Calculate Mr Wood's capital by preparing an opening balance sheet; open the ledger accounts and enter the balances at 1 January.

Enter the following transactions in the appropriate ledger accounts, then balance the accounts and extract a trial balance at 31 January.

			£
Jan.	1	Sold goods for cash (lodged)	900
	4	Paid wages by cheque	1,600
	4	Paid rent by cheque	125
	5	Sold goods for cash (lodged)	1,250
	7	Paid advertising by cheque	600
	8	Paid wages by cheque	1,500
	9	Purchased goods by cheque	1,500
	10	Paid stationery expenses by cheque	300
	11	Sold goods for cash (lodged)	2,000
	13	Paid sundry expenses by cheque	20
	14	Withdrew from bank for petty cash	50
	15	Purchased goods by cheque	900
	16	Paid wages by cheque	1,600
	17	Paid rent by cheque	225
	18	Bought stationery for cash	10
	19	Paid sundry expenses by cash	20
	20	Purchased goods by cheque	2,200
	22	Sold part of plant, at cost, (lodged)	2,000
	23	Capital introduced by proprietor (lodged)	1,200
	31	Received additional loan from Devlin (lodged)	1,000

4.

Profit (Income) Measurement

MEASURING BUSINESS INCOME—THE PROFIT AND LOSS ACCOUNT

Owners and other users of financial statements will be concerned with the overall performance of an enterprise. Success can be defined in a number of ways, e.g. sales growth, market share or even conditions of employment. However, one of the most important measures of success in today's society is 'profit'. Without profit the long-term future of a firm cannot be guaranteed. Since the drive for profits underlies the existence of most business organisations, it follows that a most important function of an accounting system is to provide information about profitability. Many types of readers of accounts, including investors, creditors and employees, are interested in the results of last year, not so much for their own sake but for their clues to the likely results of future years.

Correct measurement of the profitability of any enterprise can only be achieved when the life of the business has come to an end. However, the measurement of profits cannot be delayed until the business ceases to exist, since those involved with the business, including taxation authorities, will require regular information concerning performance. The profitability of a business has to be measured then, albeit imprecisely, each year over the life of the enterprise.

For income measurement purposes, accountants traditionally have looked to actual business transactions to provide the objective evidence that a business has been profitable or unprofitable. There are other methods, apart from the transactions approach, which could be used to measure business income. For example, comparing the valuation of the business at the start and at the end of the period. However, these other approaches are largely a matter of personal opinion and cannot be measured objectively enough for accountants to be comfortable with them, and, perhaps more importantly, for auditors to verify them.

Using the transactions approach to profit measurement, if a business buys an item for £60 and promptly sells it for £100 cash, we have objective evidence that the business has earned a profit of £40. Strictly speaking, the expression 'profit' should be used to represent the outcome of a particular transaction, with 'earnings' or 'income' reserved for the overall result of a particular time period. In Ireland, the results of the accounting period are shown in the profit and loss account for that period. In the US the more common expression is the 'earnings' or 'income' statement. Thus net profit or net income is the excess of the price of goods sold and services rendered over the cost of goods and services consumed during an accounting period. These are technical accounting terms which indicate a transactions approach to income measurement.

To determine net income in accounting terms, it is necessary to measure for a specific time period:

(*a*) The price of goods sold and services rendered; i.e. revenues.
(*b*) The cost of goods sold and services consumed; i.e. expenses.

In summary, net income or net profit equals total revenues minus total expenses. The profit and loss account, therefore, shows the results of business operations over a specific period of time, which is usually, though not always, a twelve-month period. The balance sheet on the other hand shows the financial position of the business at a particular date. In other words, the profit and loss account is a 'flow' statement, the balance sheet is a 'position' statement.

Revenues represent the price of goods sold or services rendered to customers during a given accounting period. When a business sells goods to its customers (or renders services), it receives immediate payment in cash or acquires an account receivable. Revenue represents the increase in the net asset amount of a firm. Thus when a firm sells goods (for cash), it acquires cash but it also decreases the amount of stock on hand. Since the goods will be sold for a price higher than was paid for the goods, the firm has generated revenue from this transaction.

Thus a cash receipt from borrowing does not constitute revenue but a cash sale does. The funds generated by the sale do not have to be repaid by the company. Various terms are used to describe different types of revenue. Companies selling goods usually use the term Sales to describe their major source of revenue; in professional practice of lawyers, doctors and accountants, revenue is referred to as Fees Earned. There are also miscellaneous forms of revenue including deposit interest received and rent received.

Expenses represent the cost of the goods and services used up in the process of obtaining revenues. Examples include wages and salaries for employees, rent, rates and advertising. They will also include non-cash items such as depreciation on fixed assets. A fixed asset will have a finite, useful life which extends beyond the accounting period being considered. Thus a portion of the cost of the fixed assets will be expensed over a number of accounting periods. All these costs are necessary to attract and service

customers and therefore to generate revenue. Taken together total expenses
are the 'cost of doing business', that is, the cost of the various activities
necessary to carry on a business.

Thus while revenue may be regarded as the positive factor in producing
net income, expenses are the negative factor.

The trading account

The calculation of net profit or net income can be done in two separate
stages. In the case of a manufacturing or trading firm, revenue is initially
specified and from this amount the 'cost of goods sold' is deducted. The
cost of goods sold is a special form of expense. It is in many enterprises the
major expense to be considered, and is thus generally presented separately
in the financial statements. The cost of goods sold typically comprises three
elements. Opening stock plus purchases during the accounting period represent goods available for sale. However, at the end of any accounting period
there will inevitably be a certain quantity of goods which remain unsold, e.g.
a brewery shall have barrels of beer ready for sale. The closing stock should
be deducted from the total costs of goods available for sale to provide a
'cost of goods sold' figure. In turn the cost of goods sold figure is deducted
from 'Sales' to provide a 'Gross Profit' figure. A gross loss would normally
indicate that the firm was selling its goods below cost.

Based on the trial balance of A. Hill (Exhibit 4.1), the gross profit calculation is contained in Exhibit 4.2, assuming closing stock is valued at £6,000:

Exhibit 4.1

	Debit £	Credit £
TRIAL BALANCE—A. HILL		
Bank account	8,500	
Capital account		16,000
Motor vehicle account	4,000	
Purchases account	14,900	
Sales account		16,500
Creditors account		3,800
Debtors account	2,400	
Wages account	5,000	
Light and heat account	1,500	
	36,300	36,300

The second stage in the profit measurement process is to deduct from the
gross profit all the operating expenses of the business. These would include
expenses incurred in (1) advertising and marketing the product; (2)

Exhibit 4.2

A. HILL
TRADING ACCOUNT FOR THE PERIOD ENDING............

	£	£
Sales		16,500
Less: Cost of sales:		
Opening stock	Nil	
Add: Purchases	14,900	
Deduct: Closing stock (say)	(6,000)	8,900
Gross Profit		7,600

distributing the product; (3) overall administration and accounting costs; and (4) financing the business, such as bank interest charges. In many cases the measurement of the expense is straightforward, e.g. wages. In other cases, the precise identification and measurement of expenses will not be so clear cut, and estimations will be called for as in the case of depreciation of fixed assets.

The residual between gross profit less total expenses will represent either a net profit or a net loss for the accounting period. It is the difference between the firm's accomplishments (i.e. Sales Revenue) for the period less the efforts expended (i.e. expenses incurred during the period). The net profit calculation for A. Hill is presented in Exhibit 4.3:

Exhibit 4.3

A. HILL
PROFIT AND LOSS ACCOUNT FOR PERIOD ENDED.........

	£	£
Gross profit		7,600
Less: Expenses		
Wages	5,000	
Light and heat	1,500	6,500
Net Profit		1,100

Note that the above profit and loss account shows the results of operations over a period of time. In fact, the concept of net profit (income) is meaningless unless it is related to a period of time. For external reporting purposes the period of time is usually one year. However, the accounting period of a year is often subdivided into smaller periods for management information purposes. For example, management need to know from month to month whether sales revenue is rising or falling, whether expenses are being held at the level anticipated, etc.

It is important to stress that the trading and profit and loss accounts are a fundamental and basic part of the double-entry process. Each revenue and expense account, as we have already explained, can be considered to be sub-divisions of owner's capital account. Revenues increase owner's capital whereas expenses decrease owner's capital. Thus at the end of the accounting period each revenue and expense account is transferred, within the double-entry system, to either the trading or profit and loss account. For example, the sales account of A. Hill in the previous chapter would be transferred as follows:

Sales Account					Trading Account	
		4 Bank	5,000		Sales	16,500
Transfer to		7 Debtors	9,000			
Trading a/c	16,500	13 Debtors	2,500			
	16,500		16,500			

Likewise, all the expense accounts will be transferred at the period end by way of debit to the profit and loss account and a credit entry in the relevant expense account. As a result of such transfers the balances in these accounts are reduced to zero. The profit and loss account is therefore a summary account. If the revenues (credit entries) exceed the expenses (debit entries), the profit and loss account will have a credit balance representing a net profit for the period. Conversely, if the expenses exceed the revenues, the profit and loss account will have a debit balance indicating a net loss for the period. In turn, the balance on the profit and loss account is transferred to the owner's capital account. The net impact would be the same if all revenue and expense transactions were directly entered into the owner's capital account. However, in so doing there would be a considerable loss of information since the profit and loss account would no longer be required. In other words, the profit and loss account exists because expenses and revenues are initially recorded in subdivisions of the owner's capital account. The profit and loss account is a summary of those expenses and revenues.

The computation of net profit for a year (and closing balance sheet) is illustrated using the following example, based on the trial balance extracted from the books of M. Cox at 30 June 19 . . (Exhibit 4.4). You are to assume a closing stock valuation of £1,900.

In practice, the trading account is combined with the firm's profit and loss account for computation purposes. The resulting statement is simply referred to as the profit and loss account or the income statement (Exhibit 4.5). Moreover, it is frequently presented in vertical format but it still remains an integral part of the double-entry system.

Exhibit 4.4

M. COX
TRIAL BALANCE AT 30 JUNE 19. .

	£000s Dr.	£000s Cr.
Capital		5,800
Premises	2,250	
Plant and machinery	2,010	
Loan payable (long term)		1,000
General expenses	360	
Purchases and sales	6,258	10,502
Debtors and creditors	1,524	1,479
Deposit interest received		74
Telephone	247	
Advertising	724	
Rent and rates	353	
Wages and salaries	2,172	
Cash on deposit	1,363	
Loan interest payable	94	
Stock (opening)	1,500	
	18,855	18,855

Note: closing stock is valued at £1,900.

The matching principle

Underlying the transactions approach to income measurement is the accruals or matching concept of accounting. This concept recognises revenue when earned, i.e. when realised in the form of cash or of indebtedness which is reasonably certain of being converted into cash; revenue is then 'matched' with associated costs and expenses by including them both in the profit and loss accounts for the same period. This recognises the importance of matching in any accounting period the costs or expenses associated with the generation of revenues within that accounting period.

In order to apply the matching principle, the accounting system must ensure that revenue is recognised when it is earned and that expenses are set-off against revenue in the period in which revenue is recognised. This seems at first sight to be a fairly simple task. However, as we shall see later, one major problem in income measurement is to distinguish between Capital and Revenue Expenditure.

YEAR-END EXPENSE AND REVENUE ADJUSTMENTS

The income statement starts with the sales revenue for the period from which all the expenses matched in the same period are deducted, the residue being either a net profit or a net loss. So far we have assumed that the expense payment during the period was equal to the expense incurred.

Exhibit 4.5

FINAL ACCOUNTING REPORTS
M. COX
PROFIT AND LOSS ACCOUNT FOR THE PERIOD ENDED 30 JUNE 19. .

	£000s	£000s
Sales revenue		10,502
Less: Cost of sales		
Opening stock	1,500	
Purchases	6,258	
Deduct: closing stock	(1,900)	5,858
Gross profit		4,644
Add: miscellaneous revenue—interest received		74
		4,718
Less: General expenses	360	
Telephone	247	
Advertising	724	
Rent and rates	353	
Wages and salaries	2,172	3,856
Profit before interest		862
Less: Interest payable		94
Profit after interest (net profit)		768

M. COX
BALANCE SHEET AT 30 JUNE 19. .

		£000s
Fixed Assets		
Premises		2,250
Plant and machinery		2,010
		4,260
Current assets		
Stock	1,900	
Debtors	1,524	
Cash on deposit	1,363	
	4,787	
Less: Current liabilities		
Creditors	(1,479)	3,308
		7,568
Financed by:		
Capital		5,800
Profit and loss account		768
		6,568
Long-term liability		1,000
		7,568

In reality, the expense payment rarely corresponds with the expense incurred. This is typically the case with payments in relation to insurance premiums and office supplies. Thus in order to show a true and fair view of the profit performance for the period, adjustments to some of the account balances in the ledger must be made before the financial statements are prepared. The various adjusting entries required at the end of the period may be classified into the following groups: (*a*) accrued expenses, (*b*) prepaid expenses, (*c*) revenue receivable, (*d*) deferred revenue, (*e*) adjustments for bad debts and finally depreciation of fixed assets. Each of these adjustments is now discussed in turn.

Accrued expenses

Accrued expenses or accruals represent expenses incurred prior to the accounting period in which they are paid. Interest on borrowed money is a good example of an expense which accumulates from day to day but this daily accumulation is not usually recorded in the books of account. Rather the payment of interest is recorded. However, at the end of the accounting period an adjusting entry will have to be made for any expenses which have accrued but which have not been recorded.

For example, a company has been renting a premises for £1,000 per annum. In the accounting year ended 31 December only £700 was paid and this is reflected in the rent account in the ledger as follows:

Rent account	
Bank	700

If this is the only transaction in the rent account then the balance of £700 will appear on the trial balance at the end of the year. It would be incorrect to write off only £700 to the profit and loss account since this sum does not adequately reflect the expense *incurred* during the period. Rather, the company has occupied the premises and has a legal obligation to pay rent for the twelve-month period which amounts to £1,000. The accountant, in preparing the profit and loss account, will make an adjustment at the year end to incorporate the accrual of £300. This £300 will be paid as a future transaction in a future accounting period. The adjustment, which takes place within the context of the double-entry system, will be:

DEBIT Rent (expense) account
CREDIT Accruals (liability) account

Rent account				Accruals account		
Bank	700	Transfer to			31/12 Rent	300
31/12 Accruals	300	P/L a/c	1,000			

This adjustment records the rent expense and related liability outstanding at the end of the period. In brief, the impact of the adjustment for the accrued expense is to increase the expense for the period to be transferred to the profit and loss account. Thus, the figure for rent expense in the profit and loss account will be £1,000 and £300 will be recorded as 'accruals' on the balance sheet which forms part of current liabilities. This indicates that at the end of the accounting period, £300 is owned by the firm in respect of rent.

As an alternative to using two ledger accounts to record the accrual adjustment, some accountants will make the adjustment in the rent account only. This practice is common and perfectly acceptable since the basic principle remains the same. The £300 adjustment is made to the debit side of the ledger account and this allows a transfer of £1,000 to be made to the profit and loss account at the year end. However, to complete the double-entry, the balance of £300 is carried down on the credit side of the ledger account below the underlines and is shown as a liability.

Rent account

Bank	700	Transfer to	
31/12 Bal.	300	P/L a/c	1,000
	1,000		1,000
		1/1 Bal.	300

Prepaid expenses

Prepaid expenses or prepayments represent an expense paid for prior to the period in which it was used or consumed. This occurs in the case of payments for office supplies, a portion of which are normally unused at the end of the accounting period. It also occurs in situations of expenses being paid in advance, e.g. insurance premiums or rent payments.

The rationale behind this type of adjustment is that since a portion of the payment has not been consumed, it is not an expense for the period. Rather the unexpired or unused portion represents an asset at the balance sheet date, which allows it to be carried forward and matched against the revenue of the appropriate period. In summary, prepaid expenses are assets.

For example, during an accounting period a company paid for £2,000 of heating oil of which £400 was unused at the end of the year. The ledger account for heating will show a payment of £2,000 and this will subsequently appear in the firm's trial balance.

Light and heat account

Bank	2,000

However, to transfer £2,000 to the profit and loss account under the heading of heating expenses would be incorrect since only £1,600 has been used during this period. The accountant will therefore make an adjustment at the year end to reflect this prepayment of £400.

Light and heat account

		Transfer to	
		P/L a/c	1,600
Bank	2,000	31/12 Bal.	400
	2,000		2,000
1/1 Bal.	400		

The end result of this adjustment will be twofold:

(*i*) Reduce the expense for the period to be transferred to the income statement. Thus the figure in the profit and loss account for heating expense will be £1,600 and this is the correct amount of the expense for the year.

(*ii*) Introduce 'prepayments' on the balance sheet which forms part of current assets. This indicates that at the end of the accounting period there is a stock of heating oil in the amount of £400.

If this adjustment was not made, expenses would be overstated for the year and consequently the net profit would be understated by £400. In addition, the balance sheet would be affected by the failure to make this adjustment; current assets would be understated by £400 as would owner's capital.

Revenue receivable

Revenue receivable represents revenue which has been earned during the accounting period but which has not been received in cash by the firm. Common items in this category would be rent receivable and deposit interest receivable. It is also possible that a firm might earn revenue during the current accounting period but not bill the customers until the next accounting period. This situation could occur where, for example, additional services will be performed for the same customer in the next period. In which case the sales invoice might not be prepared until the next period.

Any revenue that has been earned but not recorded in the books of account during the current accounting period should be recorded at the end of the accounting period by way of an adjusting entry. For example, a company placed £1,000 on a twelve-month deposit at an annual rate of interest of 12 per cent. During the year interest received amounted to £90. The ledger account for interest receivable will show the cash receipt of £90 and this figure will appear on the firm's trial balance.

Deposit interest received account

	Bank	90

At year end the accountant will make an adjustment and the end result of this adjustment will be twofold:

(*i*) Increase the revenue for the period to be transferred to the income statement. Thus the amount transferred to the profit and loss account in respect of interest receivable will be £120.

(*ii*) Introduce 'revenue receivable' on the balance sheet which forms part of current assets. This indicates that the firm is due to receive £30 interest in respect of its deposit account.

Deposit interest received account

Transfer to		Bank	90
P/L a/c	120	31/12 Bal.	30
	120		120
1/1 Bal.	30		

In reality, this sum would probably be included under the heading of 'prepayments'. Large organisations may include both revenue receivable and prepayments as part of their debtors total.

Deferred revenue

In some instances, customers may pay in advance for goods or services to be rendered in later accounting periods. This typically occurs in the case of clubs who collect revenue in advance through the sale of season tickets or, alternatively, members may pay two or three years' subscriptions in one lump sum.

For accounting purposes, amounts collected in advance do not represent revenue, because these amounts have not yet been earned. For example, the amounts received in respect of subscriptions will be debited to the bank account (and credited to subscriptions account). However, at the end of the accounting period some adjustment must be made to the subscriptions account for subscriptions received which relate to a future accounting period. These subscriptions received in advance can be described as deferred revenue: they can be considered to be a liability since they carry the obligations on the club to provide services in the future. In some respects the liability in the form of deferred revenue is different from other types of liabilities. This is because deferred revenue liabilities will be settled in future accounting periods by rendering services rather than making payment in cash.

For example, a golf club has 1,000 members who pay an annual subscription of £100 each. At the end of the accounting year it was discovered that all members had paid their subscription during the year and, in addition, five had paid their subscription for the following year. The subscription account will appear as follows:

Subscriptions account

	Bank (1,005 @ £100) 100,500

At the end of the year it would be appropriate to transfer only £100,000 to the club's income statement (i.e. 1,000 members at £100 each). An adjustment of £500 is therefore required in respect of deferred revenue. This can be achieved by crediting £500 to a deferred revenue account and debiting the subscriptions account. The remaining balance on the subscriptions account (£100,000) will then be transferred to the income statement at the end of the accounting period. The balance of £500 on the deferred revenue account represents a liability and appears on the balance sheet under the heading of current liabilities.

Subscriptions account		Deferred revenue account	
Deferred revenue 500	Bank 100,500		Subs. 500

It is perfectly acceptable to make the above adjustment in the subscriptions account only and this is commonly done. A debit entry of £500 is made, as usual, to the subscriptions account but it is recorded as a balance and brought down on the credit side of the account. The completed account is as follows, which shows the transfer to the income statement of £100,000.

Subscriptions account

Transfer to income a/c 31/12 Bal.	100,000 500	Bank	100,500
	100,500		100,500
		Bal.1/1	500

Adjustments for bad debts

In the previous chapter it was mentioned that an inevitable part of selling goods on credit was that bad debts will occur. Regardless of how diligent the credit control process is, some bad debts will arise in a business from errors of judgment or because of unexpected developments. Bad debts are a normal business expense and will be transferred to the profit and loss account at the end of the accounting period. Indeed, it can be argued that some bad debts are evidence of a sound credit policy. If the credit control department should become too cautious and conservative in assessing credit customers, it might avoid bad debts but, in so doing, lose profitable business by rejecting many potential and acceptable customers. When bad debts are discovered, the relevant asset account must be reduced by the amount of the bad debt (by way of a credit entry) and the bad debts expense account must be increased by the amount of the bad debt (to complete the double-entry).

In some cases, bad debts will not be known until the year following sale. This creates a problem in the context of the matching principle and profit determination. The matching principle applied to profit determination means that revenue earned during an accounting period should be matched against the expenses incurred in earning that revenue. For example, a debtor which originates from a sale in year 1 but is specified a bad debt in year 2 is an expense of year 1. Unless each year's bad debts are estimated and reflected in the accounts, the net profit will be overstated and the assets (on the balance sheet) will be overstated.

It may not be possible to tell in advance which customers will pay their account and which ones will prove to be bad. It is therefore not possible to credit the account of any customer in relation to potential bad debts. The only alternative is to credit a separate account called bad debts provision with the amount of debtors deemed to be uncollectible and bad. This bad debt provision can be described as a subdivision of the debtors account. The bad debts provision account represents an anticipated reduction in the debtors account and, as a result, it will always have a credit balance. On the balance sheet, therefore, the gross amount of debtors will be shown less a deduction for the bad debts provision. The larger the amount of the bad debts provision, the lower will be the amount of net debtors shown on the balance sheet. However, for profit determination purposes, any increase in the bad debts provision will be written-off to the profit and loss account as an ordinary business expense.

Estimating bad debts provision

There are two popular methods of estimating bad debts provision. The first is to set the provision at a constant percentage of gross debtors at the end of the account period. Typical percentages would be 5 per cent or 10 per cent. This percentage approach is simple but it is not as reliable as estimating bad debts by way of a debtors ageing schedule. The longer the debt remains unpaid, the greater the likelihood that it will not be collected in full. In recognition of this fact, the analysis of debtors by age groups can be used to determine a realistic amount of the bad debts provision. To determine this amount we estimate the percentage of uncollectible accounts for each age group of debtors. This percentage, when applied to the debtors in each group, gives the estimated bad debt portion. By adding together the estimated bad debts for all age groups, the required balance on the bad debts provision account is determined. The ageing schedule below shows how the bad debts provision could be determined. If an analysis such as this is performed every month, management will be informed continuously on the trends of collection and can take appropriate action to ease or restrict credit policy. Moreover this schedule can be used to evaluate the performance of the credit control department.

Ageing schedule of debtors

Days due	Debtors	% to be applied	Estimated bad debts
	£		£
1 – 30	15,000	Nil	Nil
31 – 60	30,000	5	1,500
61 – 90	40,000	10	4,000
91 – 120	30,000	15	4,500
Over 120	10,000	20	2,000
	125,000		12,000

This schedule indicates that a bad debts provision of £12,000 is required based on total debtors of £125,000. If the bad debts provision account has a previous balance of say, £9,000 based on last year's account, an adjusting entry of £3,000 is then required to bring the account up to the required balance of £12,000. The entry is as follows:

> DR. Bad debts account £3,000
> CR. Bad debts provision account £3,000

In summary, we are acknowledging that additional (but estimated) bad debts of £3,000 have been incurred during the accounting period and this sum is debited to the bad debts account. In turn this expense amount will be transferred to the profit and loss account. Simultaneously, we are writing down the asset debtors by £3,000. However, this reduction cannot be performed in any specific debtor's account since we do not know in advance the specific customer. Consequently, the reduction is recorded by way of a credit entry in the bad debts provision account, which as we have described above, is a subdivision of the debtors account. The balance sheet at year end will show:

Current Assets	£	£
Debtors	125,000	
Less: Bad debts		
provision	12,000	113,000

DEPRECIATION OF FIXED ASSETS

To prepare a profit and loss account and determine net profit for an accounting period, we use the matching or accruals principle. Under the matching principle, revenues are recognised when earned, i.e. when realised in the form of cash or when reasonably certain of conversion into cash; revenue is then 'matched' with associated costs and expenses by including them both in the profit and loss account for the same period. Since expenses are incurred in order to produce revenues, this year's revenues are matched with this year's expenses. To carry out the matching principle one must ensure that all expenses are recorded in the period in which they are incurred. One such expense is depreciation of fixed assets.

Fixed assets have a useful life extending over a number of years and this creates an accounting problem because to write-off the entire cost of the asset in the year of purchase to the profit and loss account would clearly be incorrect. Fixed assets will be used over a relatively long period of time, and then disposed of when it is no longer of use to the firm. Yet assets depreciate and at the end of their useful life many have a small or nil residual value.

It is important to note that it is the purpose for which the asset is used that is the determinant of its classification. A motor car in a garage business may be a current asset (i.e. stock) if the object of possessing it is to sell it to a customer. However, if the vehicle is owned by the firm for the purpose of transporting the sales manager in the course of his duties, it is classified as a fixed asset. The nature of the asset is the same in both cases, but the use to which it is put differs. It is the usage which determines the classification.

Depreciation can be defined as a measure of the wearing out, consumption or reduction in the useful economic life of a fixed asset whether arising from use, passage of time or obsolescence through technological or market changes. Accountants solve the problem of accounting for depreciation by reference to the accruals or matching concept. This means that we should write-off that portion of the costs, by way of depreciation, which has been incurred in generating sales revenue. The practical application of this regarding fixed assets is that, if an asset is deemed to last five years, then for example, one-fifth of the cost of the asset is written-off as depreciation each year to the profit and loss account. The asset will help generate revenues for five years and we match the cost of the asset with the period over which it generates revenues. Depreciation is a charge against profits for a year. It is an attempt to reflect the partial using-up of the life of the company's fixed assets. Depreciation is simply a book-keeping entry and does not involve any cash flow.

Three points are initially worth noting with regard to depreciation:

(a) Depreciation is based on the original purchase price when the asset was acquired, i.e. its historical cost. As shall be explained later, the eventual replacement cost of the asset at the end of its useful life is not used by accountants to determine annual depreciation provisions. However, in an inflationary environment, failure to anticipate increased replacement costs of fixed assets is capable of creating cash flow difficulties for the company when the asset is due for replacement.

Neither is depreciation based on the realisable value of the asset, i.e. the amount that the asset would realise if sold on the open market. The argument for this approach includes the fact that the firm intends to hold the asset, and not to sell it. In addition, the asset may have been specially produced to the firm's requirements, and thus may have considerable value to the firm despite the fact that if sold by them it would realise very little. However this accounting treatment may change if proposals by the accounting standards setting body are accepted. The proposals (ED 51) say that fixed assets should normally be stated in the balance sheet at their open market value. Revaluations should take place on a class by class basis, at least once every five years.

(*b*) The annual depreciation charge depends largely on the estimated useful economic life of the asset. As a result, it is inevitable that the written down value will differ from the ultimate sales proceeds, thereby generating a profit or loss in the year of disposal.

(*c*) Depreciation is a measurement of time and not of value.

The main factors in determining the useful economic life of a fixed asset and thus the number of accounting periods it will serve are:
—The passage of time (e.g. lease on a factory).
—Wear and tear which reflects the intensity of use and also the policy in relation to maintenance and repair.
—Obsolescence which could be a result of technological improvements.
—Rate of extraction (e.g. a gravel pit).
All four factors need to be considered when deciding on an appropriate depreciation policy.

There are three main methods of providing for depreciation on fixed assets: (1) the straight-line method; (2) the reducing balance method; (3) the machine hour method. Before examining these methods it must be emphasised that the exact amount of depreciation will not be known until the asset is ultimately disposed of. While the asset is still in use, the annual depreciation charge can only be an estimate of the amount of the asset used up during the accounting period.

To calculate depreciation we need to know or estimate:

(*a*) The cost of the asset.

(*b*) The residual or scrap value, although in many cases this will not be significant. Consequently the scrap value may sometimes be ignored in the calculation.

(*c*) The estimated useful economic life, i.e. its useful life to its present owner. Most assets (except land) have a finite useful life but this can be difficult to estimate.

Example: A company purchased an asset for £10,000 which has an estimated useful life of four years and is expected to realise £2,000 when disposed of. There will be a total of 8,000 production hours of use available from it.

Straight-line method: This method is also referred to as the fixed instalment method. The formula for calculating annual depreciation under the straight-line method is:

$$\frac{\text{Historic cost of asset less realisable value}}{\text{Estimated useful life}} \quad = \quad \text{annual charge}$$

i.e. $\quad \dfrac{£10,000 - £2,000}{4 \text{ years}} \quad = \quad £2,000 \text{ per annum}$

The straight-line method spreads the net cost evenly over the estimated useful life of the asset. This method of depreciation is very popular since it is easy to use and widely understood. Its disadvantage is that an even amount of depreciation is written-off each year yet certain assets depreciate more quickly during the initial years of their lives.

Reducing balance method: Using the reducing balance method, a pre-determined percentage is applied to the cost of the asset, and the percentage amount is the amount of depreciation for the first year. In succeeding years the same percentage is applied to the book value of the asset, i.e. cost less total depreciation written-off to date. Thus, the annual depreciation charge gets smaller and smaller each year. Its advantages are:

(*a*) If the depreciation charge in the early years is high when repairs and maintenance are expected to be low (in later years the position will be reversed), then the total annual expense associated with this asset will be relatively stable.

(*b*) The higher depreciation in early years reflects the early obsolescence associated with many fixed assets. This is appropriate where assets depreciate more rapidly in their early years compared with later years.

The appropriate percentage to use for the reducing balance method can be obtained by using the following formula:

$$R = 1 - \sqrt[N]{\frac{S}{C}}$$

Where R = annual rate of depreciation
1 = Unity, i.e. 1
N = Useful life (years) of asset
S = Scrap value at end of life
C = Historic cost of asset

It can be observed from the above formula that for the reducing balance method to apply there must be a scrap value for the asset. Exhibit 4.6 shows the appropriate reducing balance percentage given the estimated useful life and the scrap value as a percentage of historic cost. Since the above fixed asset has an estimated useful life of four years, and the scrap value is 20 per cent of cost, then the appropriate percentage to use is 33 per cent. The depreciation charges for the first two years will be as follows:

	£
Cost	10,000
Depreciation (Year 1) (33% x 10,000)	3,300
	6,700
Depreciation (Year 2) (33% x 6,700)	2,211
	4,489

Exhibit 4.6

Useful Life (Years)	Annual Depreciation Rates–Reducing Balance Method* Scrap value (S) as percentage of cost (C)				
	20%	15%	10%	5%	1%
2	55	61	68	77	90
3	41	47	53	63	78
4	33	38	43	53	68
5	27	31	37	45	60
6	23	27	32	39	54
7	20	23	28	35	48
8	18	21	25	31	44
9	16	19	22	28	40
10	15	17	20	26	37

* Based on opening book value (not cost) of asset.

Machine hour method: There are instances where a machine's life can be predicted in terms of hours of use. Using the machine hour method, the depreciable amount (cost less scrap value) is divided by the estimated running hours of the machine and an hourly rate is ascertained. Each accounting period will then be charged with an amount directly proportional to the machine usage in that period. However a record of machine running time will be required. Further, it should be recognised that during a period of low usage the machine may depreciate due to the passage of time at a rate greater than the usage indicates. In such circumstances, a conservative approach would normally be taken so that a higher depreciation charge may be applied.

Assuming the above machine had a usage pattern of 4,000 hours in its first year and 2,000 in the second, then the annual depreciation rates would be:

$$\text{Machine hour rate} = \frac{\text{Depreciable amount}}{\text{Estimated running hours}} = \frac{£10,000 - £2,000}{8,000 \text{ hours}} = £1 \text{ hr}$$

Year	Usage pattern	Annual depreciation
1	4,000 hours	£4,000
2	2,000 hours	£2,000

Accounting entries for depreciation

Depreciation involves the systematic apportionment of the cost of the asset to the income statement over the estimated life of the asset. It does not involve a cash outlay but it still represents a significant expense item for most businesses. Failure to record depreciation would result in the understatement of expenses in the profit and loss account and therefore, the overstatement of net profit.

In terms of the accounting equation depreciation reduces the net assets of the enterprise and therefore, owner's capital. The dual entry at first sight would be to debit owner's capital to record the expense and credit the asset account to record the reduction of the asset. However, we have already seen that it is usual practice to record expenses in separate ledger accounts. This is also done in respect of depreciation which is debited to a depreciation (expense) account. The credit entry could be made to the asset account, indicating a reduction in that asset. However, it is customary and more efficient to record such credits in a separate account entitled aggregate (or accumulated) depreciation account or sometimes provision for depreciation account. This aggregate depreciation account is a subdivision of the asset account. The original cost of the asset and the aggregate amount of depreciation recorded over the years can be more easily determined when separate accounts are maintained for both the asset (at cost) and the related aggregate depreciation.

The appropriate entries to record annual depreciation are:

> DR. Depreciation (expense) account
> CR. Aggregate depreciation account

The term 'depreciation' should never be confused with the term 'aggregate or accumulated depreciation'. In common with all other expense accounts the depreciation expense will be transferred to the profit and loss account at the end of the accounting period. The aggregate depreciation account, being a subdivision of the asset account, will be shown as a deduction against cost to provide a proper balance sheet amount for the asset.

The annual depreciation charges on the above fixed asset and the balance sheet presentation are summarised in Exhibit 4.7:

Exhibit 4.7

	Straight-line £	Reducing balance £	Machine hours £
Depreciation (P/L)			
Year 1	2,000	3,300	4,000
Year 2	2,000	2,211	2,000
Balance sheet			
Year 1 Cost	10,000	10,000	10,000
Less aggregate depreciation	(2,000)	(3,300)	(4,000)
BOOK VALUE	8,000	6,700	6,000
Year 2 Cost	10,000	10,000	10,000
Less aggregate depreciation	(4,000)	(5,511)	(6,000)
BOOK VALUE	6,000	4,489	4,000

Comparisons of Depreciation Methods

In relation to accounting for depreciation modern accounting practice requires:

(*a*) The disclosure in the company's financial statements of the accounting policy by way of note, i.e. disclose the assets being depreciated, the method being used and the annual rates. In addition, the depreciation charge for the year, the gross cost of the depreciable assets and the related accumulated (aggregate) depreciation must also be disclosed, as well as additions and disposals.

(*b*) The method of depreciation to be applied consistently. A change from one method to another is permissible only on the grounds that the new method will give a fairer presentation of the results and of the financial position.

(*c*) It is not appropriate to omit depreciation of a fixed asset on the grounds that its market value is greater than its book value. If account is taken of such increased values by increasing the net book value of the fixed asset in the balance sheet then depreciation should be based on the revised figure.

Disposal of fixed assets

As fixed assets wear out or become obsolete they will be scrapped, sold or traded in for new fixed assets. This is referred to as the disposal of fixed assets and accounting entries are required to record this. It will be first necessary to remove from the asset account the original cost of the asset. In addition, it is necessary to remove the accumulated depreciation to date from the aggregate depreciation account. These amounts are transferred to a temporary account entitled disposal account. For example, the above fixed assets, costing £10,000, were disposed of at the end of year four. If the company had depreciated the asset on a straight-line method over four years to give a residual amount of £2,000, the balances and transfers to the disposal account would be as follows:

Fixed asset (cost) account			Aggregate depreciation account		
		Transfer to	Transfer to		
Balance	10,000	disposal a/c 10,000	disposal a/c 8,000	Balance	8,000

Disposal account					
31/12/..	Transfer from		31/12/..	Transfer from	
	asset a/c	10,000		agg. depr. a/c	8,000

Since the residual amount (£2,000) is only an estimate, it is inevitable that assets may be sold for a price that is different from the book amount at date of disposal. The profit (loss) on disposal will be the difference between the sales proceeds and the book amount of the fixed asset. Thus, if the asset was sold for £3,000 at the end of the four years the accounting entries would be:

> DR. Bank account (with sales proceeds)
> CR. Disposal account (with sales proceeds)

Disposal account					
31/12/..	Transfer from		31/12/..	Transfer from	
	asset a/c	10,000		agg. depr. a/c	8,000
			31/12/..	Bank	3,000
31/12/..	Transfer to				
	P/L a/c	1,000			
		11,000			11,000

The completed disposal account shows the sales proceeds in the amount of £3,000. This gives a profit on disposal of £1,000 which, like other gains, is transferred to the profit and loss account for the period. If, in the above example, the asset was sold for £1,500 then the loss on disposal would amount to £500 which would ultimately be debited to the profit and loss account for year four.

The disposal of a fixed asset at book amount would result in neither a profit or a loss.

In some situations a fixed asset is traded-in against a new fixed asset. Thus, there is no sales proceeds in terms of cash entries The cash paid for the new asset, which will be reduced by the amount of the trade-in, will be debited to the fixed asset (cost) account and credited to the bank account. The trade-in value is then recorded by debiting the fixed asset (cost) account with the amount of the agreed trade-in and crediting the disposal account.

The end result is the same as if the asset was sold for cash and the full price was paid for the new fixed asset.

CAPITAL AND REVENUE EXPENDITURE

Throughout the life of a business, various expenditures must be made. Taking the example of a shopkeeper, he needs, among other things, premises from which to operate. In addition he will incur lighting and heating costs together with wages and salaries of staff. The purchase of premises is classified as capital expenditure. On the other hand expenditure which is incurred in order to carry out his trade is classified as revenue expenditure and represents the costs of carrying on the business.

Capital expenditure

Capital expenditure may be defined as any expenditure incurred in creating, acquiring, extending or improving an asset for continuing use in the business. The important point is that the benefit derived from such capital expenditure will flow over a number of accounting periods.

Examples of capital expenditure are:

—Purchase of or additions to long-term assets, e.g. purchase of premises or a lease.
—Significant extension or improvement of existing assets.
—Installation of machinery, including wages of own labour force involved in installation.

At the end of an accounting period such expenditure will appear on the face of the balance sheet under the appropriate fixed asset heading.

Revenue expenditure

Revenue expenditure may be defined as outlay incurred for earning revenue or maintaining the earning capacity of the business. The benefit derived from such expenditure is normally used up in the current accounting period. Revenue expenditure represents the day-to-day running expenses of the business.

Examples of revenue expenditure are:

—wages and salaries;
—depreciation of fixed assets;
—light, heat, rent and rates.

The importance of the distinction

The distinction between capital and revenue expenditure is important because of the implications involved when preparing financial accounting statements of a business entity. Capital expenditure is reflected on the balance sheet of a firm under the heading 'fixed assets'. Revenue expenditure, on the other hand, is charged directly to the profit and loss account of the firm and thereby reduces profit (or increases losses). If an item of expenditure is treated incorrectly in the financial statements of an entity, then the profit (loss) figure for the accounting period will be distorted, and the balance sheet will not be an accurate reflection of the financial position of a business.

For example, if the purchase of equipment is incorrectly charged to the profit and loss account in the year of purchase, then

(*a*) The 'expenses' of the year will be overstated leading to an understatement of profit and

(*b*) Fixed assets on the balance sheet will be understated.

While the *recording* of transactions of a company is a technical and objective matter using the *debit-credit* convention, the accountant must exercise a great deal of judgment in *summarising* and *reporting* the activities of the firm. The accounting treatment of research and development expenditure is but one example. Obviously, research would not be undertaken unless there was some reasonable expectation of future benefits. Thus it is possible to consider such outlay in the nature of capital expenditure. However, many research efforts prove to be worthless and therefore represent revenue expenditure. A great deal of judgment is required in deciding the amount of the expenditure to be capitalised and the amount to be written-off immediately to the profit and loss account. Not surprisingly, research and development expenditure is the topic of an accounting standard and is discussed later.

Materiality

A starting point in distinguishing between capital and revenue expenditure is the concept of materiality. The term materiality refers to the relative importance or significance of an item or event. Accountants are primarily concerned with significant information and are not overly concerned with those items which have little effect on financial statements. For example, should the cost of a pencil sharpener, a wastepaper basket, or a stapler be recorded in the asset accounts and depreciated over their useful lives? Even though more than one period will benefit from the use of these assets, the concept of materiality permits the immediate recognition of the cost of these items as an expense on grounds that it would be meaningless to undertake depreciation accounting for such low-cost assets. The reported results of the company would not differ significantly.

We must recognise that the materiality of an item is a relative matter; what is material for one business unit may not be material for another. Materiality of an item may depend not only on its amount but also on its nature.

In summary, we can state the following rule: an item is material if there is a reasonable expectation that knowledge of it would influence the decisions of prudent users of financial statements.

ACCOUNTING FOR GOVERNMENT GRANTS (SSAP 4)

Capital-based grants are grants which provide a refund of part of the purchase price of fixed assets. In Ireland a common source of such grants is the Industrial Development Authority (IDA). How should these grants be recorded and disclosed in the financial statements? Should the asset be shown at the gross or net cost and how should one account for the fact that these grants are technically repayable to the IDA, if certain conditions are not fulfilled? When one considers the magnitude of the amounts involved, it is not surprising that accounting for government grants became an early accounting standard (SSAP 4). Prior to the standard, it was possible to credit the entire amount of the grant to the profit and loss account in year of receipt, or to credit the grant to a non-distributable reserve, or to credit the grant to the profit and loss account over the useful life of the asset concerned. SSAP 4 requires capital-based grants to be credited to revenue over the expected useful life of the asset. This may be achieved by either:

(a) Reducing the fixed asset account by the amount of the grant and calculating depreciation with reference to the 'written down' amount. This is the simplest method.

(b) Treating the amount of the grant as a deferred credit, a portion of which is credited to the profit and loss account annually over the useful life of the asset. The depreciation charge is initially based on the gross cost of the asset but this is reduced in the profit and loss account by the amount of the grant credited.

Both methods of accounting for capital grants on fixed assets have the same impact on the annual profit (or loss) figure. Their balance sheet impact, however, is different. In the former case the grant is used to write down the asset and so the relevant fixed assets are shown at their reduced cost. In the latter case, fixed assets are retained at their original, gross cost. The capital grant appears on the capital/liability side of the balance sheet as a deferred credit. It will be disclosed just under shareholders' funds but it does not form part of shareholders' funds.

For example, the group balance sheet of W & R Jacob plc at 31 December 1988 showed as a long-term liability 'government grants' in the amount of £345,000. By way of explanation, the notes to the accounts indicated that 'government grants of a capital nature are set up as deferred income and are amortised separately to the profit and loss account at the same rates as the related assets are depreciated'.

The arguments in favour of method one are, first, that commercial decisions on capital investment are (or should be) made on a 'net of grants' basis and second, this method is the simplest to apply. Method two has the advantage of showing the extent to which government grants are contributing to and may be influencing the company's investment programme.

It should be noted that the standard applies only to capital-based grants. Revenue-based grants, e.g. employment grants, are always credited straight to revenue in the same period as the related expenditure.

THE REPLACEMENT PROBLEM OF FIXED ASSETS

The objective of providing for depreciation is to systematically write down the original cost of fixed assets to their estimated scrap value over their useful life. This is in accordance with the accruals or matching concept of accounting. What many people fail to appreciate is that depreciation does not generate cash funds to provide for the replacement of fixed assets, particularly when the replacement cost of the fixed assets exceeds the original historic cost. Unless this increase is specifically provided for, the firm will not have sufficient cash funds for replacement. The cash shortfall will be the difference between the replacement and the original historic cost. This point is highlighted by the following, simplified example:

Mr Hill started a travelling fishmonger's business on the 1 January 19. . His capital was £2,000 which was immediately invested in a second-hand delivery truck. The truck had an estimated life of one year with a zero scrap value. Each weekday he went to the wholesale fishmarket and purchased sufficient fish to cover his daily sales. All these sales were for cash only. His only expenses were the motoring expenses which he paid for in cash and £2,000 depreciation on the motor truck. The resultant net profit figure, after charging depreciation, was withdrawn by way of 'dividend'. At the end of the year, the truck was held to be not roadworthy. A local garage offered him another second-hand vehicle for £5,000.

Mr Hill was amazed to find that he had not got sufficient cash to provide for the replacement of his only fixed asset. Without a replacement he could not continue trading.

Since Mr Hill has withdrawn the profits by way of 'dividend' the retained profit of the firm at the end of the year is 'nil'. However, the cash position of the firm will be £2,000 at the end of the year since depreciation is a non-cash item of expenditure. In other words, by providing for depreciation in the profit and loss account, the cash which may be withdrawn by way of dividend has been curtailed. The balance sheet of the business at the end of the first year is:

MR HILL
BALANCE SHEET AT END OF FIRST YEAR

	£	£
Fixed assets		
Motor vehicle at cost	2,000	
Less: Aggregate depreciation	(2,000)	Nil
Current assets		
Cash on hands		2,000
		2,000
Financed by:		
Capital invested		2,000
Add: Retained profits		Nil
		2,000

To replace his fixed asset (motor vehicle) Mr Hill needs £5,000 cash, of which £2,000 is on hand. The cash shortfall (£3,000) represents the additional replacement cost. Unless firms specifically provide for the increased replacement costs of fixed assets, they are likely to experience a cash shortfall when replacement is necessary.

While providing for the replacement of fixed assets seems a logical thing to do, it creates two problems. First, it can be very difficult to reasonably estimate the replacement cost, not only due to inflation but especially in an environment of rapid technological change. Secondly, replacement cost depreciation will normally be higher than historic cost depreciation and thus reported profits will be reduced.

There is a second factor that can result in a cash shortfall when fixed assets need to be replaced. Most businesses need to carry certain levels of stock and many will, in addition, grant credit to customers. If Mr Hill carried £1,000 worth of stock at the year end and also had granted £500 credit to customers, his closing balance sheet would be:

MR HILL
BALANCE SHEET AT END OF FIRST YEAR (WITH STOCK AND DEBTORS)

	£	£
Fixed assets		
Motor vehicle at cost	2,000	
Less: Aggregate depreciation	(2,000)	Nil
Current assets		
Stock	1,000	
Accounts receivable	500	
Cash on hands	500	2,000
		2,000
Financed by:		
Capital invested		2,000
Add: Retained profits		Nil
		2,000

Since stock is held and credit is given to customers, Mr Hill now has only £500 cash on hands. Thus, his overall cash shortfall for the replacement is £4,500. The increased replacement cost represents £3,000 of this sum. The balance (£1,500) represents the investment in additional working capital. In any business the increased replacement cost of fixed assets, coupled with the necessity to fund additional working capital requirements, can be the major drain on the cash resources of the firm.

QUESTION 4.1 (A)

On 31 December 19. . the following balances were extracted from the books of J. O'Neill.

	Debit £	Credit £
Capital		5,600
Premises	4,800	
Plant and machinery	3,100	
Debtors and creditors	4,100	1,400
General expenses	360	
Purchases and sales	6,230	12,900
Deposit Interest received		20
Telephone	240	
Advertising	130	
Interest	170	
Wages and salaries	2,100	
Cash on hands	40	
Bank overdraft		2,290
Stock (1.1.19. .)	1,600	
Rent and rates	630	
Administration expenses	510	
Stock Exchange investments at cost	200	
Long-term loan		2,000
	24,210	24,210

* Closing stock was valued at £1,800.

Requirement:

Prepare a trading and profit and loss account for the year ended 31 December 19 . ., together with a balance sheet at that date.

QUESTION 4.2 (A)

The following balances have been extracted from the books of Joe Hayes, a sole trader, at 31 December 19 . 0:

	Dr.	Cr.
Capital invested		8,000
Debtors and creditors	3,800	2,936
Purchases	26,419	
Wages and salaries	6,287	
Advertising	3,149	
Sales		44,900
Stock (1 January)	4,100	
Rent and rates	3,986	
Postage and stationery	369	
Repairs	1,219	
Premises	10,600	
Interest on loan	400	
Plant and equipment	2,500	
Bank		1,493
10% loan		7,000
Commission paid	1,500	
	64,329	64,329

The following information is provided:
  (1) Closing stock was valued at £6,109
  (2) Provision should be made for:

	Accruals	Prepayments
Wages and salaries	268	–
Advertising	914	–
Postage and stationery	438	351
Interest	?	?

  (3) Salesmen are entitled to a commission of 5 per cent, based on sales.
  (4) Included in the rent and rates payment for the year (£3,986) in the
       above trial balance are the following payments:

Rent (for twelve months to 31 October 19. 0)	£1,200
Rates (for half year to 31 March 19. 1)	£600

  (5) The 10% loan has been in issue for a number of years.

Requirement:
Prepare a trading and profit and loss account for the year ended 31
December 19. 0 together with a balance sheet as on that date.

QUESTION 4.3 (SM)
The following is a trial balance extracted from the ledger of Mr Colombo
as on 31 March 19. :

	£	£
Investments (at cost)	5,000	
Cash at bank	10,400	
Purchases	30,854	
Sales		49,406
Distribution costs	6,606	
Rent and rates	1,060	
Heating, lighting and insurance	434	
Wages and salaries	8,912	
Postage, stationery and telephone	492	
Advertising	2,240	
Office expenses	1,546	
Legal fees	1,440	
Opening stock	6,384	
Equipment	9,180	
Motor vehicles	12,220	
Premises	20,000	
Opening capital		71,530
Dividends received on investments		240
Debtors	16,100	
Creditors		11,692
	132,868	132,868

Requirement:

Prepare an income statement for the year ended 31 March 19 . . together with a balance sheet at that date making adjustments to give effect to the following:

(*a*) The stock valuation taken in the ordinary way at cost on 31 March 19 . . was £10,740.

(*b*) The following amounts are to be provided for expenses accrued and unpaid:

Rent	£240
Office expenses	£ 70
Distribution costs	£423

(*c*) The following amounts are prepaid:

Advertising	£310
Rates	£126
Postage	£ 64

QUESTION 4.4 (SM)

From the following balances prepare J. Green's income statement for the year ended 31 December 19. . and a balance sheet as at that date.

	£
Purchases	18,682
Postage	196
Sales	49,240
Repairs	1,140
General expenses	920
Light and heat	1,040
Debtors	9,300
Advertising	2,160
Trade creditors	3,080
Stock (1 January 19. .)	7,960
Fixtures and fittings	7,000
Capital account	21,146
Premises	14,500
Rent received	690
Cash in hand	80
Rent and rates	760
Cash at bank	3,120
Wages and salaries	7,298
10% loan payable	3,000
Interest	150
Printing and stationery	350
Investments	2,500

Adjustments are required in respect of the following:

(*a*)	Accruals	Prepayments
Postage	219	–
Light and heat	114	29
Rent and rates	396	473
Wages and salaries	126	918

(*b*) Closing stock at 31 December 19. . was valued at £3,372.

(*c*) The 10% loan was in existence for a number of years.

QUESTION 4.5 (SM)

John Doyle, a wholesaler grocer, prepares accounts each year to 31 December. His rent and rates expense is recorded in a single rent and rates account and transferred to the profit and loss account as a single figure.

Details of quarterly rent payments of £2,400 each and the dates of these payments for the year ended 31 December 19 . 3 are as follows:

Quarter Ending	Rent Paid	
31 Dec. 19 . 2	3 Jan.	19 . 3
31 Mar. 19 . 3	2 Apr.	19 . 3
30 Jun. 19 . 3	28 Jun.	19 . 3
30 Sep. 19 . 3	2 Oct.	19 . 3
31 Dec. 19 . 3	5 Jan.	19 . 4

The payments in respect of rates were as follows:

Half Year Ending	Rates Paid	
31 Mar. 19 . 3	29 Dec.	19 . 2 – £540
30 Sep. 19 . 3	25 Sep.	19 . 3 – £560
31 Mar. 19 . 4	20 Nov.	19 . 3 – £560

Requirement:
Prepare the combined rent and rates account in the ledger of John Doyle for the year ended 31 December 19 . 3.
(The Institute of Chartered Accountants in Ireland)

QUESTION 4.6 (A)

Jim Hunt, a grocer, prepares accounts each year to 31 December. His rent and rates expense is recorded in a single rent and rates account and transferred to the profit and loss account at year-end as a single figure.

Details of quarterly rent payments of £1,200 each and the dates of these payments for the year ended 31 December 19 . 7 are as follows:

Quarter Ending	Rent Paid	
31 Dec. 19 . 6	3 Dec.	19 . 6
31 Mar. 19 . 7	2 Jan.	19 . 7
30 Jun. 19 . 7	29 Jun.	19 . 7
30 Sep. 19 . 7	5 Dec.	19 . 7
31 Dec. 19 . 7	9 Jan.	19 . 8

The payments in respect of rates were as follows:

Half Year Ending	Rates Paid	
31 Mar. 19 . 7	5 Jan.	19 . 7 – £720
30 Sep. 19 . 7	3 Aug.	19 . 7 – £840
31 Mar. 19 . 8	2 Dec.	19 . 7 – £840

Requirement:
Prepare the combined rent and rates account in the nominal ledger of Jim Hunt for the year ended 31 December 19 . 7.

QUESTION 4.7 (A)

Alan Smith owns a small apartment block containing four flats, each of which is rented. He prepares annual accounts to 31 December.

On 1 January 19 . 3, flats were let at a monthly rental as follows:

	£
Flat A	100 per month
Flat B	150 per month
Flat C	150 per month
Flat D	200 per month

On 1 January 19 . 3, tenants in Flats A and D were each three months in arrears and the tenant in Flat B had paid three months in advance. On 1

August 19 . 3, all rents were increased by 10 per cent per annum whereupon the tenant of Flat A immediately vacated the property. A new tenancy commenced on 1 November 19 . 3.

Mr Smith did not keep a record of the rental payments received during the year but he has confirmed to you that there is no rent owing or prepaid on any of the flats at 31 December 19 . 3.

Requirement:

Prepare the rent receivable account of Mr Alan Smith, for the year ended 31 December 19 . 3.

(The Institute of Chartered Accountants in Ireland)

QUESTION 4.8 (A)

J. O'Brien owns a house consisting of four self-contained flats. He prepares accounts to 30 June each year.

These flats were let at an annual rental as follows:

	£
Flat A	200 per month
Flat B	250 per month
Flat C	150 per month
Flat D	300 per month

On 1 July 19 . 1, all tenants were three months in arrears. On 1 October 19 . 1, rents on all flats were increased by 10 per cent per annum. The tenant of flat A vacated the property on 31 December 19 . 1. The new tenant of that flat negotiated a reduced rent of £180 per month on payment of a deposit of *£1,000*. The new tenancy commenced immediately.

The following payments were received by Mr O'Brien during the year:

	£
Flat A	3,940
Flat B	3,150
Flat C	2,385
Flat D	3,780

Requirement:

(*a*) Prepare the rent receivable account, as it would appear in the nominal ledger of J. O'Brien , for the year ended 30 June 19 . 2.

(*b*) Explain briefly the application of the accruals concept to your calculations.

(The Institute of Chartered Accountants in Ireland)

QUESTION 4.9 (SM)

The following information was extracted from the trial balance of the BTN department store on 31 May 19 . 1:

	£
Debtors	88,000
Bad debts provision	4,600

During June, the store's credit sales amounted to £42,000 and cash sales amounted to £10,000. It received £46,000 from debtors and wrote off bad debts of £3,000.

On the basis of the past experience of customers, a final estimate of bad debts is to be revised at 30 June according to the following ageing schedule of debtors.

Age of Accounts	£ Debtors	Uncollectable Estimate (%)
0 – 30 days	42,000	1
31 – 60 days	28,000	5
61 – 90 days	7,000	10
over 90 days	4,000	20
	81,000	

Requirement:
(*a*) Prepare ledger accounts to record the above information for the month of June.

(*b*) Show the figure for net debtors to be included on the balance sheet at 30 June.

(The Institute of Chartered Accountants in Ireland)

QUESTION 4.10 (SM)
Jones decided to open a small business and operated a separate bank account. During Year 1 the following transactions took place:
(1) Jones invested £25,000 by way of capital.
(2) The company bought £60,000 of goods on credit.
(3) The company paid £20,000 in wages
                 paid £10,000 in administration costs
                 paid £45,000 to creditors for goods purchased
                 paid £1,000 for sundry expenses.
(4) The company acquired and paid for the following fixed assets:
                 A premises for £10,000
                 Equipment £18,000
(5) The company borrowed £10,000 for five years from Allan, interest free.
(6) Fixed assets are to be depreciated by 10 per cent for the full year.
(7) Sold goods on credit for £94,000.
(8) Received cash from debtors £64,000 (lodged).
(9) A government grant for £2,000 was received in respect of equipment.

Note: Closing stock of raw materials was valued at £10,000. There were no closing stocks of finished goods.

Requirement:
Prepare a profit and loss account of the business for the first year of trading and a balance sheet at year end.

QUESTION 4.11 (SM)
Most balance sheets include 'fixed assets at cost less aggregate depreciation' and an item which is usually significant in most profit and loss accounts is '*depreciation*'.

Requirement:
(*a*) Define the term 'Depreciation'.
(*b*) Explain why it appears in most profit and loss accounts.
(*c*) Explain the purpose of showing fixed assets at 'cost less aggregate depreciation' in the balance sheet.
(*d*) Describe two common methods of calculating the annual charge for depreciation.
(The Chartered Association of Certified Accountants)

QUESTION 4.12 (SM)
The charge for depreciation usually represents a significant item in the accounts of most organisations.

Consider a retail organisation which owns plant and equipment which cost £70,000 in 19.5 After a useful life of ten years it is expected that the scrap value will be £10,000.

Requirement:
(*a*) Describe the straight-line method and the reducing balance method which may be used for calculating the annual depreciation charge for 19.8.
(*b*) Calculate the charge using the two methods in respect of 19.8 for the office plant and equipment described above.
(*c*) Explain briefly the purpose of depreciation.
(The Chartered Association of Certified Accountants)

QUESTION 4.13 (A)
A firm buys a fixed asset for £10,000. The firm estimates that the asset will be used for five years, and will have a scrap value of about £100, less removal expenses. After exactly two and a half years, however, the asset is suddenly sold for £5,000. The firm always provides a full year's depreciation in the year of purchase and no depreciation in the year of disposal.

Requirement:

(*a*) Write up the relevant accounts (including disposal account but not profit and loss account) for each of years 1, 2 and 3:

(*i*) Using the straight-line depreciation method (assume 20 per cent p.a.);

(*ii*) Using the reducing balance depreciation method (assume 40 per cent p.a.).

(*b*) (*i*) What is the purpose of depreciation? In what circumstances would each of the 2 methods you have used be preferable?

(*ii*) What is the meaning of the net figure for the fixed asset in the balance sheet at the end of year 2?

(*c*) If the asset was bought at the beginning of year 1, but was not used at all until year 2 (and it is confidently anticipated to last until year 6), state under each method the appropriate depreciation charge in year 1, and briefly justify your answer.

(The Chartered Association of Certified Accountants)

QUESTION 4.14 (SM)

Susan Ltd commenced business on 2 January 19 . 3. The company purchased and sold fixed assets during the three years ended 31 December 19 . 5, as follows:

					£
2 Jan. 19 . 3	Purchased	Blander	Mk 1 for	10,000	
2 Jan. 19 . 3	Purchased	Mixer	Mk 1 for	12,000	
1 Mar. 19 . 4	Purchased	Blander	Mk 2 for	15,000	
1 Sep. 19 . 4	Purchased	Mixer	Mk 2 for	14,100	
1 Apr. 19 . 5	Sold	Mixer	Mk 1 for	6,000	
1 Oct. 19 . 5	Purchased	Blender	Mk 3 for	15,000 (gross)	

but received £5,000 trade-in allowance for Blender Mk 1.

It is company policy to depreciate plant and machinery on a month-for-month basis as follows:

Blenders — 20 per cent per annum on a 'straight-line' method
Mixers — 10 per cent per annum on a 'reducing balance' method

Requirement:

Indicate clearly the impact of each of the above transactions on the annual profit and loss accounts of Susan Ltd for the 3 years ended 31 December 19 . 5

(The Institute of Chartered Accountants in Ireland)

QUESTION 4.15 (SM)

The following trial balance was extracted from the books of Albert Brown, a retailer, as at 31 December 19 . 8:

Capital account		110,000
Leasehold premises, at cost	65,000	
Wages	6,100	
Stationery	500	
Trade debtors	28,300	
Trade creditors		16,200
Fittings, at cost	28,000	
Lighting and heating	1,300	
Stock (1/1/ . 8)	20,300	
Postage and telephone	900	
Motor vehicles at cost	10,000	
Sundry expenses	400	
Cash at bank	6,700	
Selling expenses	2,800	
Purchases	193,800	
Sales		232,600
Bank term loan (short-term)		10,000
Investments (market value £6,000)	6,900	
Advertising	3,000	
Rent and rates	3,200	
Salaries	11,200	
Bank interest paid	700	
Investment income received		500
Aggregate depreciation: Leasehold premises		6,500
Motor vehicles		4,000
Fittings		9,300
	389,100	389,100

The following matters are to be taken into account in preparing the final accounts:

(1) Stock-in-trade, 31/12/ . 8 – £23,700
(2) Depreciation is to be provided on fixed assets as follows:
    (*a*) Leasehold premises: The lease is for ten years and is to be depreciated accordingly.
    (*b*) Fittings—10 per cent on cost (straight-line).
    (*c*) Motor vehicles—20 per cent on book amount (reducing balance).

Requirement:

Prepare a trading and profit and loss account for the year ended 31 December 19 . 8 together with a balance sheet as at that date.

QUESTION 4.16 (A)

You are given the following information about a sole trader.

TRIAL BALANCE 31 DECEMBER 19 . 8

	£000	£000
Bank	53	
Capital		300
Land and buildings	320	
Plant and machinery: Cost	200	
Aggregate depreciation		80
Closing stock	100	
Sales on credit		1,000
Cost of sales	600	
Operating expenses (including depreciation of 20)	140	
Bad debt written-off	2	
Debtors	100	
Accruals		5
Creditors		130
	1,515	1,515

Cash receipts—year to 31 December 19 . 8	£000
Sales	950

Cash payments—year to 31 December 19 . 8	
Purchases	560
Plant (1 January 19 . 8)	90
Operating expenses	150

The creditors figure has doubled since 1 January 19 . 8.

Requirement:

Open appropriate T accounts to enable you to calculate the items in the *opening* balance sheet at 1 January 19 . 8. Submit the summarised balance sheet at 1 January 19 . 8 and all workings.

(The Chartered Association of Certified Accountants)

QUESTION 4.17 (SM)

The following trial balance has been extracted from the books of S. Black at 31 December 19 . 8: (see next page)

The following information is available and needs to be taken into consideration before preparing final accounting reports:

	Debit £	Credit £
Purchases	19,000	
Sales		43,100
Repairs (*Notes 2 & 4*)	2,100	
Administration expenses	3,100	
Debtors	9,300	
Sales commission (*Note 3*)	1,400	
Sundry expenses	100	
Creditors		4,200
Stock (1 Jan. 19.8)	8,400	
Fixtures and fittings (*Note 4*)	4,000	
Land and buildings	15,000	
Rent received (*Note 6*)		600
Light and heat (*Note 2*)	900	
Balance at bank		400
Wages and salaries	8,600	
10% mortgage on premises		10,000
Interest (*Note 5*)	200	
Postage, telephone and stationery (*Note 2*)	700	
Deposit account	3,000	
Capital		17,500
	75,800	75,800

Note 1. Closing stock was valued at £3,500.

Note 2. Adjustments should be made for:

	Accruals	Prepayments
Repairs	£140	
Light and heat	£130	£40
Postage, telephone and stationery	£250	£60

Note 3. Commission is calculated at the rate of 5 per cent on sales.

Note 4. Included in repairs (£2,100) is a sum of £1,200 in respect of new fixtures and fittings.

Note 5. The loan was raised on 1 October 19 . 5, and interest became due from that date.

Note 6. Part of the buildings have been sub-let for a number of years at an annual rental of £1,000.

Note 7. A new motor vehicle was purchased on credit for £7,000 but no record had been made of this transaction and no invoice had been received.

Requirement:

Prepare a trading and profit and loss account for the year ended 31 December 19 . 8 together with a balance sheet as at that date.

QUESTION 4.18 (A)

The trial balance of Snodgrass, a sole trader, at 1 January 19 . 8 is as follows:

TRIAL BALANCE 1 JANUARY 19 . 8

	Dr. £000	Cr. £000
Capital		600
Fixed assets (net)	350	
Trade debtors	200	
Prepayments—rent	8	
—insurance	12	
Trade creditors		180
Accruals —electricity		9
—telephone		1
Stock	200	
Bank	20	
	790	790

The following information is given for the year:

	£000
Receipts from customers	1,000
Payments to suppliers	700
Payments for: rent	30
insurance	20
electricity	25
telephone	10
wages	100
Discounts allowed	8
Bad debts written-off	3
Depreciation	50

At 31 December 19 . 8 the following balances are given:

	£000
Trade debtors	250
Prepayments—rent	10
—telephone	2
Trade creditors	160
Accruals —electricity	7
—insurance	6
Stock	230

Requirement:

Prepare trading and profit and loss account for the year, and a balance sheet as at 31 December 19 . 8.

(The Chartered Association of Certified Accountants)

QUESTION 4.19 (SM)

Grants Ltd acquired a machine for £200,000, in respect of which it received a government grant of 25 per cent. The machine was estimated to have a ten-year life.

You are asked to show the differing accounting methods of treating the grant in accordance with SSAP 4 by showing:

(*a*) The relevant balance sheet figures at the end of year 1.

(*b*) The relevant profit and loss account figures for year 1.

QUESTION 4.20 (A)

In the year to 31 December 19 . 9, Amy bought a new fixed asset and made the following payments in relation to it:

	£	£
Cost as per suppliers list	12,000	
Less: agreed discount	1,000	11,000
Delivery charge		100
Erection charge		200
Maintenance charge		300
Additional component to increase capacity		400
Replacement parts		250

Requirement:

(*a*) State and justify the cost figure which should be used as the basis for depreciation.

(*b*) What does depreciation do, and why is it necessary?

(*c*) Briefly explain, without numerical illustration, how the straight-line and reducing balance methods of depreciation work. What different assumptions does each method make?

(*d*) Explain the term objectivity as used by accountants. To what extent is depreciation objective?

(*e*) It is common practice in published accounts in Germany to use the reducing balance method for a fixed asset in the early years of its life, and then to change to the straight-line method as soon as this would give a higher annual charge.

What do you think of this practice? Refer to relevant accounting conventions in your answer.

(The Chartered Association of Certified Accountants)

5.

Subsidiary Ledgers, Control Accounts, Books of Original Entry, Cash Control and Reconciliation

SUBSIDIARY LEDGERS AND CONTROL ACCOUNTS

While the firm has a small number of transactions and accounts, it may be convenient to maintain one ledger in which all accounts are kept. However, when the number of accounts required grows, a single ledger expands and a single individual has more than a full-time job keeping the ledger up to date. For example, a business that sells goods on credit would maintain a separate ledger account for each customer. If the business had 1,000 customers then this would require a ledger with 1,000 debtors accounts in addition to accounts dealing with other assets, liabilities etc. Also the trial balance at the end of the period would be a rather lengthy document. If the trial balance did not balance, the task of detecting the error(s) would be extremely difficult. To overcome these difficulties, the ledger may be divided up into sub-units. But a wholly random division is not satisfactory since it would be difficult to remember exactly in which section or subdivision a particular account appeared. Consequently, some rational division of the ledger accounts into 'sub-ledgers' is desirable. Generally accounts of a similar nature are segregated into separate ledgers.

The first accounts to be segregated are usually the *Debtors* accounts, and the *Creditors* accounts. These accounts are taken out of the main ledger, and form the *Debtors Ledger* and the *Creditors Ledger*, respectively. These subsidiary ledgers contain ONLY the appropriate accounts, i.e. the debtors ledger will contain all the accounts for debtors and no others, while the creditors ledger will contain all the accounts for creditors only and no other accounts. The remaining accounts, i.e. all accounts other than those for debtors and creditors are maintained in the original ledger, which is called the *Nominal Ledger*, or the *General Ledger*, so as to distinguish it from the subsidiary ledger(s). At this point, one can imagine that the writing-up of the accounts could be done by three persons, each having responsibility for one of the ledgers of the firm.

At the end of the accounting period, in order to obtain a trial balance, all the accounts in the three ledgers must be balanced and listed. If the trial balance does not balance, the error may have occurred in any one of the three ledgers. Some method of narrowing down the location of errors would obviously be desirable. In addition, with the division of responsibility allowed by subdivision of the ledger, a means of checking the activities of the individuals keeping the subsidiary ledgers is usually required. These objectives are achieved with the use of *Control Accounts*, to be maintained in the nominal ledger, associated with the subsidiary ledgers being kept by the firm.

Control accounts

Control accounts can be thought of as a *total* accounts for the subsidiary ledger in question. In the case where debtors and creditors ledgers are maintained, we would have two control accounts, a *debtors control account* and a *creditors control account*. The debtors control account balance should, at all times, be equal to the sum of all the balances on the individual debtors accounts. It is an account for *total debtors*. Similarly, the balance on the creditors control account equals the sum of the balances on the individual creditor accounts in the creditors ledger, and is therefore an account for *total creditors*. These *control* accounts are kept in the *nominal* ledger and therefore become part of the double-entry system. There is a control account for each subsidiary ledger and it is maintained in the nominal ledger. This mechanism allows a trial balance to be extracted from the nominal ledger alone. This is because the two controlling accounts represent the total amounts receivable from debtors and payable to creditors.

The entries in the individual debtors and creditors accounts in the subsidiary ledgers are not part of the double-entry system. Rather they are subsidiaries to the summarised entries in the nominal or general ledger.

Entering control accounts: The rule for writing up or posting transactions to control accounts is straightforward. Effectively, these control accounts are posted with the totals of the individual postings to the subsidiary ledger accounts. Therefore, the *debtors control account* in the *nominal* ledger is written up with the totals of the individual entries in the debtors accounts (in the debtors ledger), and the debtors control account is an asset account, just as the individual debtor accounts are asset accounts.

Example 1:
For example, suppose that Modern Products Ltd maintains a subsidiary debtors ledger, and a debtors control account in the nominal ledger. The balance at 1 January and transactions for the month of January are as follows:

Jan. 1: Balances on the debtors ledger were as follows:
     A £50.   B £75.   C £100.   D £80.
Jan. : Sales on credit to debtors were:
     A £20.   B £25.   D£50.
Jan. : Cash received from debtors:
     A £40.   C £55.   D £30.

It is apparent that the balance on the debtors control account at 1 January must be £305, the sum of the individual balances on the debtor accounts in the debtors ledger. The total of the sales to debtors for the month of January is £95, and the total cash received from debtors during the month of January is £125. The relevant *debtors control account* in the *nominal* ledger would be as follows:

Debtors Control Account

1/1 Balance	£305		
Jan. Sales	£95		
		Jan. Bank	£125
		31/1 Balance	£275
	£400		£400
1/2 Balance	£275		

The individual accounts in the subsidiary *Debtors Ledger* are as follows:

A

1/1 Bal.	£50		
Jan. Sale	£20	Jan. Bank	£40
		31/1 Bal.	£30
	£70		£70
1/2 Bal.	£30		

B

1/1 Bal.	£75		
Jan. Sale	£25		
		31/1 Bal.	£100
	£100		£100
1/2 Bal.	£100		

C

1/1 Bal.	£100		
		Jan. Bank	£55
		31/1 Bal.	£45
	£100		£100
1/2 Bal.	£45		

D

1/1 Bal.	£80		
Jan. Sale	£50		
		Jan. Bank	£30
		31/1 Bal.	£100
	£130		£130
1/2 Bal.	£100		

It can be seen that at 31January the balance on the control account in the nominal ledger is equal to the sum of the balances on the individual debtors accounts in the *Debtors* ledger.

An equivalent way to look at these entries in the control accounts and in individual debtors accounts is to regard the *Total* figure as the basis of the double entry in the *Nominal* ledger accounts. An analysis of the total entry in the *Nominal* ledger becomes a series of detailed entries in the individual debtor's accounts which, in total, make up the total entry on the control account. The debtors ledger is, therefore, a detailed record of transactions relating to debtors which mirrors the aggregate entries in the debtors control account maintained in the nominal ledger. The summary of such transactions is recorded in the debtors control account in the nominal ledger.

Nominal Ledger			Debtors Ledger	
January:	Dr. Debtors		Dr. A	£20
	control	£95	Dr. B	£25
	Cr. Sales	£95	Dr. D	£50
January:	Dr Bank	£125	Cr. A	£40
	Cr. Debtors		Cr. C	£55
	control	£125	Cr. D	£30

In all cases, the total entry in the control account in the nominal ledger is 'backed up' by a series of entries in the subsidiary ledger involving each individual debtor.

Example 2:
The following data is available for Tissues Ltd for March 198 . .

Debtors balances 1/3/9.	£5,480
Sales on credit during March	£8,430
Sales returns during March	£ 540
Cash received from debtors during March	£6,300
Discount allowed to debtors for prompt payment during March	£ 180
Bad debts written-off 31/3/9 .	£ 50

The debtors control account in the nominal ledger would appear as follows for the month of March:

Debtors control account

1/3 Balance	5,480	Sales Returns	540
		Bank	6,300
Sales	8,430	Discount allowed	180
		Bad Debts	50
		31/3 Balance	6,840
	£13,910		£13,910
1/4 Balance	6,840		

Each of these total entries in the debtors control account in the nominal ledger would be matched or backed up by a series of individual entries in the debtor accounts in the debtors ledger, and, of course, the balance on the control account should agree with the sum of all balances on the accounts in the debtors ledger.

Example 3:
The following data in relation to the creditors control account of Tissues Ltd is available for March 19. . .

Creditors balances 1/3/. .	£4,500
Purchase of goods for resale, on credit	£7,580
Goods returned to creditors	£770
Cheques paid to creditors	£6,400
Discount received from creditors	£200

The creditors control account would be as follows:

Creditors Control Account

		1/3 Balance	4,500
Purchases returns	770	Purchases	7,580
Bank	6,400		
Discount received	200		
31/3 Balance	4,710		
	£12,080		£12,080
		1/4 Balance	4,710

Again, details of these total figures would appear in the individual creditors accounts in the creditor ledger.

Benefits of control accounts: The use of control accounts achieves 'control' over the recording of entries in the subsidiary ledgers. When the time comes to balance the debtor or creditor accounts in the subsidiary ledger, a list of balances may be extracted which, in total, should agree with the balance on the relevant control account which is prepared independently, usually by a different person. In addition, the nominal ledger can be checked by a trial balance without the necessity to list the detailed debtor or creditor balances at the same time, since the control accounts, and not the individual accounts, form part of the double-entry system in the nominal ledger.

The total of the subsidiary ledger balances is compared with the balance on the control account; and where the two figures agree, the postings to the two sets of records are deemed consistent. This agreement does not verify the accuracy of the individual debtor or creditor balances, it simply verifies that the two sets of records are consistent. In turn, verification work shall be completed on the individual debtor or creditor accounts to provide assurance as to the accuracy or otherwise of the control account balance. Thus, a payment to Creditor Jones which was posted in error to Creditor Murphy's account in the creditors ledger will not be highlighted by comparing the balance on the control account with the individual balances in the creditors ledger. The two sets of balances will be an agreement. Rather, such an error would be detected by carrying out specific verification work on the individual creditors accounts, e.g., comparing individual balances against statements received from suppliers.

The use of Control accounts in this way is facilitated by the use of *Journals/Books of Original Entry.*

BOOKS OF ORIGINAL ENTRY

In a business of any size, the sheer volume of transactions would result in extensive use of the nominal ledger. Fortunately an alternative exists in the form of *Books of Original Entry/Books of Prime Entry/Day Books.* Essentially these are devices for summarising similar transactions to facilitate their subsequent recording in the nominal ledger. Where a certain type of transaction takes place on a recurring basis, a firm may decide to use a specific day book or journal to summarise all such transactions.

The books of original entry are used to accumulate details of a number of similar transactions in order to avoid the inefficiency of entering individually each transaction in the nominal ledger. Totals from the books of original entry are posted to the relevant accounts in the nominal ledger. The frequency with which the nominal ledger postings take place will depend on the accounting period. If quarterly accounts are required, then nominal ledger postings will take place at the end of each quarter. Many large companies will prepare monthly accounts so that nominal ledger postings are required at the end of each month.

An overview of the information flow in an accounting system is provided in Exhibit 5.1: (see next page)

The specific journals (or day books) used by a firm to record its transactions obviously depend on the frequency of various types of transactions. As a general case, a trading business would normally have transactions involving purchases on credit, returns of goods purchased, sales on credit, sales returned by customers, cheque payments, cash receipts from various sources and petty cash payments. The firm may therefore use a *Purchases Journal*, a *Purchases Returns Journal*, a *Sales Journal*, a *Sales Returns Journal*, a *Cheque Payments Book*, a *Petty Cash Book*, and a *Cash Receipts Book*. All transactions which do not fall naturally into any one of these areas or types would be initially recorded in a *General Journal*. The names of these books may vary from organisation to organisation.

Exhibit 5.1

Overview of Information Flow in Accounting System

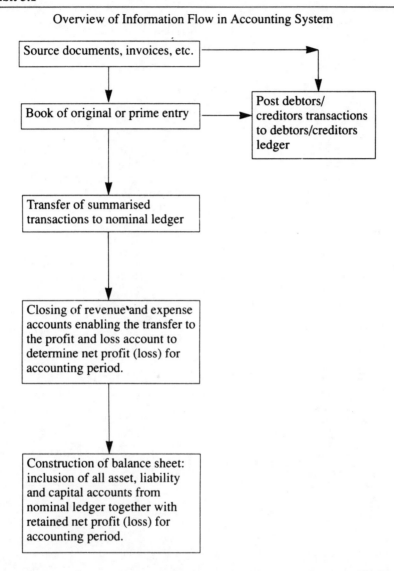

There are two problems to be overcome in writing up the books of original entry. Firstly, you must recognise the source document which gives rise to an entry in the books of account, and secondly, you must decide into which of the eight books to enter the transaction. Source documents include invoices, receipts, cheque stubs and debit/credit notes. Exhibit 5.2 provides a framework for dealing with the second problem referred to above.

Exhibit 5.2

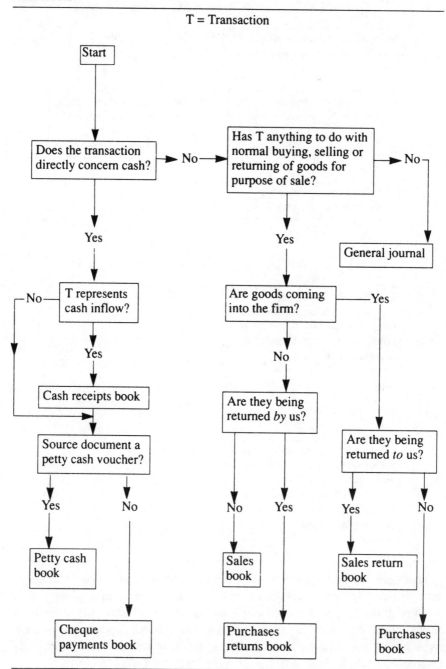

T = Transaction

Purchases Journal/Day Book

All credit purchases of goods for resale are entered and listed in the purchases day book, although some companies may also use this day book to record purchases of fixed assets and certain expense transactions. The information recorded for each transaction may include the date, the supplier (creditor), (an invoice reference), a reference to the creditors account concerned, the amount of the purchase, and perhaps an analysis of the total amount between different products purchased, if required. This journal is usually written up from approved suppliers invoices. A simple purchases journal would be as follows:

Purchases Journal

Date	Supplier	Creditors ledgers	Amount
			£
Nov. 2	F. Stapleton	C.1	275.00
Nov. 7	L. Brady	C.2	286.00
Nov. 30	F. O'Flynn	C.5	99.00
			660.00

Posting from the purchases journal can be summarised as follows:

To nominal ledger — Total: DR. Purchases account
CR. Creditors control account

To creditors ledger by way of memorandum entries. — CR. Creditors accounts in creditors ledger with individual purchases

Thus the total £660 in the purchase journal (above) is posted to two nominal ledger accounts as follows:

Purchases account

30/11 Purchases journal 660	

Creditors account

	30/11 Purchases journal 660

In addition, each transaction is posted to the relevant creditor's account in the subsidiary ledger. The individual creditors account would show:

L. Brady account

	7/11 Purchases journal 286

F. Stapleton account

	2/11 Purchases journal 275

F. O'Flynn account

	8/11 Purchases journal 99

It is important to stress that the monthly total posted to the creditors control account is equal to the sum of the credits posted to the subsidiary (creditors) ledger and that the credits posted to the subsidiary ledger are *not* part of the double-entry system.

Sales Journal

Sales of goods on credit are recorded in this journal. The sales journal is usually confined to sales of goods on credit. For each credit sale the seller will send an invoice which shows the type of goods, their specification and the amount invoiced. For its own records the company will keep a copy of the invoice and use this to write up the sales journal. Each invoice will be pre-numbered and sequenced, as this reduces the possibility of omitting to record a credit sales transaction. Detailed information on each transaction entered would normally include a date, (the invoice number), the customer, a reference to the customer's account (in the debtors ledger) and the amount of the sales invoice. There is no need to show any additional information in the sales journal, such as the type of goods involved, since this information can be found by referring to the copy invoice. The amount entered should be net of any trade discount given (but not cash discount available for

Sales Journal

Date	Supplier	Debtors ledger	Amount
Dec. 2	A. Allan	D.1	100.00
Dec. 7	B. Byrne	D.2	200.00
Dec.31	C. Cullen	D.5	300.00
			600.00

prompt payment). A simple sales journal would be as follows:
At the end of the month the sales journal is totalled. The posting to the ledgers can be summarised as follows:

To nominal ledger   Total: DR. Debtors control account
                                              CR. Sales account

To debtors ledger   DR. Debtors accounts in
by way of   debtors ledger
memorandum entries   with individual sales

Thus, the total of £600 from the above sales journal is posted to the two nominal ledger accounts as follows:

Debtors account		Sales account	
31/12 Sales journal 600		31/12 Sales journal 600	

In addition, each transaction is posted to the relevant debtor's account in the subsidiary ledger. The individual debtors accounts would show:

B. Byrne account		A. Allan account	
7/12 Sales journal 200		2/12 Sales journal 100	

C. Cullen account	
	31/12 Sales journal 300

Again it is important to note that the monthly total to the debtors control account is equal to the sum of the debits posted to the subsidiary (debtors) ledger.

Purchases Returns Journal

Returns of goods purchased, which are the subject of credit notes received from suppliers, are entered into this journal and summarised. Credit notes received would also apply to allowances claimed against, say, defective goods purchased. Details to be entered in the purchases returns journal would again be likely to include a date, the credit note number (or a reference number if entered prior to receipt of a credit note), the supplier, a reference to the supplier's account number, and the amount of the returned goods. The layout of the journal would be similar to the purchase journal.

The posting from the purchases returns journal can be summarised as follows:

To nominal ledger	Total: DR. Creditors control account CR. Purchases returns account
To creditors ledger by way of memorandum entries	DR. Creditors accounts in creditors ledger with individual returns

Sales Returns Journal

This journal would summarise all goods returned by customers, and would normally be written up from copies of *Credit Notes* issued by the vendor company to its customers. Credit notes are frequently printed in red so that they are clearly distinguishable from invoices. Goods may be returned by customers because they were of the wrong specification, defective or surplus to the customers needs. Details to be recorded in the sales returns journal would again include the date, credit note number, the customer, the account number, the amount involved, and any analysis of the amount deemed useful.

The posting from the sales returns journal can be summarised as follows:

To nominal ledger	Total: DR. Sales returns account CR. Debtors control account

To debtors ledger by way of	CR. Debtors account in
memorandum entries	debtors ledger with
	individual returns

Cheque Payments Book

The cheque payments book should list all cheques issued which are drawn on a particular bank account. Furthermore, it would record all standing orders paid by the firm, together with direct debits and bank charges. The details of each transaction recorded would normally include the date, the cheque number (where relevant), the payee, the amount of the cheque, discount received, and an analysis of the payment. This analysis would include columns for the recurring types of payments, such as payments to creditors, salaries, wages, various other expense items, and a 'sundries' or miscellaneous column in which all payments not analysed in another specific column are entered.

The cheque payments journal below contains entries for transactions which require payment by cheque. The transactions are:

Dec. 1	Paid A. White £120 by cheque and received £6 discount
Dec. 5	Drew cheque for wages, £400
Dec. 12	Purchased goods for cash, £225
Dec. 15	Drew cheque for wages £415
Dec. 21	Paid G. Green £200 less 5% discount
Dec. 31	Drew cheque for wages, £450

Cheque Payments Book

Date	Details	Cheque no	Discount recd	Cheque paid	◄——— Analysis ———►		
					Creditors	Purchases	Wages
Dec. 1	A. White	612	6	120	126		
5	Wages	613		400			400
12	Cash purchases	614		225		225	
15	Wages	615		415			415
21	G. Green	616	10	190	200		
31	Wages	617		450			450
			16	1,800	326	225	1,265

It is recommended practice that a business makes payments by cheque rather than cash since this offers a better system of control. The cheques are numbered serially, and as each transaction is entered into the cheque payments journal the cheque number is also listed. An unbroken series of cheque numbers provides an indication that every cheque written has been recorded in the accounting records.

At the end of the month the cheque payments journal is totalled and the aggregate entries on the left-hand side (£1,816) equal the aggregate entries of the analysis on the right-hand side. The posting of the entries in the cheque payments book takes place in two phases. The first phase concerns the regular posting of transactions to the individual supplier accounts in the creditors' ledger. This is done, sometimes daily, so that the individual's account is always up to date. But this is not part of the double-entry system.

At the end of the month the second phase of posting from the cheque payments journal occurs. The total of the cheque payments (£1,800) and discount received (£16) are posted to the credit sides of the bank and discount received accounts respectively. The debit entries are made to the creditors control account (£316, which includes the discount received), purchases account (£225) and wages account (£1,265).

In summary, the posting schedule from the cheque payments journal is as follows:

Posting to nominal ledger

Total cheques:	CR. Bank	£1,800
Discount Rec'd:	CR. Discount received	16
		£1,816

Analysis of cheque payments:

Creditors:	DR. Creditors control	£326
Purchases:	DR. Purchases	225
Wages:	DR. Wages	1,265
		£1,816

Posting to creditors (subsidiary) ledger:
DR. Creditors accounts in creditors ledger with cheque paid and discount received, by way of memorandum entries.

Cash Receipts Book

The cash receipts book should list all cash/cheques received and indicate that they have been lodged. The details of each receipt would normally include the date, the payer and if appropriate, the amount of cash, together with any discount allowed and the number of the receipt issued. The cash receipts book should also include an analysis indicating the various sources of cash received, e.g. debtors, cash sales, deposit interest received, together with a miscellaneous column into which all receipts that cannot be analysed in other specific columns are entered.

A typical cash receipts book is illustrated below:

Cash Receipts Book

Date	Details	Discount Allowed	Cash Rec'd	Analysis ——————→	
				Debtors	Cash Sales
Dec. 4	A. Allan	2	27	29	
16	B. Barry	4	110	114	
16	C. Conway	9	60	69	
19	Cash sales		926		926
27	A. Allan	5	195	200	
27	B. Barry	11	430	441	
31	Cash sales		643		643
		31	2,391	853	1,569

The posting from the cash receipts book, like the cheque payments book, can be viewed as consisting of two phases. First there is the regular posting, sometimes daily, of the transactions to the appropriate debtor's account. This is done frequently so that the debtor's account will always be up to date and is particularly appropriate in deciding to grant additional credit to a customer or in determining whether his account is overdue. Each debtor's account will be credited in the debtors (subsidiary) ledger with the amount of cash received, together with any discount allowed. This can be described as a memorandum entry since it does not form part of the double-entry system.

At the end of the month, the cash receipts book is totalled and one should ensure that the aggregate of the entries on the left-hand side agrees with the aggregate of the analysis columns. The total amount of cash received (£2,391) and discount allowed (£31) is posted to the debit side of the bank and discount allowed accounts, respectively. In turn, £853 is credited to the debtors control account (representing cash received plus discount allowed) and £1,569 is posted to the credit side of the sales account.

In summary, the posting from the cash receipts book is as follows:

To nominal ledger:

Total receipts:	DR. Bank	£2,391
Discount allowed:	DR. Discount allowed	31
		2,422

Analysis of cash received:

Debtors:	CR. Debtors control	£853
Cash sales:	CR. Sales	£1,569
		£2,422

To debtors ledger:
CR. Debtors accounts in debtors ledger with amount of cash received plus any discount allowed.

Petty Cash Book

This book records all petty cash payments for expense items, prior to the entering of these items in the ledger. Again, an analysis of each payment is usual to facilitate the summarisation and subsequent posting.

The petty cash book will be posted at the end of each month. The postings here will be broadly similar to those of the Cheque Payments Journal. The petty cash account should be credited with the total payments. The totals in the analysis columns, which will mainly be expense items such as postage, taxi fares etc., should be debited to the appropriate accounts. The total in the miscellaneous column is posted in individual amounts to the debit side of the appropriate accounts involved. In summary, the petty cash book can be posted as follows:

| To nominal ledger | Total payments: | CR. Petty cash |
| | Expenses | DR. Appropriate expense a/c. |

The relationship between some of the books of original entry, the nominal and subsidiary ledgers is illustrated using the following example:

Example: A trader had the following credit purchases and cheque payments:

(1)	Invoice received from A	£200
(2)	Invoice received from B	£300
(3)	Invoice received from C	£100
(4)	Cheque paid to A	£50
(5)	Cheque paid to B	£150

The entries in the appropriate books of account would be as follows:

Purchases Book (Extract)

Date	Invoice No.	Supplier	Total £	Analysis Creditors
1	A	200	200
2	B	300	300
3	C	100	100
		£600	£600

Nominal ledger posting: Dr. Purchases account £600
Cr. Creditors control account £600

Creditors ledger posting: CR. individual supplier accounts

Cheque Payments Book (Extract)

Date	No.	Name	Total	Creditors	Wages etc.
	1	A	50	50	
	2	B	150	150	
			£200	£200	

Nominal ledger posting: DR. Creditors control account £200
CR. Bank account £200

Creditors ledger posting: DR. individual supplier accounts

Each invoice and payment is posted to the individual's account in the creditors ledger as follows:

A

Cheque payments	50	Purchase journal	200	
Balance	150			
	200		200	
		Balance b/d	150	

B

Cheque payments	150	Purchase journal	300	
Balance	150			
	300		300	
		Balance b/d	150	

C

		Purchase journal	100	
Balance	100			
	100		100	
		Balance b/d	100	

The purchases journal and cheque payments book are posted to the creditors control account in the nominal ledger.

Creditors control account

Cheque payments book	200	Purchases Book	600	
Balance	400			
	600		600	
		Balance b/d	400	

Purchases account

Purchases book	600	

Bank account

	Cheque payment book	200

The individual balances must be aggregated and compared with the control account balance.

A	150
B	150
C	100
	£400

The total agrees with the balance on the control account. This agreement signifies a consistency of posting between the nominal and creditors ledgers.

General Journal

When all transactions involving cash/bank and the purchase or sale of goods are recorded in the specific journals above, only a few types of transactions remain to be recorded. These transactions are recorded in the general journal or simply, the Journal. The transactions would normally include the purchase of fixed assets on credit, the correction of errors in ledger postings or recording depreciation of fixed assets. Since it is likely that the reason for the entry in this journal will not be obvious, as all transactions and entries are dissimilar, an explanation of the entry called a *narrative* is required for each entry. Very simply, the general journal entry should set out the account(s) to be debited, the account(s) to be credited, with the appropriate amounts indicated, together with a narrative or explanation of the reason for the entry.

For example, suppose the firm wants to provide £5,000 for the depreciation of its fixed assets. Since this transaction cannot be appropriately entered in any other day book or journal it appears in the general journal of the firm as follows:

Journal

Date	Details	Dr.	Cr.
31/12	Depreciation account	£5,000	
	Aggregate depreciation account		£5,000
	(Being annual provision for depreciation on fixed assets).		

Alternatively, suppose that an error was detected in entering transactions in the nominal ledger. For example, an amount of £340 which should have been *debited* to wages account was *debited* instead to the repairs account. (The resulting trial balance would still balance!) The error should be corrected using the general journal as follows:

Journal

Date	Details	Dr.	Cr.
31/12	Wages account	£340	
	Repairs account		£340

(being correction of error—incorrect posting of £340 debit to repairs instead of wages account now rectified)

Prevention of errors

It can be seen that the postings from the journals maintain the double entry principle of equality between debits and credits in the nominal ledger. In addition, postings to subsidiary ledgers in total equal the postings to the appropriate control accounts. It can also be appreciated that the use of journals in this way to summarise transactions cuts down on the time and amount of detail in posting the general or nominal ledger. In this way, the task of maintaining accounting records can be subdivided into individual areas of responsibility, so that several people are no longer trying to update 'THE' ledger at the same time. These people may now work relatively independently in their own areas of responsibility, with periodic amalgamation of all such tasks into the nominal ledger accounts in summary form, when periodic postings take place.

However, in the processing of documentation through a typical accounting system there is significant scope for various types of error. Financial statements extracted from the accounting records are of little use if we have no assurance that they are accurate. The main controls in an accounting system to cover debtors (sales) and creditors (purchase) are:

1. All sales invoices should be double-checked before being issued. This minimises the possibility of incorrect pricing and/or arithmetic error in preparing the invoice.

2. When goods are received by the firm a goods inward docket should be prepared by the stock-keeper. This goods inward docket will indicate the type of goods received and should relate to the original order request. In turn, the goods inward docket should be matched with the supplier's invoice before payment is sanctioned. Otherwise it would be possible for a firm to pay for goods which had not been received (or which, although had been received, had not been ordered).

3. At the end of each month a statement should be sent to each debtor to show the opening balance on his account, if any, at the start of the month, together with details of credit sales, sales returns, cash paid and discount allowed. In addition to providing a reminder to the debtor that there is a balance to be paid, he will probably compare the statement received with his own records. In this way errors can be detected (and corrected) at an early stage.

Likewise, each supplier (creditor) will send us a monthly statement. Such statements should be compared with the supplier's account in the creditors ledger. Any discrepancies should be investigated and, if appropriate, the supplier should be notified.

4. At the end of the accounting period, the equality of debit and credit entries in the nominal ledger is proved by the preparation of the trial balance. When control accounts and subsidiary (debtors and creditors) ledgers are used, it is necessary to determine that each subsidiary ledger is in agreement with the relevant control account. This process is referred to as reconciling the subsidiary ledger with the control account.

The first step in the reconciliation process is the preparation of a listing of all the individual accounts in the subsidiary ledger. This listing will be totalled and the total compared with the balance on the control account in the nominal ledger. This reconciliation process is important and should be performed regularly and frequently. It may reveal errors in either the control account or the subsidiary ledger. Such errors can range from the incorrect listing of an individual's account to incorrect recording of a transaction.

If any of the above controls indicate that an error has been made, the postings and the posting sources will have to be checked to locate the error. If everything is satisfactory we have gained considerable assurance that purchases, sales, receipts, payments and postings to the nominal ledger have been correctly recorded.

CASH CONTROL AND RECONCILIATION

Of all the assets of an organisation, cash is probably the most susceptible to theft. In addition, a great many transactions involve cash in some form, i.e cash, cheques, postal orders. For these two reasons it is important to have a system of controls over cash receipts and payments. With adequate systems of control, theft of cash by employees becomes very difficult without getting caught and cash recording errors are minimised. Cash controls vary from business to business but they will generally apply to both receipts and payments.

Cash receipts will generally arise either from cash sales or collections, sometimes by post, from debtors. Each source of cash will have a different control system but the fundamental objective remains the same. The purpose of the control system is to prevent both the misappropriation of cash and recording errors. Cash sales should be recorded immediately in the cash register and a till roll receipt provided to each customer. (Some shops post notices requesting customers to ask for till receipts.) At the end of the day the shop supervisor will remove the cash drawer, count the cash and compare the total in the cash till with the total cash receipts recorded. It is inevitable that some discrepancies will occur between the recorded total and the actual cash on hand. If the discrepancy is very small it is usually ignored and the actual cash receipts are deemed to be the cash sales for the day. However, in some instances, these discrepancies are formally recorded in a 'Cash over/under account'. Some banks, for example, operate this system with each cash teller having to record the discrepancy for which he is responsible. Over a period of time the 'cash over' would normally balance out with the 'cash under'.

In order to prevent errors of recording the incorrect amount of a cash sale, some supermarkets now use electronic scanning equipment. Each product has a specific bar code and at the checkout this bar code is read by a scanning machine. The code automatically translates into a price which is printed on the receipt given to the customer. This system reduces the probability of error in recording the cash sale. However, it has other advantages in that it provides management with a detailed analysis of the different products sold. It can also be linked with a stock control system whereby each item, when sold, is automatically recorded and so management should know the amount of stock in hand at any particular time.

For cash received through the post, special control arrangements must be made. The most important feature is that at least two persons, of fairly senior rank in the organisation, should open the post each day. Ideally, the two persons entrusted with this task should be drawn from a daily roster but they would not have access to the accounting records, e. g. the debtors ledger. This arrangement does not necessarily eliminate the possibility of misappropriation. However, for fraud to take place, it would require the cooperation and agreement of the two individuals involved.

Finally, all cash received should be lodged, as soon as possible, to the business bank account. Cash payments should not be made from cash receipts.

Ideally all payments should be made by cheque and a proper control system requires that the amount and authority for each item of expenditure is verified before payment is made. If this did not exist it is possible that the firm would pay for items that it did not order, or if it did order, had not yet received. Thus, before a cheque is drawn for goods purchased, the accountant should satisfy himself that the goods were properly ordered, actually received in stock and were invoiced at the correct prices. All cheque requisitions should be supported by a voucher, signed by a senior in the organisation, requesting payment. Some organisations require that only top management authorise cheques in excess of certain limits and the majority of organisations require at least two cheque signatories. When payment is made, the invoice and supporting voucher should be stamped 'paid' to prevent the possibility of double payment.

All cheques will be pre-numbered to prevent the possibility of omitting a cheque transaction from the cash book.

The bank statement

At the end of each month (or more frequently, if required) the bank will provide the customer with a bank statement. This bank statement will show the opening balance, the individual lodgments made during the month in addition to the individual cheques presented for payment and other miscellaneous payments, e.g bank charges. The closing balance will also be printed on the bank statement.

The bank statement should be a mirror of the firm's bank account in its nominal ledger. When money is paid into the bank, the bank will debit its cash account and complete the double entry by crediting the customer's account. (The customer, on the other hand, debits his bank account in the nominal ledger.) When a cheque is written and presented for payment, the customer will credit the bank account in his nominal ledger. However, the bank will debit the customer's account by the relevant amount. Thus the bank statement shows the movement in the customer's account, according to the bank's records. For this reason, the bank statement will show the entries on the opposite sides of the nominal ledger maintained by the customer.

The bank and the firm maintain independent records. At the end of the month the accountant prepares a bank reconciliation statement to verify that these two independent sets of records are in agreement. In an ideal world the records of the customer in his ledger should exactly match those entries on the bank statement. In practice, the entries seldom agree with the major discrepancies due to timing differences. For example, cheques written and entered in the nominal ledger may not be presented for payment at the bank for a number of weeks. These are referred to as 'unpresented or outstanding (O/S) cheques'. In addition, cheques may be lodged by a firm and recorded in their nominal ledger but they may not be cleared by the bank for a few days. These are referred to as 'unpresented or outstanding (O/S) lodgments'.

In order to identify these unpresented cheques and outstanding lodgments, a bank reconciliation statement is prepared. Any remaining discrepancies between the two sets of independent records are fundamental and will be due either to error in recording or failure to record such items as bank charges. We shall return to these fundamental differences later.

There are a number of specific steps which should be taken when preparing bank reconciliation statements:

1. Compare each lodgment per the bank statement with the amount of the lodgment recorded in the firm's books. This is usually done by putting a check mark (e.g √ or B) or both the bank statement and the firm's records for each item that agrees. Any unticked lodgments represent lodgments made by the firm but not yet recorded by the bank. These should be listed as outstanding lodgments on the bank reconciliation statement and added to the closing balance reported on the bank statement.

2. Compare each cheque presented for payment per the bank statement with the amount of the cheque recorded in the firm's books. This is usually done by putting a check mark (e.g √ or B) on both the bank statement and the firm's records for each item that agrees. Any unticked cheques should be listed on the bank reconciliation statement as unpresented cheques to be deducted form closing balance reported on the bank statement.
3. Any items that remain unchecked will be due to timing differences or alternatively to more fundamental reasons such as errors (These fundamental differences will be discussed later.)
4. Prepare a bank reconciliation statement, which reconciles the balance per the bank statement with the balance as per the firm's books, using the listings of unpresented cheques and outstanding lodgments.

A recommended format for preparing bank reconciliation statements is as follows:

	£
Closing balance as per bank statement	x
Add: Outstanding lodgments	x
Less: Unpresented cheques	(x)
Closing balance per nominal ledger	xx

The closing figure per the nominal ledger is the correct figure for the firm's cash at bank and this is the amount that appears on the closing balance sheet. The above reconciliation statement proves that the differences in the closing balances between the bank's and the firm's books are due entirely to the timing of entries.

Example:

The bank account and the related bank statement of B. Hayden for the month of February are as follows:

Bank Account

DR		£			CR £
1 Feb.	Balance b/f	2,000	5 Feb. Cheque no. 20		813
2 Feb.	Lodgment	412	10 Feb. Cheque no. 21		407
9 Feb.	Lodgment	509	11 Feb. Cheque no. 22		96
9 Feb.	Lodgment	106	19 Feb. Cheque no. 23		421
15 Feb.	Lodgment	735	20 Feb. Cheque no. 24		549
22 Feb.	Cash sales (lodged)	175	21 Feb. Cheque no. 25		231
28 Feb.	Lodgment	404	28 Feb. Cheque no. 26		42
			28 Feb. Balance c/d		1,782
		4,341			4,341

Bank Statement

Date	Particulars	Debit	Credit	Balance
		£	£	£
1 Feb.	Balance forward			2,000
2 Feb.	Lodgment		412	2,412
6 Feb.	Cheque 20	813		1,599
9 Feb.	Lodgment		509	2,108
9 Feb.	Lodgment		106	2,214
12 Feb.	Cheque 22	96		2,118
15 Feb.	Lodgment		735	2,853
22 Feb.	Cheque 25	231		2,622
22 Feb.	Lodgment		175	2,797

Requirement:
You are required to prepare a statement showing your reconciliation of the closing balance on the bank statement with cash book balance on 28 February.

Solution
Comparing the individual entries on the bank statement with the bank account in the nominal ledger reveals certain differences. However, these differences are due entirely to the timing of entries. The lodgment made on 28 February (£404) has not yet been credited on the bank statement, but, presumably, will appear on the statement in early March. In addition, four cheques written by the firm have not yet been presented for payment at the bank. These outstanding cheques are numbered 21, 23, 24 and 26 respectively.

The completed bank reconciliation at 28 February appears as follows and is confined to itemising all timing differences between the two sets of books.

Bank Reconciliation Statement 28 February

			£	£
				£
Balance per Bank Statement				2,797
Add: O/S Lodgment				404
				3,201
Less:O/S cheques	– 21		407	
	– 23		421	
	– 24		549	
	– 26		42	(1,419)
Balance per nominal ledger				1,782

Fundamental differences

In all probability there will be other differences between the bank statement and the bank nominal ledger account. It is convenient to classify these as (i) entries that first appear on the bank statement and (ii) recording errors.

Some transactions concerning the company will first appear on the bank statement. For example, the bank has prior knowledge of the charges it makes for its services (e.g. for interest and fees). The main indication it gives of these charges is an entry on the bank statement. In turn, these charges should be incorporated in the firm's bank account. Other examples of such transactions include interest received, payments by standing order (S/O), direct debits and dishonoured cheques. (Dishonoured cheques represent cheques received from customers and lodged but the bank refuses payment. The most common cause for such refusal is insufficient funds on the part of the customer.) It is usual practice, on receipt of a bank statement, to update the bank account by the entry of bank charges etc. and this should always be done before reconciliation is attempted. All items would then be checked by ticking from the bank statement to the firm's bank records. The unticked items will then represent outstanding lodgments, unpresented cheques or recording errors.

Unfortunately recording errors will frequently be made. For example, a lodgment may be incorrectly totalled and listed or figures may be entered incorrectly in the firm's books. While the bank is also capable of making errors, in practice, the majority of errors are made in the firm's recording system. Where a company maintains several different accounts, one possible source of error is to record a cheque drawn on one account as a payment from another bank account. Similar errors may occur in recording lodgments. All such errors should be incorporated in the firm's bank account before a final reconciliation is made.

The following is a more comprehensive reconciliation exercise incorporating timing differences, recording errors and entries that first appear on the bank statement.

Example :

The following information has been extracted from the records of R. Harper:

Bank Account

		Dr.			Cr.
		£			£
1 Feb.	Balance b/f	2,000	5 Feb.	Cheque no. 20	813
2 Feb.	Lodgment	412	10 Feb.	Cheque no. 21	407
9 Feb.	Lodgment	509	11 Feb.	Cheque no. 22	96
9 Feb.	Lodgment	106	19 Feb.	Cheque no. 23	421

15 Feb. Lodgment	735	20 Feb.	Cheque no. 24		549
22 Feb. Cash Sales (lodged)	175	21 Feb.	Cheque no. 25		123
28 Feb. Lodgment	404	28 Feb.	Cheque no. 26		42
28 Feb. Lodgment	276	28 Feb.	Balance c/d		2,166
	4,617				4,617

Note: You are informed by the bank that ALL entries on the statement are correct.

Bank Statement

Date	Particulars	Debit £	Credit £	Balance £
1 Feb.	Balance Forward			2,000
2 Feb.	Lodgment		412	2,412
6 Feb.	Cheque 20	813		1,599
9 Feb.	Lodgment		615	2,214
12 Feb.	Cheque 22	96		2,118
12 Feb.	S/O term loan	100		2,018
15 Feb.	Lodgment		735	2,753
22 Feb.	Cheque 25	231		2,522
22 Feb.	Lodgment		185	2,707
24 Feb.	Bank charges	25		2,682

Requirement:

You are required to prepare—

(a) a statement showing the balance which would appear in Mr Harper's cash book on 28 February, after making all necessary adjustments;

(b) a statement showing your reconciliation of the closing balance on the bank statement with corrected cash book balance on 28 February.

Solution

Comparing the cheques per the bank account with the bank statement reveals that cheques numbered 21, 23, 24 and 26 have not yet been presented for payment. In addition, both lodgments made on the 28 February have not yet been credited by the bank. (The lodgments made on 9 February have been aggregated by the bank).

However, two transactions appearing on the bank statement should be incorporated in the firm's own records. These are the standing order (S/O) for the term loan and also the bank charges. The closing balance on the firm's bank account (£2,166) in the nominal ledger will, thus, be reduced by £125. However, two recording errors have been detected since the bank have informed you that all entries on their statement are correct. The lodgment on

22 February was £185 and not £175 and cheque numbered 25 should have been listed in the firm's books as £231 and not £123. These two errors should be incorporated in the firm's records before final reconciliation is made.

(A) Adjusted Cash Book Balance:

	£
Balance (original) per Cash Book	2,166
Add: Error in Lodgment	10
Less: Cheque error (231 -123)	(108)
Less: Term loan	(100)
Less: Bank Charges	(25)
	1,943

(B) Bank Reconciliation Statement 28 February

		£
Balance per Bank Statement		2,682
Add: O/S Lodgments	404	
	276	680
Less: O/S cheques – 21	407	
– 23	421	
– 24	549	
– 26	42	(1,419)
Balance per nominal ledger (adjusted)		1,943

QUESTION 5.1 (A)

The following information relates to a company for a recent account period:

	£
Opening creditors	4,600
Credit purchases	54,000
Credit purchases returned	6,000
Payments to suppliers	39,000

Requirement:

Prepare a creditors control account (in the nominal ledger) from the above information.

QUESTION 5.2 (SM)

The following information relates to a company for a recent accounting period:

	£
Opening debtors	5,100
Cash received from customers	49,000
Credit sales	63,000
Refunds paid to debtors for overpayments	2,000
Balances in debtors ledger set off against creditors ledger (contra entries)	3,000

Requirement:

Prepare a debtors control account (in the debtors ledger) from the above information.

QUESTION 5.3 (A)

The following summarised information was extracted from the cheque payments book of a business for an accounting period:

Discount received	Bank	Creditors	Wages
£	£	£	£
10	140	90	60

Requirement:

Show how the above summarised information would be posted to the nominal and subsidiary ledgers of the company.

QUESTION 5.4 (SM)

D. Daly maintains both a nominal ledger (containing a debtors control account) and a subsidiary debtors ledger. The following transactions took place during the month of January:

Sales Journal

Date	Details	Invoice No.	£
Jan. 4	A. Albert	201	98
10	B. Ball	202	196
6	A. Albert	203	147
20	C. Casey	204	152
25	D. Dunne	205	76
28	B. Ball	206	294
			963

Requirement:

Post the transactions overleaf to the nominal and subsidiary ledgers, as appropriate.

Cash Receipts Book

Date	Details	Discount Allowed	Cash	Analysis Debtors	Cash sales
Jan. 9	A. Albert		50	50	
19	B. Ball	6	190	196	
19	A. Albert		48	48	
24	Cash sales		900		900
26	D. Dunne		76	76	
30	B. Ball	4	290	294	
31	Cash sales		600		600
		10	2,154	664	1,500

(The Institute of Chartered Accountants in Ireland)

QUESTION 5.5 (SM)

A. Brown maintains both a nominal ledger (containing debtors and creditors control accounts) and subsidiary debtors and creditors ledgers. The following entries appear in his books of original entry:

Sales Journal

Date	Details	Invoice No.	Amount
			£
Dec. 3	A. Allan	117	29
Dec. 9	B. Barry	118	114
Dec. 15	C. Conway	119	69
Dec. 21	B. Barry	120	841
Dec. 26	A Allan	121	430
Dec. 31	D. Dunne	122	721
			2,204

Cash Receipts Book

Date	Details	Discount Allowed	Cash Rec'd	Analysis Debtors	Cash sales
Dec. 4	A. Allan	2	27	29	
16	B. Barry	4	110	114	
16	C. Conway	9	60	69	
19	Cash sales		926		926
27	A. Allan	5	195	200	
27	B. Barry	11	430	441	
31	Cash sales		643		643
		31	2,391	853	1,569

Purchases Journal

Date	Details	Amount
Dec. 4	A. White	126
8	B. Grey	841
12	C. Green	465
16	B. Grey	168
20	C. Green	912
24	A. White	973
26	D. Brown	246
		3,731

Cheque Payments Book

Date		Details	Discount Received	Cheque Paid	◄——— Analysis ———►		
					Creditors	Purchases	Wages
Dec.	5	A. White	6	120	126		
	9	B. Grey	11	830	841		
	13	Cash purchases		210		210	
	16	B. Grey	8	160	168		
	21	C. Green	5	195	200		
	26	A. White		473	473		
	27	D. Brown	6	240	246		
	30	Wages		916			916
			36	3,144	2,054	210	916

Requirement:

Post the above entries in the nominal and subsidiary ledgers and show the debtors and creditors balances in the subsidiary ledgers at 31 December. (The Institute of Chartered Accountants in Ireland)

QUESTION 5.6 (A)

(a) Why are many accounting systems designed with a purchase ledger (creditors ledger) control account, as well as with a purchase ledger (creditors ledger)?

(b) The following errors have been discovered in the accounting records:

(i) A invoice for £654 has been entered in the purchase day book as £456;

(ii) A prompt payment discount of £100 from a creditor had been completely omitted from the accounting records;

(iii) Purchases of £250 had been entered on the wrong side of a supplier's account in the purchase ledger;

(iv) No entry had been made to record an agreement to contra an amount owed to X of £600 against an amount owed by X of £400;

(*v*) A credit note for £60 had been entered as if it was an invoice.
State the numerical effect on the purchase ledger control account balance of
correcting each of these items (treating each item separately).
(The Chartered Association of Certified Accountants)

QUESTION 5.7 (SM)
(*a*) You are given the following balances at 1 January 19 . 1 :
Debtors £10,000; Bank overdraft £5,000; Provisions for doubtful debts
£400. You ascertain the following information: £
   Sales for the year 19 . 1 (all on credit)   100,000
   Sales return for the year 19 . 1   1,000
   Receipts from customers during 19 . 1   90,000
   Bad debts written-off during 19 . 1   500
   Discounts allowed during 19 . 1   400
At the end of 19 . 1 the provision for doubtful debts is required to be 5
per cent of debtors, after making a specific provision for a debt of £200
from a customer who has gone bankrupt.   £

Sales for the year 19 . 2 (90 per cent on credit)   100,000
Sales returns for the year 19 . 2
   (90 per cent relating to credit customers)   2,000
Receipts from credit customers during 19 . 2   95,000
Debtor balances settled by contra against creditor
   balances during 19. 2   3,000
Bad debts written-off during 19 . 2 (including
   50 per cent of the debt due from the customer
   who had gone bankrupt, the other 50 per cent
   having been received in cash during 19 . 2)   1,500
Discounts allowed during 19. 2   500

At the end of 19 . 2 the provision for doubtful debts is still required to be
5 per cent of debtors.

Requirement:
(*a*) Write up the debtors and provision for doubtful debts accounts for
19 . 1 and 19. 2, bringing down the balances at the end of each year and
showing in those accounts the double entry for each item.
(*b*) The normal accounting approach with credit sales, as illustrated in
part (*a*) above, is to recognise revenue on the sale when it is made, and then
to allow for the possibility of some bad debts.
   Outline, by reference to appropriate accounting conventions, the justification for this approach.
(The Chartered Association of Certified Accountants)

QUESTION 5.8 (SM)

The trial balance of Happy Book-keeper Ltd, as produced by its book-keeper includes the following items:

Sales ledger control account	£110,172
Purchase ledger control account	£78,266

You have been given the following information:

(1) The sales ledger debit balances total £111,106 and the credit balances total £1,334.
(2) The purchase ledger credit balances total £77,777 and the debit balances total £1,111.
(3) The sales ledger includes a debit balance of £700 for business X, and the purchase ledger includes a credit balance of £800 relating to the same business X. Only the net amount will eventually be paid.
(4) Included in the credit balance on the sales ledger is a balance of £600 in the name of H. Smith. This arose because a sales invoice for £600 had earlier been posted in error from the sales day book to the debit of the account of M. Smith in the purchase ledger.
(5) An allowance of £300 against some damaged goods had been omitted from the appropriate account in the sales ledger. This allowance had been included in the control account.
(6) An invoice for £456 had been entered in the purchase day book as £654.
(7) A cash receipt from a credit customer for £345 had been entered in the cash book as £245.
(8) The purchase day book had been overcast by £1,000.
(9) The book-keeper had been instructed to write-off £500 from customer Y's account as a bad debt, and to reduce the provision for doubtful debts by £700. By mistake, however, he had written off £700 from customer Y's account and *increased* the provision for doubtful debts by £500.

Requirement:

Record corrections in the control accounts. Attempt to reconcile the sales ledger control account with the sales ledger balances, and the purchase ledger control account with the purchase ledger balances.
(The Chartered Association of Certified Accountants)

QUESTION 5.9 (A)

The following information has been extracted from the records of P. Rock:

Bank Account

Dr.			Cr.
	£		£
1 Feb. Balance b/f	2,000	5 Feb. Cheque No. 20	318
2 Feb. Lodgment	393	10 Feb. Cheque No. 21	265
9 Feb. Lodgment	416	11 Feb. Cheque No. 22	192
9 Feb. Lodgment	524	19 Feb. Cheque No. 23	234
15 Feb. Lodgment	387	20 Feb. Cheque No. 24	459
22 Feb. Cash sales (lodged)	185	21 Feb. Cheque No. 25	117
28 Feb. Lodgment	364	28 Feb. Cheque No. 26	26
28 Feb. Lodgment	291	28 Feb. Balance c/d	2,949
	4,560		4,560

Note: You are informed by the bank that all entries on the statement are correct.

Bank Statement

Account No. 63161

P. Rock   Bank of Leinster

Date	Particulars	Debit £	Credit £	Balance £
1. Feb.	Balance Forward			1,971
2 Feb.	Lodgment		129	2,100
2 Feb.	Cheque 15	100		2,000
2 Feb.	Lodgment		393	2,393
6 Feb.	Cheque 20	318		2,075
9 Feb.	Lodgment		940	3,015
12 Feb.	Cheque 22	192		2,823
12 Feb.	S/O term loan	120		2,703
15 Feb.	Lodgment		387	3,090
22 Feb.	Cheque 25	127		2,963
22 Feb.	Lodgment		184	3,147
24 Feb.	Bank charges	2		3,145
26 Feb.	Dividend		15	3,160

Requirement:

You are required to prepare:

(a) a bank reconciliation statement on 1 February;

(b) a statement showing the balance which would appear in Mr Rock's cash book on 28 February, after making all necessary adjustments; and

(c) a statement showing your reconciliation of the closing balance on the bank statement with the corrected cash book balance on 28 February.
(The Institute of Chartered Accountants in Ireland)

QUESTION 5.10 (SM)
The following information has been extracted from the records of B. Cullen:

Bank Account

		Debit £			Credit £
3 Feb.	Lodgment	1,412	1 Feb.	Balance b/d	938
10 Feb.	Lodgment	516	1 Feb.	Cheque no. 317	912
10 Feb.	Lodgment	619	2 Feb.	Cheque No. 318	423
16 Feb.	Lodgment	713	13 Feb.	Cheque No. 319	291
21 Feb.	Lodgment	27	18 Feb.	Cheque No. 320	417
26 Feb.	Lodgment	93	22 Feb.	Cheque No. 321	612
28 Feb.	Lodgment	146	24 Feb.	Cheque No. 322	26
28 Feb.	Balance c/d	98	26 Feb.	Charges	5
		3,624			3,634

Note: you are informed by the bank that all entries on the statement are correct.

Bank Statement

Date	Particulars	Debit £	Credit £	Balance £
1 Feb.	Balance Forward			(719) O'drawn
2 Feb.	Lodgment		1,000	281
2 Feb.	Cheque 318	423		(142) O'drawn
2 Feb.	Lodgment		1,412	1,270
6 Feb.	Cheque 317	914		356
10 Feb.	Lodgment		1,135	1,491
14 Feb.	Cheque 319	291		1,200
14 Feb.	S O term loan	100		1,100
16 Feb.	Lodgment		713	1,813
21 Feb.	Cheque 315	1,219		594
21 Feb.	Lodgment		26	620
26 Feb.	Bank charges	15		605
28 Feb.	Dividend		15	620

Requirement:

You are required to prepare a statement showing your reconciliation of the closing balance on the bank statement with the corrected cash book balance on 28 February.

(The Institute of Chartered Accountants in Ireland)

QUESTION 5.11 (A)

The following information relating to the bank account of Mr S. Rodgers has been presented to you:

		£
1st June	Bank balance (per nominal ledger — Dr.)	297

Lodgments

2nd June	lodgment	8,273
5th June	lodgment	1,923
16th June	lodgment	2,495
16th June	lodgment	3,042
21st June	lodgment	1,928
22nd June	lodgment	462
30th June	lodgment	48

Cheque Payments

3rd June	cheque no. 60	1,117
5th June	cheque no. 61	438
11th June	cheque no. 62	8,778
15th June	cheque no. 63	3,000
19th June	cheque no. 64	590
21st June	cheque no. 65	711
30th June	cheque no. 66	522

The following bank statement for the month of June has been received:

Money Bank

	S. Rodgers		Bank Statement	
Date	Particulars	Debit £	Credit £	Balance £
1st June	Balance			1,200
2nd June	Lodgment		260	
2nd June	Lodgment		8,273	9,733
4th June	Cheque No. 49	371		9,362
5th June	Cheque No. 58	792		
5th June	Cheque No. 60	1,117		
5th June	Lodgment		1,923	9,376
16th June	Lodgment		5,537	14,913
21st June	Cheque No. 61	438		
21st June	Cheque No. 64	590		

21st June	Lodgment		1,948	15,833
22nd June	Cheque No. 65	711		
22nd June	Lodgment		462	15,584
25th June	S/O	275		15,309
30th June	Bank Giro		192	15,501

Note: You are informed by the bank that all entries on their statement are correct.

Requirement:
You are required to:
(a) Prepare a statement showing your reconciliation of the closing balance on the bank statement with the corrected nominal ledger balance at 30th June; and
(b) explain briefly which items, if any, in your bank reconciliation statement would require further investigation.
(The Institute of Chartered Accountants in Ireland)

QUESTION 5.12 (SM)
The following information relating to the bank account of Mr R. Stephens has been presented to you:

		£
1st May	Bank balance (per nominal ledger — Dr.)	1.000

Lodgments

2nd May	lodgment	3,180
5th May	lodgment	2,650
16th May	lodgment	1,920
16th May	lodgment	4,593
21st May	lodgment	3,875
22nd May	lodgment	364
30th May	lodgment	26

Cheques Payments

3rd May	cheque no. 50	1,261
5th May	cheque no. 51	2,792
11th May	cheque no. 52	1,900
15th May	cheque no. 53	5,943
19th May	cheque no. 54	7,541
21st May	cheque no. 55	19
29th May	cheque no. 56	1,949

The following bank statement has been received for the month of May:

Bank Statement
Account No. 69324

R. Stephens   Bank of Leinster

Date	Particulars	Debit £	Credit £	Balance £
1st May	Balance			1,500
2nd May	Lodgment		3,180	
2nd May	Lodgment		400	5,080
4th May	Cheque No 50	1,261		3,819
5th May	Cheque No 49	900		
5th May	Cheque No 51	2,792		
5th May	Lodgment		2,650	2,777
16th May	Lodgment		6,513	9,290
21st May	Cheque No. 52	1,900		
21st May	Cheque No. 53	5,945		
21st May	Lodgment		3,878	5,323
22nd May	Cheque No. 55	19		
22nd May	Lodgment		364	5,668
25th May	S/O loan	1,000		4,668
29th May	Dividend		15	4,683

Note: You are informed by the bank that all entries on their statement are correct.

Requirement:
You are required to prepare
(*a*) a bank reconciliation statement on 1st May:
(*b*) a statement showing the bank balance which would appear in Mr Stephen's nominal ledger at 31st May, after making the appropriate adjustments:
(*c*) a statement showing your reconciliation of the closing balance on the bank statement with the corrected nominal ledger balance at 31st May; and
(*d*) a balance sheet extract at 31st May, to show 'Cash at bank.'
(The Institute of Chartered Accountants in Ireland)

6.

Accounting for Manufacturing Operations

THE IMPORTANCE OF STOCK AND ITS VALUATION

It used to be said some years ago, in jest, that when drawing up the annual accounts of companies, the first figure to be set down was the desired profit, then all the other ascertainable figures, until the closing stock figure emerged as a balancing amount! This sentiment is certainly echoed in the introductory remarks of SSAP 9, *Stocks and Work in Progress,* which was issued in May 1975 (and revised in August 1988):

> No area of accounting has produced wider differences in practice than the computation of the amount at which stocks and work in progress are stated in the financial accounts. This statement of standard accounting practice seeks to define the practices, to narrow the differences and variations in those practices and to ensure adequate disclosure in the accounts.

Closing stocks represent as much as 25 per cent of the historic cost assets of many large companies. This is a considerable proportion and its magnitude would probably apply to many small, family companies as well. Thus, the closing stock valuation is always likely to be significant in the context of the calculation of cost of goods sold (which is shown below for a retail company):

Opening stock	400
Add: Purchases	3,200
Less: Closing stock	(500)
Cost of Goods Sold	3,100

Since gross profit is calculated by deducting cost of goods sold from sales revenue it follows that the valuation of closing stock will have a substantial impact on the gross profit (and net profit) figure of any trading enterprise. As a general rule, the higher the closing stock the higher the reported profit will be. Likewise, the lower closing stock, the lower will be the reported profit.

The valuation of closing stock is obtained by counting the physical units on hand at the end of the accounting period and multiplying this figure by the correct valuation placed on each item in stock. The physical count is referred to as periodic inventory or physical stock-take. Taking and pricing stock items is a time-consuming process that is usually done only once a year and is completed as near to balance sheet date as possible.

However, the physical stock-take is subject to counting errors or pure oversight. Accordingly, companies maintain a perpetual inventory system. This system records all receipts and issues of stock on an appropriate stock or bin card with a running balance of the physical items in stock being maintained. Complementary to this system will be a physical count system to ensure the accuracy of the accounting records. The constant monitoring associated with a perpetual inventory has the following advantages:

—Accurate stock counts thus facilitating stock-taking.
—Prevents the company running out of stock, and stock control is greatly improved with an obvious impact on cash flow.
—Greater security over stock.

For stock valuation purposes, SSAP 9 is specific: stocks must be valued at the 'lower of cost or net realisable value.' Net realisable value (NRV) is the amount expected to be received from sale of the product less any additional expenditure to be incurred on or before disposal, e.g. selling expenses. This approach is emphasised in the Companies (Amendment Act, 1986 which states that if the current realisable value of any current asset is lower than its purchase price (or production cost) the amount to be included in respect of that asset shall be the net realisable value. If net realisable value is in excess of cost (which it should be if the company is to trade profitably) then cost is used for valuation purposes. However, if net realisable value is less than cost, then the eventual sale will produce a loss. As shall be explained later, one of the fundamental principles underlying the preparation of financial statements is that of prudence. The prudence concept in this context requires that the anticipated loss should be recognised as soon as it is apparent. By valuing this stock at NRV, the probable loss is recognised in the period to which the goods were acquired or when this becomes apparent rather than in the subsequent period in which they were sold.

The principal method of comparing cost with NRV is to aggregate the cost figures for specific groups or categories of stock items, and then compare the cost figures with the net realisable value for the same items. Select the lower for valuation purposes.

Example:

A company produced the following data in relation to its closing stock levels:

	Historic cost	Replacement cost	Net realisable value
	£	£	£
Category A	8,000	9,500	8,600
Category B	7,600	6,750	7,000
Category C	12,400*	16,000	13,100
	28,000	32,250	28,700

* The historic cost of Category C stock has been computed as follows:

		£
Purchases during year (in sequence):	250 @ £30 =	7,500
	300 @ £35 =	10,500
	200 @ £40 =	8,000
		26,000
Units sold during period:	200 @ £40 = 8,000	
	160 @ £35 = 5,600	13,600
Closing stock valuation		12,400

Requirement:

Compute the valuation of the above stock in compliance with SSAP 9 which requires that stock should be valued at the lower of cost or net realisable value.

Solution: Replacement cost is not an acceptable method for valuing stocks and so the replacement cost figures are *irrelevant*. Cost can be determined in a number of ways. However, the method used above is that of LIFO (Last In First Out) which is not specifically allowed under SSAP 9. Consequently, we use the First In First Out (FIFO) method, which shall be explained fully later. Using this method, the most recent acquisitions are assumed to be held in closing stock. Therefore:

Closing stock (units) (750-360) = 390 units

	£
(valuation) 200 units @ £40 =	8,000
190 units @ £35 =	6,650
Cost (FIFO)	14,650

Computation of closing stock valuation

	Historic cost	NRV	SSAP 9
	£	£	£
Category A	8,000	8,600	8,000
Category B	7,600	7,000	7,000
Category C	14,650	13,100	13,100
	30,250	28,700	28,100

Note: £28,100 is the amount that should be included in the financial statements in respect of closing stock valuation.

THE DETERMINATION OF COST AND SSAP 9

The main difficulty with stock valuation is to determine *cost*. Initially we consider the case of a retail company and then consider the more complex situation of a manufacturing concern.

Common methods of determining 'cost' in a retail company would be the First In First Out (FIFO), Last In First Out (LIFO) and AVERAGE cost. All three bases require (1) separate identification of each item of stock; and (2) measurement of the physical stock on hand at the end of the current year.

FIFO: The most common base is FIFO, which assumes that the first unit to be acquired is the first unit to be sold. Thus, if two items are in stock which have been purchased on different dates, it is the *older* unit which is first to be sold. Under the FIFO method of stock valuation, the valuation of closing stock will be based on relatively recent acquisitions. Its common usage is due to its acceptability for both financial accounting and taxation purposes. SSAP 9 requires us to choose the method that provides the fairest approximation to actual cost. Since it would be normal to sell older stock first, FIFO would be an appropriate valuation base.

LIFO: Under LIFO the calculation of the cost of stock is on the assumption that the most recent purchases are taken to production or sold first and the closing stock on hand represents the earliest purchase or production. However, it is not normal to sell the newer stock first, hence LIFO is not favoured. Also, LIFO is not usually an appropriate method of stock valuation because it often results in stocks being stated in the balance sheet at amounts that bear little resemblance to recent cost levels. Nevertheless, some people would argue that the LIFO method of stock valuation results in a more realistic profit figure. Current revenue is matched with the most recent cost of purchase and so holding gains on price level changes are excluded. However, the stock valuation recorded on the balance sheet may be out of date and unrealistic. The main impact of these two methods (FIFO and LIFO) of closing stock valuation can be seen in a period of rapidly rising input prices. In such inflationary periods, the LIFO method will provide the lower stock valuation and therefore the lower profits.

AVERAGE: The third method of determining cost is referred to as the average cost basis. Average cost is computed by dividing the total cost of goods available for sale by the number of units available for sale. This computation gives a weighted-average unit cost, which is then applied to the units in closing stock. The average method would be appropriate where goods are selected randomly for sale. Consider the following example, using the purchase and sale of identical articles:

Exhibit 6.1

January	Quantity Purchased	Unit Price
2nd	12	£5
10th	8	£6
21st	10	£7
	30	

Sales were 25 units, leaving 5 units in stock at the end of the period.
What is the cost of goods sold, and what is the value to be placed on the closing stock?

FIFO method: With this method, it is assumed that the goods are sold in strict purchase order: the oldest items are sold first. Goods sold are valued on the basis of the oldest purchase price paid. Hence, the cost of goods sold is

$$
\begin{aligned}
12 \times £5 &= 60 \\
8 \times £6 &= 48 \\
5 \times £7 &= \underline{35} \\
&\quad £143
\end{aligned}
$$

Closing stock is determined by considering the cost of the most recent purchases.

Hence, closing stock is $5 \times £7 = £35$

LIFO method: Closing stock is valued at the cost of the oldest goods purchased. From the example above, the closing stock of five units would be valued at £5 each.

$$
\begin{aligned}
& & & £ \\
\text{Hence, cost of goods sold } 7 \times £5 &= & & 35 \\
8 \times £6 &= & & 48 \\
10 \times £7 &= & & \underline{70} \\
& & & £153
\end{aligned}
$$

Closing stock is $5 \times £5$ $= £25$

AVERAGE COST METHOD: Using this method, the average cost of all purchases during the accounting period together with the opening stock is calculated, and the cost of sales and closing stocks are based on that figure. In the example the weighted-average method figures would be:

January	Number	Price	£
2	12	£5	60
10	8	£6	48
21	10	£7	70
	30		£178

Average cost: £178/30 = £5.93 per article
Cost of goods sold: 25 x £5.93 = £148.35 (rounded)
Closing stock is thus 5 units x £5.93 = £29.65

The varying results arising from using these three methods can be seen in this summary.

	Cost of goods sold £	Closing stock £
FIFO	143	35
LIFO	153	25
Average (weighted)	148.35	29.65

With respect to the figures used above, the different results arising from choosing one method as opposed to the others would not be great, but with stocks of say £50m, a significant difference would appear.

It should be noted that in accordance with SSAP 9 (Stocks and work in progress), LIFO is not acceptable for external reporting purposes and is not acceptable to the Revenue Commissioners as a basis for taxation computations. In addition, LIFO is not allowed under the provisions of the Companies (Amendment) Act, 1986. The act states that purchase price (or production price of stocks) may be valued at either first in, first out (FIFO), weighted-average or a similar method and the method chosen must appear appropriate to the directors.

The accounting convention of consistency applies most forcefully in this instance. The convention of consistency comes into play whenever a choice must be made between methods of valuation of assets (and the apportionment of expenses/revenues to accounting periods). This convention suggests that the same accounting method should be used by a business from year to year. The interpretation of accounting information is often done by comparison with previous years. The financial statements of one year need to be viewed in the context of the previous years accounts—hence the need for consistency. Thus, the method chosen to value stocks should be applied consistently over accounting periods. The consistency convention also suggests that users of financial statements need to be told if methods have changed and what are the effects of these changes. Consequently, any change in the method of stock valuation must be disclosed in the accounting report and an indication must be given of the impact of the change.

ACCOUNTING FOR PRODUCTION COSTS

So far in our discussion we have concentrated on stock valuation for retailing concerns. Now we switch our attention to manufacturing companies. In many respects, retail companies and manufacturers are similar. Both businesses earn their revenue by selling products. However, the essential difference is that the retail concern buys its goods in a ready-to-sell condition.

Thus the retailer's cost of goods sold is based upon the cost of goods purchased. The manufacturer, on the other hand, produces the goods it sells. Therefore, its cost of goods sold is based on the costs incurred in manufacturing these goods.

A typical manufacturer buys raw materials and converts them into finished goods. Thus, the first basic cost of a manufacturer is that of raw materials. The raw material for a furniture manufacturer includes timber, springs and various types of foam and fabric. The terms raw materials and finished goods are defined in the context of each manufacturing firm. For example, the fabric may be the raw material of the furniture manufacturer, but it represents the finished goods of the textile manufacturer.

In converting raw materials into finished goods, a manufacturer will incur direct labour. This represents the wages paid to factory employees who work directly on the products being manufactured. Direct labour costs typically include the cost of machine operators, assembly line workers and others who work on the goods by hand or with tools.

All manufacturing costs other than raw material and direct production labour are called factory or production overhead. Production overheads are those production costs that cannot be traced entirely to a specific product. For example, factory rent relates to the entire production operation as distinct from a specific unit produced. Therefore, there are three types of basic manufacturing costs, namely, direct labour, direct materials, and production overhead. Examples of factory or production overhead cost include:

(*a*) *Indirect labour*:
supervisory salaries;
maintenance salaries;
plant security service

(*b*) *Factory occupancy costs*:
depreciation of buildings;
insurance and rates on buildings;
repairs and maintenance of buildings

(*c*) *Plant and machinery costs*: ,
depreciation of plant and machinery;
maintenance of plant and machinery

The items above represent a few examples of factory overhead costs,but it is not possible to compile an exhaustive list of all factory overhead costs. For this reason, factory or production overhead will basically consist of all costs incurred in the manufacturing process other than raw materials and direct (production) labour. It should be noted that selling and administrative costs do not relate to the production process and should never be included in factory overhead. Certain costs such as insurance may be applicable partly to factory operations and partly to administration. In such case, these costs should be apportioned among factory overhead and administration costs.

The manufacturing account

It has been stated above that the essential difference between a manufacturer and a retailing concern is that the former produces the goods it sells, the latter buys its goods in a ready-to-sell condition. Thus, for a manufacturing concern it is necessary to prepare a manufacturing account to reflect the cost of goods produced during the period. A typical manufacturing account is reproduced below.

Raw materials become a manufacturing cost when they are consumed rather than when they are purchased. The cost of raw materials consumed during an accounting period comprises of the opening stock plus purchases less any raw materials on hand at the end of the period.

FRANK MANUFACTURING COMPANY
MANUFACTURING ACCOUNT FOR YEAR ENDED 31 DECEMBER 199 .

	£	£
1. Raw materials consumed:		
Opening stock of raw materials		25,000
Add: Purchases of raw materials		140,000
Cost of raw materials available for use		165,000
Less: Closing stock of raw materials		(20,000)
Cost of raw materials consumed		145,000
2. Direct labour		300,000
Prime Cost		445,000
3. Factory Overhead:		
Indirect labour	90,000	
Rent and rates	16,000	
Depreciation of plant	11,000	
Depreciation of buildings	10,000	127,000
Manufacturing costs incurred during the period		572,000
Add: Opening work in progress		84,000
Less: Closing work in progress		(98,000)
Cost of finished goods manufactured		558,000

It is important to note the adjustment made in the manufacturing account in respect of opening and closing work in progress. The figure £572,000 represents the total of manufacturing costs incurred during the relevant accounting period. To find the production cost of goods *completed* in the period, the value of work in progress at the start must be brought into consideration since, presumably, it would have been completed during the accounting period. On the other hand, closing work in progress must be deducted since it has not, by definition, been finished and so must be carried forward to the next accounting period.

When the cost of finished goods manufactured is ascertained, it is transferred to the firm's trading account, taking the place where normally purchases are shown. Thus, the trading account of Frank Manufacturing would appear:

FRANK MANUFACTURING COMPANY
TRADING ACCOUNT FOR THE YEAR ENDED 31 DECEMBER 199 .

	£	£
Sales		780,000
Cost of goods sold:		
Opening stock of finished goods	38,000	
Cost of finished goods manufactured	558,000	
Cost of goods available for sale	596,000	
Less: Closing stock of finished goods	(45,000)	551,000
		229,000

The item amounting to £551,000 in the trading account is described as the cost of goods sold and it represents the cost of the finished goods which were actually sold during 199 .. The £558,000 in the trading account represents the cost of goods manufactured, which has been transferred from the manufacturing account.

ABSORPTION AND DIRECT COST VALUATION METHODS

The stocks of a manufacturing concern will consist of the following categories:

(*a*) raw materials
(*b*) work-in-progress
(*c*) finished goods

(*a*) *Raw materials*: There are treated in the same manner as goods for re-sale. Note is taken of the price paid, the method of calculation (e.g. FIFO), and of net realisable value at the balance sheet date.

(*b*) *Work-in-progress*: This consists of partly finished products. Their cost will be determined on the same basis that is used for valuing finished goods.

(*c*) *Finished goods*: Finished goods will be valued at cost of production (subject to the lower of cost/net realisable value rule). Although the goods are available for sale to a customer, revenue cannot be recognised until the goods have been sold.

In a manufacturing company, the definition of cost of production can be complex. We have seen that it will usually include three elements, namely, raw materials, direct labour and production overheads. Clearly the raw materials used to make the product must be included, i.e. direct materials including transport charges. These materials can be physically traced to the product, e.g. wood for golf clubs, fabric in clothes etc.

The second cost ingredient in manufactured goods is the direct labour which is performed on the product. You could go into the factory and verify this work being performed, e.g. welding, assembly. Without such direct labour the product would never be produced.

The third cost ingredient is manufacturing overhead. Overhead is simply the aggregate of indirect expenses (e.g. factory light and heat) and indirect labour (e.g. factory supervisors). By their nature such costs are necessary for production, but they can't be physically traced to an individual product. For example, light and heat is incurred in respect of total production and not only for a single product. In addition, it is legitimate to include in production overhead interest on capital borrowed to finance the production of stock, to the extent that it accrues in respect of the period of production. Thus the total cost structure of a manufacturing company can be displayed as follows, with only the costs associated with production being assigned to closing stock valuation:

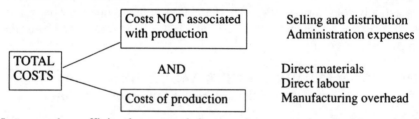

It cannot be sufficiently stressed that costs *not* associated with production should *never* be assigned to closing stock. Thus, administration costs represent costs associated with administering the business, as distinct from producing goods.

The major problem with respect to the valuation of closing stock is the accounting treatment of 'manufacturing overhead' and this is an area in which financial and management accounting overlap. It is also an area of controversy and it leads to two separate schools of thought, namely, 'absorption' and 'variable'. The controversy concerns *only* the accounting treatment of *fixed* production overhead. A fixed cost is one that remains unchanged for a given period, even when the volume of output changes. Thus, the cost of rent is a fixed cost since it remains unchanged whether business is booming or slack. Obviously, this is true only within a given or relevant range of activity. If, for example, volume were to increase three-fold, the company may have need to acquire larger premises and hence incur greater rental costs.

A variable cost is one which changes in proportion to the volume of output. Alternatively stated, a variable cost is one that is constant per unit of output. A typical example of a variable cost is raw materials. As output expands, more materials are needed, yet the amount of raw material input per unit produced remains constant. In defining variable costs, it is also important to stress that the relationship between variable costs and output is valid for a given range of activity. For example, purchases of raw materials beyond a certain amount may generate quantity discounts which would have an impact on the variable cost/output relationship.

The absorption school argues that both fixed and variable production overheads should be included in stock valuation since they have been incurred in 'bringing the product to its present location and condition'. Thus, you cannot produce without incurring fixed production cost. In addition, they would point out that the classification between fixed and variable production overhead is vague and imprecise.

The variable costing school argues that fixed production costs are associated with providing productive capacity as distinct from using it. Fixed overheads would be incurred regardless of the level of output. They should not be included in stock valuation, but written-off in total to the profit and loss account immediately.

SSAP 9 resolves the argument by requiring companies to use the 'full' or 'absorption' method of stock valuation for financial accounting purposes. Cost is defined in SSAP 9 as being that expenditure which has been incurred in the normal course of business in bringing the product to its present location and condition. This expenditure should include, in addition to the cost of purchases, such costs of conversions as are appropriate to the location and condition of the product. Clearly conversion costs include production overhead, and SSAP 9 indicates that it is the classification of overheads according to their function (e.g. production overheads, administration overheads, etc.) which is the distinguishing characteristic rather than a classification system with respect to volume, i.e. fixed and variable overheads.

However, for management accounting, i.e. internal purposes, the company may use whatever method it likes. The difference between the reported net profit figures under both absorption and variable costing methods will be entirely attributable to accounting treatment of fixed production overhead.

Example:
A manufacturing company produces only 10,000 units of similar output annually. Direct material and direct labour costs amount to £1 and £2, respec-

tively. Each unit is machine processed for 30 minutes and production overhead is to be assigned to units of production on the basis of machine hours.

Total annual overhead is estimated as follows:

Machine power (variable)	£5,000
Other factory overheads (fixed)	£10,000
Administration expenses	£10,000

Requirement:

Calculate appropriate overhead absorption rates on the basis of machine hours and compute the valuation of 1,000 units of closing stock under both absorption and variable costing.

Production overhead recovery rates are designed to apportion production overhead to individual units. The overhead recovery rates is calculated by the formula:

$$\frac{\text{'£' Production overhead to be recovered}}{\text{Activity base}}$$

One popular activity base is that of machine hours. The overhead to be apportioned to each unit is therefore the overhead rate per machine hour multiplied by the machine hours per unit. The appropriate overhead recovery rates are:

Overhead to be absorbed	Absorption Costing £	Variable Costing £
Machine power	5,000	5,000
Other factory overheads	10,000	Not applicable
Overhead to be absorbed	£15,000	£5,000
Machine hours	5,000 hours	5,000 hours
Overhead absorption rate (Overhead/hours)	£3 per machine hr	£1 per machine hr
Closing stock valuation:	£	£
Direct materials	1.00	1.00
Direct labour	2.00	2.00
Production overhead (30 mins)	1.50	0.50
Production cost (per unit)	4.50	3.50
Total valuation (1,000 Units)	£4,500	£3,500

There are two important points to note in the above example. First, administration costs should not be included in stock valuation since they do not represent a cost of production. Second, the difference between overhead per unit under absorption and variable costing is explained by the treatment of fixed production overhead.

The differences in net profit for internal purposes between variable and absorption costing methods can be significant. Generally, absorption costing will provide less volatile net income figures relative to variable costing. However, over the life of the enterprise the *total* profit figures will be identical.

The difference in net profit between the two valuation methods depends on the changes in opening and closing stock levels. Basically, there are only three possible situations in relation to movements in stock levels during an accounting period:

(*a*) *Production equals sales*: Both methods will provide identical net profit figures.

(*b*) *Production exceeds sales (i.e. stock build-up)*: Absorption costing provides the relatively higher profit figures because a portion of the fixed production overhead attributable to production will be included in closing stock. The essence of absorption costing is that an enterprise could boost its reported profit performance by overproducing and thus building up its stock at the end of an accounting period. Thus, reported profit will depend on production as distinct from sales performance.

(*c*) *Sales exceed production (i.e. stock run-down)*: When stock levels are declining, variable costing will provide the relatively higher profit figure. This is because under variable costing, only the fixed overheads applicable to the period in question are being written-off.

Under an absorption costing system, the overheads for the period in question are being written-off *in addition* to a portion of the previous period's fixed overheads which were included in opening stock.

QUESTION 6.1 (SM)

Two students, Peter and Paul, are equal partners in a joint venture which involves them, on a part-time basis, in buying and selling sacks of product F. The transactions for the six months ended 30 September were as stated below. You are to assume that purchases at the unit costs given were made at the beginning of each month and that the sales were made at the end of each month at the fixed price of £1.50 per sack.

| Month | Purchases | | Sales |
| | Sacks | Unit Cost | Sacks |
		£	
April	1,000	1.00	500
May	500	1.20	750
June	1,000	1.00	Nil
July	Nil	—	600
August	500	1.20	650
September	500	1.30	600

In October, Peter and Paul held a meeting to review their financial position and to share out the profits, but there was disagreement because each partner had priced the issues on a different basis. Peter had used FIFO and Paul had used LIFO. It was however, agreed that the stock remaining at the end of September should be stored until next April.

Requirement:
(*a*) Show the records which each student kept of the transactions.
(*b*) Show the amount each student ought to receive if the whole of the profit arising from each method of pricing the issues were distributed.

QUESTION 6.2 (SM)

A project to manufacture a new product is under consideration by the management of Belfield Products. The following information applies:

Selling price per unit	£6
Advertising and promotion costs	20% of sales price
Variable manufacturing costs	£1.20 per unit
Variable selling expenses	4% of sales price

Fixed production costs are estimated at £8,000 per month and the normal production capacity is 10,000 units. Fixed administration costs will amount to £3,000 per month. Production and sales will be:

	July	August	September	Total
Production (units)	5,000	5,000	5,000	15,000
Sales (units)	3,000	5,000	7,000	15,000

Requirement:
(*a*) Indicate closing stock valuations for July under both absorption and variable costing methods.
(*b*) Prepare a forecast profit statement for the above three months under both variable and absorption costing.
(The Chartered Association of Certified Accountants)

QUESTION 6.3 (A)

The draft profit and loss account of the Stamp Company, which makes widgets, is shown below.

During the period, 100 widgets were produced of which ten remained in stock at the year end. Closing stock is valued at the same price as they are sold to customers.

Requirement:
Calculate the correct valuation of closing stock.

	£	£
Sales		270,000
Costs incurred in year		
Direct materials and labour	100,000	
Production overheads	70,000	
	170,000	
Less: Closing stock	30,000	140,000
Gross profit		130,000
Administration costs		100,000
Net profit		30,000

QUESTION 6.4 (A)

D. Murphy, a furniture manufacturer, extracted the following trial balance from his books on 30 June 19 . 2:

	Debit £	Credit £
D. Murphy: capital account		8,150
Freehold property at cost	9,200	
Plant and machinery (cost—£10,000)	4,700	
Motor vehicle (cost—£8,000)	1,500	
Stock of raw materials, 1 July, 19 . 1	4,720	
Stock of finished goods, 1 July, 19 . 1	10, 940	
Trade debtors	5,800	
Bank overdraft		9,600
Trade creditors		4,900
Bad debts written-off	700	
Bad debts provision		500
Purchases of raw materials	27,400	
Duty on purchases of raw materials	2,040	
Direct wages	21,900	
Factory power	2,400	
Factory light and heat	1,200	
Rent and rates	800	
General office salaries	3,800	
General office expenses	5,000	
Drawings	2,900	
Bank charges	100	
Sales		81,950
	105,100	105,100

The following additional information is available:

(1) Stocks at 30 June 19. 2, were as follows:

Raw materials	£5,100
Finished goods	£7,200

(2) Rent and rates are to be apportioned as follows:

Factory	(3/4)
Office	(1/4)

(3) Depreciation is to be provided as follows

Plant and machinery	10% on cost
Motor vehicles	10% on cost

(4) Amounts outstanding at 30 June 19 . 2, were as follows:

Rent and rates	£560
General office salaries	£100

(5) Amount paid in advance at 30 June 19 . 2, was as follows:

Factory power	£130

(6) The bad debts provision should be adjusted to 2½% of trade debtors.

Requirement:
Prepare

(*a*) A manufacturing, trading and profit and loss account for the year ended 30 June 19 . 2.

(*b*) A balance sheet as at that date.

(The Institute of Chartered Accountants in Ireland)

QUESTION 6.5 (A)

From Snag Manufacturing Company's adjusted trial balance of 31 December 19 . 4, the following account balances have been obtained:

	£
Raw materials stock, 1 January 19 . 4	75,000
Work in progress, 1 January 19 . 4	21,200
Finished goods stock, 1 January 19 . 4	50,000
Purchases	198,000
Sales	300,000
Direct labour	125,000
Indirect factory labour	40,000
Sales and office salaries	49,000
Factory light and heat	35,000
Factory insurance	6,000
Machine and plant maintenance	8,000
Purchase returns	3,000
Miscellaneous factory overheads	6,000
Depreciation—factory building	9,000
Depreciation—plant and machinery	39,000
Factory rates	3,600
Bad debts written-off	7,000
Administration expenses	5,000

In addition, you are reliably informed that, for the year ended 31 December 19 . 4, raw materials costing £187,000 were consumed, the cost of goods manufactured was £440,000 and the cost of goods sold was £430,000.

Requirement:
Calculate each of the following:
(a) closing stock of raw materials;
(b) closing stock of work-in-progress;
(c) total factory overheads for year;
(d) closing stock of finished goods;
(e) the unit costs of direct raw materials based on the production of 100,000 unites and 200,000 units respectively;
(f) the unit costs of depreciation of plant and machinery based on the production of 100,000 units and 200,000 units respectively.
(The Institute of Chartered Accountants in Ireland)

QUESTION 6.6 (SM)
You are advising the owner of a small retail store which has just completed its first year of trading. The store, buys and sells two different categories of items—X and Y. All transactions are conducted on a credit basis.

You are presented with the following information regarding purchases and sales during the year:

Commodity	Period	Purchases on Credit	Sales on Credit
X	Jan.-Mar. 19 . 1	1,000 units - £5 each	500 units - £10 each
	Apr.-Jun. 19 . 1	2,000 units - £6 each	1,000 units - £11 each
	Jul.-Sep. 19 . 1	3,000 units - £7 each	2,000 units - £13 each
	Oct.-Dec. 19 . 1	4,000 units - £8 each	3,000 units - £13 each
Y	Jan.-Mar. 19 . 1	500 units - £10 each	100 units - £20 each
	Apr.-Jun. 19 . 1	1,000 units - £11 each	500 units - £21 each
	Jul.-Sep. 19 . 1	1,500 units - £12 each	1,000 units - £22 each
	Oct.-Dec. 19 . 1	2,000 units - £13 each	1,500 units - £23 each

Payments to creditors during the year amounted to £110,000 and cash received from customers amounted to £135,000.

You have decided to create a bad debt provision equivalent to 10 per cent of debtors at 31 December 19 . 1.

Requirement:
(a) Calculate the closing stock valuation using the following bases:
(i) first in, first out method,
(ii) last in, last out method;

(*b*) Prepare the trading and profit and loss account for the year ended 31 December 19 . 1, assuming a closing stock valuation of £65,700.
(The Institute of Chartered Accountants in Ireland)

QUESTION 6.7 (A)

A retail store sells two different categories of commodity—X and Y. During a single trading period, purchases and sales of these two commodities were as follows:

Commodity	Purchases	Sales on Credit
X	100 units @ £5 each 200 units @ £6 each 300 units @ £7 each	400 units @ £11 each
Y	200 units @ £10 each 400 units @ £11 each	500 units @ £15 each

At the end of the trading period it was decided to create a provision of 5 per cent on credit sales to cover bad debts.

Requirement:
(*a*) Calculate the closing value of stock, using the first in, first out method.
(*b*) Prepare a trading and profit and loss account for the above period.
Note: There was no opening stock.
(The Institute of Chartered Accountants in Ireland)

QUESTION 6.8 (A)

You are advising the owner of a small retail store which has just completed its first year of trading on 31 December 19 . 2. The store buys and sells two different categories of commodity—A and B.

You are presented with the following information regarding purchases and sales during the year:

Commodity	Period	Purchases on Credit		Credit Sales		Cash Sales	
		Units	£	Units	£	Units	£
A	Jan.-Mar. 19 . 2	1,500 @ 5 each		400 @ 10 each		200 @ 10 each	
	Apr.-Jun. 19 . 2	1,500 @ 6 each		1,100 @ 11 each		500 @ 10 each	
	Jul.-Sep. 19 . 2	3,500 @ 7 each		2,500 @ 13 each		500 @ 12 each	
	Oct.-Dec. 19 . 2	3,500 @ 8 each		2,500 @ 13 each		600 @ 12 each	
B	Jan.-Mar. 19 . 2	500 @ 10 each		200 @ 20 each		200 @ 19 each	
	Apr.-Jun. 19 . 2	1,250 @ 11 each		400 @ 21 each		400 @ 20 each	
	Jul.-Sep. 19 . 2	1,250 @ 12 each		1,100 @ 22 each		100 @ 21 each	
	Oct.-Dec. 19 . 2	2,000 @ 13 each		1,400 @ 23 each		300 @ 22 each	

Payment to creditors during the year amounted to £95,000 and cash received from debtors amounted to £142,000. Discounts allowed during the year amounted to £2,400 and discounts received amounted to £1,800.

You have decided to create a bad debt provision equivalent to 10 per cent of debtors at 31 December 19 . 2.

Requirement:
(a) Prepare debtors and creditors control accounts to record the above information.
(b) Calculate the closing stock valuation using the first in, first out method (FIFO).
(c) Prepare the trading and profit and loss account for the year ended 31 December. 19 . 2, assuming a closing stock valuation of £21,800.

(The Institute of Chartered Accountants in Ireland)

QUESTION 6.9 (A)
You are the auditor of Groucho Ltd which commenced business on 1 January, 19 . 6, processing and selling a single product.

You are given the following information:
(1) 1 tonne of raw material, when processed, makes 1 tonne of finished product.
(2) 100 tonnes of raw material were purchased each week in 19 . 6.
(3) The ex-works cost of raw material was £100 per tonne on 1 January 19 . 6, and this increased to £120 per tonne from 1 October 19 . 6. Customs duty and carriage costs throughout the year were £5 and £15 per tonne respectively.
(4) Labour costs on conversion and variable production overhead costs were £10 and £20 per tonne respectively.
(5) Fixed production overhead costs for all levels of activity, administrative expenses and selling expenses for the year ended 31 December 19 . 6, were £196,000, £50,000 and £25,000 respectively.
(6) The finished product was sold for £215 per tonne and the delivery cost (included in the selling price) was £8 per tonne.
(7) There were 52 production weeks in 19 . 6.
(8) At 31 December 19 . 6, the company had stocks of 400 tonnes of raw material and 600 tonnes of finished product. There was no work-in-progress.
(9) The selling price of the product will remain at £215 per tonne during 19 . 7. There is adequate demand for the product.
(10) All overheads are expected to continue at their 19 . 6 level.

Requirement:
You are required to write a letter to the accountant of Groucho Ltd setting out the calculation of the value of stocks for inclusion in the financial statements for the year ended 31 December 19 . 6.

(The Institute of Chartered Accountants in Ireland)

7.

Accounts from Incomplete Records

Some businesses do not have a full double-entry book-keeping system from which to prepare year-end financial statements. There are many reasons for this. Perhaps the business is small in size with only a few transactions. In such case, a full double-entry book-keeping system would be an expensive luxury. In other cases, there may not be the necessary accounting expertise in the business. In an extreme case, it is possible that due to damage or loss, some of the accounting records may be missing.

In all these cases, profit will need to be calculated to satisfy, for example, the needs of the Inspector of Taxes. It is now common to refer to such situations as preparing accounts from incomplete records. Depending on the incompleteness of the records, it will be necessary for the accountant to do work ranging from the logical deduction of missing figures to pure guesswork based on the limited information available. Preparing accounts from incomplete records occurs regularly in practice and is a favourite accounting examination topic. For teaching purposes, it is useful to divide the subject into four different areas namely, preparing a statement of affairs, preparing full financial statements for a period, determining stock destroyed by fire and finally, determination of the amount of cash misappropriated.

STATEMENT OF AFFAIRS

In some cases, the accounting records of a business may have been destroyed, lost or improperly maintained during a period and this creates difficulties when preparing financial statements. The best that can be done is to prepare a statement of closing assets and liabilities from whatever information is available (usually an opening balance sheet will be available). Some of this information will be obtained from external sources such as the bank statement and statements received from suppliers. Other information will be based on representations made by the owners.

The accountant is aided by the knowledge that any increase in capital (owner's equity) during the period must be attributable to profit, assuming no capital has been introduced or withdrawn during the period. The situation is represented by the following equation:

Opening				Capital				Closing
Capital	+	Net profit	+	introduced	−	drawings	=	Capital

Usually four of the above five variables can be the estimated, with differing degrees of reliability, by the accountant. The opening capital figure should be available from the previous balance sheet whereas the closing capital figure will be equal to the net assets at the end of the accounting period. Clearly, the amount attributed to closing net assets will be dependent on the values assigned to the various assets and liabilities. The personal records of the proprietor may indicate the amount of additional capital contributed during the period but the figure for drawings is often imprecisely estimated.

Drawings represent sums of money (or other assets) withdrawn by the proprietor. It is customary for a proprietor, who depends upon the business for his living, to withdraw sums of money at regular intervals for personal expenses, or he may withdraw goods if they happen to be useful to him. Such withdrawals are withdrawals of capital. They represent a reduction of capital but are not a reduction of profit. Thus, if a business generates £1,000 in profit which is withdrawn by the proprietor in cash, it would be incorrect to claim that the business had not made any profit.

If these four variables can be quantified in money terms, then the residual in the above equation will represent the net profit earned during the period.

Unfortunately, there is no guarantee that the closing capital figure, obtained by the listing of all assets and liabilities, is correct. Some items may be incorrectly included or excluded whereas others may be included at an incorrect amount. Likewise the amount of capital introduced may be incorrect and, in many cases, the figure for drawings would be a reasonable estimate rather than the exact amount. Thus, the computation of net profit, by such a method, cannot be assumed to be accurate. At best, the net profit computed is only an estimate. A further limitation of this approach is that it does not provide sufficient information for owners and managers in planning and controlling the business since there is no information on expenses and revenues.

EXAMPLE

John won £5,000 and decided to set up in business as a retailer. He borrowed £1,000 from his father, purchased a van for £4,000 and paid the balance into a bank account which was maintained in the name of the business. He banked all receipts and made all payments by cheque. His accounting records have been kept haphazardly but you ascertain for his first year of trading that:

1. His father has been repaid £600.
2. Unsold stock at the end of the year cost £800.
3. His closing bank statement shows a favourable balance of £860, but from his cheque book you discover that a cheque for £68, written during the period, had not been presented to the bank.
4. The balance on the suppliers' statement for the last month of the year amounted to £674. On checking you find that:

   (i) A cheque for £88, written during the period, has not been credited by the supplier;

  (ii) Goods for £45 shown on statements had not been received at the end of the year;

 (iii) An invoice charged at £847 should have been at £836.

5. Sales invoices not paid at the end of the year totalled £875.
6. The van is to be depreciated at the rate of 10% per annum.

Requirement:

You are required to ascertain how much profit the business has generated during the year.

Solution: The first step in this profit measurement process is to prepare a closing statement of affairs, listing and valuing all assets and liabilities. The statement of affairs is really a balance sheet under a different names. However, the term balance sheet is generally used in the context of double-entry book-keeping. John's closing balance sheet or statement of affairs, based on the information provided, is as follows:

Balance Sheet at End of Year One

	£	£
Fixed assets (at book value)		3,600
Current assets		
Stock	800	
Debtors	875	
Bank (W1)	792	2,467
		6,067
Financed by:		
Closing capital (balancing figure)		5,137
Loan from father		400
Creditors (W2)		530
		6,067

Since the opening capital was £5,000 and the closing capital amounted to £5,137, the difference between the two figures (£137) must represent the net profit, in the absence of either additional capital introduced or drawings during the period.

(W1) Computation of closing bank balance

Balance per bank statement		860
Less: Unrepresented cheque		(68)
		792

(W2) Computation of closing creditors

Balance per statement (given)		674
Less:	Cheque in transit	(88)
	Goods not delivered	(45)
	Error on invoice	(11)
		530

It is obvious that the reliability of the above net profit figure depends entirely on the accuracy of the identification and subsequent valuation of assets and liabilities. If a considerable length of time expires between the financial year end and date of preparation of the statement of affairs, then this facilitates the verification of assets and liabilities. However, if the statement of affairs is prepared shortly after financial year end then there is little time available for extensive verification work to be completed.

PREPARATION OF FINANCIAL STATEMENTS

Many small businesses will record their transactions only in a cash book, detailing receipts and payments, and maintain a debtors and creditors ledger. In addition, some note will be kept of various assets and liabilities on hand at the start and end of the accounting period. This is the most common case of preparing accounts from 'Incomplete records'. However, one assumes that an adequate record of all cash/bank transactions has been maintained and that the listing of closing debtors and creditors is complete and accurate. The cash/bank account summary, when combined with opening and closing assets and liabilities, can be used to reconstruct appropriate nominal ledger accounts prior to the preparation of a complete set of financial statements. In so doing, the accountant will have to make logical assumptions regarding missing figures that he will encounter in the various ledger accounts. However, the accountant will be aware that the risks of fraud and theft are much higher when there is no complete double-entry accounting system.

It is useful to approach the preparation of accounts from incomplete records in a systematic fashion. The first step is to reconstruct an opening balance sheet from the assets and liabilities listed. Usually, the opening capital figure will not be provided but this can easily be obtained by subtracting total assets from total liabilities. In other words, we acknowledge that capital (or owner's equity) is the residual between assets and liabilities with its valuation being dependent on the valuation placed on all assets and liabilities. It is then recommended to open a ledger account for each balance sheet item, in particular accounts for cash, bank, debtors control and creditors control.

The cash and bank accounts should be reconstructed from the information available. (In many cases, the summarised bank account will be provided, especially in examination-type questions.) The bank account should contain a record of all lodgments and cheque payments, bank charges etc. made during the period. The cash account should record all lodgments and miscellaneous payments made from cash. In the absence of double-entry, the amount paid to suppliers is known, but the value of purchases is not; likewise lodgments will be known but not the value of sales revenue. In addition, payments for the various expenses are known but these may not correspond to the expenses incurred during the period.

Once the cash and bank accounts have been properly reconstructed and balanced, the double-entry should be completed for all the information given and this will ultimately generate data such as sales, purchases and business expenses for the period. It is inevitable that there will be 'missing' figures in some of the ledger accounts and the accountant must make a logical assumption on the nature of such items. In particular, the missing figure in the debtors control account will, in most instances, represent sales on credit for the period and the missing figure in the creditors control account will represent purchases on credit for the period.

When all the transactions have been posted by way of double-entry, year end adjustments should be made for accruals, prepayments, depreciation, disposals of fixed assets and bad debts. This final step should now lead to the preparation of a trading, profit and loss account for the period together with a closing balance sheet.

EXAMPLE

C. Lately, a sole trader, prepares his accounts annually to 31 December. His purchases and sales are on a cash and credit basis. The summary of his bank account on 31 December 19 . 1, was as follows:

	£		£
Balance 1 January, 19 . 1	5,575	Salaries	15,294
Lodgments	47,497	Sundry expenses	4,642
		Light and heat	642
		Creditors	29,673
		Rates—first moiety to	
		30 June 19 . 1	1,200
		Balance 31 Dec. 19 . 1	1,621
	53,072		53,072

You are supplied with the following additional information on 31 December 19 . 1:

(1) Part of the premises are sub-let at an annual rental of £1,500. A cheque for the annual rental had been lodged to Mr Lately's private bank account.

(2) Mr Latley had banked his cash takings after making the following payments:

	£
Sundry expenses	914
Salaries	2,873

(3) Details of other assets and liabilities are as follows:

	31 December 19 . 0	31 December 19 . 1
	£	£
Premises	15,000	15,000
Stock at cost	7, 135	8,258
Debtors	9,993	8,209
Creditors	5,400	16,450
Salaries due but unpaid	910	346
Motor vehicle (net) (Reg—RNI 14)	2,800	Note 4

(4) On 30 September 19 . 1, a new motor vehicle was purchased from the Easy Motor Co. to replace RNI 14. The details were as follows:

	£
New vehicle (cost)	5,000
Trade-in allowance	2,400

No invoice has yet been received from the Easy Motor Co. and no record of this transaction has been made in the books.

(5) Depreciation is to be provided on motor vehicles at 20% per annum with a full year's depreciation provided in year of disposal but none in year of acquisition.

(6) Bad debts of £932 are to be written off.

Requirement:
You are required to prepare

(a) The trading and profit and loss account for the year ended 31 December 19 . 1; and

(b) The balance sheet as on that date.

Solution: The first thing to be done is to estimate Mr Lately's opening capital by preparing a statement of affairs. The difference between the amount of aggregate assets and aggregate liabilities represents capital (owner's equity).

Computation of capital at 1 January 19 . 1	£	£
Assets: Bank	5,575	
Premises	15,000	
Stock	7,135	
Debtors	9,993	
Vehicles	2,800	40,503
Less Creditors		(5,400)
Accruals		(910)
Opening capital		34,193

The summarised bank account has been presented so that it need not be reconstructed. However, it is necessary to reconstruct other nominal ledger accounts, in particular the cash account, debtors control and creditors control accounts.

Cash account

		Lodgments	47,497
. : Debtors	51,284	Sundry	914
		Salaries	2,873
	51,284		51,284

On the credit side of the cash account we have recorded the amount of lodgments (which are debited to the bank account), sundry expenses and salaries paid out of cash receipts (which are, in turn, debited to the appropriate expense account). However, there must be a debit entry in the cash account amounting to £51,284. It is logical to assume that this represents the amount of cash received from customers. Thus, the double-entry is to debit the cash account with £51,284 and credit the debtors control account with the same amount.

Debtors control account

1.1 . Balance	9,993		Cash	51,284
. . Sales	49,500	31.12	Balance	8,209
	59,493			59,493

The debtors control account will now record the opening and closing balances (given) together with the amount of cash received from debtors (£51,284). The missing figure on the debit side of the debtors control account must therefore represent credit sales for the period. Thus, the debtors control account is debited with £49,500 and the sales account is credited with this amount. (This sales account figure will eventually be transferred to the trading account.)

Creditors control account

	Bank	29,673	1.1.	Balance	5,400
31.12	Balance	16,450	∴	Purchases	40,723
		46,123			46,123

The creditors control account will record the opening and closing balances (given) together with the total of cheques paid to suppliers. The missing figure on the credit side of the creditors control account must represent purchases during the period. Thus, the creditors control account is credited with £40,723 and this amount is debited to the purchases account. (The purchases figure will, in turn, be transferred to the trading account.)

In preparing accounts from incomplete records, it is recommended that the entire double-entry book-keeping process is complete in the appropriate nominal ledger accounts together with all year-end adjustments. The main adjustments are for the accrual of salaries, rates, bad debts write-off and the amount owing for the new car purchased together with the disposal of the old vehicle. The appropriate ledger accounts are as follows:

Salaries

	Bank	15,294	1.1	Balance	910
	Cash	2,873		P/L account	17,603
31.12	Balance	346			

Rates

	Bank	1,200			
31.12	Balance	1,200		P/L account	2,400

Debtors control

1.1	Balance	9,993		Cash	51,284
	Sales	49,500		Bad debts	932
			31.12	Balance	7,277
		59,493			59,493

Motor vehicle

1.1	Balance	2,800		Disposal	2,800
	Trade in (disposal)	2,400			
31.12	Balance	2,600	31.12	Balance	5,000

Disposal account

	Vehicles	2,800		Trade-in	2,400
				Loss (P/L)	400

Sundry expenses account

Bank	4,642			
Cash	914	P/L account	5,556

Light and heat account

Bank	642	P/L account	642

Rent received account

P/L account	1,500	Drawings	1,500

Drawings account

Rental income	1,500	Transfer to capital	1,500

Bad debts account

Debtors	932	P/L account	932

Depreciation account

Aggregate depreciation	1,000	P/L Account	1,000

Aggregate depreciation account

31.12	Balance	1,000	Vehicle	1,000

Based on the above, the trading, profit and loss account of C. Lately for the year ended 31 December 19 . 1 and balance sheet at that date are:

C. LATELY
TRADING AND PROFIT AND LOSS ACCOUNT FOR
THE YEAR ENDED 31 DECEMBER 19 . 1

	£	£
Sales		49,500
Cost of Sales:		
Opening Stock	7,135	
Purchases	40,723	
Less: closing stock	(8,258)	(39,600)
Gross profit		9,900
Rental Income		1,500
		11,400
Salaries	17,603	
Light and Heat	642	
Rates	2,400	
Sundry expenses	5,556	
Loss on sale	400	
Bad debts	932	
Depreciation	1,000	(28,533)
Net loss for period		(17,133)

Balance Sheet at 31 December 19 . 1

Fixed Assets:	Cost	Depreciation	£
Premises	15,000	—	15,000
Vehicles	5,000	1,000	4,000
	20,000	1,000	19,000
Current Assets:			
Stock		8,258	
Debtors		7,277	
Bank		1,621	
		17,156	
Current liabilities			
Trade creditors	16,450		
Creditors (car)	2,600		
Accruals	1,546	20,596	(3,440)
			15,560
Financed by:			
Opening capital			34,193
Less: Drawings			(1,500)
Less: Net loss			(17,133)
			15,560

STOCK DESTROYED BY FIRE

If stock is destroyed by fire or otherwise, it is necessary to calculate the value of these goods, especially in the context of claiming insurance. Some companies maintain a perpetual inventory system which means that all purchase and sale of stock items are automatically recorded on stock cards. This allows for quick and easy ascertainment of stock on hand. However, many businesses do not maintain such a system and the only way that they can ascertain stock is to undertake a physical stock-take. This involves counting each item of stock on hand and then correctly valuing it. Because this is a time-consuming exercise, physical stock-take is usually done once a year, just at the financial year end.

However, if stock is destroyed by fire, physical stock-taking becomes an impossibility. In such circumstances, the accountant will estimate closing stock on hand with reference to the normal gross profit margin of the business.

Gross profit, it will be recalled, is the difference between sales revenue and cost of sales. It is customary to express this gross margin as a percentage of sales. Thus, based on the following trading account, the gross profit percentage is 20%.

TRADING ACCOUNT FOR THE YEAR ENDED 31 DECEMBER 19.1

	£	£
Sales		55,000
Cost of Sales:		
Opening stock	9,000	
Purchases	40,000	
Less: Closing stock	(5,000)	(44,000)
Gross profit		11,000 (20%)

However, it is possible to express the same gross profit in terms of mark-up on cost. Since the gross profit of £11,000 is based on a cost of sales of £44,000, then the mark-up on cost is 25%. It is very important to stress that the gross profit, in money terms, remains at £11,000. However, the method by which this can be expressed in percentage terms differs. Some accountants prefer to use the gross margin as a percentage of sales; others will refer to mark-up on cost. Although the percentages sound different, they both relate to the same information but expressed in different ways.

It is important to be able to convert from gross margin as a percentage of sales to mark-up percentage on cost. One method of conversion is always to use a base of 100. For example, if the gross profit to sales is 50%, then the sales price is equivalent to 100. The mark-up on cost is 100% as follows:

Assumed selling price	100
Gross margin	50 (50% of sales)
Therefore, the cost of goods sold is	50
And the mark-up on cost is	100%

On the other hand, if the mark-up on cost is 25%, then let the cost price be equal to a base of 100. The gross margin to sales percentage is 20% as follows:

Assumed cost price	100
Add mark-up on cost	25 (25% on cost)
Equals the anticipated sales price of	125

In applying the normal gross profit percentage to determine the amount of stock destroyed, the accountant implicitly assumes that the gross margin is constant from one period to another. This assumption may not be valid especially in the context of pilferage, increased or reduced selling prices. However, in many retail businesses, gross profit margins are reasonably stable. Indeed, for many pubs and lounges, the fall in a gross profit percentage between accounting periods is often attributed to cash misappropriation.

A constant gross profit margin allows the accountant to estimate the 'cost of goods sold' from the sales figure. The 'cost of goods sold' figure, it will be recalled, comprises opening stock plus purchases less closing stock. Of these three items, the valuation of opening stock should be available from the previous balance sheet and purchases for the period can be determined from the accounting records. The amount of closing stock will be the balancing figure in the cost of goods sold computation. This closing stock will correspond to the cost of stock destroyed by fire, assuming none has been salvaged.

EXAMPLE

On 11 May 19 . 7, a fire destroyed the entire stock of Mr Crowley, a retail merchant. He sells one product line which yields a gross margin on sales of 20%.

The following information has been extracted from the books:

(1)	*1 January 19 . 7*	*11 May 19 . 7*
Trade debtors (gross)	£8,109	£13,209
Trade creditors	6,518	6,466
Stock in hands	24,800	Unknown

(2) Cash movements during this period from 1 January 19 . 7 to 11 May 19 . 7 were as follows:

	£
Cheque payments for purchases for re-sale	62,052
Receipts from customers (banked)	81,900

Requirement:

You are required to determine the cost of goods destroyed by fire on 11 May 19 . 7.

Solution: In this instance, it is necessary to reconstruct both the debtors and creditors control accounts to determine sales and purchases for the period.

Debtors control account

1.1. . 7 Balance	8,109			
Sales	87,000			
		Bank account	81,900	
		11.05. . 7 Balance	13,209	
	95,109		95,109	

Creditors control account

		1.1. . 7	
Bank	62,052	Balance	6,518
11.05. . 7		Purchases	62,000
Balance	6,466		
	68,518		68,518

Since both sales and purchases are now known, the 'cost of goods sold' can be computed. The starting point is the sales figure of £87,000 on which a 20% gross margin is earned and, therefore, cost of sales must equal 80% of sales revenue. Thus:

	£
Sales (total)	87,000
Cost of goods sold	69,600 (80%)

The missing figure in the cost of goods sold computation represents closing stock as follows:

Opening stock (given)	24,800
Purchases (total)	62,000
Less: Closing stock	(17,200) (balancing figure)
Cost of sales (above)	69,600

Thus, on the assumption that no stock was salvaged, the stock destroyed by fire amounted to £17,200.

DETERMINATION OF CASH MISAPPROPRIATED

It was stated in a previous chapter that cash is the asset which is most easily misappropriated. Consequently, it is not uncommon that accountants are asked to estimate the amounts of money that may have been misappropriated during an accounting period. At best, the accountant will provide a reasonable estimate of the money involved but the degree of accuracy will depend crucially on the firm's anticipated gross profit margin and plausible reasons for changes in this ratio.

The accountant should always be in a position to ascertain correctly the cost of goods sold from the accounting records available. Using this figure he will then be able to estimate anticipated sales revenue, based on the normal gross profit margin. Thus, if cost of sales are £100,000 and the firm expects a gross profit margin on sales of 20%, then there is a reasonable expectation of sales revenue in the amount of £125,000, shown as follows:

Cost of sales	£100,000
Gross profit	
(20% on sales is	
equivalent to 25% on cost)	25,000
Anticipated sales	125,000

If actual sales are registered at £118,000, then there is a possibility of cash misappropriation in the amount of £7,000—the difference between anticipated sales and recorded sales.

EXAMPLE

A. Count owns a small retail shop which was managed by U. Take. The manager, who left on 31 December 19 . 7, was suspected of cash pilferage. The company has sought your advice in determining the amount of cash which may have been misappropriated for the recent six-month period.

Your enquiries establish the following:

	1 July 19 . 7	31 December 19 . 7
	£	£
Stock at cost	9,234	13,532
Trade creditors	17,321	13,421
Trade debtors	3,886	9,010

During the period ended 31 December 19 . 7, takings of £60,857 had been received from customers (immediately lodged) and cheques amounting to £58,198 had been paid to suppliers for goods purchased.

The company's gross profit margin on sales is estimated at $33\frac{1}{3}\%$.

Requirement:

You are required to estimate the amount of cash misappropriated for the period.

Solution: The first step is to reconstruct both the debtors and creditors control accounts in order to obtain purchases and sales figures for the period. (In practice both these figures are readily available from the accounting records.) However, the sales figure (£65,981) cannot be relied upon since there is a suspicion of theft. Theft is easily achieved, for example, by employees undertaking the cash received/sales figure and retaining the difference between actual cash received and cash recorded.

Debtors control account

1.7. . 7 Balance	3,886		
∴ Sales	65,981		
		Bank account	60,857
		31.12. . 7 Balance	9,010
	69,867		69,867

Creditors control account

	Bank	58,198	1.7. . 7	Balance	17,321
31.12. . 7	Balance	13,421	. .	Purchases	54,298
		71,619			71,619

The extent of the cash misappropriated can be estimated using the gross profit margin normally generated by this business. Assuming that purchases have been properly accounted for and that there are no errors in the valuation of opening or closing stocks, the cost of goods sold can be computed as follows:

	£
Opening stock	9,234
Purchases	54,298
Less: Closing stock	(13,532)
Cost of goods sold	50,000

This cost of goods sold figure can be used to approximate the real sales figure using the anticipated gross profit margin. In this case the gross margin is 33⅓% of sales which is equivalent to a mark-up on cost of 50%. Thus, the anticipated sales and estimated cash shortfall are as follows:

Cost of goods sold (above)	50,000
Gross margin	25,000 (50% on cost)
Estimated sales	75,000
Actual sales	65,981 (per debtors control account)
Estimated cash shortfall	9,019

In other words, sales amounting to £75,000 were anticipated during the period, assuming a normal gross profit margin of 33⅓%. Since recorded sales were £65,981, the difference between anticipated and recorded sales (£9,019) could be attributed to cash misappropriated. However, it should be stressed that there are many reasons for a fall in the gross profit margin over different accounting periods and the precise cause is especially difficult to determine in a company which sells different products at different margins. In such a case, it is entirely plausible that the gross profit margin may fall (or increase) due to a change in the overall sales mix of products.

QUESTION 7.1 (A)

Ms Ryan was made redundant in April 19 . 6 and she started up a small retail business on 1 May 19 . 6. She opened a business bank account with her accumulated savings of £5,000 and arranged a short-term loan from her local bank in the amount of £2,000 and overdraft facilities for £3,000. Simultaneously she purchased a three year lease on a suitable business premises for £3,000 with responsibility for rates of £600 per annum.

At the end of the first accounting year you have been requested by Ms Ryan to prepare final accounting reports. However, you find that the accounting records were incomplete. After some investigation you obtain following information:

(1) Personal drawings from the business bank account in the sum of £40 per week for the fifty-two week period were made.

(2) Shop equipment was purchased for £3,000. The equipment has an estimated useful life of five years with an estimated resale value of £500 and is to be depreciated on a straight-line method.

(3) Total payments to the bank in respect of the term loan during the year amounted to £1,100 which includes £120 interest. At the end of the year £150 interest was accrued on the term loan. The agreed overdraft limit remained at £3,000.

(4) A payment of £900 was made for rates on 5 May 19 . 6, and payments in respect of miscellaneous expenses during the accounting year to 30 April 19 . 7 amounted to £4,000.

(5) The bank statement for the current account on 30 April 19. 7 showed a debit balance of £414, but from the cash book you discover that a recent deposit in the bank's night safe of £800 has not been credited by the bank and cheques amounting to £269 have not been presented. In addition, the bank statement reveals bank interest and charges, £55, and a dishonoured cheque, £68 which have not been recorded in the cash book.

(6) The suppliers' statements at 30 April 19 . 7 amounted to £1,750. On checking these statements you discover that:

(i) A supplier's invoice charged at £93 should have been charged at £39;
(ii) A cheque payment £243 has not been credited by a supplier;

(7) Closing stock was valued at selling price and amounted to £2,100. The average mark up on cost was 25%.

(8) Sales invoices unpaid at end of year amounted to £1,900.

Requirement:
You are required to:
(*a*) Prepare a bank reconciliation statement at 30 April 19 . 7;
(*b*) Prepare a balance sheet of the business at 30 April 19 . 7 and indicate clearly the profit (loss) made during the year ended on that date;
(*c*) Explain briefly the disadvantages of this method of profit measurement.

QUESTION 7.2 (SM)

Ms Smith was made redundant in November 19 . 4. During an inactive Christmas, she resolved to set up her own business. On 2 January 19 . 5, she opened a business bank account with her accumulated savings of £4,000 and arranged a short-term loan from her local bank in the amount of £2,000 and overdraft facilities for £3,000. Simultaneously she purchased a two-year lease on a suitable business premises for £3,000 with responsibility for rates equivalent to £400 per annum and any necessary repairs.

At the end of the first accounting year you have been requested by Ms Smith to prepare final accounting reports. However, you realise that the accounting records were kept haphazardly.

After some investigation you ascertain the following information:

(1) Personal drawings in the amount of £25 per week for the fifty-two week period were made.

(2) Fixtures and fittings were purchased for £3,000. They have an estimated useful life of five years with an estimated resale value of £500.

(3) Total payments to the bank in respect of the loan during the year amounted to £1,200 which includes £300 interest. At the end of the year £100 interest was accrued. The agreed overdraft limit remained at £3,000.

(4) A payment of £800 was made for rates on 5 January 19 . 5, and payments in respect of necessary repairs amounted to £500.

(5) The bank statement for the current account on 31 December 19 . 5 showed a debit balance of £1,260, but from the cash book you discover that a recent deposit in the bank's night safe of £494 has not been received by the bank and cheques amounting to £156 have not been presented.

In addition, the bank statement reveals bank charges, £15, and a dishonoured cheque, £75, which have not been recorded in the cash book.

(6) The suppliers' statements at 31 December 19 . 5, amounted to £1,960. On checking these statements you discover that:

(i) A supplier's invoice charged at £37 should have been charged at £73;

(ii) A cheque for £158 has not been credited by a supplier;

(iii) Goods for £314 have been received and included in closing stock valuation but have not been shown on the statements.

(7) Closing stock was valued at selling price at £1,600. The average mark-up on cost was 25%. Sales invoices unpaid at end of year amounted to £1,200.

Requirement:

You are required to:

(a) Prepare a bank reconciliation statement at 31 December 19 . 5;

(b) Prepare a balance sheet of the business at 31 December 19 . 5, and indicate clearly the profit (loss) made during the year ended on that date;

(*c*) Calculate the current ratio at 31 December 19 . 5;

(*d*) Summarise the comments relevant to your profit calculation.

(The Institute of Chartered Accountants in Ireland)

QUESTION 7.3 (SM)

John Bull won £5,000 in the national lottery and decided to set up in business as a retailer on 1 January 19 . 4. He borrowed £3,000 from his father and purchased a six-year lease on a suitable premises for £6,000, plus responsibility for rates equivalent to £200 per annum. The remaining cash was placed in a business bank account.

During his first year of trading, accounting records were kept haphazardly but the following information is available:

(1) His father was repaid £1,000 plus interest of £200.

(2) Personal drawings of £900 were made.

(3) A payment of £300 was made for rates on 2 January 19 . 4.

(4) A second-hand motor vehicle was purchased for £2,000 which, at the end of the year, had depreciated by £400.

(5) The bank statement on 31 December 19 . 4, showed a credit balance of £960 but from the cash book you discover that a payment of £84 for wages has not been presented and a recent lodgment of £124 for December cash sales has not yet been received by the bank.

(6) The suppliers' statements for the month of December totalled £740. On checking this figure you discover that:

    (i) A cheque for £94 has not been credited by a supplier:

   (ii) Goods for £216 have been received and included in closing stock valuation but have not been shown on the statements;

  (iii) A supplier's invoice charges at £54 should have been at £45.

(7) Closing stock was valued at selling price at £1,500. The average mark-up on cost was 25%. Sales invoices unpaid at end of year amounted to £1,300.

Requirement:

You are required to:

(*a*) Calculate how much profit (loss) the business made during the year ended 31 December 19 . 4;

(*b*) Calculate the current ratio at 31 December 19 . 4;

(*c*) Explain briefly your opinion on this method of calculating profit.

(The Institute of Chartered Accountants in Ireland)

QUESTION 7.4 (A)

Derek Brady is a retailer. He has not kept proper books of account. His purchases and sales are on a strict credit basis. The following is a summary of Mr Brady's bank account on 31 December 19 . 2:

	£		£
Balance (1.1.19 . 2)	360	Wages	8,980
Lodgments	49,855	Sundry (Note 1)	5,360
From deposit account	1,045	Creditors	17,820
Balance (31.12. 19 . 2)	5,295	Staff loan (Note 2)	600
		Motor vehicle (Note 5)	4,800
		Rent and rates	1,550
		General expenses	14,480
		Drawings	1,965
		Transfer to deposit account	1,000
	56,555		56,555

The following additional information is supplied:

(1) Sundry payments included in the bank account consist of:

	£
General expenses	2,400
PAYE and PRSI deductions	2,960
	5,360

(2) The staff loan was made on 1 April 19 . 2, for twelve months at a 10% rate of interest.

(3) Discount allowed to customers during the year amounted of £1,255. Discount received from suppliers amounted to £1,980.

(4) (i) All cash received was lodged to the bank, except for the following amounts paid by cash:

	£
Personal expenses	2,250
General expenses	640

   (ii) Deposit interest received amounted to £45.

(5) A new motor vehicle was purchased on 1 January 19 . 2, as follows:

	£
Cost price of new vehicle	5,600
Less: trade-in allowance	800
	4,800

(6) Depreciation is to be provided on motor vehicles at 10% per annum, based on book value.

(7) Details of other assets and liabilities are as follows:

	1 Jan. 19 . 2	31 Dec 19 . 2
	£	£
Creditors	700	2,900
Debtors	4,000	5,000
Motor vehicle	1,000	?
Stock at cost	1,900	2,400
PAYE and PRSI deductions	220	270
Wages due	400	450

Requirement:

You are required to prepare for Mr Brady:

(*a*) A trading and profit and loss account for the year ended 31 December 19 . 2;

(*b*) A balance sheet as at that date.

(The Institute of Chartered Accountants in Ireland)

QUESTION 7.5 (SM)

The following is a letter which you receive from a business friend of yours, Mr Brian Ward, whose accounting records are improperly kept.

Dear John,

Thank you for your kind offer to help me in organising my accounts. As you know, I recently won £10,000 in the Prize Bonds, which I received in December 19 . 5, and decided to commence my own business as a contractor. I purchased a JCB digger on 2 January 19 . 6 for £6,500 which I hope will last for 5 years.

Business was slow at first but picked up eventually. I kept a note of all work done, and on 31 December 19 . 6 I had received cheques totalling £4,714 from various customers which were lodged. This does not include work done just before Christmas which I did not get a chance to invoice and which amounts to £360.

I have incurred very few expenses during the year except for repair bills. I added these up the other day and the cheque payments amounted to £572. Some other cheques which I wrote were in respect of insurance of £245, which coincides with the calendar year, and £416 in respect of petrol and diesel oil. The bank charged me £95 interest as I had a small overdraft during the year.

The debit balance per my bank statement on 31 December 19 . 6, was £2,498 but I noticed that a cheque for £200, which I gave my wife as a Christmas present, had not yet been presented.

I wrote a few other non-business cheques during the year. I do not know for how much exactly as I did not fill in the cheque stubbs properly. Best to say that if there is any money missing then it should be charged to me by way of drawings.

I hope from what I have said that you can prepare some sort of accounts for me. Don't forget to provide for your own accountancy fee of £100.

Yours etc.,
Brian Ward

Requirement:
You are required to prepare for Mr Ward:
(*a*) A profit and loss account for the year ended 31 December 19 . 6;
(*b*) A balance sheet as on that date.
(The Institute of Chartered Accountants in Ireland)

QUESTION 7. 6 (SM)

D. Cooper is in business as a dealer in electrical equipment and has not kept proper books of account.

You obtain the following information:
(1) Trading assets and liabilities

	1 July 19 . 0	*30 June 19 . 1*
	£	£
Total debtors	12,500	13,500
Total creditors	12,000	14,000
Stock on hands	15,000	13,200
Balance at bank	8,750	13,308
Cash on hands	750	400
Capital	25,000	?

(2) Movements in the cash and bank accounts during the year were as follows:

	£
Cash payments for purchases for resale	4,250
Cash drawings by proprietor	2,700
Cheque payments to suppliers	35,900
Wages paid from bank	25,400
Sundry expenses paid from cash takings	3,142
Total lodgments to bank	65,858

(3) During the year, bad debts amounting to £2,450 were written off, discounts amounting to £950 were allowed and discounts amounting to £637 were received.

(4) During the year the proprietor withdrew stock costing £587 for private purposes. No record has been made in the books in respect of this stock.

(5) During the year sales on credit amounted to £62,000.

Requirement:
You are required to prepare:

(*a*) The nominal ledger accounts to record the above transactions;

(*b*) The trading and profit and loss account for the year ended 30 June 19 . 1;

(*c*) A balance sheet as on that date.

(The Institute of Chartered Accountants in Ireland)

QUESTION 7.7 (A)

The entire stock in trade of B. O'Hara, a small trader, was destroyed by fire on 30 April 19 . 2, with the exception of a small quantity which had cost £308. An estimate of the value of the stock destroyed is required and you obtain the following information:

(1) Accounts are prepared annually to 31 December.

(2) The rate of gross profit is constant each year.

(3) Purchases as shown in the purchases journal were £36,592 for the year 19 . 1 and £9,216 for the period 1 January 19 . 2 to 30 April 19 . 2.

(4) Sales as shown in the sales journal were £45,420 for the year 19 . 1 and £11,612 for the period 1 January 19 . 2 to 30 April 19 . 2.

(5) Stock at cost on 31 December 19 . 0 was £9,369 and on 31 December 19 . 1, was £9,625.

(6) During March 19 . 2 sales amounting to £37 were returned by a customer.

Requirement:
You are required to compute the cost of stock destroyed by fire on 30 April 19 . 2.

(The Institute of Chartered Accountants in Ireland)

QUESTION 7. 8 (SM)

On August 11 19 . 7 a fire destroyed the entire stock of Mr Patterson, a retail merchant. He sells two categories of goods as follows:

	Percentage mark-up on cost
Category A	25%
Category B	33⅓%

The following information has been extracted from the books:

(1)	1 January 19 . 7	11 August 19 . 7
Trade debtors (gross)	£8,027	£11,000
Bad debts provision	1,000	2,000
Trade creditors	6,492	4,925
Stock in hands		
Category A	16,843	Unknown
Category B	8,106	Unknown
Cash on hands	900	1,200

(2) Cash movements during the period from 1 January 19 . 7 to 11 August 19 . 7 were as follows:

	£
Cheque payments for purchases for re-sale	59,126
Cash till lodgments arising from credit sales	83,555
Cash till payments to creditors for goods for resale	1,800

(3) Bad debts amounting to £760 were written off and bad debts recovered amounting to £48 were received and immediately lodged during the period. In addition, discounts allowed amounted to £612 and discounts received amounted to £641.

The mix of purchases and sales consists of:

Category A	70%
Category B	30%

Requirement:

You are required to:

(a) Reconstruct cash, debtors and creditors control accounts for the above period;

(b) Compute the cost of goods destroyed by fire on 11 August 19 . 7. (The Institute of Chartered Accountants in Ireland)

QUESTION 7.9 (SM)

Rough Ltd owns a retail shop which is managed by John Smith. The manager was dismissed on 31 December 19 . 7 for cash pilferage and the company has sought your advice in determining the amount of the loss for the recent six-month period.

Your enquiries establish the following:

1.	1 July 19 . 7	31 December 19 . 7
	£	£
Stock at cost	9,234	11,234
Trade creditors	17,321	14,123
Trade debtors	3,498	6,124
Provision for bad debts	1,000	1,500
Cash on hands	300	400

2. During the period ended 31 December 19 .7, takings of £54,927 had been lodged to the business bank account after payment of the following items:

	£
Creditors	3,561
Sundry expenses	278
Wages	1,934
Refunds to customer in respect of overpayments	157

3. During the period, cheque payments to suppliers for goods amounted to £54,637.
4. Bad debts amounting to £2,486 were written off in November 19 . 7.
5. Discounts allowed amounted to £88 during the period.
6. The company's gross profit margin on sales is estimated at 33⅓%

Requirement:
You are required to:
(*a*) Reconstruct cash, debtors and creditors control accounts for the six months ended 31 December 19 . 7;
(*b*) Determine the amount of cash misappropriated for that period.
(The Institute of Chartered Accountants in Ireland)

QUESTION 7.10 (SM)
Mr Murphy owns a retail shop which is managed by A. Codd. Mr Murphy is suspicious that Codd is misappropriating the funds of the shop. You have been asked to investigate the matter and are provided with the following data:

	1 July 19 . 0 £	30 June 19 . 1 £
Stock at cost	5,942	4,462
Debtors	19,000	9,000
Bad debts provision	1,900	2,900
Creditors	12,000	16,000
Accrued expenses	2,000	Nil
Balance at bank	6,000	15,463
Cash on hands	2,000	1,000

The following additional information is supplied in respect of operations during the year:

	£
Sales invoiced to customers	60,000
Receipts issued in respect of cash sales	9,863
Purchases of goods on credit for re-sale	58,000
Purchases paid by cheque	4,000
Total lodgments	70,863
Cash takings were banked after making the following payments:	
(i) Sundry expenses	1,000
(ii) Drawings	2,900
Bad debts written off	2,500
Contra adjustment between debtors and creditors ledgers	2,000
Discounts allowed to debtors	1,600
Discounts received from creditors	2,600
Stock withdrawn by the proprietor at selling price	600

All goods were priced to yield a 20% gross profit on sales.

Requirement:

You are required to compare anticipated sales with recorded sales and show the estimated shortfall.

(The Institute of Chartered Accountants in Ireland)

Financial Statements and
Regulation of Limited Companies

Financial Statements of Limited Companies

INTRODUCTION TO LIMITED COMPANIES

Businesses run by sole proprietors and partnerships are very common today, especially among small enterprises and professional firms. However, these forms of business leave their owners carrying full personal responsibility for the liabilities of their undertakings. If the assets of the business prove insufficient to meet its liabilities, then the owners of the business are liable to meet these liabilities from their personal assets. In addition, these forms of enterprise have limited access to capital since they tend to be relatively small. The limitation of this business structure was exposed during the rapid industrialisation of the UK in the mid-nineteenth century—the start of the industrial revolution. The industrial revolution led to the creation of large manufacturing enterprises which needed access to large amounts of capital in order to finance the acquisition of fixed assets and working capital items such as stocks and debtors.

The problem was therefore how to encourage a sufficient number of individuals to invest capital into an organisation and simultaneously protect them from unscrupulous and/or incompetent managers. Otherwise the investors might expose their entire estates to possible claims by creditors. The problem was solved by a new business structure—the limited liability company, with the protection of 'limited liability' for all shareholders. Such companies had two important features, namely, (1) limited liability and (2) separate legal entity.

Limited liability

This concept basically means that if a limited company is experiencing financial difficulties, the creditors, e.g. banks, can look only to the company's assets for repayment of their outstanding claims. The creditors cannot ask the shareholders to pay any more cash into the company should the company's assets be insufficient to meet their claims. Once the shareholder has paid into the company the amount of share capital which he agreed to invest, then no further claims can be made against him by anyone dealing with the into the company the amount of share capital which he agreed to invest, then no further claims can be made against him by anyone dealing with the company. This feature of companies has been a major incentive in providing capital for companies. It has provided the prime protection that investors, especially those not participating in the management of the enterprise, have needed.

In contrast, if the assets of a sole trader or partnership are insufficient to meet the claims of creditors, these creditors can look to the owners' personal assets for repayment. The liability of owners of an 'unincorporated' business is unlimited.

Under current legislation in Ireland it is difficult for the courts to 'lift the veil' of limited liability. However, the Companies Bill, 1987 proposes that, in certain circumstances, the veil of limited liability can be lifted and that a person can be made personally liable for a company's liabilities. This provision is intended to be a potent deterrent to persons who would abuse the protection afforded under that of limited liability.

Nevertheless, creditors, including lending institutions, are placed at a certain disadvantage when providing finance to limited companies. The practice has therefore developed, especially among banks, of asking the directors of limited companies to personally guarantee liabilities.

An alternative way by which lenders/creditors protect themselves when dealing with a limited company is to secure their loan, i.e. they acquire a charge or special claim on the assets of the company. Such security is legally given by way of a debenture deed and the providers of finance are referred to as the debenture holders. The debenture holders are given prior claim on the assets of the company over the unsecured creditors and a specific date for the repayment of the loan. Such prior claims must be registered with the Registrar of Companies and are available for public inspection.

Debentures will either be fixed or floating:

Fixed: A fixed debenture is secured on a specific asset, e.g. land and buildings. This gives the debenture holder a legal interest in the assets concerned as security for the loan. However, if the proceeds of selling the assets charged are insufficient to pay the debenture holders in full, then the debenture holders rank equally with unsecured creditors for the shortfall.

Floating: This is a general charge on the assets of a company. The debenture holder has no legal interest in the assets unless and until an event specified in the debenture deed occurs or the company goes into liquidation or ceases to trade. However, in some circumstances, a floating charge is postponed to certain other interests—such as later created fixed charges unless these are precluded by the terms of the floating charge.

As long as the borrower operates within the confines of the debenture deed, the lenders have no control over the company. However, if a company fails to meet the conditions of a debenture deed, e.g. payment of interest, the debenture holders have the right to appoint a receiver. The role of the receiver is to take physical possession of the assets of the company. Some assets may be sold but in many cases the receiver will try to continue running the company, because a company can normally be sold as a going concern for more than its break-up value.

A more modern device used to protect trade creditors is to sell stock to a limited company subject to 'retention of title'. This means that ownership of the stock only passes to the purchaser on payment for the goods. If the goods are not paid for when a company goes into liquidation then the seller may repossess the goods, even though a liquidator or receiver has been appointed. Trading in goods subject to 'retention of title' is fairly common in Europe and is becoming increasingly popular in Ireland. However, for 'retention of title' to be effective in law there are, at least, two essential features:

(*a*) The purchaser must have been notified of the retention clause before the sale was agreed.

(*b*) The goods in question must be in their original state and separately identifiable.

Separate legal entity

The second feature of limited companies is that, upon incorporation, the company becomes a separate legal entity, separate from that of its members. Thus, it is the company as a body corporate, and not its members, which enters into contracts and incurs liability in respect of such contracts. The company is considered a 'person' under law; it can sue and be sued.

The concept of legal entity was clearly exemplified in the famous case dating from the last century: Salomon v. Salomon & Co. Ltd. Salomon converted his sole proprietorship business into a limited company and lent the company £10,000 under a secured charge. On liquidation, the company's secured charge was repaid leaving the unsecured creditors with nothing. The action, taken by unsecured creditors to prevent repayment of the secured loan, failed, since the company was considered by the law to be a different person altogether from the subscribers to the company.

The legal entity is 'a body corporate . . . having perpetual succession' irrespective of the death or change of members. Thus a limited company continues in existence until liquidated. The death of a shareholder does not affect the legal continuity of the company. This is in complete contrast to the situation which arises on the death of a sole trader, where there is technically a cessation of business, with all the legal consequences which such an event entails.

Formation of limited companies

The formation or creation of a corporate body as a limited company, commonly referred to as 'registering a company', is relatively straightforward. Any two persons may form a (private limited) company by following the procedures laid down by the Companies Act, 1963 for registration.

Formation of a company is achieved through registration with the Registrar of Companies (an officer of the Department of Industry and Commerce). There are a number of documents which need to be filed with the Registrar at the time of application and soon after incorporation. The two most important documents are the Memorandum of Association (Memorandum) and the Articles of Association (Articles).

Memorandum of Association: The Memorandum sets out, informing the public, the basic facts relating to the company. It is an important document since it states the objects and powers of the company and provides the company with its form and framework.

The Memorandum of every company must state:

(*a*) the *name* of the company with 'limited' or 'public limited company' as the last word(s) of the name. However, a company may change its name by special resolution with the approval of the Minister for Industry and Commerce.

(*b*) the *objects* of the company which would include the areas of activity in which the company operates or intends to operate. It is usual for the Memorandum to contain one main objects clause followed by a number of clauses of ancillary objects. A company only has the power to carry out the objects specified in its Memorandum or anything which is reasonably incidental thereto. If any act is performed which, though legal in itself, is not authorised by the objects clause(s), it is ultra vires (beyond the powers of) the company and becomes void.

This can have serious consequences for the company and those dealing with it. There is now a call for the elimination of the ultra vires doctrine on the grounds that innocent people and organisations trading with a company cannot reasonably be expected to check the company's powers under its Memorandum. In order to protect against charges of ultra vires, the practice has grown of providing companies with all-embracing objects.

A company may, to the extent specified in the Companies Act, 1963, alter its objects, subject to confirmation in certain circumstances by the court.

(*c*) that the *liability* of shareholders is *limited*. The liability of a shareholder of a company limited by shares is confined to the amount unpaid on the shares for which he has agreed to subscribe. Thus, if the issued share capital of a limited company is fully paid up, then shareholders owe no liability to the company. The total amount payable per share is normally the nominal value of the share fixed in the Memorandum.

(*d*) the *authorised* share capital with which the company proposes to be registered and its division into shares of a fixed amount. However, a company may increase its authorised share capital by ordinary resolution and on the payment of additional ad valorem stamp duty.

It is important to understand the meaning of authorised share capital: it is the amount of capital specified in the Memorandum and represents the amount up to which the company is authorised to issue capital. It is not the amount which the company has raised by issuing shares, e.g. a company may have an authorised share capital of £100,000 but an issued share capital of £2.

Articles of Association: The Articles of Association regulate the internal workings or management of the company. In effect, they are a set of rules and regulations which the company may draw up on its own or adopt as a model set of articles contained in Table A of the Companies Act, 1963. This table automatically applies to any company which does not draw up its own articles. The model set of articles, as set out in Table A of the Companies Act, 1963 includes the following:

(*a*) the rights of shareholders including any restriction on the transfer of shares;

(*b*) the procedure for general meetings;

(*c*) the election, retirement and powers of directors;

(*d*) the declaration of dividends;

(*e*) the procedure for winding up the company.

The Articles of Association are subject to the Memorandum and cannot confer or include any powers beyond those contained in the Memorandum. The Articles can be altered at any time by special resolution of the shareholders, that is, with the approval of 75 per cent of those voting.

Books of account

The Companies Act, 1963 states that proper books of account are required to record all receipts and payments, all sales and purchases and all assets and liabilities.

Proper books of account should be such that they explain the transactions and the financial position. They should contain day-to-day entries for all cash received and paid and include where appropriate: (1) Annual stock sheets; (2) Records of goods sold and purchased, with sufficient detail to enable the goods, the purchasers and sellers to be identified (except in the case of sales in the retail trade).

In other words, these books must provide sufficient detail to give a true and fair view of the company's affairs and to explain its transactions. The essential principle is that there should be a sound basis for the recording of relevant economic events. They should be retained to enable the annual financial statements to be prepared and audited.

PUBLIC AND PRIVATE LIMITED COMPANIES

Limited companies may be registered as either public or private. At the time of writing, there are approximately 500 public companies registered in Ireland and 108,000 private companies. Only a public limited company may offer its shares to the public. Consequently, a stock exchange quotation is impossible for a private company. There are other important distinctions. Chiefly, a private company must have between 2 and 50 members and a minimum of two shareholders for incorporation. A minimum of seven persons is required for incorporation of a public company and the maximum is governed by the number of shares the company proposes to issue. In addition, the right to the transfer of shares of a private company is restricted, whereas shares are generally transferable in a public company. Therefore, to be a public limited company (plc), a company must:

(*a*) have a minimum of seven members;
(*b*) allow its shares to be, generally speaking, freely transferable;
(*c*) have a minimum issued share capital of £30,000;
(*d*) have a Memorandum which states that it is a plc;
(*e*) have a name that ends with 'public limited company', or 'plc'.

Many public companies have their shares listed, i.e. quoted on the Stock Exchange. There are various ways of 'going public' and a merchant bank or stockbroker is normally retained to advise in this regard. For instance, existing shareholders may sell off some of their shares direct to the public and/or financial institutions. In the latter case, the institutions would agree to make available a certain percentage of their shares to the public in order to create a market. Alternatively, cash may be raised for the company through selling off new shares to the public.

Exhibit 8.1 shows the main advantages and disadvantages of going public but it is not exhaustive:

Exhibit 8.1

Going Public—Advantages

1. A company has more ready access to equity capital, usually essential to fund a developing business. A private company is restricted in this regard.
2. Existing shareholders can realise some of their capital for private use and still maintain a significant shareholding.
3. A shareholding in a public company almost always has a higher value attributed to it than an equivalent private company shareholding because it is a marketable instrument.
4. Shares may be issued as consideration for acquiring other companies.
5. A company may become better known with increased credibility in its business dealings with customers, suppliers, banks, etc.

Going Public—Disadvantages

1. If the company has serious problems, financial or otherwise, it may receive a great deal of publicity.
2. The management is more accountable, and to a wider audience, for its performance.
3. There is a certain, indefinable, level of additional work associated with being a public company, e.g. half-yearly figures, annual reports, annual general meetings, maintaining PR relationships with the media.
4. There is a tremendous pressure on the company to produce increasingly better results each year.

TYPES OF SHARE CAPITAL AND DIVIDENDS
Share capital
The different meanings attributed to the word 'capital' can cause misunderstanding to the layperson. The main legal distinctions are:

(*a*) *Nominal* or authorised capital: the nominal or authorised capital is set out in the Memorandum which must state the division of the authorised capital into fixed nominal amounts, e.g. the nominal share capital of the company is £200,000 divided into one million shares of 20p each.

(*b*) *Issued* capital: that part of authorised capital that has been issued by the company.

(*c*) *Called up* capital: applicable where shares are partly paid for. This represents that part of issued capital that has been called up for payment, e.g. 75p of a £1 share.

Classes of share capital
The Memorandum may divide the share capital into classes and the rights attaching to each class are recorded in the Articles of Association. In the majority of companies, the rights attaching to shares are rarely changed.

Owners are called shareholders, because in return for the capital which they subscribe, they own a share in the company. The degree of control which a particular shareholder can exercise will depend on the number of shares which he holds and, more importantly, the type of share which he owns. Broadly speaking, there are two classes of share capital: *preference* share capital and *ordinary* (or equity) share capital.

A *preference* shareholder, under normal terms, is entitled each year to a dividend at a specified rate out of the profits, before anything is paid to the ordinary shareholders. Thus, a holder of one 10% preference share with a nominal value of £1 will receive an annual dividend of 10p—the dividend being related to the invested capital rather than the company's profitability. Unless preference shares are declared to be non-cumulative they are entitled to a cumulative dividend, (i.e. if a dividend is not paid in any year because of insufficient profits, the dividend is carried forward to be paid in a future year, before any dividend is paid on the ordinary shares). The word cumulative is usually included in the description (e.g. 7% cumulative preference shares).

Under the Articles, preference shareholders are usually also entitled to preference with respect to the return of capital in the event of the company being wound up, but only to the extent of the par value of their shares (the ordinary shareholders being entitled to the remainder of the assets).

A company may have different groups or levels of preference share capital, issued usually at different times, and possibly at different fixed rates of dividend, depending on the money market conditions prevailing at the time of issue and also taking into account the order of priority, e.g.

1st 6% preference share capital.
2nd 9% preference share capital.

A slight variation to preference shares is that of a participating preference shares. These shares entitle their holders to participate in profits in addition to their fixed dividend rate. In years of buoyant profits, participating preference shareholders receive a higher dividend than normal.

On occasions, shares are issued as redeemable preference shares. Investors may not wish to make a permanent investment in a company. To cater for such investors, a finite life is given to certain preference shares. At the end of this finite life the company redeems it, i.e. it buys back the preference shares, (the investor receives the original capital subscribed). In Ireland, redeemable preference shares have been used to provide tax-efficient remuneration for executives. Dividends paid out of manufacturing profits are favourably treated for income tax purposes. For example, a shareholder in receipt of dividends taken out of manufacturing profits will be assessed to income tax purposes based on half the dividend received, subject to certain limits. This represents a considerable tax saving and naturally there is special tax legislation to counter possible abuse of this arrangement.

ORDINARY shares are the real risk shares. The ordinary shareholders are entitled to all profits not appropriated by prior charges, such as preference dividends. As a result, they stand to gain most when high profits are made and to suffer most when losses are incurred. In addition, the ordinary shareholders share between themselves any surplus capital that might remain after the liquidation of the company.

The rights of the preference and ordinary shareholders are generally those outlined in Exhibit 8.2:

Exhibit 8.2

General Rights of Preference and Ordinary Shareholders		
	Preference	Ordinary
Right to dividend	Prior claim	None
Amount of dividend	Fixed rate	Fluctuating
Voting rights	None	Yes
Liquidation	Prior claim to repayment of capital, but do not participate in any surplus.	Entitled to residue, if any.

The reason for having different types of share capital is that it provides the company with flexibility in raising funds. Companies will attract funds from a variety of sources, and the providers of these funds may have different attitudes concerning an acceptable mix of risk and rewards. Some investors are content with stable returns at relatively low risk and preference share capital would meet such needs. Other investors may be prepared to accept a great deal of risk, with the possibility of obtaining greater returns and instead purchase the ordinary shares of a company.

Companies have seen the popularity of preference share capital diminish with changes in the structure of the corporate taxation system. Interest on borrowings are tax deductible, whereas dividends to preference (or ordinary) shares are not. Thus, borrowings generally provide a more flexible and tax efficient way of providing a range of securities which can be packaged to appeal to investors.

LOAN CAPITAL

In theory, the ideal source of finance is one where a firm can obtain the maximum amount of money for the required period of time, paying the minimum rate of interest and having to provide the minimum of security. In practice, a firm may have to obtain the finance required from a source other than its first wish. In raising finance, one normally thinks of the bank overdraft or term loans. It may often happen that the term loan will not be granted by the bank so it is essential that alternative sources of finance exist. Before raising finance, it is essential that the firm be clear on all the implications of raising the money. These implications include the following:

(a) The costs associated with the different sources of finance, i.e. is it dearer to obtain a loan from a commercial bank than from a merchant bank?

(b) How does the finance affect the capital structure of the company?

(c) If the finance is raised by means of loans, the interest on them is tax deductible. This means that if, for instance, the firm had to pay £500 interest per annum on a loan, this amount can be written-off as an expense against profits for taxation purposes.

(*d*) If the finance is raised by issuing shares there is no tax concession because the return to shareholders is a dividend not interest. Dividends represent an appropriation out of profits so there is no tax concession for the firm.

(*e*) The security required. This must be adequate if the finance is to be raised by borrowing rather than by issuing shares. The security required by the bank may be the deeds of the premises. If these have already been given as security for another loan it follows that the firm may not be able to raise the extra finance unless, of course, some person acceptable to the bank agrees to act as a guarantor.

(*f*) When has the money to be repaid? If the money is required for a long-term project, it is important that the repayments be spread over a suitable period of time. If this were not the case, it would mean that the loan plus interest would have to be repaid before the purpose of the loan had an opportunity to pay its way.

(*g*) Why is the money required?

(*h*) What are the existing financial commitments of the firm?

The impact of gearing on profits

Gearing or *Leverage* is the term which relates the ordinary share capital investment in a company to loan capital. Borrowing involves financial risk since it requires the company to make annual, fixed commitments in the form of interest and, perhaps, partial repayment. Every increase in borrowed funds increases this financial risk. However, there is a potential income benefit arising from the possibility of investing fixed interest borrowings to produce a return higher than the cost.

In the simplest of terms the traditional theory of gearing maintains that if a company can borrow funds at a fixed cost of, say, 16 per cent and can earn 20 per cent on the funds then the 4 per cent difference will accrue to the ordinary shareholders. Return to ordinary shareholders is thus boosted by the gearing effect. If the company's profits fall, then the return to ordinary shareholders will fall more quickly than if their capital structure had been ungeared. This situation is illustrated by way of the following example:

Capital structure of two companies

	Company A £	Company B £
Ordinary shares	500,000	200,000
Debenture 10%	—	300,000
	500,000	500,000
Total assets	500,000	500,000

Note that whilst both companies have the same total capital employed of £500,000 (and total assets), they differ in the way that the capital has been raised. Company A has all ordinary share capital (owners' equity), while Company B has part ordinary share capital and part loan capital. Note also that loan capital carries a fixed rate of return (i.e. in this example, 10 per cent). With both companies earning £100,000 before interest in a particular year, and ignoring tax for simplicity, the division of the £100,000 would be as in Exhibit 8.3:

Exhibit 8.3

	Company A £	Company B £
Profit before interest	100,000	100,000
Less: Interest	—	30,000
Profits available to shareholders	100,000	70,000
Shareholders' funds	500,000	200,000
Return on shareholders' funds %	20%	35%

Company B, which is relatively highly geared, generates a return on shareholders funds of 35 per cent compared to 20 per cent for Company A. The difference between the overall return to shareholders becomes even more dramatic if profits increase in a subsequent year. For example, assume that all available profits were distributed to shareholders by way of dividend in the first year. In such case, opening and closing shareholders' funds will be the same amount for both companies. If the profits of both companies in the following year are £200,000 then the division of earnings would now be as per Exhibit 8.4:

Exhibit 8.4

	Company A £	Company B £
Profit before interest	200,000	200,000
Less: Interest	—	30,000
Profits available to shareholders	200,000	170,000
Shareholders' funds	500,000	200,000
Return on shareholders' funds %	40%	85%

For the subsequent year, the ordinary shareholders in Company A have earned 40 per cent. The earnings have doubled from one year to the next, and so have the earnings of the shareholders. The relationship between the earnings of Company A and shareholders' investment is linear. The ordinary shareholders in Company B have earned 85 per cent in the second year, despite the fact that the earnings of the company have only doubled compared to the previous year. A summary is provided in Exhibit 8.5:

Exhibit 8.5

	Company A			Company B		
	First Year	Second Year	Change	First Year	Second Year	Change
Return on shareholders' funds	20%	40%	100%	35%	85%	143%

The move from the first to the second year's results is of benefit to shareholders in Company B. It should be noted that if results were to be reversed, so that the third year again saw profits of £100,000, it would be shareholders of Company A who would be better protected. The above example has an important message in that the imaginative use of gearing can boost the return available to a company's ordinary shareholders!

MEETINGS AND ROLES OF DIRECTORS AND THE COMPANY SECRETARY
Meetings
An annual general meeting (AGM) of the members of a company must be held at least once every calendar year.

The rights of shareholders to attend such meetings and to vote, as well as the procedure for exercising votes, will be contained in the Articles of Association of the company. Votes at meetings are usually taken in the first place on a show of hands, one vote per member present, but on a poll the

Articles usually provide for one vote per share held. Generally, the Articles also provide that when a vote is taken by a poll, proxies may be used. This means that shareholders not present at a meeting may, by prior arrangement, exercise their vote on a proxy form for or against each resolution to be considered.

Preference shareholders are not normally entitled to vote at meetings unless their interests are affected by the resolution being considered, or their dividend is in arrears, or there is a resolution to wind up the company to be voted on during the meeting.

It is the ordinary shareholders, therefore, who normally exercise control over a company. They, as a body, delegate to the board of directors the day-to-day management of the company.

Directors

The Companies Act defines a director as 'any person occupying the position of director by whatever name called', and provides that directors are officers of the company.

Appointment of directors: The procedure for the appointment of directors is governed by the Articles and these usually provide that directors shall be appointed by the members in a general meeting. Appointments to the position of director are usually made either because the person involved:

(*a*) owns a large part of the equity share capital;

(*b*) has special knowledge or ability which he will use to the benefit of the company;

(*c*) is the nominee of a large shareholder.

Any person may be a director except an undischarged bankrupt or a person convicted of certain offences. In addition the Companies Bill, 1987 proposes that a person convicted of a serious 'commercial type' offence will be automatically disqualified for at least five years from holding a directorship in any company. In addition, directors of companies going into insolvent liquidation may be unable to set up a new company unless it meets a certain set of requirements including greater capitalisation as a protection to its creditors.

It is common, but by no means universal, for the Articles of a public company to provide that a director shall hold a certain number of shares in the company as a share qualification. Details of directors and of their share and debenture holdings in the company and associated companies must be maintained in a register. Directors are required to make full disclosure of their interest in any contract with the company, and of dealings in the company's shares or debentures and those of associated companies. The interest in shares or debentures of the director's family must also be reported. They are also required to disclose any other directorships they hold.

Retirement of directors: The retirement of directors is also dealt with by the Articles and it is common for these to provide that a proportion (say one-third) of the directors shall retire by rotation at each AGM and to go on to provide that those retiring by rotation or otherwise shall be eligible for re-election.

Duties of directors: As officers of the company, directors have many obligations and responsibilities. A director is entrusted with the powers given to him in the Articles of Association and is said to be a trustee of the company's money and property. They have a duty to make the best use of the assets with which they have been entrusted by the shareholders. The directors are regarded as acting as the company's agents when entering into transactions on behalf of the company, which imposes on them duties of loyalty and good faith. Their duties are to the company as a whole and not to the individual shareholders.

In addition, under the Companies (Amendment) Act, 1983 directors are required to call an extraordinary general meeting of the company if they become aware that the value of the net assets have fallen to half or less than half of the called-up share capital of the company. The meeting is to consider whether any, and if so what, measures should be taken to deal with the situation.

The preparation of the annual financial statements to be presented to shareholders is the sole responsibility of the directors. They may delegate that responsibility to a committee of the board, the financial director, or accountant, but they retain the final responsibility for their accuracy. Two of them sign the accounts, often the chairman, managing director or financial director.

Chairman

The Chairman of a company (Chairman of the Board of Directors) is appointed by his fellow directors. In many cases, the chairman is an executive member of the board, taking the leading part in the day-to-day overall management and control of the company.

Large companies sometimes appoint to that office a well-known public figure with a high reputation in the business world or in politics. In many cases he is a figurehead. Under the Articles, the chairman often has a casting or second vote. It is customary when called upon to use a casting vote that he does so to maintain the status quo.

Non-executive directors

Companies often employ non-executive directors involved in a part-time counselling function. In addition, they are also seen as bringing in outside expertise and contacts which the company employing them could not afford and/or would not need on a full-time basis.

They normally only attend meetings of the board of directors and meetings of shareholders. Notwithstanding their limited participation, these part-time directors are as responsible as the executive directors to the members and for the fulfilment of the obligations of officers and directors under the Companies Acts.

The company secretary

Every company must have a secretary who is an officer of the company. The duties of a secretary are mainly of an administrative nature; they will vary of course with the size and nature of the undertaking but normally include the following formal responsibilities:

(*a*) Issue of notices of and attendance at meetings of directors and of members, and making minutes of the proceedings.

(*b*) Responsibility for keeping the company's books and registers and for making official returns to the Registrar of Companies. In practice the accountant is usually directly responsible to the board for keeping the books of account.

(*c*) Custodian of the company's seal which is applied to the deeds, share certificates and other official documents in the presence of the director/s and secretary who also sign.

THE ROLE OF AUDITORS

The term auditor is derived from the Latin verb 'audire'—to hear. In Roman times it was the function of certain individuals to listen to a 'calling' of the receipts and payments in order for him to ascertain that they were correct.

Modern audits and auditors result from the status of limited liability companies. These companies, because of their privilege of limited liability, must satisfy a number of requirements as laid down in the Companies Acts.

One such requirement is that directors must present, each year, financial statements to shareholders showing the financial position and performance of the company. In order to protect the position of shareholders, it is reasonable that the directors' financial statements be checked. Thus, company law requires that independent experts add their *opinion* as to whether the financial statements show a true and fair view. These independent experts are the auditors and the auditors' report must form part of the annual financial statements.

The Companies Act, 1963 in Ireland requires a company, once in every calendar year, to present to its members an audited profit and loss account and a balance sheet. These documents are required to be drawn up to give a *true* and *fair* view of the profit or loss for the financial year and the state of affairs at the end of the financial year. The expression 'true and fair' has now been accepted by the European Community. The use of this expression by auditors does not mean that they are guaranteeing that the financial statements are correct. Rather the auditor is implying that in his *opinion* the financial statements have been drawn up honestly, to give a balanced view of the performance and position of the company. This balanced view is necessary, bearing in mind that there are several different user groups interested in a company's performance.

In relation to auditors and the annual audit, a number of fundamental points should be made:

1. An auditor must be a member of a body of accountants recognised by the Department of Industry and Commerce. One result of this provision is that the auditing of company accounts is the only accounting field on which there are legal restrictions on entry. Anyone can put up a brass plate outside his office and call himself an accountant but to audit the financial statements of limited companies one must be a member of one of the professional accountancy bodies.

2. The task of the auditors is to 'audit' rather than prepare the completed financial statements. In this context, auditors report to the shareholders/members of the company. Their report is based on the evidence which they have examined during the course of their audit. Much of the time on audit is spent confirming that the procedures of the company are adequate to record the transactions of the year and that there is adequate division of responsibilities within the enterprise to prevent fraud and error. This is called an audit of internal control. Thus, one of the most common questions asked by auditors is 'Who opens the post?' If only one person opens the post then this facilitates possible cash misappropriation. If they are not satisfied with the system of internal control, auditors will make recommendations to the directors and check the transactions of the business more thoroughly to ensure that they have been correctly recorded.

In many small companies, by definition, there does not exist an adequate system of internal control. Furthermore, many would argue that the annual audit of such small companies is an unnecessary activity and is simply an expensive burden on small businesses. The accountancy profession in the UK has made submissions to the government suggesting the relaxation of the small companies audit requirements. The thrust of these discussions is that small companies should be allowed to discontinue their audit requirement subject to the unanimous approval of all shareholders. However, this proposal was not favoured by either the UK treasury or the taxation authorities. These have persuaded the UK government that the annual audit requirement helps to prevent fraud and ensures that the tax assessments are based on reliable information. The UK government concluded that none of the alternatives (of the small company audit) offers sufficient advantages to justify abolition. The Institute of Chartered Accountants in Ireland which dominates the Irish auditing profession had made its support clear for retaining the audit requirement on many occasions. Officially, it argues, not because it sees this as protecting some area of work for its members but because it is convinced of the benefits of an annual required audit, not only to the company audited, but to shareholders, creditors, taxation authorities and the community at large. However, it is likely that this issue will be resolved in the context of the Commission of the European Community. A recent draft by the EC Commission, in an attempt to ease the burdens on smaller enterprises which result from their compliance with legislation and regulations, proposes a mandatory exemption for all small companies for the compulsory audit requirement.

3. Statutory auditors are a legal requirement for all limited companies and the auditor has specific responsibilities placed on him by the Companies Act, 1963. The most fundamental responsibility is the expression of a 'true and fair' opinion to shareholders. He has the right to attend the annual general meeting and to be heard thereat on any part of the business which concerns him as auditor.

Acting as a spur to the responsibility of the auditors is their knowledge that they can be sued for damages by parties who have suffered by relying upon any misleading information on which the auditors have expressed an opinion. Such actions for professional negligence are common in the US and insurance premiums for professional indemnity have risen dramatically, such so that some American accountancy firms are now practising without insurance cover. Some accountants are now questioning the system of professional indemnity which encourages action against them.

Auditors are effectively restricted from practising in the form of a limited liability company. The Companies Act prevents a body corporate from carrying out an audit. It is likely that there will be important changes in this area over the next decade. For example, a recent Companies Act in the UK allows incorporation of accountancy firms.

In relation to the auditors' report the following matters must be expressly stated:

(*a*) if they have not obtained all the information necessary for the purpose of their audit;

(*b*) if proper books of account have been kept;

(*c*) if the financial statements are not in agreement with the books of the company;

(*d*) that the financial statements give the information required by the Companies Acts, 1963 to 1986;

(*e*) an *opinion* that the financial statements show a true and fair view of the financial position and profit performance for the period under review. It is not easy to pin down the precise meaning of these deceptively simple looking words in this context. They basically mean that the overall impression given by the accounts is not a misleading reflection of the real state of affairs. The expression of an *opinion* on the financial statements is the primary legal objective of any audit;

(*f*) whether a situation exists under the Companies (Amendment) Act, 1986 that requires the holding of an extraordinary general meeting, i.e. the net assets of the company are half or less thar half of the amount of the called-up share capital.

4. The auditor must be independent of the directors. Professional independence is a concept fundamental to the accountancy profession. It is essentially an attitude of mind characterised by integrity and an objective approach to professional work. Thus, an auditor should be, and be seen to be, free in each professional assignment he undertakes of any interest which might detract from objectivity. In reality, this independent and objective attitude can be difficult to achieve. As a result, the proposed EC 8th Directive on Company Law requires auditors to be independent—but allows each member state to set its own rules. However, the European Commission wants to harmonise these rules; some continental member states restrict auditors from supplying other services to audit clients believing that this prejudices independence. In these circumstances, the Irish (and UK) accountancy profession will have to persuade many civil servants of the benefit which accrues to companies through being able to call upon a broad range of services from their auditors. The Irish (and UK) accountancy profession will have to put forward a convincing case if their view is to prevail. Understandably, the implementation of this proposed directive is not expected for a considerable length of time.

Independence is achieved, in theory, since auditors remuneration is determined by shareholders in the general meeting, although in most cases the shareholders, in turn, give the directors authority to fix the remuneration. Such remuneration must be disclosed in the accounts. This disclosure requirement applies only to the audit fee but does not apply to fees in respect of consultancy or taxation work provided by the firm of auditors to the company. Annual audit fees for large multinational corporations will run into millions of pounds.

5. Subsidiary to the main purpose of the audit, which is the expression of an opinion, is the detection of fraud and errors. The primary responsibility for the detection and prevention of fraud lies with management. It is not the auditors' duty to detect fraud. Several legal cases have established this principle. For example in Catterson and Sons (1937) the judge attached considerable weight to the directors' failure to institute proper systems of internal control when deciding that the auditors had not been negligent in

their failure to uncover fraudulent activity. He stated that: 'The first fact which often seems to be lost sight of is that the primary responsibility for the accounts of the company is with those who are in control of the company, that is to say the directors.'

Nevertheless, auditors must reach an independent conclusion and they may be held negligent if they fail to do so. For example, it would be most unwise to rely solely on representations made by management during the course of the audit.

The courts expect an auditor to exercise reasonable care and skill in the conduct of an audit, but what is reasonable care and skill depends on the particular circumstances. However, he has a duty to examine the books and records of the company and in the conduct of normal auditing work (i.e. checking and vouching), fraud and errors may be revealed. Thus the auditors are not negligent merely by failing to discover fraud taking place in a company but the failure to detect it may be an indication of negligence.

6. Under normal circumstances, the statutory auditor is automatically reappointed at the annual general meeting. Extended notice must be given to remove an auditor at the AGM, and a copy of the resolution must be given to the auditor. The retiring auditor is entitled to make written representations which must be circulated to all shareholders.

Types of audit reports

Audit reports may be either 'clean', i.e. unqualified, or 'qualified'. This distinction can be helpful to the reader of financial statements and it is worth explaining the differences in some detail.

Unqualified: In this report the auditors express their opinion that the financial statements show a true and fair view. This is the situation that should exist for all companies.

Qualified: If the auditor is unable to give a clean report, then he should qualify it in relation to the material matters about which he has reservations. All reasons for the qualification should be given, together with a quantification of its effect, if possible.

There are two types of qualified audit report resulting from (1) uncertainty or (2) disagreement. Each category is then subdivided according to whether the subject matter of the uncertainty or disagreement is material or fundamental (so important and significant as to undermine the view given by the financial statements taken as a whole).

An *uncertainty qualification* will be warranted where there is uncertainty which prevents the auditor from forming an opinion on a matter. This in turn is subdivided into:

(*a*) material uncertainty, e.g. failure to verify stock valuation.

(*b*) fundamental uncertainty, e.g. unable to form an opinion. This could result from limitations in the scope of the audit due to lack of information, and is referred to as a 'disclaimer of opinion'.

A *disagreement qualification* will result where the auditor can form an opinion on the matter but this conflicts with the view given by the financial statements. This situation in turn is subdivided into:

(*a*) material disagreement, which relates to a particular item, e.g. method of stock valuation or inappropriate accounting policies. This is a fairly common form of qualified audit report and is due to the technical infringement of an accounting standard.

(*b*) fundamental disagreement, which is the most extreme position, in that the auditor is saying that in his opinion the accounts do not show a true and fair view. This is referred to as an 'adverse opinion'.

In each of these four cases the recommended wording for the auditor's opinion paragraph in the audit report is as follows:

—Material uncertainty   :   'subject to'
—Fundamental uncertainty   :   'unable to form an opinion to'
—Material disagreement   :   'except for'
—Fundamental disagreement   :   'do not give a true and fair view'
                                       (called an adverse opinion).

Apart from qualification, if the directors and auditors fail to resolve their disagreement over a particular matter, the latter may resign or a resolution may be put at the AGM not to reappoint the auditors.

The retiring auditor has the right to make representations at such an AGM. Also, it is an ethical requirement for accountancy firms not to accept an audit unless they are satisfied with the reasons for the departure of the previous auditors. Consequently, auditors are in a fairly strong position to get their point of view accepted by the directors.

A typical auditors' report for Irish companies is presented opposite.

REPORT OF THE AUDITORS

To the members of X Limited

We have audited the financial statements on pages . . to . . in accordance with approved Auditing Standards.

In our opinion the financial statements give a true and fair view of the state of affairs of the Company at 31 December 199 . and of its profit and source and application of funds for the year then ended and give the information required by the Companies Acts, 1963 to 1986.

The net assets of the Company, as stated in the balance sheet on page . . are more than half of the amount of its called-up share capital and, in our opinion, on that basis there did not exist at 31 December 199 ., a financial situation under which section 40 (1) of the Companies (Amendment) Act, 1983 would require the convening of an extraordinary general meeting of the Company.

In our opinion, the information relating to the year ended 31 December 199 . given in the Directors' report on pages . . to . . is consistent with the financial statements, and proper books of account have been kept by the Company.

We have obtained all the information and explanations we considered necessary for the purpose of our audit. The Company's balance sheet is in agreement with the books of account.

A Company
Chartered Accountants

9.

Financial Statements and Company Law

PRESENTATION OF FINANCIAL STATEMENTS AND COMPANY LAW

The format and content of financial statements published by limited companies is controlled by the Companies Act, 1963 and more recently the Companies (Amendment) Act, 1986. The 1963 act (s. 149) requires the profit and loss account and balance sheet of a company to give a true and fair view of the profit or loss and the state of affairs of the company and requires the financial statements to comply with the requirements of the sixth schedule of that act. Decisions on matters of measurement lay with the company directors, their professional advisors and auditors, and on just what constituted a true and fair view.

The essence of the 1963 act was that the financial statements should show a true and fair view and contain certain specified information. However, the manner of presentation was largely a matter for the directors of the company to decide.

The Companies (Amendment) Act, 1986 translates into law the provisions of the EC fourth directive in relation to the preparation and publication of annual financial statements of both public and private limited companies, subject to certain exemptions. It imposes on all limited companies incorporated in the Republic of Ireland the obligation to present their financial statements in standard formats. The requirements of the act do not apply to unlimited companies, branches of foreign companies or to dormant companies which have not previously carried on trading activities. The act came into effect on 1 August 1986 and applies to all accounting periods commencing after 31 December 1986. Thus, for many Irish companies the financial statements for the accounting period beginning on 1 January 1987 will be governed by this act.

One main implication of the 1986 act is the removal of the exemption under section 128 of the Companies Act, 1963 whereby private limited companies were not required to file their financial statements with the companies registration office in Dublin Castle. Another feature is the distinction between shareholder's accounts and filed accounts—less information is available to the public than to the shareholders. Accounts for presentation at the annual general meeting (AGM) must be circulated in advance to shareholders (and others who may be entitled to receive them). These financial statements are referred to as 'shareholders accounts'. They must give a true and fair view of the profit (or loss) for the year and of the state of affairs at the balance sheet date. However, the accounts which must be filed in the companies registration office are referred to as the 'accounts to be filed' or simply the 'filed accounts'. Certain disclosure exemptions are given for the filed accounts of medium-sized and small companies. Nevertheless each profit and loss account must give a true and fair view of the profit (or loss) for the year and each balance sheet must give a true and fair view of the state of affairs at the balance sheet date.

The information shown in the act is the minimum requirement. Additional information may be provided. However, there are fixed formats for the financial statements. The order and heading of the standard formats must be adhered to, though in the profit and loss account rearrangement and adaptation is permitted where the special nature of a company's business requires it.

There are two types of format for the balance sheet reflecting the choice between a vertical (list) and a horizontal (account type) layout. There are however, four choices of format for the profit and loss account, allowing for two methods of aggregating costs in the trading part of the profit and loss account, both of which can be in either vertical or horizontal form. (These formats are reproduced in the appendix to this chapter.) The choice of a particular balance sheet format does not limit the choice as to which profit and loss format one must use, or vice versa.

The 1986 act also creates two new classes of company, namely, small and medium-sized companies, for which one can modify the format and reduce disclosure requirements for the filed accounts. However, this concession for small and medium-sized companies can only be availed of by private companies. Public limited companies must file shareholders' accounts with the companies registration office in Dublin Castle.

The reliefs for small and medium-sized companies apply to the format of the financial statements and the content of the notes and consequently affect the amount of information disclosed. The categories of companies under the act are defined in terms of the balance sheet totals, turnover and average numbers of employees engaged throughout the year. These tests must be met for consecutive years, although there are commencement rules which modify this.

The classification between small and medium-sized companies is determined by meeting at least two of the following criteria:

	Small company	*Medium-sized company*
(a) Turnover not exceeding	£IR. 2.5m.	£IR10.0m.
(b) Balance sheet total not exceeding	£IR1.25m.	£IR5.0m.
(c) Average number of persons employed not exceeding	50	250

Turnover means the amount derived from the provision of goods and services falling within the company's ordinary activities. It will, therefore, automatically exclude VAT on sales. Where the financial year is not of twelve months' duration the turnover threshold must be adjusted proportionately.

The balance sheet total is defined as the aggregate of fixed and current assets, i.e. gross assets. Thus a significant increase in stocks, financed by borrowings, could result in the company exceeding the balance sheet total threshold—even though net assets remain the same.

The average number of employees is initially calculated for each week in the financial year. The sum of weekly numbers is then divided by the number of weeks in the financial year to get the average. A summary of requirements relating to shareholders' and filed accounts is provided below:

	Large AGM	Filed	Medium AGM	File	Small AGM	File
Profit and loss account	Full	Full	Short	Short	Short	No
Balance sheet	Full	Full	Full	Abridged	Abridged	Abridged

The term 'full' above is intended to indicate that there are no exemptions for preparing and filing full accounts. The short profit and loss account allow companies to net certain items against turnover and start the profit and loss account with a figure described as gross profit. (Small companies do not have to file the profit and loss account and this is one of the significant concessions of the act). The abridged balance sheet is less detailed than the full balance sheet and can contain aggregate figures, e.g. the total for tangible fixed assets without any analysis between plant, land and buildings or fixtures and fittings, etc.

A typical set of financial statements issued to members of a company might contain the following information:

1. Notice of Meeting
2. Chairman's Statement
3. Report of Directors
4. Balance Sheet
5. Profit and Loss Account
6. Statement of Source and Application of Funds
7. Notes to the Accounts including Accounting Policies
8. Report of the Auditors

1. *Notice of Meeting*: This will relate to the Annual General Meeting (AGM). The Articles of Association will specify what business may be conducted at the AGM, and usually includes:

    1.1 approval of the report and financial statements;

    1.2 the declaration of dividends;

    1.3 the re-appointment of directors;

    1.4 the re-appointment and remuneration of auditors.

Most of these matters are non-controversial, and as a result the AGM of many companies takes very little time. Some AGMs of large, Irish publicly quoted companies take less than twenty minutes!

2. *Chairman's Statement*: This represents a statement of company policy and future prospects, even though it is somewhat general or vague on occasions. This statement tends to be a personal view of the company's activities and performance and the environment in which the company operates.

3. *Report of the Directors*: This is a potentially important source of information about the company and it must include:

    3.1 state of the company's affairs;

    3.2 details of any change during the financial year in the nature of the business of the company or its subsidiaries, or in the class of business in which the company has an interest, whether as a member of another company or otherwise.

    3.3 amounts to be carried to reserves;

    3.4 recommended dividend;

The Companies (Amendment), 1986 Act also requires it to include:

    3.5 a fair review of the development of the company's business during the year;

    3.6 particulars of any important events affecting the company since the end of the financial period;

    3.7 an indication of likely future developments in the business of the company.

4. *Balance Sheet*: The balance sheet is one of the two central accounting reports required by statute. It is the responsibility of the directors to report

via the financial statements to shareholders. The Companies (Amendment) Act, 1986 laid down some important rules concerning the way in which published accounts are presented. For example, there are two types of format for the balance sheet, reflecting the choice between a vertical and a horizontal layout.

The balance sheet shown in Exhibit 9.1 indicates some of the principal features of these reporting requirements. However, readers are encouraged to obtain a set of published financial statements to gain a better impression of the full effect and width of the information provided. A public company's financial statements may be obtained, for example, by writing to the company secretary at the company's registered office.

Exhibit 9.1

BALANCE SHEET PRESENTATION (FORMAT 1)   a

Balance Sheet at 31 December 199 .   Reference

	£	Reference
Fixed Assets		b
Intangible assets	x	c
Tangible assets	x	d
Financial assets	x	e
	x	
Current Assets		b
Stocks	x	f
Debtors	x	
Cash at bank and in hand	x	
	x	
Creditors (amounts falling due within one year)		
Bank loans and overdrafts	x	
Trade creditors	x	
Taxation and social welfare	x	g
	x	
Net Current Assets	x	
Total Assets Less Current Liabilities	x	
Creditors (amounts falling due after more than one year)		h
Bank loans	x	
Debenture loans	x	
	x	
	x	
Capital and Reserves		
Called up share capital	x	
Share premium account	x	
Revaluation reserve	x	
Profit and loss acount	x	
	x	

Reference to balance sheet

(*a*) Format 2 allows for horizontal presentation of the balance sheet.

(*b*) All assets must be classified as either 'fixed' or 'current'. Fixed assets are classified under the headings intangible, tangible and financial. Fixed assets are those defined as assets which are intended for use on a continuing basis in the company's activities. all other assets are current assets.

(*c*) Includes goodwill and capitalised development costs.

(*d*) Sub-divided, as appropriate, into:

—land and building

—plant and machinery

—fixtures and fittings

(*e*) This includes investments listed on a recognised Stock Exchange (market values must be shown) and long-term investments in other companies.

(*f*) Sub-divided into:

—raw materials

—work in progress

—finished goods and goods for resale

(*g*) Taxation amounts must be shown separately, i.e. amounts owing for corporation tax, PAYE, VAT and income tax.

(*h*) Sub-divided as for creditors falling due within one year (this item could be shown in the lower section of the balance sheet, together with capital and reserves.)

5. *Profit and Loss Account*: The profit and loss account is the second accounting report required by statute. The requirements for proper presentation of the profit and loss account are not as rigorous as those for the balance sheet. Exhibit 9.2 indicates the main items to be expected in a published profit and loss account for a company without subsidiaries. There are four choices of format for the profit and loss account, allowing for two methods of aggregating costs in the trading part of the profit and loss account, both of which can be in either horizontal or vertical form.

Reference to profit and loss account:

(*a*) The term sales is not used. Turnover must be analysed by

— class of business

— geographical markets

unless this information, in the opinion of the directors, would seriously prejudice the company's interests.

(*b*) Other headings may be added here, as considered appropriate. An example might be research and development expenses written-off.

(*c*) This would normally be derived from investments in companies not considered to be either subsidiary or associated companies of the reporting company.

Exhibit 9.2

PROFIT AND LOSS ACCOUNT PRESENTATION

Profit and loss account for year ended 31 December 199 .

		£000	Reference
Turnover		x	a
Less: cost of sales		x	
Gross profit (loss)		x	
Less: Distribution costs	x		
Administration expenses	x		b
		x	
		x	
Other operating income	x		
Income from financial assets	x		c
		x	
		x	
Interest receivable	x		
Less: Interest payable	x		
		x	
Profit on ordinary activities, before taxation		x	
Less: Tax on profit on ordinary activities		x	d
Profit on ordinary activities, after tax		x	
Extraordinary items (net of taxation)		x	e
Profit (loss) for the financial year		x	
Dividends paid and proposed		x	f
Profit retained for year		x	g
Profit brought forward at 1 January 199 .		x	
Profit carried forward at 31 December 199 .		x	

(*d*) The 1986 act requires analysis of the taxation charge.

(*e*) Extraordinary items are those items not related to the ordinary trading activities of the company, e.g. costs of closing a subsidiary company.

(*f*) Dividends may only be paid out of *distributable profits*. The Companies (Amendment) Act, 1983 defines distributable profit as accumulated realised losses (which have not been written off in a capital reduction of reorganisation)'.

Hence, unrealised profits are not distributable, and past realised losses must be made good before current realised profits can be distributed. It is therefore no longer possible for a company to pay dividends out of current profits unless past losses have been made good. Also, accumulated unrealised profits (e.g. unrealised surpluses arising from the revaluation of fixed assets) will not be available for dividend payments.

This definition of distributable profit requires a distinction between a *realised profit or loss* and an *unrealised profit or loss*. A realised profit means that the company will receive cash as opposed to a book profit which will not give rise to any immediate cash and is termed unrealised.

Public Limited Companies are subject to a further restriction when calculating distributable profit. They may only pay a dividend where, after the dividend, net assets are equal to or greater than the total of issued share capital plus undistributable reserves. Distributable profits for a public company will, therefore, be net realised profits less any net realised losses. In effect, if a company's unrealised profits are less than its unrealised losses, the deficit must be covered by realised profits before a dividend can be paid.

(g) Retained profits are distributable reserves and are available for distribution as dividend. This is sometimes done possibly when, in an exceptionally bad trading year, the profits of a company are insufficient to meet a level of dividends which may be the policy of the directors to maintain.

Retained profits (or revenue reserves) will not normally represent cash. Indeed, there are many companies that have large reserves and at the same time large bank overdrafts. The profits made have been invested in stocks, fixed assets, investments or in providing more goods on credit to customers (debtors).

6. *Statement of Source and Application of Funds*: This statement is not a legal requirement but rather a requirement of the accountancy profession. This statement is required by SSAP 10, and forms part of the audited financial statements (chapter 15).

7. *Notes to the Accounts*: these notes will disclose the major accounting policies adopted by the company. In addition, the notes will provide break-downs of figures in the profit and loss account and balance sheet. Much of this detailed financial information is required by law, e.g. analysis of turnover.

8. *Report of the Auditors*: In accordance with company law every limited company must have auditors who are appointed by the shareholders at the Annual General Meeting. The reality is that auditors are recommended by the directors who request shareholders to confirm their appointment. The Companies Act 1963 requires that auditors report to *shareholders*, as distinct from directors, whether the financial statements show a true and fair view.

SHARE PREMIUM ACCOUNT AND BONUS SHARE ISSUES

When a company issues shares at incorporation, it will normally issue the shares at their par or nominal value. This par value represents the legal liability attaching to that share and will be stated in the company's Memorandum of Association. Typical par values are 25p or £1 per share. After a number of years, the company may have traded profitably and, in order to raise additional capital for expansion, the directors may wish to issue additional shares. It is probable that the value of each share will far exceed its original, par value. Thus, the directors may want to issue the additional shares at a premium. This would be particularly the case of a quoted company where the market price of the share currently exceeds the par value.

Example:

ABC Ltd, a private company, has decided to issue an additional 75,000 Ordinary shares of £1 each at a price of £1.50 each. The current balance sheet of the company is:

	£
Cash on hands	150,000
Financed by:	
100,000 ord. shares of £1 each	100,000
Profit and loss account	50,000
	150,000

Based on the above balance sheet, the net asset amount per share is £1.50 (i.e. £150,000/100,000 shares), and this is the price at which the new shares are issued. When the company makes the rights issue it shall receive £112,500 cash (i.e. 75,000 shares at £1.50). The balance sheet immediately following the issue is:

	£
Cash on hands	262,500
Financed by:	
175,000 ord. shares of £1 each	175,000
Share premium	37,500
Profit and loss account	50,000
	262,500

The net assets backing per share remains at £1.50 (i.e. £262,500/175,000 shares). It should be noted that only the nominal amount received for the shares issued is taken to the share capital account (i.e. 75,000 shares at £1 each). The premium received is taken to a separate and special share premium account and would be disclosed separately under the general heading on the balance sheet of Capital and Reserves. A share premium account is not distributable to shareholders by way of a dividend. In other words, once the cash equivalent to the share premium is received, it is locked into the company.

In accordance with Irish company law, one use of a share premium account is to pay up *bonus shares* to be issued by the company. In such circumstances, no cash will be received by the company. Rather, it is a paper transaction and the accounting treatment is to transfer an appropriated portion of the share premium account to the share capital account.

EXAMPLE:

Based on the above balance sheet the company decides to make a 'one for five' bonus share issue. Thus, for every five shares held, a shareholder will receive one bonus share. In all, 35,000 additional shares are issued to existing shareholders. The balance sheet immediately following the bonus issue is:

	£
Cash on hands	262,500
Financed by:	
210,000 ord. shares of £1 each	210,000
Share premium	2,500
Profit and loss account	50,000
	262,500

From the company's point of view, the impact of the bonus issue is largely cosmetic. No cash has been received.

In logic, the true financial position of the shareholders in the company is unaffected. Admittedly, the net asset backing per share has declined as a result of the bonus issue to £1.25 (i.e. £262,500/210,000 shares) but as compensation the shareholder now holds six shares where previously he held five. Thus, five shares at £1.50 each are equivalent to six shares at £1.25 each.

The intangible benefit of such a manoeuvre is that additional shares are now in issue. In some cases shareholders may sell part of their additional shares, thereby increasing the number of shareholders in the company. The share price should automatically fall after a bonus issue, if logic prevails. This 'cheaper' price may make the share more attractive to potential investors.

DISSOLUTION OF LIMITED COMPANIES

A company may be dissolved for a variety of reasons, such as the fulfilment of an object, (e.g. in the case of a mining company, when the mine is worked out) and insolvency.

Dissolution of a company may take place only in accordance with the Companies Acts:

(*a*) By being struck off the register of companies in the case of a defunct company

(*b*) By order of the court without winding up to facilitate reconstruction.

(*c*) Liquidation by winding up, which may be in one of the following ways:

(*i*) winding up by the court (compulsory liquidation);
(*ii*) voluntary winding up, which may be either;

—a members' voluntary winding up, or

—a creditors' voluntary winding up.

The most common grounds for winding up by the court is that the company is unable to pay its debts. A company shall be deemed unable to pay its debts if, for example a creditor to whom the company is indebted in a sum exceeding £50, has served on the company a demand in writing requiring the company to pay the sum so due, and the company has for three weeks thereafter neglected to pay the sum.

For the purposes of conducting the proceeding in winding up a company, the court may appoint a liquidator or liquidators. The liquidator is vested with many powers including that of selling the property of the company or carrying on the business of the company so far as may be necessary for the beneficial winding up.

A voluntary winding up of a company will commence when the appropriate resolution has been passed by the members. Within fourteen days of passing the resolution the company must advertise it in the *Iris Oifigiuil*.

Where the directors of a company make and file with the Register of Companies, a declaration of solvency within twenty eight days preceding the passing of a resolution to wind up voluntarily, then the winding up will be a *members' voluntary winding up*. Otherwise it will be a *creditors' voluntary winding up*. The declaration of solvency expresses the opinion of the directors, or a majority of them, that the company will be able to pay its debts within twelve months and embodies a statement of the company's assets and liabilities. In a creditors' voluntary winding up, the creditors may appoint a liquidator, and may also appoint a committee of inspection, consisting of not more than five persons. Through meetings of creditors they are able to exercise control over the winding up.

The liquidator

Briefly, the duties of a liquidator are to realise the assets of the company and to distribute the proceeds to creditors on an equitable basis after observing the legal priorities. If there is any surplus after meeting all the liabilities (unlikely except in a members' voluntary winding up), he will distribute that surplus to members equitably; observing any priorities provided for in the Articles. In all cases the liquidator must report on all his acts as a liquidator, keep proper books and account for all receipts and payments. He must make appropriate returns and reports to the court, to the Registrar, to the creditors and members. The liquidator must hold general meetings of the company and meetings of creditors in certain cases, at which to report on the conduct of the liquidation. A final meeting of the company must be convened when the liquidation has been completed. In the case of a *com-*

pulsory winding up, the liquidator must obtain a dissolution order from the court and, in any winding up where creditors have been concerned in the liquidation, a final meeting of creditors must also be held.

The receiver

Although the function of the receiver is not to liquidate the company, his role can be discussed here since there is often confusion in the minds of the public as to the difference between liquidators and receivers.

When a company wishes to issue loan capital it can offer the lender some specific security on the loan. If it does so, the loan is called a debenture. The company enters into a debenture deed which places a charge on the assets of the company, provides for interest payments and eventual repayment of the loan. If the company defaults on any conditions of the debenture deed, the debenture holders can appoint a receiver. The function of the receiver is to take physical possession of the assets. He has the legal right to sell off the assets and use the proceeds of the sale ro repay the debenture holders in full. Any surplus remaining is then paid to the company. In theory, the company can then continue trading. However in many cases receivership is a symptom of severe liquidity problems, lack of profitability, and eventual liquidation of the company is inevitable.

In some instances, the receiver continues to run the company so that it can be sold as a going concern and realise more than its breakup value. In such circumstances, the company continues in existence, although with different owners. Thus, the appointment of a receiver does not necessarily mean the liquidation of the company. Liquidation is the function of the liquidator. However, the appointment of a receiver could be the first step in the eventual liquidation of the company.

APPENDIX
Companies (Amendment) Act, 1986
Balance sheet formats

Format 1

A. Fixed Assets

   I. Intangible assets
     1. Development costs
     2. Concessions, patents, licences, trade marks and similar rights and assets
     3. Goodwill
     4. Payments on account

II. Tangible assets
  1. Land and buildings
  2. Plant and machinery
  3. Fixtures, fittings, tools and equipment
  4. Payments on account and assets in course of construction

III. Financial assets
  1. Shares in group companies
  2. Loans to group companies
  3. Shares in related companies
  4. Loans to related companies
  5. Other investments other than loans
  6. Other loans
  7. Own shares

B. Current Assets

I. Stocks
  1. Raw materials and consumables
  2. Work in progress
  3. Finished goods and goods for resale
  4. Payments on account

II. Debtors
  1. Trade debtors
  2. Amounts owed by group companies
  3. Amounts owed by related companies
  4. Other debtors
  5. Called up share capital not paid
  6. Prepayments and accrued income

III. Investments
  1. Shares in group companies
  2. Own shares
  3. Other investments

IV. Cash at bank and in hand

C. Creditors: amounts falling due within one year

  1. Debenture loans
  2. Bank loans and overdrafts
  3. Payments received on account
  4. Trade creditors
  5. Bills of exchange payable

    6. Amounts owed to group companies
    7. Amounts owed to related companies
    8. Other creditors including tax and social welfare
    9. Accruals and deferred income

D. Net current assets (liabilities)

E. Total assets less current liabilities

F. Creditors: Amounts falling due after more than one year
    1. Debenture loans
    2. Bank loans and overdrafts
    3. Payments received on account
    4. Trade creditors
    5. Bills of exchange payable
    6. Amounts owed to group companies
    7. Amounts owed to related companies
    8. Other creditors including tax and social welfare
    9. Accruals and deferred income

G. Provisions for liabilities and charges
    1. Pensions and similar obligations
    2. Taxation, including deferred taxation
    3. Other provisions

H. Capital and reserves

    I. Called up share capital
    II. Share premium account
    III. Revaluation reserve
    IV. Other reserves

        1. The capital redemption reserve fund
        2. Reserves for own shares
        3. Reserves provided for by the articles of association
        4. Other reserves

    V. Profit and loss account

Format 2

ASSETS

A. Fixed Assets

   I. Intangible assets
1. Development costs
2. Concessions, patents, licences, trade marks and similar rights and assets
3. Goodwill
4. Payments on account

   II. Tangible assets
1. Land and buildings
2. Plant and machinery
3. Fixtures, fittings, tools and equipment
4. Payments on account and assets in course of construction

   III. Financial assets
1. Shares in group companies
2. Loans to group companies
3. Shares in related companies
4. Loans to related companies
5. Other investments other than loans
6. Other loans
7. Own shares

B. Current Assets

   I. Stocks
1. Raw materials and consumables
2. Work in progress
3. Finished goods and goods for resale
4. Payments on account

   II. Debtors
1. Trade debtors
2. Amounts owed by group companies
3. Amounts owed by related companies
4. Other debtors
5. Called up share capital not paid
6. Prepayments and accrued income

   III. Investments
1. Shares in group companies
2. Own shares
3. Other investments

   IV. Cash at bank and in hand

LIABILITIES

A. Capital and reserves

   I. Called up share capital

   II. Share premium account

   III. Revaluation reserve

   IV. Other reserves

      1. The capital redemption reserve fund
      2. Reserve for own shares
      3. Reserves provided for by the articles of association
      4. Other reserves

   V. Profit and loss account

B. Provisions for liabilities and charges

      1. Pensions and similar obligations
      2. Taxation, including deferred taxation
      3. Other provisions

C. Creditors

      1. Debenture loans
      2. Bank loans and overdrafts
      3. Payments recived on account
      4. Trade creditors
      5. Bills of exchange payable
      6. Amounts owed to group companies
      7. Amounts owed to related companies
      8. Other creditors including tax and social welfare
      9. Accruals and deferred income

Companies (Amendment) Act, 1986.
Profit and loss account formats

Format 1

      1. Turnover
      2. Cost of sales
      3. Gross profit or loss
      4. Distribution costs
      5. Administrative expenses
      6. Other operating income

7. Income from shares in group companies
8. Income from shares in related companies
9. Income from other financial assets
10. Other interest receivable and similar income
11. Amounts written off financial assets and investments held as current assets
12. Interest payable and similar charges
13. Tax on profit or loss on ordinary activities after taxation
15. Extraordinary income
16. Extraordinary charges
17. Extraordinary profit or loss
18. Tax on extraordinary profit or loss
19. Other taxes not shown under the above items
20. Profit or loss for the financial year

Format 2

1. Turnover
2. Variation in stocks of finished goods and in work in progress
3. Own work capitalised
4. Other operating income
5. (*a*) Raw materials and consumables
   (*b*) Other external charges
6. Staff costs:
   (*a*) Wages and salaries
   (*b*) Social welfare costs
   (*c*) Other pension costs
7. (*a*) Depreciation and other amounts written off tangible and intangible fixed assets
   (*b*) Exceptional amounts written off current assets
8. Other operating charges
9. Income from shares in group companies
10. Income from shares in related companies
11. Income from other financial assets
12. Other interest receivable and similar income
13. Amounts written off financial assets and investments held as current assets
14. Interest payable and similar charges
15. Tax on profit or loss on ordinary activities
16. Profit or loss on ordinary activities after taxation
17. Extraordinary income
18. Extraordinary charges

19. Extraordinary profit or loss
20. Tax on extraordinary profit or loss
21. Other taxes not shown under the above items
22. Profit or loss for the financial year

Format 3

A. Charges

1. Cost of sales
2. Distribution costs
3. Administrative expenses
4. Amounts written off financial assets and investments held as current assets
5. Interest payable and similar charges
6. Tax on profit or loss on ordinary activities
7. Profit or loss on ordinary activities after taxation
8. Extraordinary charges
9. Tax on extraordinary profit or loss
10. Other taxes not shown under the above items
11. Profit or loss for the financial year

B. Income

1. Turnover
2. Other operating income
3. Income from shares in group companies
4. Income from shares in related companies
5. Income from other financial assets
6. Other interest receivable and similar income
7. Profit or loss on ordinary activities after taxation
8. Extraordinary income
9. Profit or loss for the financial year

Format 4

A. Charges

1. Reduction in stocks of finished goods and in work in progress
2. (*a*) Raw materials and consumables
   (*b*) Other external charges
3. Staff costs:
   (*a*) Wages and salaries
   (*b*) Social welfare costs
   (*c*) Other pension costs

4. (*a*) Depreciation and other amounts written off tangible and intangible fixed assets

  (*b*) Exceptional amounts written off current assets
5. Other operating charges
6. Amounts written off financial assets and investments held as current assets
7. Interest payable and similar charges
8. Tax on profit or loss on ordinary activities
9. Profit or loss on ordinary activities after taxation
10. Extraordinary charges
11. Tax on extraordinary profit or loss
12. Other taxes not shown under the above items
13. Profit or loss for the financial year

B. Income

1. Turnover
2. Increase in stocks of finished goods and in work in progress
3. Own work capitalised
4. Other operating income
5. Income from shares in group companies
6. Income from shares in related companies
7. Income from other financial assets
8. Other interest receivable and similar income
9. Profit or loss on ordinary activities after taxation
10. Extraordinary income
11. Profit or loss for the financial year

QUESTION 9.1 (A)

The following balances have been presented to you for Rodgers Ltd, a retail company, as at 31 January, 198 .

	£
Sales (95 units)	2,750
Opening stock (40 units)	400
Purchases	1,188
Buildings (*Note 6*)	4,000
Fixtures at cost (*Note 5*)	600
Fixtures—aggregate depreciation	192
Rent and rates (*Note 2*)	240
Cash	40
Salaries and wages	70
Bank overdraft	970
Debtors	600
Ordinary share capital of 50p each	800

Creditors	710
Ordinary dividend—paid	30
10% preference share capital (*Note 8*)	200
Loan (*Note 3*)	1,000
Profit and loss account	1,006
Advertising	170
Bad debts written-off	200
Light and heat (*Note 4*)	90

The following information is also provided:

Note 1. Purchase of goods were recorded during the year as follows:

Date	Units Purchased	Unit price	£
March	26	£10	260
June	40	£14	560
December	23	£16	368
	89		1,188

Note 2. The rent and rates payment of £240 includes a payment of £30 covering the period January-March 198.

Note 3. The loan was raised at the start of August and carried a 12 per cent annual rate of interest.

Note 4. The light and heat payment of £90 includes a stock of heating oil, unused at year end, valued at £25.

Note 5. The fixtures have a useful life of five years with an estimated residual value of £120. Depreciation is based on the straight-line method.

Note 6. Buildings have been owned for a number of years, originally cost £6,000 and now have a book value of £4,000. Depreciation is based on book value at the annual rate of 10 per cent.

Note 7. Taxation, based on the profits for the year, is estimated at £100.

Note 8. The preference dividend is proposed and a final ordinary dividend of 5p per share.

Requirement:
Prepare a profit and loss account for the year ended 31 January, 198 . for presentation to the board of directors (but not for publication).

QUESTION 9.2 (SM)
The trial balance of J.R. Ltd as on 31 December 19 . 6 is as follows:

	Dr.	Cr.
Preference shares of £1 each		50,000
Ordinary shares of 50p each		100,000
Profit and loss account		66,000
Sales		450,000

Cost of sales, including depreciation	225,000	
Stock 31.12.19 . 6	15,000	
Wages	70,000	
Motor expenses	16,000	
Administration expenses	63,000	
Debenture interest	10,000	
Directors remuneration	18,000	
Plant and machinery — (net)	200,000	
Motor vehicles — (net)	28,000	
Debtors and creditors	78,000	48,000
Balance at bank	35,000	
Debentures		80,000
Taxation (basd on profits – 19 . 6)	21,000	
Preference dividend	5,000	
Ordinary dividend	10,000	
	794,000	794,000

Requirement:
Prepare a profit and loss account for the year ended 31 December 19 . 6.

QUESTION 9.3 (A)
The nominal ledger of Stanton Concrete Ltd had the following balances as of the end of its accounting year dated 31 December 19 . 8. The accountant needed to devise appropriate headings and prepare a balance sheet.

Profit and loss account	43,500
Revaluation reserve	7,200
Share capital (ordinary)	77,000
7.5% loan	68,700
Cash	1,000
Stock and work in progress	55,800
Motor vehicles at cost	34,500
aggregate depreciation	16,000
Plant and machinery at cost	92,900
aggregate depreciation	47,100
Investments (short-term) at cost	9,300
Current taxation due	15,700
Creditors and accruals	59,700
Debtors and prepayments	79,600
Freehold land and buildings	85,800
aggregate depreciation	11,300
Proposed dividend	3,800
Bank overdraft (secured)	8,900

Requirement:
Prepare a balance sheet at 31 December 19 . 8, based on the above information.

QUESTION 9.4 (SM)

(*a*) Indicate the basic restrictions being placed on distributing profits for both private and public limited companies.

(*b*) Applying the restrictions, indicate the amount which could be distributed by way of dividend in each of the following companies as a private company and as a plc:

RELEVANT EXTRACTS FROM BALANCE SHEETS

	Company X £	Company Y £	Company Z £
Called-up share capital	100	150	1,000
Surplus (deficit) on revaluation	600	(100)	——
Capital profit (realised)	400	——	——
Revenue profit (loss)			
brought forward	200	250	(800)
Current year's profit (loss)	100	(100)	100
Liabilities	350	80	100

(The Institute of Chartered Accountants in Ireland)

QUESTION 9.5 (SM)

The following is the balance sheet of Wolf Ltd at 31 May 19 . 1.

BALANCE SHEET AT MAY 19 . 1

	£	£
Fixed assets		4,000
Current assets	1,251,000	
Less: Current liabilities	1,200,000	
Net current assets		51,000
Total assets less current liabilities		55,000
Financed by:		
Called-up share capital		250,000
Profit and loss account		(195,000)
		55,000

Requirement:

Draft a note to the board, outlining any obligations on the directors in relation to the state of affairs as indicated by the above balance sheet and the action to be taken and any time limits.

(The Institute of Chartered Accountants in Ireland)

QUESTION 9.6 (A)

You are given the following trial balance of Grace Ltd as at 31 December 19 . 7, as prepared by the firm's book-keeper. All figures are in £000s:

	Dr.	Cr.
Share capital (200,000 50p shares)		100
Share premium		50
Profit and loss balance 1 January 19 . 7		100
Debentures (10% interest p.a.) issued in 19 . 4		100
Stock	200	
Motor vehicles	100	
Motor vehicles depreciation 1 January 19 . 7		60
Machinery	120	
Machinery depreciation 1 January 19 . 7		50
Buildings at cost 1 January 19 . 7	230	
Sales		750
Purchases	350	
Discounts	2	
Returns	2	
Carriage	2	
General expenses	200	
Advertising	10	
Creditors		200
Debtors	200	
Provision for doubtful debts		6
Debenture interest	5	
Bank balance		5
	1,421	1,421

You are also given the following information:

(a) The book-keeper, in an attempt at simplification, has posted both discounts received and discounts allowed to the discounts account. He has also posted both returns inwards and returns outwards to the returns account, and both carriage inwards and carriage outwards to the carriage account.

Discounts received were actually £1,000
Returns outwards were actually £1,000
Carriage outwards was actually £1,000

(b) The following items are already included in general expenses:
  (i) Rates for the 12 months to 31 March 19.8, £4,000;
  (ii) Insurance for the 12 months to 31 December 19 . 8, £2,000.
    Half of this amount relates to the managing director's private yacht.
(c) Your own charges of £1,000 for accountancy services need to be included.
(d) A debtor of £20,000 has gone bankrupt. The provision for doubtful debts is required to be 5% of debtors.

(*e*) A dividend of 5p per share is proposed.

(*f*) Closing stock is £180,000.

(*g*) Depreciation of £20,000 is to be provided on the motor vehicles and of £10,000 on the machinery. The buildings are to be revealed by £30,000.

Requirement:

Prepare a profit and loss account and balance sheet for Grace Ltd for the year (for internal purposes).

(The Chartered Association of Certified Accountants)

QUESTION 9.7 (SM)

The trial balance of Toby Ltd at 31 December 199 . is as follows:

	£	£
Share capital – £1 ordinary shares		10,000
Profit and loss account		19,000
Sales and purchases	61,000	100,000
Sales returns and purchase returns	2,000	4,000
Sales and purchase ledger control accounts	20,000	7,000
Land	40,000	
Buildings and Plant (at cost, and depreciation to 1 January 199.	50,000	22,000
Debentures (10% p.a. interest)		30,000
Opening stock	15,000	
Operating expenses	9,000	
Administration expenses	7,000	
Selling expenses	6,000	
Bank		8,000
Disposal account		7,000
Suspense account		3,000
	210,000	210,000

You are also given the following information:

(1) 1,875 new shares were issued during the year at £1.60 per share. The proceeds have been credited to the suspense account.

(2) Sales returns of £1,000 have been entered in the sales day book and debtors as if they were sales.

(3) The book-keeper has included the opening provision for doubtful debts of £800 in the selling expenses account in the trial balance. The provision is required to be 5% of debtors.

(4) A standing order payment of £1,000 for rates paid in December has not been entered. Rates are included under administration expenses. This payment covered the half-year to 31 March following 199.

(5) Closing stock is £18,000.

(6) No debenture interest has been paid.

(7) The £7,000 balance on the disposal account represents the sales proceeds of a fully depreciated item of plant, costing £10,000. No other entries (except bank) have been made concerning this disposal.

(8) Depreciation at 10% on cost should be provided on the plant and buildings

Requirement:
Prepare a trading, profit and loss account for the year, and balance sheet as at 31 December 19 . ., in good order, taking account of the above notes. (The Chartered Association and Certified Accountants)

QUESTION 9.8 (SM)
The summarised trial balance of Helen Ltd at 31 December after the calculation of the net operating profit, was as follows:

	Dr. £	Cr. £
Ordinary shares of 50p each		10,000
10% preference shares of £1 each		9,000
10% debentures		8,000
Fixed assets at net book value	35,000	
Current assets	30,100	
Creditors		20,000
Capital redemption reserve		5,000
Share premium		4,000
Profit and loss balance 1 January		3,000
Debenture interest	400	
Preference dividend	450	
Net operating profit for year		8,450
Interim ordinary dividend	2,000	
Corporation tax		500
	67,950	67,950

The following is to be taken into account:
(1) A building, net book value currently £5,000 is to be revalued to £9,000.
(2) Preference dividends of £450 and a final ordinary dividend of 10p per share are to be proposed.
(3) The balance on the corporation tax account represents an overprovision of tax for the previous year. corporation tax for the current year is estimated at £3,000.

Requirement:
(*a*) Prepare completed final accounts for internal use, within the limits of the information available. Ignore taxation except as specifically stated in the question.

(*b*) What are reserves in the context of limited companies, and what essential features distinguish reserves from debentures and share capital? Explain briefly the differences between capital and revenue reserves, using the reserves in the balance sheet of Helen Ltd for the purpose of illustration. (The Chartered Association of Certified Accountants)

QUESTION 9.9 (SM)

The trial balance of Hall Ltd on 31 May 19 . 8 was presented as follows:

TRIAL BALANCE

	Dr. £	Cr. £
Sales		610,000
Cost of sales	420,000	
Stock (31 May 19.8)	220,000	
Wages and salaries	84,000	
Rent, rates and insurance	1,200	
Directors' remuneration	4,000	
Administration expenses	7,100	
Debenture interest	1,600	
Light and heat	2,400	
Audit fees	1,500	
Preference dividend	1,000	
Interim ordinary dividend	2,000	
Ordinary shares of 50p each		200,000
10% preference shares of £1 each		20,000
Profit and loss account—1 June 19.7		9,400
Bank overdraft		6,400
10% debentures		50,000
Machinery (cost £200,000)	127,000	
Motor vehicles (cost £25,000)	15,000	
Debtors and creditors	53,000	42,000
Bad debt provision		2,000
	939,800	939,800

You are provided with the following additional information:
(1) Audit fees of £2,000 have not been paid at the end of the year.
(2) During the year rates in the amount of £600 for the year ended 30 November 19 . 8 were paid.
(3) Depreciation is to be provided on fixed assets at the following rates, with a full year's depreciation being provided in year of acquisition and none in year of sale:

      Machinery   20 per cent per annum on cost
      Motor vehicles 20 per cent per annum on book value

(4) Provision is to be made for the preference dividend and a dividend of 3p on the ordinary shares.

(5) Machinery costing £4,000 with a book value of £1,700 was sold during the year for £2,800. This amount has not yet been received and no record has been made of this transaction.

(6) Bad debts of £1,800 are to be written-off and the bad debt provision is to be maintained at 5 per cent of trading debtors.

(7) Administration expenses include £1,000 paid to a director by way of an interest-free loan.

(8) The authorised share capital consisted of £600,000 dividend into 800,000 ordinary shares of 50p each and 200,000 10% cumulative preference shares of £1 each.

Requirement:

(*a*) The trading, profit and loss and profit and loss appropriation accounts for the year ended 31 May 19 . 8.

(*b*) A balance sheet as at that date.

QUESTION 9.10 (A)

R. Jones Ltd commenced trading on 1 January 19 . 6. The following draft balance sheet has been prepared prior to audit from the books as on 31 December 19 . 6.

	£	£	£
Fixed assets at cost			
Equipment			25,000
Motor Vehicles			11,000
			36,000
Current assets			
Stock		10,000	
Debtors		9,000	
Bank		12,000	
Cash		400	
		31,400	
Less:			
Current liabilities			
Director's loan account	2,000		
Creditors	7,000	9,000	22,400
			58,400
Financed by:			
Share capital			50,000
Profit for year			3,400
Long-term loan (12%)			5,000
			58,400

You ascertain that adjustments are required in respect of the following matters:

(1) The director's loan account was repaid in full on 29 December 19 . 6 but this transaction was inadvertently omitted from the books of the company.

(2) A debtor of the company who owes £2,000 went into liquidation on 24 December 19 . 6. You are reliably informed that 20p in the pound is the expected recovery.

(3) No interest was provided on the long-term loan raised on April 19 . 6.

(4) An analysis of stock revealed the following:

Cost	Net realisable value	Replacement cost	Sales value
£	£	£	£
10,000	9,000	11,000	13,000

(5) It is company policy to provide for a full year's depreciation on all fixed assets in year of acquisition at the following annual rates:
   —equipment: 20 per cent on cost,
   —motor vehicles: 25 per cent on the reducing balance method.

(6) A bad debt provision is to be created at 10 per cent of debtors.

(7) Cash on hands only amounted to £290. The discrepancy is to be written-off.

(8) Rates in the amount of £1,200 were written-off to the profit and loss account. This payment was made on 1 Febrauary 19 . 6, in respect of the fifteen month period ending 31 March 19 . 7.

Requirement:
   (*a*) Re-draft the balance sheet at 31 December 19 . 6.
   (*b*) Highlight the main limitations associated with calculating depreciation of fixed assets under the historic cost system.

10.

Accounting Standards and Financial Statements—1

THE DEVELOPMENT AND ROLE OF ACCOUNTING STANDARDS

In the early 1960s accountancy practice was considered by some to be 'largely a matter of taste'. This description was unfortunately valid since there were no definitive rules governing how the wide range of transactions and events should be reported in a company's financial statements. Admittedly, the Companies Act, 1963 was in existence but its main stipulation was that financial statements should show a 'true and fair' view of the reporting company's financial position and profit performance. However, the interpretation of this 'true and fair' requirement was left to the directors and company auditors and it was probable that different firms of auditors would accept different profit figures for the same firm for the same accounting period. In some cases this profit differential could be significant.

While the accountancy profession was conscious of this phenomenon little was done to improve the situation until a few incidents occured in the UK which brought widespread attention to the flexibility of accounting practice. These incidents shall be described later but they resulted in widespread criticisms of the accountancy profession its plethora of accounting principles, the flexibility of accounting practice, inadequate disclosure and the lack of a theoretical foundation for the preparation of financial statements. Sir Ronald Leach, the then president of the Institute of Chartered Accountants in England and Wales, reported that he 'was besieged by members demanding action from the council to stem the mounting criticism in the press'. Part of the accountants' unease was possibly provoked by the suggestion that government intervention was likely in regulating financial reporting—in the absence of appropriate action by the accountancy profession.

The response of the accounting profession in the UK was the setting up in December 1969 of an accounting standards steering committee (ASSC) sponsored by the Institute of Chartered Accountants in England and Wales and in which all of the major accounting bodies in these islands subsequently participated. This committee was to promote accounting standards along the following lines:

(*a*) To narrow the range of difference and variety in accounting practice.

(*b*) To require disclosure of accounting policies adopted by the reporting entity.

(*c*) To require disclosure of departures from definitive accounting standards. Thus, significant departures in financial statements from applicable accounting standards would have to be noted and explained in the financial statements.

(*d*) Wider exposure for major new proposals on accounting standards.

The English Institute was quickly joined on the ASSC by representatives of the Institute of Chartered Accountants in both Scotland and Ireland. In 1971 the committee was expanded to include representatives of the Association of Certified Accountants and the Institute of Cost and Management Accountants and, in 1976, by representatives from the Chartered Institute of Public Finance and Accountancy. On 1 February 1976 the Committee changed its name to the Accounting Standards Committee (ASC), and is now the representative of all the major accountancy bodies in the United Kingdom and Ireland. At the time of writing, the ASC has issued over twenty Statements of Standards Accounting Practice (SSAP), some of which have been withdrawn or amended. However in August 1990 the ASC will be replaced by a Financial Reporting Council (FRC) which will have overall responsibility for accounting standards. The FRC will have two operating sections: the Accounting Standards Board (ASB) for drafting accounting standards and a review panel which will be concerned with the examination and questionaing of departures from accounting standards.

Flexibility and plethora of accounting principles

As indicated above, there were a few well-publicised incidents regarding the flexibility of accounting practice which preceded the foundation of the ASC. These dramatic cases had an enormous effect on public opinion and there is no doubt that several such cases, coming close together as they did, were a severe blow to the image of the accountancy profession.

(*a*) *Rolls Razor Ltd*: In 1964 the sudden collapse of Rolls Razor Ltd a few weeks following the publication of audited annual accounts that gave no indication of financial difficulties, provoked many penetrating questions in the financial press about the adequacy of published accounts.

(*b*) *AEI/GEC Takeover Bid*: this controversial affair, which brought to the public's attention the extent of the difference which could emerge between two sets of figures based of the same circumstances, was particularly concerned with the valuation of stocks and work in progress. The ASC has now issued SSAP 9, which seeks to define certain acceptable practices with respect to the computation of the amount at which stocks and work in progress are stated in the financial statements, in order to narrow the differences and variations in those practices and to ensure adequate disclosure. But this accounting standard was not available when, in 1967, the General Electric company (GEC) made its bid to take over Associated Electrical Industries (AEI). It must be emphasised that there was no question of fraud involved with respect to the production of figures which was the focus of the public's attention.

In October 1967 the Board of AEI forecast a pre-tax profit of approximately £10m. for the year ended 31 December 1967 as part of its defence against a takeover bid from GEC. However, this particular forecast was made nearly ten months into the year to which it related. It was prepared in a manner consistent with the principles followed in preparing recent published annual accounts.

In the event, the GEC bid was successful. When, however, the AEI results were published, they disclosed a GEC loss of £4.5m. for 1967! This represented a difference of some £14.5m. compared to the original profit forecast—a staggering difference which required an explanation. It was acknowledged by GEC that only £5m. of this difference was a matter of fact, while the remaining £9.5m. was attributable to 'adjustments which are mainly matters of judgment'. One such area of judgment was the valuation of stock and the provision for obsolescence. The AEI directors concluded in respect of the shortfall of £14.5m. 'we think it incredible that such a difference could occur . . . unless there were massive changes in the management policy, and in the policies and principles of accounting especially in the valuation of stocks and work in progress'.

The financial press was left a little incredulous and curious about the diversity of accounting practices and the consequent validity of forecasts and published accounts. It was obvious that there were a number of accounting methods available for reporting transactions, and this facilitated the forecast or reported profit figure to be largely at the discretion of management. These were the circumstances that hastened the arrival of the accounting standards programme.

(*c*) *Pergamon Agreement with Leasco*: In June 1969 Mr Robert Maxwell announced that he had agreed to sell out his company to the American Leasco Data Processing Equipment Corporation. However, on 21 August of that year, Leasco and its advisors, Rothschild and Sons, announced that they did not intend to proceed with the offer. This decision was in breach of the city code on takeovers and mergers , since a bidder who does not make a formal offer within a reasonable period must be prepared to justify the circumstances of the case to the Panel on Takeovers and Mergers. On 27

August 1969 the City panel issued a statement accepting Leasco's explanation of its withdrawal from the proposed offer. It was clear that Pergamon had adopted what would now be termed highly aggressive accounting policies.

For example, the audited profits of Pergamon Press Ltd shown in the accounts for the year ended 31 December 1968 were slightly in excess of £2m. The highly reputable firm of auditors, Price Waterhouse, was asked to undertake an investigation into the company's financial affairs. Their subsequent lengthy report recommended many adjustments to the accounts, resulting in the net profit of less than £500,000. The public comment on this large difference in net profit involving different firms of accountants and auditors, cast further doubt on the flexibility of the accounting practice and did little for the reputation of the accountancy profession.

One of the reasons for the reported difference in the net profit was attributable to transactions between Pergamon Press Ltd, a public company, and a private company in which Mr Maxwell had a family interest. They were not subsidiary companies and so there was no requirement to integrate the accounts of the family company with that of the Pergamon Press group. Goods were sold at artificial prices between these companies. Furthermore, the valuation of closing stock items was questionable. For example, certain books included in closing stock were valued at cost, although an examination of subsequent sales statistics showed that they were sold at reduced rates to libraries and students. Also, no stock value was attributable to back issues of scientific and other learned journals. However, in 1968 the company changed its method of accounting and brought back issues into stock at £341,000. Profits increased by a corresponding amount. The investigating accountants did not dispute the inclusion of these items in stock but they were of the opinion that the same basis must be used in respect of the opening stock. If so, opening stock would have been increased by £326,000, showing an overall improvement in net profit of only £15,000!

Not suprisingly there were some severe comments in the press. The editorial of *Management Today* (October 1970) stated '. . . issues raised by the events at Pergamon are important, because they touch the vital nerve of the corporate system. Good management, wise investment and intelligent comment depend alike on being able to trust figures produced by the company's accountants, accepted by its directors, and approved by its auditors.' It continued, 'a profit which arrives from the upward valuation of shares is not a profit at all. No new money has come into the company.' Pointing out that the original accounts of Pergamon should show a £2m. deterioration in the net cash position in the year in which reported profit was £2m. the editorial pleaded '. . . the cash story is the one on which management accounting is based . . . there should be a legal requirement to record the cash story for the year and explain the discrepancies between these accounts and the profit and loss statement'. (An accounting standard designed to show the sources and application of funds and the resultant change in the company's liquid position was published to have effect from 1 January 1976—see chapter 15.)

Robert Maxwell subsequently wrote to his shareholders and stated that 'accountancy is not the exact science which some of us once thought it was'. No doubt there was an element of 'tongue in cheek' about this remark. However, the accountancy profession in these islands was about to launch its programme for accounting standards.

Programme for accounting standards

The above incidents highlighted the flexibility of the accounting practice which existed. Companies had the incentive to utilise this flexibility to boost the reported profits and thus the share price and thereby improve overall market value. Alternatively, conservative accounting practice would reduce profits, share price and overall market valuation, making the company a possible target for a takeover bid. A similar situation could also arise where a company wished to raise additional finance from lending institutions. These institutions are not impressed with low profitability, so that management have the motivation to present their financial statements in the most favourable manner possible.

It is appropriate to note some of the main areas of difference and variety of accounting practices. These areas would subsequently be narrowed by the promotion of accounting standards.

1. Not reporting results (profits/losses) of closely connected companies, other than subsidiaries. Thus artificial profits could be generated by the reporting company by selling stock or other assets at grossly inflated prices to a connected company which was not part of the regarding group (SSAP 1).

2. Definition and calculation of earnings per share (SSAP 3).

3. Writing-off 'non-recurring' or 'abnormal' items directly against reserves, especially when these items were in the nature of expenses (SSAP 6).

4. Accounting for government grants received (SSAP 4).

5. Valuation of closing stock, since the higher the value assigned, the greater the reported profits for the year in question and closing valuation per balance sheet (SSAP 9).

6. Capitalisation of research and development costs rather than writing them off immediately to the profit and loss account as and when incurred. Thus, current profits would be artificially high (SSAP 13).

Another SSAP issued in the early years should be noted. The basic philosophy of accounting standards is contained in SSAP 2—*Disclosure of*

Accounting Policies—and it is arguably the most important accounting standard. (Indeed it is a pity that it was not issued as SSAP 1.) This standard states the broad, fundamental assumptions underlying the preparation of financial statements and requires that the firm's accounting policies be disclosed in those financial statements.

Role of accounting standards

The ASC was formed against a background when financial reporting practices came under increased scrutiny and criticism. The accountancy profession's perception of the role of accounting standards, contained in the explanatory foreword of its SSAPs, can be summarised as follows:

(a) SSAPs describe approved methods of accounting for application to all financial statements intended to give a true and fair view of the financial position and profit or loss.

(b) Members who assume responsibilities in respect of financial accounts are expected to observe accounting standards.

(c) Significant departures in financial accounts from applicable accounting standards should be disclosed and explained.

(d) Methods of financial accounting evolve and alter in response to business and economic needs. From time to time new accounting standards will be developed and established standards will be reviewed.

In other words, accounting standards must be applied to all financial statements that purport to give a true and fair view, although it is recognised that a particular accounting standard may not be appropriate for all present and future situations. In the event of non-compliance, a company is expected to explain the reasons for and the effects of the departure from the relevant accounting standard. Thus, accounting standards would narrow the areas of difference in accounting practice and improve disclosure.

The ASC was originally established with a membership consisting entirely of qualified accountants with a specific number of places being allotted to each of the six member bodies. In 1982 the constitution of the ASC was changed to enable membership to be more representative of users. Membership has now been broadened to include 'user-members' who would probably not be accountants, such as representatives from the CBI, Stock Exchange, Banks and Pension funds and also non-voting members representing the (UK) Treasury and the (UK) Department of Trade and Industry.

The ASC prepares SSAPs for adoption by the professional accountancy bodies. The procedure preceding the issue of an accounting standard is briefly as follows: the ASC identifies an area of accounting practice which it believes a recommendation is necessary and establishes a working party to prepare a draft standard. When the draft has been approved by the ASC, it is issued for discussion and comment as an Exposure Draft (ED) for a period typically of three to six months. At the end of this period the ASC reviews the ED in light of the submissions it has received and amends it as it thinks appropriate. The proposed new accounting standard has to be approved of by the Councils of each of the Institute of Chartered Accountants in England and Wales, The Institute of Chartered Accountants of Scotland, The Institute of Chartered Accountants in Ireland, The Chartered Association of Certified Accountants, The Chartered Institute of Cost and Management Accountants and The Chartered Institute of Public Finance and Accountancy. The Institute of Chartered Accountants in Ireland, therefore, directly participates in the development of accounting standards through regular meetings with the ASC, on which it is represented, and by communication verbally and in writing, of comments on the exposure drafts and other relevant matters. Indeed, many of the accounting standards, when referring to legislation, will separately mention Irish circumstances. However the role of the ASC will be assumed by the new Accounting Standards Board (ASB) and it shall issue standards on its own authority.

In addition to SSAPs and EDs, the ASC in 1984 introduced a new form of consultative document, the Statement of Intent (SOI), designed to give an early indication of how the ASC proposes to deal with a particular accounting matter. The ASC also introduced in 1983 the Statement of Recommended Practice (SORP), to give guidance on specialised areas of accounting where an SSAP would not be justified. Unlike accounting standards, these are not mandatory on members of the accountancy bodies, but they are consistent with accounting standards in that they help to define accounting practice in the particular area or sector to which they refer.

Enforcement and legal status

In order to have authority and status, SSAPs must be capable of enforcement. Members of the accountancy profession must comply with accounting standards when preparing accounts which are intended to show a true and fair view. Members in practice must 'qualify' their audit report, if there is unjustified non-compliance with an SSAP and/or inappropriate accounting policies apply. Any significant departure from applicable accounting standards should be disclosed by way of note to the financial statements, explained, and the financial effects should be estimated and, if material, disclosed. The accountant/auditor who unjustifibly ignores the application of SSAPs to financial statements may face disciplinary action by the professional body of which he is a member.

It should be noted that the principal method of ensuring compliance with accounting standards is through the professional accountancy bodies. Enforcement of accounting standards is achieved, for example, by making enquiries about non-compliance and by persuasion. In the case of blatant disregard for accounting standards, there is the option of bringing disciplinary charges against members who are responsible for this. However, this is an approach which has not been adopted to date. In general, standards have been well observed by quoted companies. Furthermore, for listed companies the Council of the Stock Exchange expects the accounts of limited companies to be prepared in conformity with the SSAPs. This provision adds significantly to the status and authority of accounting standards.

The final dimension to the enforcement process is the legal status of accounting standards. Accounting standards per se are not incorporated in either the Companies Act, 1963 or the Companies (Amendment) Act, 1986. However, the legislation requires that all companies must show a true and fair view of the state of affairs at balance sheet date and of the profit or loss for the accounting period. However, any legal dispute as to whether financial statements show a true and fair view can only be resolved by a judge in a court of law. In making such a decision it is probable that the courts would look for guidance on this question from the ordinary practices of professional accountants. Thus the court will treat relevant accounting standards as strong professional evidence of good accounting practice. Departure from accounting standards, without adequate disclosure and/or justification, may be interpreted by the courts as not showing a true and fair view.

This position was clarified in the case of Lloyd Cheyham and Co. Ltd v. Littlejohn and Co. (QB 1984 No. 4032). In his judgment, delivered on 30 September 1985, The Hon. Mr Justice Woolf said

> As to the proper treatment of such statements [i.e. SSAPs] . . . while they are not conclusive . . . they are very strong evidence as to what is the proper standard which should be adopted and unless there is some jusification, a departure from this will be regarded as constituting a breach of duty. It appears to be important that this should be the position because third parties in reading the accounts are entitled to assume that they have been drawn up in accordance with the approved practice, unless there is some indication in the accounts which clearly states that this is not the case.

In addition, section 5 of the Companies (Amendment) Act, 1986 embodies in law a number of accounting principles which are already established as fundamental accounting concepts in SSAP 2, i.e. going concern, accruals, consistency and prudence. All company accounts must now incorporate these four concepts as a matter of law. Thus, in effect SSAP 2 has a legal status. SSAP 2 has already been regarded as the most fundamental accounting standard. It explains some of the assumptions on which all other accounting standards rest. It can be said that SSAP 2 explains the very language of accounting, or that which must be taken for granted without question, as the foundation stone upon which all other arguments are stated. The non-application of accounting standards could well be considered in a court of law as a breach of company legislation governing the preparation of a company's financial statements.

FUNDAMENTAL ACCOUNTING CONCEPTS (SSAP 2)

SSAP 2 (issued in November 1971) is arguably the most important of all the accounting standards in that it is applicable to all material aspects of financial statements rather than to a particular problem. The main objective of SSAP 2 is to establish, as standard accounting practice, the disclosure of clear explanations of the accounting policies followed by companies. In this context, the standard may be perceived as an active agent in enhancing the quality of financial reporting.

The importance of SSAP 2 was duly acknowledged in the Companies (Amendment) Act, 1986 which incorporated under 'Accounting Principles' the essential concepts which were first formulated in SSAP 2. In brief, SSAP 2 contains the arguments on which all other accounting standards are based. Disclosure of financial information necessarily improves the quality of financial statements in that it may assist the reader in evaluating the effect of selecting accounting policies on the results of the entity, regardless of the fact that the policy adopted may be totally inappropriate. It promotes clarity and also (to an extent) uniformity in financial reporting.

If users of financial statements are to be able to understand and interpret them, they should be aware of the main assumptions/concepts on which those financial statements are based. Four fundamental accounting concepts are listed in SSAP 2 as follows:

(*a*) The going-concern concept.
(*b*) The accruals or matching concept.
(*c*) The prudence concept or the concept of conservatism.
(*d*) The consistency concept.

There is no discussion in the standard justifying the choice of the four concepts selected. What does fundamental mean? The lack of such a conceptual justification is a major fault in the standard. Undoubtedly, the concepts outlined are important but it is not conclusively apparent from SSAP 2 that they are the most important ones.

The going-concern concept

The going-concern concept is wholly different from that of the other three concepts included in SSAP 2. The assumption that a business is a going concern has to be justified in order to satisfy compliance; whereas for the other three concepts, it is a departure that would have to be justified. Unless there is evidence to the contrary, it is assumed that the business will continue in operational existence for the foreseeable future. All of this means that both the profit and loss account and balance sheet assume no intention or necessity to liquidate the business or to significantly curtail the scale of operation.

Thus, the accountant does not normally value the assets of the company on the basis of what they may realise on a liquidation. Rather, assets will be shown at cost and in the case of fixed assets, at (historic) cost less aggregate depreciation. Cost less aggregate depreciation represents the unexpired historic cost. Fixed assets are only written off when there has been a permanent impairment to their future value to the firm. The going-concern concept provides the basis for the preparation of financial statements. However, the prudence concept is more dominant in the valuation of current assets.

What is meant by the term 'continue to operate for the foreseeable future'? One view is that the ability of an enterprise to remain in operational existence depends on its solvency. So long as a firm can remain solvent, that is, pay its debts as they become due, it can continue in operational existence whatever the extent of its losses. Continued losses, of course, will eventually render the firm insolvent, as it runs out of cash and its bankers refuse to provide further finance. 'Foreseeable future' means that the business will not be liquidated within a span of time necessary to carry out present contractual commitments or to use up assets according to the plans and expectations currently held.

The general assumption of the going-concern concept has a number of implications under the existing system of accounting:

(*i*) It provides justification for the use of a historical cost system of valuation. Fixed assets are intended for use, not sale. Therefore, liquidation values are inappropriate and consequently, historical cost is the proper valuation base.

(*ii*) The second major implication of going-concern is that it provides justification for measuring the position of an entity at a point in time other than in the event of liquidation. There is, therefore, a connection between going-concern and periodic reporting.

(*iii*) With periodic reporting on the progress of an entity and the related recognition of earning power, the profit and loss account emerges as the most important of the financial reports.

(*iv*) With emphasis on the profit and loss account, the major focus of attention turned to the most appropriate form of income measurement, with the accruals concept eventually emerging as superior. Thus, the going-concern concept is also linked with the accruals or matching concept.

(*v*) Given the major focus of attention on the profit and loss account, the balance sheet virtually became meaningless as a statement of value. It became nothing more than a link between two profit and loss accounts and remains so to this day under the historical cost system of accounting.

Indeed, a recent research paper published by the Institute of Chartered Accountants in Scotland described the balance sheet as:

a hotchpotch of costs, valuations, and adjusted figures which indicate neither the worth of an entity as a whole nor the separate worths of its individual components.

Since the fundamental accounting concerns are defined as broad basic assumptions underlying the periodic accounts of a business enterprise, it would appear that the assumption of going-concern is correctly included in this classification under the existing system of accounting.

The accruals concept

The accruals concept follows directly from the going-concern assumption. Accrual accounting emphasised transactions and events which have cash consequences rather than cash receipts and payments.

The accruals concept is a difficult concept to describe, although most accountants clearly understand what is meant by it, at least in situations which are commonly encountered. The concept means that revenues (e.g. sales income) are recognised as they are earned, usually at the date of a transaction with a third party, not necessarily when the cash flow relating to the transaction is received. Thus, when revenues are generated, they are reflected in the firm's profit figure for that period.

Moreover, expenses are accrued, i.e. acknowledged as having been incurred, in the same period as that in which the corresponding revenue was generated. Expenses are therefore 'matched' with revenues only in so far as as this relationship can be established or justifiably assumed. Hence, the term 'matching' concept is often used in place of the accruals concept.

In many situations, the application of the accruals concept is straight-forward. At the end of an accounting period, sales transactions may have been completed, but the cash has not yet been received. Such sales represent revenues for the period but cash receipts for the next period. Likewise, a company will make year-end adjustments for rent due or bank interest receivable. In the same way that revenues will rarely equal receipts, neither will expenses equal cash payments. Payments may be made this year but relate to the next accounting period, for example rent paid in advance. Alternatively, some expenses incurred this year may not be paid until next year, e.g. rent paid in arrears.

The accruals/matching concept is often the most difficult to apply when preparing financial statements, in particular with the treatment of expenses.

There are a number of major difficulties in relation to expense determination. Firstly, there are few costs which can be *directly* associated with revenues but there are a large number of costs which are indirectly associated with revenues. Many costs are indirectly necessary if revenue is to be earned but these cannot be directly associated with the earned revenue, e.g. overhead expenses of the business. Secondly, in certain periods there will be a measurable expiration of costs having no direct association with the revenues earned in the particular period, but for which there is no justification in allowing them to be carried forward to be written-off in future periods. The basic problem with the matching concept is the implication that expense determination is a direct function of revenue recognition, whereas in fact expenses are determined quite independently of revenue. Take, for example, an extensive marketing campaign associated with launching a new product. How much of this expenditure should be written-off against profit immediately? Similar problems occur when dealing with research and development expenditure and expenditure on developing information systems.

With regard to revenues, the general rule is that recognition takes place only when revenues are reasonably assured of being realised. There are, however, two major exceptions to this rule. Firstly, revenue may be recognised during production. This may happen with services provided on a time basis and with the recognition of revenue on long-term contracts. Secondly, in some situations, revenue recognition prior to receipt of cash may be inappropriate. This usually happens when the degree of uncertainty is very high, e.g. hire purchase contracts where some deferment of revenue income is common practice.

While these exceptions result in inconsistencies in revenue recognition they do not, of themselves, distort the matching process.

There is general support for the belief that earnings of a period measured by accruals is regarded as superior to those measured on a cash basis. For example, modern business activities are extremely complex, involving long production processes in which output is the joint result of numerous inputs acquired at various times. Business is largely conducted on credit so that the acquisition or sale of goods and services is commonly separated from the related cash outlay or receipt by a creditor or debtor.

Whatever the conceptual validity of the matching concept, it is the method which in practice is applied almost universally to the measurement of income. Consequently, the accruals concept is correctly included as a fundamental accounting concept. It should, however, be remembered that while it is a fundamental concept under the present system of accounting, the accruals concept is only one possible method of income measurement. To date however, it has, despite its problems, emerged as more acceptable than any alternative.

The major implication of the accruals concept is in relation to its effect on the balance sheet. While the going-concern concept provides justification for the balance sheet as a link between two profit and loss accounts, the matching concept is the process by which such a balance sheet is derived. Under the matching process, assets are viewed as those resources acquired for production which have not yet reached the point in the business process where they may be treated as cost of sales or expenses. Thus, it is argued, the balance sheet is virtually meaningless as anything other than a list of balances.

The prudence concept

The prudence concept is also known as the concept of conservatism. Prudence is the concept whereby revenue and profits are not anticipated, but are recognised by the inclusion as part of income only realised in the form of cash or when the ultimate cash realisation can be assessed with reasonably certainty. Provision is made for all known liabilities, whether the amount of these is known with certainty or its the best estimate in the light of the information available.

The origin of the prudence concept can be traced to the last century and, in particular, to the formation of limited liability companies. The owners of such companies were prohibited by company law from withdrawing dividends except out of profits. However, the definition and measurement of profits was left to the emerging accountancy profession. In order to avoid breaking the law it is understandable that accountants adopted a conservative attitude to reporting business income. Thus, revenues were not anticipated unless they were reasonably assured of being received in cash. Conversely, provision was made for all known liabilities and losses.

The intention of this asymmetrical approach is to introduce a bias which will tend to understate profits. Although such a concept might at first sight be thought of as being appropriate for creditors, it might, in fact, damage shareholders' interest. Thus a shareholder may sell his shares at a low price, because the financial statements show low profits and low asset valuations (revaluation of land and buildings is not universal accounting practice). To complicate matters, accountants have failed to satisfactorily resolve the issue of accounting for changing prices. This has led to overstatements of profits in an inflationary environment since, for example, depreciation is not provided on the replacement cost of productive fixed assets. In periods of rising prices, adherence to the 'historic' cost convention has the very opposite effect than that which the prudence concept would seem to require.

In practice, the doctrine of conservatism is evident throughout the accounting standards. To cite three examples:

i) SSAP 9 requires that stocks be valued at the lower of cost or net realisable value (thus reporting losses, if applicable, before the disposal of stocks). In addition, SSAP 9 requires that provision be made for all foreseeable losses on long-term contract work in progress despite the fact that work may not yet have started on contracts entered into by the balance sheet date.

ii) SSAP 12 requires that provision for depreciation of fixed assets having a finite useful life should be made by allocating the cost (or revalued amount) less estimated residual values of the assets as fairly as possible to the periods expected to benefit from their use. The omission of the depreciation charge on the grounds that market value was greater than book value is no longer acceptable.

iii) SSAP 13 provides that all research and development expenditure should be written-off in the period incurred unless very stringent conditions are met, which would justify it being carried forward.

The prudence concept may be inconsistent with the accruals concept. To this extent, the fundamental concepts outlined in SSAP 2 are internally inconsistent. For example, it may be expected that a particular asset has an expected useful life, at a given usage level, of ten years if properly serviced and maintained. It may, however, be prudent to recognise, based on the knowledge of the technology currently being developed, that obsolesence after five years is a strong possibility, especially if past experience supports such a view. The normal application of the accruals concept would suggest that the cost of the asset should be charged over the ten successive accounting periods in which the benefits of its use are likely to be recorded. For reasons of prudence, however, the standard requires that in this case, a five-year period should be used, giving rise to higher depreciation charges throughout.

Ironically, excessive use of the conservatism principle results in distorting the results of an enterprise over an extended period of time. The adoption of an extremist policy in applying the prudence concept would result significantly in the understatement of profits in early years followed by corresponding overstatements, in later years, thereby defeating the objective of caution inherent in the concept. The effect of such an extreme application of the doctrine may be more or less serious, depending on the circumstances of the company. Excessive use of the doctrine may be used to build up secret reserves to hide management inefficiency, or to manipulate the price of a company's shares.

The consistency concept

This is, perhaps the most straightforward concept. Its application requires consistency of accounting treatment of like items within each accounting period and from one period to the next. In other words, if a particular method of reporting a transaction is adopted by a business, then it should continue to use that method of accounting in successive accounting periods. For example, if a firm adopts a policy of depreciating its fixed assets on a straight-line basis, then it should continue to use this method in following accounting periods.

However, such a concept could prevent progress if applied too rigidly. If a more appropriate accounting method was discovered, it could not be applied because it would be inconsistent with the past! Fortunately, the consistency concept is not an absolute rule of accounting. Firms are allowed to change their accounting methods if a more appropriate accounting method is available. Consistency is reinforced by SSAP 6 which requires restatement of prior years in the event of a change of accounting policy, the object being to facilitate comparisons.

Thus, some inconsistency of accounting treatment is acceptable in the context of changing an accounting method to a better one or following a change in the law or the introduction of an accounting standard.

Consistency must be understood to relate to the accounting policies themselves, rather than the detail of their application. A reduction in the period over which the cost of an asset is written-off does *not* represent a change of depreciation policy, nor does it represent a breach of the consistency principle. The policy of charging the cost against the revenue of respective accounting periods (by means of a specified method such as 'straight-line', 'reducing balance', etc.) remains consistently in force, despite the alteration in the write-off period due to changed circumstances.

The alternatives

It was mentioned previously that there is no discussion in the standard justifying the choice of the four concepts selected. However, the importance of these four concepts to the preparation of financial statements can be appreciated by contemplating what might happen if they did not apply.

The alternative to the going-concern concept is that of liquidation or the 'gone' concern concept. The abandonment of the assumption would have a significant effect on the content of financial statements. Such a move would necessitate all assets (including fixed assets) being valued on a liquidation basis. This liquidation concept would reflect the estimated value that assets would realise if the assets were disposed of. However, determining such values can be extremely difficult and largely depends on the assumptions one makes regarding the market in which the assets are sold. Is it a forced or orderly sale? Are the assets being sold in a piecemeal way or as a unit? Such estimates could not be verified, especially relative to the historic cost price of the asset. Moreover, fluctuating net realisable values would generate annual unrealised profits/losses which could be misleading to users of financial statements.

The adoption of the liquidation concept would most probably also result in increased liabilities for the reporting entity (e.g redundancy payments claims).

It is interesting to note that liquidation values automatically apply to the valuation of current assets such as debtors and stocks. In valuing debtors for balance sheet purposes, provision must be made for estimated bad and doubtful debts. Moreover, stocks must be valued at the lower of cost or net realisable value.

The alternative to the accruals/matching concept is the cash basis of accounting which only recognises revenues and expenses when actual cash is received or paid. Under this method of accounting, the 'profit' position is likely to be distorted. Indeed, it could be deliberately distorted by post-poning payment of expenditure until a future accounting period. This simple method of accounting (it does not require a great deal of expertise) is sometimes used by small non-profit organisations, e.g. clubs.

The alternative to the prudence concept is that of optimism. Optimism in managers is a common phenomenon, but if it is reflected in the preparation of financial statements, then the reliability of such statements would be questionable and the comparability of statements between companies would be virtually impossible.

The alternative to the consistency concept is that of inconsistency. With inconsistency of accounting treatment, the comparability of financial statements of the same business over accounting periods would be impossible, in addition to the comparision of financial statements between companies. Accounting reports would become largely a matter of taste.

Other concepts

It should be noted that SSAP 2 does not provide any theoretical justification for adopting the above four concepts. Indeed, two other concepts could easily have been added, namely, the materiality concept and the concept of objectivity.

The use of the word 'material' in relation to accounting matters is intended to give scope to a reasonably wide interpretation according to the variety of circumstances which can arise. It is not possible or desirable, therefore, to give a precise definition of such an expression. By literal definition, the adjective 'material' can vary in meaning from 'significant' to 'essential'. In an accounting sense, however, a matter is material if its non-disclosure, mis-statement or omission would be likely to distort the view given by the financial statements or other statements under consideration.

Certain items of expenditure are sometimes insignificant in relation to the total expenditure of the enterprise. Thus, the classification of items such as ashtrays or coat hangers into either revenue or capital expenditure will not significantly influence the reported performance of the financial position of the business. Coat hangers, for example, last for many years and should theoretically be classified as capital expenditure and thus included under fixed assets on the balance sheet. However, because the expenditure on such items is usually insignificant for most businesses they will not be treated as assets. Rather they will probably be written-off immediately and in whole to the income statement. Thus it is immaterial whether the prudence or accruals concepts are applied to this insignificant amount of expenditure.

Materiality can only be considered in relative terms. In a small business £1,000 may be material, whereas £1m. may not be when classifying the expenditure of a very large undertaking. (Indeed, large reporting entities will 'round' the accounting numbers in the financial statements to the nearest million pounds.) Those responsible for preparing and auditing financial statements must decide which, out of the many facts available to them, are the ones that have a real bearing on the true and fair view which the accounts must give. In some circumstances, a difference of about 10 per cent might be acceptable, but in other cases a difference of 3 per cent may be too much. While percentage comparisions can, if properly used, constitute broad useful guides, it should be noted that they are no more than rough rules of thumb, and should not be applied indiscriminately, without regard to particular circumstances.

Many accountants believe that objectivity is one of the most important desirable qualities. Unfortunately, it is not clear that all accountants attach the same meaning to the word. It is probably true that most accountants believe that objectivity is virtually synonymous with verifiability, i.e. that accounts should, as far as possible, be based on information which is capable of independent verification, and should exclude items which depend on personal opinion and judgment.

Objectivity seeks to ensure that verifiable information is used in the preparation of financial statements. Thus, fixed assets can be physically identified in addition to their legal ownership and the cost price paid for them. Objectivity seeks to acquire evidence which one would reasonably accept and thus attempts to eliminate an element of judgment in preparing financial statements.

However, no set of financial statements can be completely objective. Areas such as depreciation of fixed assets, provision for bad debts, and valuation of stocks always require informed judgment. Consequently, there are other understandings of the term 'objectivity'. This interpretation follows on from, inter alia, *The Corporate Report* which stated:

> The information presented should be objective or unbiased in that it should meet all proper user needs and be neutral in that the perception of the measurer should not be biased towards the interest of any one user

group. This implies the need for reporting standards which are themselves neutral as between competing interests.

(Accounting Standards Steering Committee, The Corporate Report, Institute of Chartered Accountants in England and Wales, 1975)

The difference between traditional objectivity (which equals verifiability) and the more recent interpretation of objectivity is an extremely important one which will have an increasing impact on accounting practice. For example, the recent controversy regarding accounting for brand names and newspaper titles is a debate about, inter alia, the interpretation of the objectivity concept.

In Ireland, Independent Newspapers plc incorporated the group's newspaper titles in their 1987 financial statements at a valuation of £48 million. This valuation (which amounted to 58 per cent of all fixed assets) represented the amount that it was estimated could be realised if the newspaper titles were to be disposed of on their own, unaccompanied by the assets and other rights and interests which go into making up the business of the group as a whole. Independent Newspapers were only following the trend set in the UK where, for example, Rank Hovis McDougall put £678m. worth of new assets (representing more than fifty brand names) onto its balance sheet.

Accounting bases

SSAP 2 explains that the basic concepts are capable of practical implementation in a variety of ways, depending on the nature of the transactions or balances in question, the nature of the business and the particular circumstances prevailing. The methods by which the concepts may correctly be applied are referred to in SSAP 2 as 'accounting bases'.

Accounting bases are the methods developed for applying the fundamental accounting concepts to financial transactions and items for the purpose of the financial accounts and, in particular:

(a) for determining the accounting periods in which revenue and costs should be recognised in the profit and loss account; and

(b) for determining the amounts at which material items should be stated in the balance sheet.

Accounting bases have developed over time in respect of different transactions and different businesses. In many areas of accounting, there are a number of bases available for use in relation to a particular transaction. For example, depreciation of fixed assets may be provided on a straight-line, reducing balance or usage (e.g. machine hours) method. The complexity and diversity of a business renders the total and rigid uniformity of bases impracticable.

Accounting bases provide rational and consistent methods for arriving at numbers for inclusion in the financial statements. The directors must exercise their judgment in selecting one of these alternative methods and the selected method is referred to as an accounting policy. The significance of accounting bases is that they provide limits to the area subject to the exercise of judgment and a check against arbitrary, excessive or unjustifiable adjustments where no other objective yardstick is available.

SSAP 2 outlines a number of examples of matters where different accounting bases are recognised. Since SSAP 2 was published a number of items listed have been dealt with in later SSAPs, thus reducing the elements of choice that existed at the time SSAP 2 was published. For example, research and development expenditure is now the subject of a separate accounting standard, as is the accounting treatment of government grants, to name but two.

Accounting policies

Accounting policies are the specific accounting bases selected and consistently followed by a business enterprise as being in the opinion of the directors appropriate to its circumstances and best suited to present fully its results and financial position. Since the accounting policy followed can significantly affect the reported results and financial position, the policies followed in dealing with the material items must also be explained. This is natural enough, given the range of permissible bases. Also, without explicit disclosures, the financial statements would lack an inherent intelligibility and comparability with financial statements of the following accounting periods and with other reporting entities. Accounting policy notes should be clear, fair and as brief as possible. SSAP 2 views adequate disclosure of the accounting policies as essential to the fair presentation of financial accounts. An example of an accounting policy note is as follows:

> All expenditure on research and development relating to the activities of the company is charged to the profit and loss account in the financial period in which it is incurred.

SSAP 2 requires that the accounting policies which are followed for dealing with items judged material or critical in determining the profit or loss for the year, and also when stating the financial position of the company, should be disclosed by way of notes to the accounts. In practice, accounting policy notes are given in four major circumstances:

(*a*) Where the accounting policy adopted is not normal for the industry.

(*b*) Where the accounting policy adopted in the current period differs from that applied in the previous period.

(*c*) Where there are a number of permissible bases.

(*d*) Where an explanation of the accounting base permitted is considered necessary in order to inform the user or where it is required by an accounting standard.

The objective of the ASC in seeking increased disclosure through SSAP 2 illustrates an attempt to improve the quality of financial statements. However, little attention had been paid to the much more important issue of 'relevance' of accounting numbers to users. Whatever the ultimate result of the debate concerning relevance to users, one point is evident—disclosure will always be necessary. If accounting practice is to fulfil its objectives, consensus must be reached on a system that will be both relevant to users and practical for accountants. In respect of any system which is ultimately adopted as being conceptually superior to the current reporting system there will still be a need for:

(*a*) The fundamental concepts on which the system is based, and

(*b*) The particular accounting policies adopted in the preparation of the financial statements.

To the extent that SSAP 2 deals with these crucial questions under the system of accounting currently in use, the financial statements will be relevant and useful. However, it should not be regarded as a substitute for a conceptual framework for accounting. The American Financial Accounting Standards Board (FASB) has defined such a conceptual framework as a 'coherent system of inter-related objectives and fundamental concepts that can lead to consistent standards and that prescribe the nature, function and limits of financial accounting and financial statements'. In the USA the need for such a framework in developing coherent and consistent standards has long been recognised, and work on developing a framework has been continuing since the mid-1970s. The recent Deering Report in the UK stated that further work on a conceptual framework is desirable but that it should be undertaken on a modest scale.

Such a framework, slow both in developing and being accepted, requires recognition of accounting applications and the information needs of the various user groups. Until it is developed, SSAP 2 provides only a description, at the most basic level, of the building blocks with which financial statements are constructed.

EARNINGS PER SHARE (SSAP 3) AND EXCEPTIONAL and EXTRAORDINARY ITEMS (SSAP 6)

The need to define earnings per share (EPS) arises because of the importance that investors and security analysts attach to the price earnings (P/E) ratio of the company. The price earnings ratio of a company is calculated as follows:

$$\text{Price earnings ratio} \quad = \quad \frac{\text{Market price of ordinary shares}}{\text{Earnings per share}}$$

Therefore, if a company could manipulate its reported earnings, then the EPS would be affected as well as the price/earnings ratio and this might influence investors, either actual or potential. The EPS figure must now be shown on the face of the profit and loss account of all quoted companies.

The accounting standard (SSAP 3) defines EPS as:

> Profit on ordinary activities (i.e. after exceptional items, minority interests, taxation and preference dividends, but before extraordinary items) attributable to the ordinary shareholders divided by the number of ordinary shares in issue.

Exceptional and extraordinary items were subsequently defined in SSAP 6 which was issued in January 1974 (and revised in August 1986). It requires all exceptional and extraordinary expenses (with some exceptions) to be accounted for through the profit and loss account for the year and *not* through reserves. Thus, the ASC favoured the 'all-inclusive' concept of profit, as distinct from the 'current operating performance' concept of profit which would include only normal, recurring activities of the company.

However, SSAP 3 stipulates that EPS should be calculated with reference to normal activities only (including *exceptional* items). However, profits/losses from abnormal activities, i.e. *extraordinary* items, while they also pass through the profit and loss account, will not affect the EPS calculations. In essence, exceptional items pass through the profit and loss account 'above the line', i.e. they are deducted in arriving at net profit before tax. On the other hand, extraordinary items are deducted 'below the line' in the profit and loss account. Thus, the crucial matter in calculating EPS is often the distinction between extraordinary and exceptional items.

Extraordinary items are defined as those material items which derive from transactions or events that fall outside the ordinary activities of the company and which are therefore expected not to recur frequently or regularly. They do not include exceptional items nor do they include prior year items merely because they relate to a prior year. Examples of extraordinary items would be:

(*a*) The discontinuance of a business segment, either through termination or disposal.

(*b*) Profit/loss on sale of investment not acquired with the intention of resale, such as investments in subsidiary and associated companies.

(*c*) Provision made for the permanent diminution in value of a fixed asset because of an extraordinary event during the accounting period.

(*d*) Profits/losses resulting from expropriation of assets by foreign governments or via nationalisation.

Extraordinary items will be shown in the profit and loss account net of taxation. Thus, the tax consequences are automatically grouped with that item and *not* with the tax charge on ordinary items.

Exceptional items are defined as those items which, whilst deriving from transactions or events that fall within the ordinary activities of the company, need to be disclosed separately by virtue of their size or incidence, if the financial statements are to give a true and fair view.

Ordinary activities are any activities which are usually undertaken by the company and any related activities in which the company engages in furtherance of, incidental to, or arising from those activities. They include, but are not confined to, the trading activities of the company. Examples would be:

(*a*) Abnormal charge for bad debts or stock write-off.

(*b*) Reorganisation, rationalisation costs related to *continuing* activities. (Note: discontinuance would constitute an extraordinary item.)

(*c*) special contributions to pension funds.

A typical profit and loss account which combines the requirements of both SSAP 3 and SSAP 6 is shown in Exhibit 10.1.

Exhibit 10.1

	£
PROFIT AND LOSS ACCOUNT FOR YEAR ENDED . . .	
Turnover	25,000
Profit on ordinary activities	
before taxation	4,181
Tax on profit on ordinary activities	1,559
Profit on ordinary activities after taxation	2,622
Extraordinary gain (net of tax)	150
Profit for the financial year	2,772
Dividends paid (*Note 1*)	1,710
Profit retained for year	1,062
Profit brought forward	2,985
Profit carried forward	4,047
Earnings per share (*Note 2*)	16.4p

Note 1:   Dividends:
Preference dividends   290
Ordinary dividends 1,420 (i.e. 10p per share)

Note 2: There are 14,200 ordinary shares in issue and, therefore, earnings available to ordinary shareholders equals £2,332 (i.e. £2,622—290), divided by the number of ordinary shares in issue (14,200). The resultant figure, 16.4p (i.e. £2,322/14,200) is the EPS. The extraordinary gain has been excluded from the EPS calculation in accordance with SSAP 3.

It should be noted that the distinction between extraordinary and exceptional items can, on occasions, be very difficult. However, this distinction must be made due to the impact on earnings per share calculations. The important distinctions between extraordinary and exceptional items are summarised in Exhibit 10.2

Exhibit 10.2

	Extraordinary	Exceptional
1. Significant?	Yes	Yes
2. Included in P/L and disclosed	Yes—net of tax	Yes—gross
3. Nature of item	*Outside* normal activities of the business	*Within* normal activities of the business
4. Expected occurence	Infrequent and irregular	Abnormal in incidence but can be frequent
5. Impact on EPS	No	Yes

QUESTION 10.1 (SM)

The production and publication of financial statements of companies are governed by the Companies Act, the Accounting Standards Committee and the Accounting Standards Board.

Requirement:
(*a*) Explain the role of each of these
(*b*) Explain the relationship between them
(*c*) Describe, briefly, the differences between the factors controlling the production of internal and external financial statements.
(The Chartered Association of Certified Accountants)

QUESTION 10.2 (SM)

The Oddities Company Ltd is involved in a wide range of diverse activities. The book-keeper in currently preparing the annual accounts to 30 November 199 . and has asked for your help in deciding what should be included or omitted from these accounts.

Indicate with reasons how you would deal with each of the following queries in the Company's accounts. By how much would each of these queries affect the profit of Oddities?

The queries that the book-keeper has are:

(*a*) Sold £34,000 of goods to International Buyers Ltd on credit. All the goods have been delivered, but payment has not been received.

(*b*) Machinery Ltd has ordered £75,000 of spares from Oddities Ltd. Oddities Ltd has £15,000 of the spares for the contract in stock, but the balance has had to be ordered from suppliers. Delivery is expected on 15 December. Machinery Ltd will only accept delivery of the goods if the order is completed in full. The gross profit on spares is 20 per cent.

(*c*) Prior to the end of the last financial year the company invoiced Experimental Research Ltd for £30,000 for goods. They have paid £20,000 to date, but rumours now circulating suggest that Experimental Research Ltd are in financial difficulties. The credit control department is experiencing difficulties trying to obtain the amount due. The goods originally cost £22,000.

(*d*) Confused Ltd place an order for some machinery which you have manufactured specially for them. They paid a £10,000 deposit with their order, the contract price being £65,000. They have now changed their long-range plans and no longer require the machinery and you have agreed to accept the £10,000 deposit as the cancellation fee. You believe you can persuade Multitech Ltd, a company manufacturing similar products to Confused Ltd, to buy the machinery. Multitech have shown considerable interest and it looks as though a sale is likely at a price of about £60,000. The machinery cost £45,000 to manufacture.

(*e*) Received a payment for £13,500 for goods supplied in the previous financial year. The customer to whom you had supplied these goods was thought to be a bad credit risk, and you had written-off the account as a bad debt in the profit and loss account of the previous accounting period.

(*f*) Mrs A. C. Dentprone was unfortunately hurt whilst trying to operate the 'Oddities Yoghurt maker'. She badly damaged her hand and claims to have suffered not only physically but also mentally. Oddities' legal advisors are of the opinion that her claim for £5,000 in respect of the physical damage to her hand is reasonable, and that there is no defence, but her claim for £100,000 in respect of mental and psychological strain has only a 5 per cent chance of success, depending upon the attitude of the judge.

(The Chartered Association of Certified Accountants)

QUESTION 10.3 (A)

Detailed below are *extracts* from the summarised draft accounts for Contract Contractors Ltd.

BALANCE SHEET AS AT 30 SEPTEMBER 19 . 8

	£000
Current assets	
Stock	860
Debtors	660
Cash	15
Current liabilities	
Creditors	820
Capital and reserves	
Called-up share capital	1,000
Profit and loss account	100

Included in the profit and loss account is a contract to supply Metal Tools Ltd with tools and dies for an invoice value of £600,000 during 19 . 9. The £600,000 contract is included in the 19 . 8 sales figure, and the debtors figure included £390,000 for the Metal Tools account in respect of this contract. The undelivered portion has not been included in stock since it has been, in theory, sold.

The contract specified the exact number of items to be supplied. On 30 September 19 . 8, the position on the contract was:

Goods delivered and invoiced	£300,000
Payments received	£210,000

The Metal Tools Contract costings were: £000s

Production cost	560,000
Anticipated profit	40,000
	600,000

When you questioned the managing director of Contract Contractors Ltd about this, he stated the following:

(1) Accounting principles recognise revenue when a contract is made

(2) The goods are manufactured and costings were as budgeted.

Do you agree with the managing director? Why?

(The Chartered Association of Certified Accountants)

QUESTION 10.4 (SM)

The Barry Company plc is considering raising £12 million to finance an expansion programme. Its current balance sheet shows:

	£000
Fixed assets	13,600
Net current assets	8,400
Ordinary share capital (£1 each)	10,000
Revenue reserves	12,000

Its most recent profit statement shows:

	£
Profit before tax	5,500
Corporation tax	(2,200)
Profit before tax	3,300
Ordinary dividends	792
	2,508

The additional investment is expected to generate £2 million additional pre-tax profits during the forthcoming period. The corporation tax rate will remain at 40 per cent. Without the additional investment pre-tax profits will remain static.

Three financing options are available:

1. issuing debentures at 16 per cent;
2. issue of 12% preference shares;
3. rights issue to ordinary shareholders at £6.

Requirement:

(*a*) Compute forecast earnings per share for each of the three financing options;

(*b*) show the composition of capital employed for each of the three financing options.

QUESTION 10.5 (SM)

During December 19 . 7 your client paid £10,000 for an advertising campaign. The advertisements will be heard on local, independent radio stations from 1 January 19 . 8 to 31 December 19 . 8. Your client believes that as a result sales will increase by 60 per cent in 19 . 8 (over 19.7 levels).

Requirement:

You are required to write a memorandum to your client explaining your views on how this item should be treated in the accounts for the three years 19 . 7 to 19 . 9. Your answer should include explicit reference to at least three relevant accounting conventions, and to the requirements of *two* classes of user of published financial statements.

QUESTION 10.6 (A)

Most companies now include in their annual report and accounts a section headed 'Accounting Policies'. Specify five subheadings that might be dealt with in this section of the report giving details of the type of information that you would expect to be provided.

QUESTION 10.7 (SM)

(*a*) Explain what is meant by basic earnings per share

(*b*) From the information below relating to A Ltd calculate the basic earnings per share for the year ended 31 December 19 . 1

A Ltd
SUMMARY PROFIT AND LOSS ACCOUNT FOR YEAR ENDED
31 DECEMBER 19 . 1

			£000
Profit before tax and extraordinary items			700
Corporation tax on the profit for the year			260
Profit after taxation			440
Extraordinary items less tax			30
Profit after extraordinary items			410
Dividends:	Preference	80	
	Ordinary	150	230
Retained profit			180

There were 1m. ordinary shares of £1 each throughout the year.

QUESTION 10.8 (SM)

Unusual Ltd has sales of £6 million and pre-tax trading profits of £1 million before taking account of the following items:

(1) Costs of £750,000 incurred in terminating production at one of the company's factories.

(2) Provision for an abnormally large bad debt of £500,000 arising on a trading contract.

(3) Currency exchange surplus amounting to £7,500 arising on remittances from an overseas depot.

(4) Profits of £150,000 on sale of plant and machinery written-off in a previous year when production of the particular product ceased.

(5) An extra £100,000 contribution by the company to the employees pension fund.

How should these items be treated with reference to SSAP 6?

QUESTION 10.9 (A)

    (*a*) How does SSAP 6 define extraordinary and exceptional items?

    (*b*) State, giving your reasons, whether you consider the following to be extraordinary or exceptional items and state what additional information might be necessary to reach a firm decision on:

    (*i*) The profit on the sale of shares in a subsidiary company.

    (*ii*) Amounts received in settlement of insurance claims for consequential loss of profits.

    (*iii*) The impact of a change in the basis of taxation.

    (*iv*) Redundancy costs.

    (*v*) Loss on the disposal of a fixed asset.

(The Chartered Association of Certified Accountants)

11

Accounting Standards and Financial Statements—2

ACCOUNTING FOR VALUE-ADDED TAX (SSAP 5)

Value-added Tax (VAT) was introduced in Ireland on 1 November 1972. Its introduction was entirely due to our impending membership of the European Community, whose principal objective is to establish a fully integrated economic community. If this could be achieved, Europe would become a dominant economic and political force in the world. However, for a unified European Community to exist, variations in the tax systems and tax rates from one member state to another would have to be eliminated. Otherwise, these variations would distort the movement of goods and services (capital and labour) within the community. This consideration led to the need for tax harmonisation between member states which would include harmonisation of taxes on spending, income and capital.

One immediate problem was that the various member states had different taxes levied on spending. Ireland, for example, had turnover and wholesale taxes and these were replaced with a value-added taxation system with effect from 1 November 1972. The legislation is based on the EC's sixth VAT directive.

VAT is a turnover tax, charged on goods sold and supplied within Ireland in the course of business, and on the importation of certain goods and services. Thus, the payment of VAT is automatic for customers. However, the remittance of VAT to the Revenue is done by the various business entities which are registered for VAT. In this context, businesses are acting as unpaid tax collectors but nevertheless incur certain costs in doing so.

Registration

Generally, a person must register for VAT if his turnover from those goods and services which are liable for VAT exceeds £32,000 per annum. Service businesses are liable to register if turnover exceeds £15,000 per annum (a business below these limits may elect to register if it wishes). The effect to these limits is that, generally speaking, the publican or newsagent must register for VAT if his receipts exceed £32,000 per annum; the person providing services such as accountants or architects must register if their annual receipts exceed £15,000. Registration automatically imposes certain obligations. The major ones include:

(*a*) The requirement to account for and remit the VAT due to the Collector General for every taxable period. Each taxable period is a period of two months commencing 1 January, 1 March etc. and so there are six taxable periods in each calendar year. The VAT return and payment is due between 10th and 19th of the month following each taxable period. Thus the VAT return for January–February is due between 10 and 19 March. Failure to make the appropriate return and payment can result in penalties, including interest charges.

In an attempt to reduce the administrative burden on small businesses the Finance Act 1989 enables the Collector General to authorise persons (businesses) to make an VAT return and pay their VAT on an annual basis. This concession applies mainly to small businesses, but the Collector General must consider certain factors before issuing an authorisation; this may be issued conditionally or unconditionally and may be withdrawn by him.

(*b*) The need to issue an invoice for each taxable supply of goods to another taxable person. This invoice must include the name and address of the person issuing the invoice, the VAT registration number, the description of the goods and services, the rate of VAT and the amount and the name and address of the customer. The term 'supply' represents the transfer of ownership of the goods. (Obviously this requirement is modified in the case of some cash sales, since one would not expect to receive an invoice for the purchase of the morning paper.) Thus, the VAT invoice is only strictly necessary where the transaction is between taxable persons, i.e. where the person supplying the goods is liable for VAT and the customer wants to obtain a credit for VAT paid. In other circumstances, there is no obligation on taxable persons to supply such an invoice even though VAT will be automatically included in the price. Indeed, the supplier, in such circumstances, is not required to indicate his VAT registration number on such invoices.

Each business registered for VAT will charge VAT at the appropriate rate on its sales of goods and services. However, in computing VAT liability at the end of the period, the person is entitled to claim a deduction, known as input credit, for VAT borne on purchases or importation of goods and services. However, credit is not allowed for entertainment expenses, petrol and hotel bills, among other items.

The main rates of VAT at the time of writing are zero, 10 per cent and 23 per cent. The zero rate indicates that no VAT should be charged on certain goods and they include food, clothing and footwear for children under eleven and books. The 10 per cent rate applies to building materials, adult clothing, adult footwear and newspapers. The 23 per cent rate applies to most services and luxury goods, including television and electrical goods.

In addition to the above rates certain goods and activities are exempt. An exempt person may not register for VAT and would not charge for it on his goods or services. Exempted activities include education, betting, medical, dental and optical services, banking and insurance.

Accounting entries for VAT

The accounting entries for VAT become very simple if one considers the business as acting like an unpaid tax collector. The business has the obligation to charge out VAT at the appropriate rate on its sales. Thus, the invoice price will include VAT and the firm expects to receive the full amount in due course. On its purchases, the firm will suffer VAT and the VAT–inclusive cost will subsequently be discharged by payment.

In computing the VAT return at the end of the period, the difference between VAT charged on sales invoices and VAT borne on purchases (inputs) should be remitted to the Collector General. (If VAT on inputs exceeds VAT on sales, a refund will be due.)

Example:

The TVA Company is registered for VAT and the appropriate rate for its goods is 10 per cent. During the recent accounting period, the following transactions occured:

January 2   Sales on credit to A Ltd, £5,000 plus 10% VAT.
January 15   Purchases on credit from X Ltd, £3,000 plus 10% VAT.
February 3   Purchases on credit from X Ltd £6,000 plus 10%
February 21   Sales on credit to A Ltd £8,000 plus 10%.
February 27   Paid entertainment expenses £1,000 plus 10% VAT.
February 28   Received £5,500 from A Ltd.

Sales for the period amounted to £13,000 plus VAT at 10 per cent. Thus, the VAT on sales amounts to £1,300. VAT on purchases (inputs) amounted to £900. Since the VAT on entertainment expenses cannot be recovered, the end of period VAT liability must be £400 (£1,300–£900). The VAT on purchases and sales will be recorded in the VAT account. The balance on this account will indicate the liability in respect of VAT (or a VAT refund due). The total amount of the purchases and sales transactions (i.e. the VAT–inclusive price) will be recorded in the creditors/debtors ledger, as appropriate. However, the purchases and sales account will always record the VAT–exclusive amount. In turn, the profit and loss account will show purchases and sales at the VAT–exclusive price. The main ledger entries would appear as follows:

Purchases account			Sales account	
15/1 X Ltd 3,000				2/1 A Ltd 5,000
3/2 X Ltd 6,000				21/2 A Ltd 8,000

Debtor A Ltd account			Creditor X Ltd account	
2/1 Sales 5,500	28/2 Bank 5,500			15/1 Purchases 3,300
21/2 Sales 8,800	29/2 Bal. 8,800	29/2 Bal. 9,900		3/2 Purchases 6,600
14,300	14,300	9,900		9,900
1/3 Bal. 8,800			1/3	Bal. 9,900

Value-added tax account		
15/1 Purchases 300	2/1 Sales	500
3/2 Purchases 600	21/1 Sales	800
28/2 Bal. 400		
1,300		1,300
	1/3 Bal.	400

The trading and profit and loss account at the end of the period will have the following entries:

Sales	£13,000
Purchases	£9,000
Entertainment expenses	£1,100

The VAT on entertainment expenses is not recoverable, so that the entire cost is borne by the company. The purchases and sales figures in the profit and loss account reflect that the company is acting as a tax collector. The tax charged on its sales cannot be retained; the VAT on purchases reduces any potential liability.

The balance sheet will show the following:

Current Assets

Debtors	£8,800

Creditors (amounts due within one year)

Creditors	£9,900
VAT	£400

Accounting for VAT on a cash basis

A VAT-registered business must normally account for VAT on the basis of the invoices issued to customers. However, it may opt to account for VAT on the basis of cash received, where more than 90 per cent (by value) of its sales are to unregistered customers. Accounting for VAT on a cash basis eliminates the cost of funding the VAT when accounting for VAT on an invoice basis. For example, in the illustration above the company is liable for a VAT payment of £400 even though it has not yet received payment for some of its sales. However, prior approval of the Revenue must be obtained to account for VAT on the cash basis. Accounting for VAT on a cash basis can create a slight difficulty since the trader will know only the gross amount of the receipts which will automatically include VAT. This problem is easily overcome if one knows the relevant rate of VAT.

For example, a trader had cash receipts of £55,000 during a period and the relevant rate of VAT was 10 per cent. For accounting purposes he will need to extract the net amount of the sales and the appropriate amount of VAT. Let an index of 100 represent the VAT–exclusive price, therefore, the VAT–inclusive price must represent 110. Thus:

VAT–inclusive price = 110 = £55,000 (cash receipts)
VAT–exclusive price = 100/110 x £55,000 = £50,000 (cash sales)
VAT on sales = 10/110 x £55,000 = £5,000

Obviously, the situation gets a little complicated in the case of sales at different rates of VAT. The Revenue are prepared to accept returns showing *estimated* sales at different rates. However, the Revenue have clearly indicated how to arrive at such sales figures, based on purchases and the profit margin thereon. Thus, the trader must maintain adequate records relating to all his purchases.

There is a final point worth noting in relation to VAT. Since VAT liability is determined by the selling price, it is only fair that this liability should be reduced if cash discounts are made or goods returned etc. A taxable person may adjust his VAT liability in respect of returned goods, discounts or bad debts. However, in the case of bad debts, prior approval should be obtained from the Revenue before this adjustment is made. It is surprising the number of small businesses which do not take advantage of this concession.

ACCOUNTING FOR RESEARCH AND DEVELOPMENT COSTS (SSAP 13)

Expenditure on research and development can represent a considerable outlay for some firms and its accounting treatment will have a significant impact on a firm's reported profit performance and balance sheet position. The accounting problems for research and development arise because such expenditure is incurred with a view to providing benefits in the future. Thus, it can be viewed in the nature of capital expenditure and so could be written-off over a number of years. However, in many cases, when benefits do arise they cannot be specifically identified with research and development costs expended. There is also the very real problem that in many cases it is not known whether or not research and development costs will provide future benefits.

The ASC has found it difficult to produce an acceptable accounting standard on this matter. The main problem was the extensive lobbying from the aerospace and electronics industries in the UK. The ASC initially wanted in their exposure draft (ED 14) all R & D expenditure to be written-off in the year in which it was incurred, but the aerospace and electronics industries objected to this treatment. These industries spent considerable sums on research and development. Clearly the accounting treatment of such an important item was relevant to these companies, especially since most were engaged in government contracts. Such contracts generally allowed the contractor to cover his costs in addition to a profit margin based on a percentage of *capital employed*. Thus, it was in their interest to capitalise such expenditure which, in turn, would boost their capital employed figures and profit margins on contracts. In other words, if the provisions of ED 14 were followed, reported profits would dramatically fall, which would automatically reduce capital employed, and hence the profit allowed on government contract would also be reduced.

The accounting standard (SSAP 13) distinguished between research and development expenditure with separate accounting treatments for each category:

(*a*) *Pure research*: experimental or theoretical work undertaken primarily to acquire new scientific or technical knowledge for its own sake rather than directed towards any specific aim of application.

(*b*) *Applied research*: original or critical investigation undertaken in order to gain new scientific or technical knowledge and directed towards a specific practical aim or objective.

(*c*) *Development*: use of scientific or technical knowledge in order to produce new or substantially improved materials, devices, products or services, to install new processes or systems prior to the commencement of commercial production or commercial applications, or to substantially improving those already produced or installed.

In the case of both pure and applied research the standard requires that this expenditure be written-off in the profit and loss account in the year in which it was incurred. The rationale for this treatment is that no one period is expected to benefit from the expenditure.

Development expenditure should also be written-off in the year of expenditure, except in the following circumstances when it may be deferred to future periods:

(*a*) there is a clearly defined project;

(*b*) the related expenditure is separately identifiable;

(*c*) the outcome of such a project has been assessed with reasonable certainty as to its technical feasibility and its ultimate commercial viability.

This standard is more concerned with the prudence rather than the accruals concept since development expenditure must also be written-off in the year in which it was incurred. However, where the 'commercial success' of development expenditure is reasonably certain, the company may defer charging development expenditure to the extent that its recovery can be reasonably regarded as being assured. Thus, the standard requires the application of the prudence concept, except in clearly defined circumstances in relation to *development* expenditure only. However, a company may decide to write-off its development expenditure even though it complies with the above criteria.

There is an interesting interaction between SSAP 13 and the Companies (Amendment) Act, 1983. This act was concerned with the amount of profits which a firm could distribute. Section 45A of this act, concerning the treatment of development costs, provides that where the development costs are shown in a company's accounts any amount shown as an asset in respect of those costs shall be treated as a realised loss for the purpose of determining profits available for distribution. Thus, even though a company capitalises its development costs in accordance with recognised criteria, when determining profits available for distribution such development costs are treated as revenue expenditure.

It is also interesting to note the social process by which this standard was drafted and approved. It can be argued that accounting standard setting is a political process subject to inevitable pressures and compromises. In such cases, accounting arguments which propose 'theoretically correct views' become ammunition for the various participants in the debate. The overriding question is whether the content of financial statements satisfy the information needs of users.

POST-BALANCE SHEET EVENTS (SSAP 17) AND ACCOUNTING FOR CONTINGENCIES (SSAP 18)

Post-balance sheet events

Frequently there will be events occurring after balance date which may have an impact on the previous set of financial statements. SSAP 17 (*Accounting for Post-balance sheet Events*) directs our attention to such events. The accounting standard distinguishes between 'adjusting events' and 'non-adjusting events' and recommends appropriate accounting treatment.

Adjusting events are those events which provide additional evidence relating to conditions existing at balance sheet date. Even if they have occurred *after* balance sheet date, the standard requires that the amounts should be included in the financial statements. Examples of adjusting events are:

(*a*) Notification of the insolvency of a debtor.

(*b*) The discovery of errors which show that the draft financial statements were incorrect.

In both of the above circumstances the information was received on a *post-*balance sheet date but provided additional evidence relating to conditions existing at the balance sheet date. Consequently, the valuation of debtors will be revised and the errors eliminated from the financial statements.

Non-adjusting events also arise after the balance sheet date but concern conditions which did not exist at that time. Examples of non-adjusting events include:

(*a*) Government action, such as nationalisation.

(*b*) Loss of fixed assets as a result of a catastrophe such as fire or flood.

Because they do not relate to conditions pertaining at balance sheet date they do not result in changes of the amounts in the financial statements. They may, however, be of such materiality that their disclosure is required by way of note to the accounts to ensure that the financial statements are not misleading.

Accounting for contingencies

A contingency is defined in SSAP 18 as 'a condition which exists at balance date, where the outcome will be confirmed only on the occurrence or non-occurrence of one or more uncertain future events'. Thus, a contingent liability represents the *possibility* of a future obligation.

An excellent example of a contingent liability is that of a court action where the company is in the position of defendant. If the outcome is successfully defended, no damages will be awarded against the company. Alternatively, if the case goes against the company, it will involve significant liabilities. Perhaps the most common form of contingency noted in the financial statements of public companies is that related to government grants. Such grants are repayable if certain, specified conditions are not complied with. A typical note to the accounts would therefore read, 'There are contingent liabilities to repay in certain circumstances in whole or in part grants of £ . . . . received on certain grant aided assets'. Other examples are financial guarantees on behalf of other parties and product warranties issued to customers and still unexpired. Contingencies may also be favourable items as in insurance claims in respect of losses incurred or litigation likely to benefit the company. By their nature contingent liabilities are insufficiently concrete to warrant specific provisions being made for them in the accounts, and none is in fact made. Rather, it is adequate to disclose the nature of the contingent liability by way of note to the financial statements.

In deciding whether a liability should be classified as a contingent liability, one must be aware of the over-riding concept of prudence. Quite simply, if there is a material contingent loss which can be estimated with reasonable accuracy then it should be accrued and provided for in the financial statements. Otherwise it should be disclosed by way of note to the accounts. In keeping with the concept of prudence contingent gains would only be stated by way of note.

The standard avoids any attempt to determine categorically when the outcome of a contingency is sufficiently clear to warrant adjustments to the accounts. However, the auditing practices committee (APC), which is a committee of the six major accountancy bodies in these islands, made some attempt in this regard. They offered the following guidance on a 'rule of thumb' basis, which should be regarded as no more than a guide to a starting point for evaluating particular situations.

| | Contingent | |
Likelihood of crystallisation	Assets	Liabilities
1. Remote	Do not disclose	Do not disclose
2. Possible—probable	Do not disclose	Disclose by way of note
3. Highly probable	Disclose by way of note	Make specific provision
4. Virtually certain	Accrue	Make specific provision

The above guide serves to indicate when it is permissible to recognise gains, either by way of note or accrual in the accounts, and when it is permissible to allow losses or liabilities merely to be noted, as opposed to being provided in the accounts. In other words, it is necessary always to give careful consideration to the question of whether a potential gain or loss is genuinely a contingency at all.

In many cases, notes on contingent liabilities are of no real significance, for no liability is expected to arise, and none does. Occasionally, the important points to watch for are a sharp rise in the total sums involved, and liabilities that may arise outside the normal course of business, especially in the nature of guarantees.

ACCOUNTING FOR LEASED ASSETS (SSAP 21)

In recent years, a large amount of all new capital expenditure in Ireland has been financed through the mechanism of leasing. Among the assets financed in this way have been ships, aeroplanes, motor vehicles and plant and machinery. The principal advantage of leasing is that the lessee can use the asset immediately. Although the lease agreement is signed, he does not have to pay an immediate sum equivalent to its purchase price. Essentially, the lessee rents the asset over a number of years. The benefit to the lessor is that the cost of the asset can be written-off quickly for corporation tax purposes, since it is the owner and not the user who qualifies for tax allowances on the cost of the leased asset.

Traditionally, leasing was considered to be 'off balance sheet' financing. Since the lessee company did not own the asset, it did not appear on the balance sheet and neither did the financial obligations attaching to the lease. As a result the balance sheet, it was argued, did not provide an adequate picture of the total indebtedness of the firm. In addition, since the asset was not owned it was not necessary to provide for depreciation on the asset. Apart from the pure convenience of not having to calculate annual depreciation rates, the profit and loss account would reflect only the lease payments since this was the strict legal form of the lease agreement. Not suprisingly, financial ratios relating to overall profitability and gearing levels were not strictly comparable between companies that purchased their fixed assets outright and those who acquired them by way of lease arrangements.

As this growth in leasing developed, there was considerable pressure on accountants to record and disclose the substance of transactions, rather than their strict legal form. In particular, the pressure for recognition that the substance of the transaction was that the user enjoyed the use of the asset as if he owned it. Therefore the company should account for the asset as if it owned it. To explain the accounting treatment of leased assets it is first necessary to distinguish between financial and operating leases.

A *Finance* lease is one where the user of the asset (lessee) leased pays nearly the full cost of the asset (90 per cent +) plus finance charges over a primary lease period to which the user is irrevocably committed. The lease term is normally divided into a primary period and a secondary period. The lessee guarantees to pay rent in the primary period and this part of the contract is legally binding and non-cancellable. (The lessor earns the bulk of the profit during the primary period.) In the secondary period the lessee has the option to continue with the use of the asset for which he will pay a nominal rent to the lessor. The lessee will be responsible for maintenance and insurance.

An *operating* lease involves the lessee paying a rental for the hire of an asset for a period of time which is normally substantially less than its useful economic life. The lessor retains the risks and the rewards of ownership for repairs, maintenance and insurance. Under an operating lease, only the rental will be taken into account in the financial statements of the lessee.

Current thinking, contained in an accounting standard (SSAP 21), differentiates between these two types of leases. Under an operating lease, only the rental payments will be reflected in the profit and loss account of the lessee. In relation to finance leases the accounting standard requires the lessee to show the asset in its balance sheet, along with a recognition that the obligation under the lease represents a liability which should also appear in its balance sheet. This form of accounting for finance leases is described as *capitalisation of leases.*

Whilst the arithmetic leading to calculation of the asset and liability to be entered into the books of the lessee can be complex, the underlying thinking is not, and is explained in the simplified example as follows:

Example:

A firm enters into a finance lease on 1 January 19 . 1. The agreement provides for a primary period of five years, with rentals of £10,000 per annum, payable in advance. The secondary period, commencing in the sixth year, calls only for a nominal rental. The estimated useful life of the asset is eight years, and if purchased outright by the lessee would have cost £41,700. For simplicity, taxation is to be ignored. The calculations need to be performed before accounting entries are made as follows:

Exhibit 11.1

	Balance at 1 Jan. (1)	Payments made on 1 Jan. (2)	(3) (1) – (2)	Interest* for year (4) 10% x (3)	Balance at 31 Dec. (5) (3) + (4)
	£	£	£	£	£
19 . 1	41700	10000	31700	3170	34870
19 . 2	34870	10000	24870	2487	27357
19 . 3	27357	10000	17357	1735	19092
19 . 4	19092	10000	9092	908	10000
19 . 5	10000	10000	Nil	Nil	Nil
		£50,000		£8,300	

* The rate of interest is calculated by obtaining the interest implicit in the lease, which is the rate of interest which equates the £41,700 cost and the annual payments of £10,000, having due regard to the timing of the cash flows. The rate is 10%

Accounting entries by lessee to reflect capitalisation

1. Set up both asset and liability at £41,700. This corresponds to the present value of minimum lease payments, i.e.:

DR. Leased asset a/c   £41,700

CR. Lease obligation a/c   £41,700

2. The accumulated interest charges are recorded since they will also have to be paid:

DR. Finance charge suspense a/c   £8,300

CR. Lease obligation a/c   £8,300

3. The annual lease payment of £10,000 will be recorded as follows:

DR. Lease obligation a/c   £10,000

CR. Bank a/c   £10,000

4. At the end of the year, the asset will be depreciated. Depreciation will be based over five years. using straight-line depreciation, the annual charge will be £8,340, thus:

DR. Depreciation a/c   £8,340

CR. Aggregate depreciation a/c   £8,340

5. The profit and loss account will bear an interest charge (col. 4) each year. In the first year, the entries will be:

DR. Interest expense a/c   £3,170

CR. Interest suspense a/c   £3,170

6. The outstanding liability (col. 5) will appear in the balance sheets at year ends subdivided into short- and long-term components.

Extracts from the profit and loss accounts for the five-year period will be as follows:

Expense heading	Year 1	Year 2	Year 3	Year 4	Year 5
Depreciation	8,340	8,340	8,340	8,340	8,340
Interest	3,170	2,487	1,735	908	Nil *

* Since payments are made at the start of the year, no interest is payable in year five.

Balance sheet extract will be as follows:

Fixed Assets	Year 1	Year 2	Year 3	Year 4	Year 5
	£	£	£	£	£
Tangible asset—cost	41,700	41,700	41,700	41,700	41,700
Aggregate depreciation	8,340	16,680	25,020	33,360	41,700
Creditors (amounts falling due within one year)	7,513*	8,265	9,092	10,000	Nil
Creditors (amounts falling due after more than one year)	27,357	19,092	10,000	Nil	Nil

*Payment for year   £10,000

less interest for year 2   (2,487)

                                    7,513 etc

THE FUTURE OF ACCOUNTING STANDARDS

Undoubtedly, the existence of SSAPs have improved the quality of financial reporting. Extensive policy notes are now a normal part of financial statements and there is a broad consistency in reporting the financial impact of transactions and events. The consultative process in the development of accounting standards has widened the exposure of accounting practice to various interested parties including the Stock Exchange and financial analysts. Awareness of accounting issues has been enhanced by this exposure.

The ASC has seen its workload increasing dramatically during the 1980s. Much of the committee's time during that period has been spent on revising existing standards, some as a result of changing company legislation. Concurrently with the effort to update SSAPs, the ASC was aware of a growing emphasis on the literal interpretation of accounting standards. For example, some companies have recently included 'brands and newspaper titles' as an asset on their balance sheet. The wide variety of accounting for brands is potentially dangerous. Indeed, the attitude of 'what is not prohibited by an accounting standard must be acceptable' is gaining acceptance. Such attitudes are being used to circumvent recommended accounting practices which prove onerous or disagreeable. Some accounting policies adopted by companies can be politely stated as being 'aggressive' while others are quite 'creative'. This is in spite of the explanatory foreword to the accounting standards which states that 'in applying accounting standards, it will be important to have regard to the spirit and reasoning behind them . . . they do not supersede the exercise of an informed judgment in determining what constitutes a true and fair view in each circumstance'.

The ASC has always avoided the 'cookbook' approach to accounting standards setting, maintaining that professional judgment should be allowed determine the appropriateness of certain treatments in differing circumstances. However, the legalistic interpretation of standards will only compound the problem of inconsistency in the absence of specific, clear regulations.

The ASC has to work with limited resources. As a part-time voluntary committee with a small secretariat, a 'fire-fighting' approach has to be adopted. Also the ASC exists within a cumbersome structure. The structure such that each of the six accountancy bodies that comprise the consultative committee of accountancy bodies (CCAB) has a right veto the pronouncements of the ASC. Thus, there is the necessity to command broad support for its proposals, which results often in compromise and diluted accounting standards. Accounting standards tend to be documents which are 'acceptable' rather than controversial. On occasions, there is a total 'U-turn' in drafting an accountancy standard. For example, in the attempt to draft an accounting standard on changing prices where the original standard (SSAP 7) was withdrawn and replaced by an entirely different standard (SSAP 16), which in turn was withdrawn but not replaced.

Not suprisingly, timeliness is not a characteristic which the ASC has been able to demonstrate. It is compounded by the increasing complexity of the various accounting issues with which it is faced. For some time now, there have been concerns, sometimes conflicting, on the nature and role of accounting standards. When companies, for various reasons but mainly for self-interest, departed from standards, views were expressed that there should be greater enforceability. At the same time, other voices expressed concern that accounting standards were being promoted to take over rather than to support professional judgment. Yet again, other concerns expressed were that, because accounting standards were developed and promoted by the accountancy profession alone, they did not carry sufficient weight to ensure full compliance, particularly in the more sensitive areas of measurement and valuation. Indeed, the ASC has been criticised for giving an exalted credibility to financial statements by using the title statement of *standard* accounting practice for its pronouncements which suggests that there is only one acceptable accounting treatment for the topic covered.

Other criticisms are that the ASC is too slow in dealing with emerging issues; that the ASC's recommendations are compromises without foundation in sound principles; and that the standards are produced in a haphazard manner in response to accounting abuses as distinct from clearly defined segments of an overall strategy to improve financial reporting.

It is against such criticisms that the ASC appointed the Deering Committee in November 1987 to investigate the making of accounting standards. The report makes recommendations for fundamental changes in the process of setting accounting standards. Moves to advance these recommendations are now being made, and if they are fully implemented will result in the formation of a powerful standards-setting authority. This Financial Reporting Council (FRC) will have two main divisions: an Accounting Standards Board (ASB) which will draft and issue accounting standards and a Review Panel which will monitor compliance with accounting standards. Standards will be definitive with strictly limited user discretion. Among the recommendations made by Deering are:

(*a*) The concern should be with increasing the quality and timeliness of accounting standards and reducing the permitted options.

(*b*) New accounting standards should be developed by a new Accounting Standards Boards, with a full-time chairman and technical director. The Board would issue standards on its own authority.

(*c*) The Accounting Standards Board should establish a capability of high standing to publish authoritative, though non-mandatory, guidance on emerging issues.

(*d*) On the basis of a cost-benefit test, the proposed Accounting Standards Board should express a clear view on the extent to which accounting standards should apply to small companies.

(*e*) Accounting standards should carry a statement of the principles underlying them and of the reasons why alternatives were rejected.

(*f*) There should be a general presumption in any legal proceedings that all accounting standards will have the support of the courts.

(*g*) A top-level Financial Reporting Council should be created. The council would guide the standard-setting body on work programmes and issues of public concern and would act as a powerful proactive public influence for securing good accounting practice.

(*h*) A review panel should be set up to examine contentious departures from accounting standards by large companies.

(*i*) Standards should remain the responsibility of auditors, preparers and users of financial statements; there should not be a general move towards incorporating them into law. But to facilitate the effect of published financial reporting, government should introduce legislation along the following lines:

- (*i*) In the case of all large companies, directors should be required to state in the notes to the accounts whether these are drawn up in accordance with applicable accounting standards and to draw attention to any material departures.
- (*ii*) There should be a new statutory power under civil law for certain authorised bodies to apply to the courts for an order requiring the revision of accounts that do not give a true and fair view.
- (*iii*) A small levy should be added to the annual fees paid by all companies to the Companies Office to assist in meeting the cost of setting and monitoring accounting standards

The necessary legislation has already been passed in the UK and enabling legislation is expected for Ireland in the near future. Consequently, in Ireland and the UK the development of accounting standards will be taken over by an independent organisation funded from a multiplicity of sources, including government, and reporting to a widely representative Financial Reporting Council. Standards will not have explicit legal backing but will have legal recognition. Furthermore, compliance monitoring and review functions will feature in the new machinery. Such mechanisms will undoubtedly improve the credibility of the accountancy profession as well as the quality of financial reporting in these islands.

QUESTION 11.1 (SM)

You are advising the owner of a small retail store which has just completed its first year of trading on 31 December 19 . 6. The store buys and sells only one category of commodity which is liable to a 10 per cent VAT rate.

You are presented with the following information regarding purchases and sales (exclusive of VAT) during the year: (see overleaf)

Period	Purchases on Credit Units	Credit Sales Units	Cash Sales Units
Jan.-Mar. 19 . 6	1,500 @ £5 each	400 @ £10 each	200 @ £10 each
Apr.-Jun. 19 . 6	1,500 @ £6 each	1,100 @ £11 each	500 @ £10 each
Jul.-Sep. 19 . 6	3,500 @ £7 each	2,500 @ £13 each	500 @ £12 each
Oct.-Dec. 19 . 6	3,500 @ £8 each	2,500 @ £18 each	600 @ £12 each

Payments to creditors during the year amounted to £63,000 and cash received from debtors amounted to £92,000. Payments in respect of VAT amounted to £4,500.

Requirement:

(*a*) Prepare summarised debtors and creditors control accounts to record the above information.

(*b*) Calculate the closing stock valuation using the first in, first out, method (FIFO);

(*c*) Prepare the trading account for the year ended 31 December 19 . 6, assuming a closing stock valuation of £20,000.

(The Institute of Chartered Accountants in Ireland)

QUESTION 11.2 (SM)

The following figures have been extracted from the records of Orange Ltd for the year to 31 December 19 . 6:

	1 Jan. 19 . 6 £	31 Dec. 19 . 6 £
Creditors	20,000	25,000
Debtors	10,000	12,000
VAT Account	5,000 cr	?
Summary of transactions for the year		
Invoiced sales including VAT		220,000
Sales returns including VAT		1,100
Bank payments		
Trade creditors including VAT		206,000
Revenue commissioners for VAT		3,000

Note: (1) There is a uniform rate of VAT of 10 per cent on all purchase and sales transactions.

Requirement:

(*a*) Prepare the ledger accounts necessary to record the above transactions for the year ended 31 December 19 . 6.

(*b*) Indicate the entries to be included in the firm's trading account for the year ended 31 December 19 . 6.

(The Institute of Chartered Accountants in Ireland)

QUESTION 11.3 (SM)

Explain clearly the following terms as an accountant would understand them:

(*a*) Financial accounting.

(*b*) Realisation.

(*c*) Matching.

(*d*) Materiality.

(The Chartered Association of Certified Accountants)

QUESTION 11.4 (SM)

The Companies (Amendment) Act 1986 allows small companies to file with the Registrar of Companies modified accounts which contain less detail than the full accounts filed by large companies.

The Accounting Standards Committee gives no such exemption to small companies from its Statements of Standard Accounting Practice.

Do you consider that the Accounting Standards Committee approach to financial statements of small companies is justified?

State your reasons.

(The Chartered Association of Certified Accountants)

QUESTION 11.5 (SM)

The Explanatory Foreword to the Statements of Standard Accounting Practice issued by the Accounting Standards Committee in August 1986 states:

(*a*) Statements of Standard Accounting Practice are developed in the public interest by the Accounting Standards Committee.

(*b*) In applying accounting standards, it will be important to have regard to the spirit of and reasoning behind them.

Discuss the significance of *both* of these statements.

(The Chartered Association of Certified Accountants)

QUESTION 11.6 (SM)

Thatcher is managing director of Grocers Company and has written to you asking you to explain to her certain aspects of her company's accounts which she does not understand. You are required to write a letter explaining in simple and concise terms the following matters which she has raised:

(*a*) Stocks:

Stocks stand in the balance sheet at £20,000. However, according to Thatcher, they have a selling price of £30,000 and would cost her at least £24,000 to purchases at current prices. Why the lower figure?

(*b*) Fixed assets: Extract from balance sheet:

	Cost	Depreciation	
	£	£	£
Land and buildings	50,000	(1,000)	49,000
Motor vehicles	30,000	(22,000)	8,000
Equipment	1,000	(999)	1

Thatcher is puzzled over the following points:

(1) depreciation of 2 per cent on land and buildings has never been charged before, and she reckons they are worth £75,000;

(2) the motor vehicles are four years old and are now worth only £7,000. They will cost £50,000 to replace, which she plans to do at the end of the year;

(3) the equipment is five years old but still works well and is worth £500.

You should incorporate in your answer an explanation of what depreciation is and why a charge is made against profit each year.

QUESTION 11.7 (SM)

During the course of a year Newprods Ltd incurred expenditure on many research and development activities. Details of three of them are given below.

Project 3.

To develop a new compound in view of the anticipated shortage of raw material currently being used on one of the company's processes. Sufficient progress has been made to suggest that the new compound can be produced at a cost comparable to that of the existing raw material.

Project 4.

To improve the yield of an important manufacturing operation of the company. At present, material input with a cost of £100,000 p.a. becomes contaminated in the operation and half is wasted. Sufficient progress has been made for the scientists to predict an improvement so that only 20 per cent will be wasted.

Project 5.

To carry out work, as specified by a creditworthy client, in an attempt to bring a proposed aerospace product of that client into line with safety regulations.

Costs incurred during the year were:

Project	3	4	5
	£	£	£
Staff salaries	5,000	10,000	20,000
Overheads	6,000	12,000	24,000
Plant at cost			
(life 10 years)	10,000	20,000	5,000

Requirement:

(*a*) State the circumstances in which it may be appropriate to carry forward research and development expenditure to future periods.

(*b*) Show how the expenditure on projects 3, 4 and 5 would be dealt with in the balance sheet and profit and loss account in accordance with SSAP 13.

QUESTION 11.8 (SM)

(*a*) How does SSAP 18 Accounting for Contingencies define a contingency?

(*b*) What information should be disclosed in financial statements with regard to contingencies?

(*c*) State, with reasons, how you would account for the following items:

(*i*) The directors of a company have discovered a painting in a cupboard and have sent it to an auction house, who have confirmed that it should sell for £1m. in the following month's auction.

(*ii*) A claim has been made against a company for injury suffered by a pedestrian in connection with building work by the company. Legal advisers have confirmed that the company will probably have to pay damages of £200,000 but that a claim can be made against the building sub-contractors for £100,000.

(*iii*) A company uses 'recourse factoring' whereby the company agrees with the factor to re-purchase any debts not paid to the factor within 90 days of the sales invoice date. In the year ended 30 June 19.7 the factored credit sales of the company were £2m. of which £1.8m. had been paid to the factor, £150,000 was unpaid but due within 90 days and £50,000 was unpaid for more than 90 days.

(*iv*) The manufacturer of a snooker table has received a letter from a professional snooker player, who was defeated in the final of a major snooker competition, threatening to sue the manufacturer for £1m. being his estimate of his loss of earnings through failing to win the competition, on the grounds that the table was not level.

(The Chartered Association of Certified Accountants)

QUESTION 11.9 (SM)

(*a*) Give a definition of the following:

(*i*) Off-balance sheet finance;

(*ii*) Window-dressing.

(*b*) Discuss how the Accounting Standards Committee has tackled *both* of these issues.

(The Chartered Association of Certified Accountants)

QUESTION 11.10 (A)

You are the Financial Controller of Liffey Ltd and are finalising the company's accounts for the year ended 31 December 19 . 6 before approval by the board of directors on 31 March, 19 . 7. The draft accounts, which have been prepared by your assistant, show a turnover of £9m. and a profit before tax of £750,000.

You are given the following information:

(1) A customer went into liquidation on 21 March, 19 . 7, at which date the balance owing was £450,000. The liquidator has indicated that the assets will be insufficient to pay secured and preferential creditors in full. The balance owing (by the customer) at 31 December, 19 . 6 was £400,000.

(2) The profit before tax is arrived at after charging £75,000 redundancy and other costs associated with the closure of one of the company's factories.

(3) A director of the company was dismissed on 30 June 19 . 6, and received an ex-gratia payment of £40,000.

(4) During January 19 . 7 modification was received of a claim by a customer for £20,000 arising out of a fire at his home which he alleged was the result of a malfunction of an electrical appliance which had been manufactured by Liffey Ltd are of the opinion that the claim is reasonable and that the company should offer £17,000 in settlement.

The company does not carry product liability insurance.

(5) Included in the draft balance sheet at 31 December 19 . 6 is a freehold property shown at book value of £125,000. In February 19   7 the company completed negotiations to sell the property for £750,000. The proceeds were received in March 19 . 7. Taxation of £180,000 will be payable on the profit on sale.

(6) Shannon Ltd alleges that Liffey Ltd has infringed a patent registered by Shannon Ltd and is claiming £400,000 as damages. The legal advisors to Liffey Ltd are of the opinion that there is an 80 per cent chance that the company will not be held liable by the courts and a 20 per cent chance that the company will be required to pay the claim in full.

(7) A contingent liability of £40,000 has been disclosed in the financial statements for the year ended 31 December 19 . 5, following a violation by Liffey Ltd of a sales contract in which there were penalty clauses. In February 19 . 7 a compromise was reached and Liffey Ltd paid the customer £30,000 in settlement.

Requirement:

Explain, with reasons, the accounting treatment which you consider Liffey Ltd should follow in respect of items (1) to (7) above, in preparing the financial statements for the year ended 31 December 19 . 6. You are not required to draft extracts from the financial statements.

QUESTION 11.11 (SM)

Mr George Green is a sole trader who has produced the following receipts and payments account for the year ended 31 December 19 . 3:

Receipts	£	Payments	£
Lodgments	93,248	Balance at Bank	
Transfer from deposit		1 January 19 . 3	6,017
account	1,020	Wages and PAYE	9,127
Receipt from creditors	34	Creditors	49,876
		Rent and rates	816
		Light and heat	5,129
		VAT	3,800
		Telephone	803
		Transfer to deposit	
		account	1,000
		Balance at bank on	
		31 December 19 . 3	17,734
	94,302		94,302

Mr Green also provides you with the following information:

(1) All purchases and sales are on credit. The VAT rate, which applies only to purchases and sales, is 20%

(2) The book value of the premises on 31 December 19 . 2, was £15,000. The original cost of the premises was £40,000. Depreciation should be provided at the rate of 20% per annum, using the reducing balance method.

(3) Details of other assets and liabilities are as follows:

	31 December 19 . 2	31 December 19 . 3
	£	£
Stock at cost	9,423	9,010
Debtors	4,250	15,879
Creditors	2,310	6,366
Wages due	292	618
VAT due	1,200	?

(4) During the year, discounts allowed were estimated at £1,026 and discounts received amounted to £924.

(5) Lodgments were made to the bank after making the following payments:

	£
Payments to creditors	678
light and heat	219
Refunds to debtors	198

(6) It is estimated that one quarter of the light and heat expense should be treated as drawings.

(7) During the year contra entries amounting to £1,200 were recorded in the debtors and the creditors ledgers.

Requirement:
You are required to prepare:

(*a*) A trading and profit and loss account for the year ended 31 December 19 . 3;

(*b*) A balance sheet as at that date.

(The Institute of Chartered Accountants in Ireland)

12.

Accounting for Groups of Companies

AMALGAMATION AND INTEGRATION OF COMPANIES

Corporate mergers and acquisitions have been a common phenomenon during the past twenty years and are set to continue throughout the 1990s. A number of top-quality Irish companies—Smurfits, Cement Roadstone, Allied Irish Banks and Bank of Ireland—have become significant international entities by means of international acquisitions. For example, in 1978/79 the Smurfit Group generated 78 per cent of its sales in Ireland and the UK. Ten years later the same market accounted for only 20 per cent of the group's revenue. Currently, more than 80 per cent of the Smurfit Group profits are generated in North America. Another example is that of Food Industries plc which dominates the domestic scene as a result of local takeovers and amalgamations in recent years.

The process of amalgamation leading to the domination of markets by large firms can be thought of as inevitable. It also leads to the concentration of industry and the reduction of competition within an economic system. However, it can be claimed that the process is desirable, because it allows individual firms to combine in order to compete in world, rather than national, markets. While accepting that amalgamations can lead to a reduction in competition, it is argued that appropriate government action or action by the European Community can alter the rules of the game to ensure that competition is kept alive.

Mergers and acquisitions

In order to grow, a company can expand its product range, enter new markets with existing products or diversify into a totally new business, for example, Carroll Industries plc, which has recently diversified into targeted direct marketing and aquaculture. A company wishing to grow by breaking into a new geographical market could hire more salesmen and marketing staff, and rent offices and showrooms in the new area. This effort is generated from within the company, and can be described as internal growth.

Alternatively, the company could decide to grow by amalgamation. Rather than spend resources on a thrust into the new market, the capital could be used to buy a company already in that market. This is external growth—growth by acquisition—which is now a well-accepted part of corporate strategy. Legally, mergers can be distinguished from acquisitions, but from a financial viewpoint there is rarely a significant difference.

In a merger situation, the businesses of the amalgamating companies continue after amalgamation. In many cases, the amalgamating companies are of comparable size and some of the members of the amalgamating companies are able to remain members of the enlarged business unit. As the businesses are to continue, the members of all the amalgamating companies should, as members of the new unit, be able to retain some control of future decisions.

In an acquisition, the members of the acquired company agree (however reluctantly) to give up ownership of their company. Amalgamations can be classified as either *horizontal, vertical* or *conglomerate*. The difference is indicated in Exhibit 12.1:

Exhibit 12.1

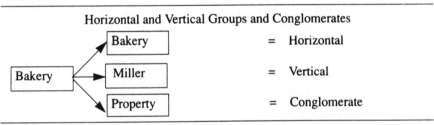

Horizontal and Vertical Groups and Conglomerates

Bakery = Horizontal

Bakery → Miller = Vertical

Property = Conglomerate

Horizontal amalgamation is the amalgamation of business units engaged in the same stage of the production or service process (i.e. amalgamation of bakery companies). Horizontal takeovers are undertaken to capture specific markets, to increase market share or to eliminate competition. Capital intensive industries often find it easier to buy market share rather than to develop new sales. Vertical integration is the amalgamation of business units engaged in the related stages of a productive or service process (i.e. amalgamation of bakery companies with milling companies). Vertical buyers are seeking acquisitions that will enable them to gain greater efficiencies through integration, either forward by buying distributors and/or retail outlets or backward by acquiring supply and/or manufacturing capability, e.g. the takeover of Dakota, the print and packaging firm, by Carrolls. Dakota produced all the packets for Carrolls so that vertical integration made good economic sense. Vertical integration can also take place across international boundries since manufacturers have good reason to integrate backwards to protect the supply of their raw materials.

Conglomerate amalgamation is the amalgamation of business units engaged in productive or service processes with no immediate business links. The era of the conglomerate in Ireland occurred in the late 1960s/ early 1970s when conglomerates such as Fitzwilton were formed. Apart from growth aspirations, there are numerous reasons why companies amalgamate. Chiefly:

(*a*) where there is a shortage of raw materials. In these circumstances, a company may try to ensure a source of supply by buying companies producing the relevant raw materials.

(*b*) where there is over-capacity in an industry. This is often found in declining industries, and has been a feature of some amalgamations in recent years. Amalgamations in these circumstances aim to reduce competition and to help stabilise prices.

(*c*) because of the desire to obtain technology, management or special skills controlled by another.

(*d*) to achieve economies of scale.

CONSOLIDATED BALANCE SHEETS (SSAP 14)

The most frequently encountered method of arranging amalgamations is where one company acquires control of another company by purchasing a majority of its voting shares. This leads to a common structure of a holding company with a number of operating subsidiary companies. The holding or parent company owns either all or the majority of shares of these subsidiary companies. A typical group structure can be depicted as follows:

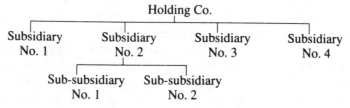

In some cases, the parent or holding company is a non-trading company. It may simply hold the investments in the subsidiary companies, many of which can be trading in different countries with their own subsidiaries. The parent company of a vast group could comprise merely an office with a few legal and financial staff.

If the financial statements of the group were to show the assets, liabilities and profit of the holding company, this would be very misleading. For example, without consolidation of earnings the holding company would show as income only dividends received from its subsidiaries. In addition, the performance and financial position of all the subsidiary companies would not be revealed. Therefore, according to company law the shareholders of the holding company must receive 'group accounts' which can be presented in a number of alternative ways. However, SSAP 14 requires a single set of *consolidated* accounts (subject to exceptions) for the group using what is referred to as the acquisition method.

The basic technique of consolidation involves adding together all the external assets and external liabilities of the group. Thus, any inter-group loans are automatically cancelled out in addition to eliminating inter-company trading and profits. It is simplistic but nevertheless accurate to suggest that the aim of consolidation accounts is to produce a set of accounts for the group as if it were a single operating entity. In other words, the concept of separate legal entity is set aside for accounting reporting purposes. The basic features of consolidated (i.e. group) accounts are:

(*a*) Inter-company transactions are eliminated from group accounts.

(*b*) The share capital in the consolidated balance sheet is only that of the parent company of the group.

(*c*) In the majority of cases, the fixed and current assets, together with liabilities of all the companies, can be aggregated and included in the consolidated balance sheet. This applies irrespective of whether the subsidiaries are wholly owned or not. Thus we see the total fixed assets etc., controlled by the group.

(*d*) In the process of consolidation, the share capital and pre-acquisition reserves of the subsidiary companies are set against the price paid for the shares which will be shown on the balance sheet of the parent company. Any excess of the investment over the capital and reserves at the date of acquisition is called *goodwill arising on consolidation.*

The treatment of goodwill arising on consolidation has aroused controversy from time to time. Some companies write the goodwill off against reserves as soon as they can, and this automatically removes it from the balance sheet. Other companies leave goodwill on the balance sheet and write-off a portion of it annually to the profit and loss account. In SSAP 22, the accountancy profession agreed that goodwill arising as a result of consolidation should be treated in either of two ways:

(*i*) it should be written-off immediately against group reserves. (This is the preferred treatment according to the standard.)
(*ii*) it should be written off systematically against group profits over its estimated useful life.

However, more recent proposals by the accountancy profession (ED 47) recommend that goodwill be shown on the balance sheet as an asset and depreciated over its estimated useful life.

(*e*) The process of consolidation does not take place within the books or records of any of the companies involved. There is no 'double entry'. Rather, consolidation is computed in separate workings outside normal accounting records. Thus goodwill arising on consolidation appears only in the consolidated accounts and *not* in the accounts of the individual companies.

(*f*) It is important to identify whether all the subsidiary's shares are held by the holding company (a wholly owned subsidiary) or whether it is a partially owned subsidiary, i.e. there are outside shareholders. This latter situation will give rise to the phenomenon of minority interests. For balance sheet purposes, the value of minority interests corresponds to the proportion of net assets of the subsidiary which is not owned by the holding company. This calculation is entirely due to the consolidation technique whereby the assets etc. of all the subsidiary companies are aggregated (see (*c*) above) even though some of them are not wholly owned. We shall see later that minority interests will also appear on the consolidated profit and loss account.

Example:

The balance sheet of Peter Ltd and its subsidiary, Pan Ltd, are set out below for the year ended 31 December 19 . 1. Peter Ltd has held its shares in Pan Ltd since the date of Pan's incorporation.

	Peter Ltd £	Pan Ltd £
Fixed assets	140,000	150,000
Investment in Pan Ltd (80,000 £1 ordinary shares)	100,000	
Current assets	60,000	65,000
Loan to Pan Ltd	10,000	
	310,000	215,000
Financed by:		
Ordinary shares of £1 ea	120,000	100,000
Revaluation reserve	55,000	40,000
Profit and loss account	105,000	50,000
	280,000	190,000
Current liabilities	30,000	15,000
Loan from Peter Ltd		10,000
	310,000	215,000

Requirement:

You are required to prepare a consolidated balance sheet of the group as at 31 December 19 . 1.

Exhibit 12.2

CONSOLIDATED BALANCE SHEET AT 31 DECEMBER 19 . 1

Fixed assets

Tangible assets (*Note 1*)	290,000
Intangible assets (*Note 2*)	20,000
Current assets (*Note 1*)	125,000
	435,000

Financed by

Share capital (*Note 3*)	120,000
Revaluation reserve (*Note 4*)	87,000
Profit and loss account (*Note 4*)	145,000
Minority interests (*Note 5*)	38,000
Current liabilities (*Note 1*)	45,000
	435,000

Note 1: Schedule of assets and liabilities

	Peter Ltd £	Pan Ltd £	Total £
Fixed assets	140,000	150,000	290,000
Current assets	60,000	65,000	125,000
Current liabilities	30,000	15,000	45,000

Note 2: Intangible assets—Goodwill arising on consolidation

Cost of investment (Peter's books)	100,000
Share capital acquired (80% x £100,000; Pan's books)	80,000
Reserves acquired	Nil
Goodwill, since cost of acquisition exceeded capital and reserves acquired	20,000

In SSAP 22, the accountancy profession agreed that goodwill arising on consolidation should be treated in either of two ways:

1. It should be written off immediately against group reserves.

2. It should be written off systematically against group profits over its estimated useful life.

More recent proposals from the ASC recommend that goodwill should be shown on the balance sheet as an asset and depreciated over its estimated economic life.

Note 3: the share capital in the consolidated balance sheet is always that of the parent (holding) company.

Note 4:	Capital reserves £	Revenue reserves £
As per Peter's books	55,000	105,000
Add: 80% share of Pan's reserves	32,000	40,000
	87,000	145,000

Note 5: Minority interests   £

Share capital of Pan Ltd	(20% x £100,000)	=	20,000
Capital reserves of Pan Ltd	(20% x £40,000)	=	8,000
Revenue reserves of Pan Ltd	(20% x £50,000)	=	10,000
			38,000

Note 6: The inter-company loan is eliminated, being an asset in Peter's books and a liability in Pan's books.

Definitions of a subsidiary company

We have looked at the concept and technique of preparing group accounts. However, we have ignored the regulatory environment within which consolidation takes place. The Companies Act 1963 and SSAP 14 broadly specify that a company shall be deemed to be a subsidiary of another if that other either:

(a) is a member of it and controls the composition of the board of directors; or

(b) holds more than half of the nominal value of its equity share capital; or

(c) the first mentioned company is a subsidiary of a company which itself is a subsidiary, i.e. a sub-subsidiary.

The term 'equity share capital' means all share capital which carries the right to participate beyond a specified amount in a liquidation. Thus, preference shares carrying a fixed dividend and having no voting rights may neverthe-less be 'equity' share capital for this purpose if they are entitled to participate beyond a fixed amount in the surplus assets, if any, on a liquidation.

Standard accounting practice

In accordance with standard accounting practice a holding company should prepare group accounts in the form of a single set of consolidated financial statements covering the holding company and its subsidiaries, both at home and abroad.

Financial statements of all subsidiary companies should have the same accounting year-end as the holding company. This conforms with the legal requirement that the directors of the holding company should ensure that the financial year-ends coincide unless there is good reason.

The two principal exceptions to the requirement of preparing group accounts are:

(*a*) A subsidiary should be excluded from consolidation where its activities are so dissimilar from those of other companies within the group that consolidated financial statements would be misleading and that information for the holding company's shareholders and other users of the statements would be better provided for by presenting separate financial statements for such a subsidiary.

(*b*) If the subsidiary company operates under severe restrictions which significantly impair control by the holding company over the subsidiary's assets and operations for the foreseeable future, it should be excluded from consolidation.

Where these exceptions are availed of, the reason for the exclusion from group accounts must be stated in the financial statements. In addition, the Companies Act 1963 stipulates that the financial statements of such an excluded subsidiary must be available to shareholders, on request.

CONSOLIDATED PROFIT AND LOSS ACCOUNTS (SSAP 14)

The consolidated profit and loss account will show the *aggregated* sales (to external parties), profit and tax figures of the group. Because of this, aggregation may include subsidiary companies which are not wholly owned, and an adjustment must be made for a 'minority interest' share in the group profits. This adjustment is fairly simple since the share of the after-tax profit due to the minority shareholders in subsidiary companies is shown as a deduction from group profit to arrive at 'profit attributable to the company'. A typical consolidated profit and loss account appears in Exhibit 12.3

Exhibit 12.3

CONSOLIDATED PROFIT AND LOSS ACCOUNT FOR YEAR ENDED . .

	£m
Turnover	4,300
Operating costs	4,226
Profit on ordinary activities before taxation	74
Tax on profits on ordinary activities	28
Profit on ordinary activities after tax	46
Minority interests	10
Profit after tax and minority interests	36
Dividends (ordinary)	15

Profit retained for year	21
Profit brought forward	16
Profit carried forward	37

Note: EPS calculation will be based on £36m. divided by the number of ordinary shares in issue. Thus, minority interests are automatically deducted in computing EPS.

In the above example, and in most cases in practice, minority interests are a deduction from group profit after taxation. In other words, having included all the profit after tax of the subsidiary in the group profit and loss account, the accountant then deducts that portion of profits attributable to minority interests. It can happen that minority interests are *added* to profit on ordinary activities after tax. Such a treatment generally reflects that the subsidiary company traded at a loss for the period. Since the entire loss (a negative item) is included in the group profit and loss account 'above the line', then the adjustment for minority interests must be positive.

Finally, the absence of minority interests in the group profit and loss account indicates that all the subsidiary companies are wholly (100 per cent) owned.

Example:

The following are summarised profit and loss accounts of H Ltd and its 80 per cent subsidiary, S Ltd. There is no inter-company trading and H Ltd has held its shares in S Ltd since the date of incorporation

PROFIT AND LOSS ACCOUNTS FOR YEAR ENDED 31 DECEMBER 19 . 1

	H Ltd	*S Ltd*
Turnover	125,000	63,000
Operating costs	106,000	52,000
Operating profit	19,000	11,000
Taxation	7,000	6,000
Profit on ordinary activities after tax	12,000	5,000
Profit brought forward	10,000	5,000
Profit carried forward	22,000	10,000

Requirement:

Prepare a consolidated profit and loss account for the year ended 31 December 19 . 1.

The consolidated profit and loss account appears in Exhibit 12.4: (see overleaf)

Note 1: £10,000 + 80% x £5,000

Note 2: EPS would be based on profit of £16,000

Exhibit 12.4

CONSOLIDATED PROFIT AND LOSS ACCOUNT FOR YEAR
ENDED 31 DECEMBER 19 . 1

	£
Turnover	188,000
Operating costs	158,000
Profit on ordinary activities before tax	30,000
Tax on profit on ordinary activities	13,000
Profit on ordinary activities after tax	17,000
Minority interests (20% x £5,000)	1,000
Profit after tax and minority interests	16,000
Profit brought forward (note 1)	14,000
Profit carried forward	30,000

ACCOUNTING FOR ASSOCIATED COMPANIES (SSAP 1)

It has been seen that the Companies Act 1963 requires consolidation where one company acquires a majority interest in the equity of another. It was left to the accounting profession to note that there was a growing practice among companies of acquiring a substantial, but not a controlling, interest in other companies, and that the mere disclosure or inclusion of dividend income arising from these investments did not give the investing company's shareholders adequate information about the sources of their income nor the manner in which their funds were being employed.

The accounting profession decided that for such substantial, but not controlling, interests, an additional form of group accounts should be employed. This accounting treatment is known as *equity accounting*. The requirement for this equity accounting was to be an investing company— associated company relationship, and details are to be found in SSAP 1.

Definition of 'Associated Company'

A company (not being a subsidiary of the investing group or company) is an associated company of the investing group or company if:

(a) the interest of the investing group or company is effectively that of a partner of joint venture or consortium and the investing group or company is in a position to exercise a significant influence over the company in which the investment is made; or

(b) the interest of the investing group or company is for the long term and is substantial and, having regard to the disposition of the other share-holdings, the investing group or company is in a position to exercise a significant influence over the company in which the investment is made.

In both cases, it is essential that the investing group or company exercises significant influence by participating in the financial and operating policy decisions of the associated company, including the distribution of profits, but not necessarily control over those policies. Representation on the board of directors is indicative of such participation, but it will neither give conclusive evidence of it nor be the only method by which the investing company may participate in policy decisions.

There are three important terms introduced by the above definition, namely, 'long-term nature', 'substantial holding' and 'significant influence'.

Whether or not an investment is held for the long term depends on a number of factors. One such factor is the reason for which the investment was acquired and so the relationship between the investor and investee will have to be examined. Where there is a trading relationship between the two and the investment in the investee is an extension of the trade of the investor, the relationship can be assumed to be long term, provided there is no intention to dispose of it. On the other hand, if the purpose of the investment is to achieve capital growth and the decision to hold it or dispose of it depends on the performance of the investment, then the investment will not be considered as being long term.

The holding must be substantial in the context of the size of the holding in the investee company and not in relation to the accounts of the investor. SSAP 1 does not specifically define what the size of this holding should be.

The final requirement of the definition of an associated company is that the investing company is in a position to exercise a significant influence. This term is, unfortunately, very difficult to define. It is also very subjective because influence may be exerted in many ways. It is important to note that influence is not the same as control. If control is exercised over the other company then it becomes a subsidiary company. SSAP 1 states that 'significant influence over a company essentially involves participation in the financial and operating policy decisions of that company (including dividend policies)'. Whether a significant influence exists or not will depend on a number of factors including board representation, trading relationships and the size of the holding. The accounting standard states that if the investing company has a holding of 20 per cent or more of the equity voting rights in a company, it should be presumed that the investing company has the ability to exercise significant influence over that company unless it can be clearly demonstrated otherwise.

(*a*) *Profit and loss account*: include the investing company's proportion of the associated company's results. If the investing company owns, say, 28 per cent of the shares of an associated company, then it will add to its own results 28 per cent of the associated company's profit before tax. It should be described as 'share of profits of associated companies'. Also, it should include 28 per cent of the tax attributable to the share of profits of the associated company. These items should be disclosed separately in the consolidated profit and loss account. The net impact of these adjustments is to include 28 per cent of the associated company's after-tax profits in the profit and loss account.

(*b*) *Balance sheet*: the investing company will already show the cost of the investment in the associated company in its balance sheet. To this must now be added the investing company's share of the post-acquisition retained profits (and other reserves) of the associated company. This will be balanced by the increase in reserves in (*a*) above. The computation for balance sheet purposes will be:

Cost of the investment	£x
add: (*less*) the investing company's share of	
post-acquisition retained profits	
(or losses) and reserves	£x
	£xx

Example:

A Ltd purchased 40 per cent of the shares of B Ltd for £670,000 on 1 January 19 . 1. At that date the net assets of B Ltd amounted to £1.5m. In 19 . 1 B Ltd made a profit of £200,000 but no dividends were declared or paid. The extract from the consolidated balance sheet at 31 December 19 . 1 would be as follows:

EXTRACT FROM BALANCE SHEET OF INVESTING COMPANY

Fixed assets		. . .
Financial assets (*note 1*)	670	
Add: investing company's share		
of post-acquisition profits		
and other reserves (40% x £200,000)	80	
		750
		£. . .
Financed by		. . .
Called-up share capital		
Profit and loss account	. . .	
Add: investing company's share of		
post-acquisition profits and reserves	80	
		£. . .

Note 1 The investment in the associated company is:	£
share of net assets acquired (40% x £1.5 million)	600
goodwill arising (£670,000-£600,000)	70
	670

The importance of definitions

The distinction between subsidiary and associated companies and other company investments has enormous implications for financial reporting purposes. The following simplified example illustrates this:

Year 1. H Ltd holds 19 per cent of B Ltd, but B Ltd is not deemed to be an associated company since H Ltd is not in a position to exercise a significant influence over B Ltd.

B Ltd makes pre-tax profits of £10m. but distributes only £1m. of dividends.

Result: Contribution to H's profits of £190,000 representing 19 per cent of the dividend received since B Ltd is not an associated company.

Year 2. H Ltd increases its shareholding in B Ltd to 30 per cent and appoints several directors to B's board. B now becomes an associated company of H Ltd since it now has board representation and is in a position to exercise significant influence.

B Ltd produces identical results to the previous year.

Result: Contribution to H's profits of £3m. (30 per cent x £10m.) thus considerably increasing H Ltd's profits and shareholders' funds.

Year 3. H Ltd removes its directors from B's board and, in relation to the disposition of other shareholdings which changed during the year, it is deemed unable to exert significant influence over B Ltd. Consequently, B Ltd is no longer an a associated company.

B Ltd reports a loss of £5m. for the year.

Result: Rather than disclosing its share of B's losses in excess of £1m. nothing will appear in H's income statement because, presumably, no dividend income was received!

There is no doubt that some window dressing in relation to classification of subsidiary, associate and related companies does take place. It is unlikely that the mechanics would be as simple or blatant as the above example portrays. This is because the accounting standard relating to associated companies was revised in April 1982 to specifically counteract such devices. For example, the original definition of an associated company referred to a 20 per cent shareholding in a company and this, perhaps, tended to cause accountants to apply a quantitative test rather than make a subjective judgment which takes account of the ability of the investing company to exercise significant influence over the investee company. The revised standard relating to associated companies made no reference to a 20 per cent shareholding in its definition, so that an associated company could exist with, say, only a 16 per cent equity shareholding, but yet not exist with an equity holding of 40 per cent. The revised standard does, however, state that where the investing company holds 20 per cent or more of the equity voting rights, there is a presumption that the investee company is an associated company, which may be rebutted only if the investing company can clearly demonstrate that it is not in a position to exercise significant influence.

The essential differences between subsidiary and associated companies and other investments (i.e. less than 20 per cent shareholding) are summarised in Exhibit 12.5:

Exhibit 12.5

| | Nature of investment | | |
| | *Subsidiary* | *Associated* | *Other Shareholding* |
	50% plus	20%—49%	20% (*Note 1*)
Accounting treatment	Acquisition method of consolidation	Equity method of accounting	Record only transactions
Impact on group sales	All included in group sales	None	None
Profit impact on group profit	All profits of subsidiary are included with adjustment for minority interests	Share of profits	Dividend received
Impact on group balance sheet	All assets and liabilities included	Share of retained profits added to assets and reserves	None
Minority interests	Yes, if less than 100%	No	No

Note 1: This quantitative test (of 20 per cent) is no longer directly relevant in determining an associated company. The relevant fact is whether the investing company is able to exercise significant influence over the investee company. However, a 20 per cent shareholding provides a cut-off point in helping to determine whether or not the investing company is in a position to exercise significant influence.

QUESTION 12.1 (A)

The following balance sheets were drawn up immediately after H Ltd (holding company) had acquired 100 per cent control of S Ltd (subsidiary company). You are to draw up a consolidated balance sheet, treating goodwill arising on consolidation as an asset.

H LTD BALANCE SHEET

	£
Assets:	
Investment in S: 100 shares	110
Stock	80
Bank	10
	200
Financed by:	
Share capital	200

S LTD BALANCE SHEET

	£
Assets:	
Stock	70
Bank	30
	100
Financed by:	
Share capital	100

QUESTION 12.2 (SM)

The following balance sheets were prepared immediately after H Ltd acquired control of S Ltd. You are required to prepare a consolidated balance sheet at 31 December 19 . 1, treating goodwill arising on consolidation as an asset.

H LTD BALANCE SHEET AT 31 DECEMBER 19 . 1

	£
Assets:	
Investment in S Ltd: 3,000 shares	3,300
Fixed Assets	2,000
Stock	500
Debtors	100
Bank	100
	6,000
Financed by:	
Called-up share capital of £1 each	6,000

S LTD BALANCE SHEET AT 31 DECEMBER 19.1

	£
Assets	
Fixed Assets	1,800
Stock	700
Debtors	300

Bank	200
	3,000
Financed by:	
Issued share capital of £1 each	3,000

QUESTION 12.3 (A)

The following balance sheets were prepared immediately after H Ltd acquired control of S Ltd on 31 December 19 . 1. You are required to prepare a consolidation balance sheet at 31 December 19 . 1, treating goodwill arising on consolidation as an asset.

H LTD BALANCE SHEET AT 31 DECEMBER 19 . 1

	£
Assets:	
Investment in S Ltd: (2,400 shares)	1,400
Fixed assets	800
Stock	800
Debtors	600
Bank	400
	4,000
Financed by:	
Share capital	4,000
	4,000

S LTD BALANCE SHEET AT 31 DECEMBER 19 . 1

	£
Fixed Assets	1,100
Stock	500
Debtors	300
Bank	100
	2,000
Share capital (50p each)	2,000
	2,000

QUESTION 12.4 (SM)

The following balance sheets relate to H Ltd and its two subsidiary companies, S1 and S2, which were acquired on the date of their incorporation on 31 December 19 . 1. You are required to prepare a consolidated balance sheet at 31 December 19 . 1, based of the above data, assuming that goodwill arising on consolidation is treated as an asset.

H LTD BALANCE SHEET AT 31 DECEMBER 19 . 1

Assets:	£
Investment in subsidiaries: S1 Ltd. (3,000 shares)	3,800
S2 Ltd (3,200 shares)	5,700
Fixed assets	5,000
Current assets	2,000
	16,500
Financed by:	
Share capital	10,000
Profit and loss account	6,500
	16,500

S1 LTD BALANCE SHEET AT 31 DECEMBER 19 . 1

Assets:	£
Fixed assets	2,000
Current assets	1,500
	3,500
Financed by:	
Share capital of £1 each	3,000
Profit and loss account	500
	3,500

S2 LTD BALANCE SHEET AT 31 DECEMBER 19 . 1

Assets	£
Fixed assets	5,000
Current assets	2,000
	7,000
Financed by:	
Share capital of £1 each	4,000
Profit and loss account	3,000
	7,000

QUESTION 12.5 (A)

The following represents the summarised profit and loss accounts of H Ltd and its subsidiary, S Ltd. S. Ltd was acquired at the date of incorporation which was 1 January 19 . 1. You are required to prepare a consolidated profit and loss account for the year ended 31 December 19 . 1.

	H Ltd		S Ltd	
	£	£	£	£
Turnover		100,000		100,000
Operating costs		20,000		70,000
Net profit before tax		80,000		30,000
Less: corporation tax	35,000		14,000	
proposed dividend	30,000		NIL	
		65,000		14,000
Profit retained for the year		15,000		16,000
Profit brought forward		10,000		Nil
Profit carried forward		25,000		16,000

H Ltd owns 75 per cent of the shares in S Ltd.

QUESTION 12.6 (SM)

The following represents the summarised profit and loss accounts of H Ltd and its subsidiary, S Ltd. S Ltd was acquired at date of incorporation which was 1 January 19 . 1. You are required to prepare a consolidated profit and loss account for the year ended 31 December 19 . 1.

	H Ltd		S Ltd	
	£	£	£	£
Turnover		1,000,000		500,000
Operating costs		414,000		300,000
Profit on ordinary activities before tax		586,000		200,000
Less: corporation tax	254,000		98,000	
proposed dividend	180,000		Nil	
		434,000		98,000
Profit retained for year		152,000		102,000
Profit brought forward		300,000		Nil
Profit carried forward		452,000		102,000

H Ltd own 60 per cent of the shares of S Ltd.

QUESTION 12.7 (A)

The summary balance sheets of Predator plc and Victim plc at 31 May 19 . 8 are set out below, as prepared under the historical convention.(see overleaf)

	Predator plc Cost £000	*Victim plc* Cost £000
Shares £1 each	80	20
Revenue reserve	60	12
	140	32
Net assets	140	32

On 1 June 1988 predator plc gives £3 per share in cash for 80 per cent of Victim plc's share capital.

Requirement:

Prepare the summary consolidated balance sheet for Predator plc and its subsidiary at 1 June 19 . 8:

(The Chartered Association of Certified Accountants)

QUESTION 12.8 (A)

(a) How does SSAP 1 Accounting for Associated Companies define an associated company?

(b) The abbreviated balance sheets of Cable plc on 31 December 19 . 0 and 19 . 6 are set out below.

	19 . 0 £000	19 . 6 £000
Net tangible assets	300	400
Goodwill	50	50
	350	450
Ordinary shares	200	200
Revenue reserves	150	250
	350	450

Wire plc acquired 30% of the ordinary share capital of Cable plc on 1 January 19 . 1 at a cost of £150,000. The net tangible assets in Cable plc are stated at their fair values.

Requirement:

Show how the investment in Cable plc should be stated in accordance with SSAP 1 Accounting for Associated Companies in the consolidated balance sheet of Wire plc at 31 December 19 . 6.

(The Chartered Association of Certified Accountants)

13.

Accounting for Changing Price Levels

INCOME MEASUREMENT AND CAPITAL MAINTENANCE CONCEPTS

There is probably no single area in accounting which is surrounded by as much confusion and debate as that of 'inflation accounting'. Indeed the term 'inflation accounting' is misleading but has gained acceptance. The debate is basically about how best to measure business income during a period in which there has been a significant increase in price levels.

Changes in price levels, either in the form of inflation or deflation, undermine historic cost accounts, and call into question their validity. Inflation is a general increase in prices that cause a fall in the purchasing power of money. In Ireland inflation is measured by the movement in the consumer price index (CPI). The CPI is based on the weighted average basket of representative goods and services purchased by consumers. Thus changes in, say, mortgage interest rates or bus fares will impact on the consumer price index.

The CPI is produced quarterly by the Central Statistics Office in Dublin. The (mid-November) index for 1979 to 1989 (with mid-November 1975 taken as a base of 100) is set out below and indicates that, since 1975, average consumer prices have increased fourfold!

Index of consumer prices in Ireland

Year	Index	% annual change in index
1975	100.0	———
1979	167.2	———
1980	197.7	18.2%
1981	243.8	23.3%
1982	273.8	12.3%
1983	302.0	10.3%
1984	322.3	6.7%
1985	338.1	4.9%
1986	348.8	3.1%
1987	359.5	3.0%
1988	369.1	2.6%
1989	386.3	4.6%

Source: Central Statistics Office

The effects of price changes on financial statements are evident when considering the valuation of assets on the balance sheet. The measuring unit, i.e. the £, on which successive accounts are prepared is not a stable yardstick. Nowhere is this more apparent than in the case of fixed assets. Each asset is recorded at its historic cost and, for balance sheet purposes, successive acquisitions are aggregated even though they were purchased at different times. Indeed, the total for fixed assets may include a variety of costs and valuations of certain assets. Moreover, the comparability of successive accounting periods becomes dubious since, for example, a company's sales would inevitably increase. But how much of this increase was real and how much was due to price increases?

The impact on profit is more complicated. Profit is determined with reference to the matching principle, whereby revenues recognised in the profit and loss account are matched against the costs of earning that revenue. However, the costs that are matched with revenue in preparing traditional profit and loss accounts are the historic costs. Thus, historic costs are matched against current revenues. One example is that of depreciation of fixed assets which is provided with reference to the historic cost of the fixed asset. Yet, one year's usage of a machine with no scrap value and a five-year life may more realistically be said to incur a charge of one-fifth of the replacement cost of the asset rather than one-fifth of its historic cost. It is both prudent and realistic to depreciate fixed assets on their replacement rather than historic cost.

A second complication concerns the cost of sales, which is based on the historic cost of stock. The consumption or using-up of stock can be said to involve an expense that is equivalent to their replacement cost rather than the original historic cost. If a business uses an item of stock in a particular way, then, generally speaking, that item must be replaced so that the effective cost, especially in terms of cash flow, is based on the replacement cost.

A third problem with conventional profit and loss accounts during a period of inflation concerns monetary assets and liabilities. Monetary items are those assets and liabilities fixed in money terms regardless of changes in the general price level. Examples are cash, debtors, creditors and other forms of borrowing. Monetary items cannot maintain their purchasing power during a period of inflation since their prices cannot increase. Thus, a company that holds monetary assets during a period of inflation incurs a loss of purchasing power. If an individual maintains £1,000 in cash during a year where inflation was measured at 20 per cent, then that individual has lost purchasing power equivalent to £200. In other words, at the end of the year the individual would need £1,200 to maintain his purchasing power but he has only £1,000. Conversely, a company that borrows money during periods of inflation is making a gain, in the sense that the money that will have to be repaid will be worth less in real terms. Hence, in an inflationary period, a gain will be registered by holding monetary liabilities but losses will be incurred in respect of holding monetary assets.

It can be seen from the above that the historic cost profit is overstated during a period of inflation by the failure to provide for the replacement cost of fixed assets and stock. However, this is slightly counterbalanced by the impact of holding net monetary liabilities. Not surprisingly, during the high inflation era of the 1970s many companies experienced cash flow problems especially in respect to the replacement of fixed assets. Unless this overstatement of net profit is recognised, the usefulness of accounting data for decision making may be significantly reduced. For example, the magnitude of dividend payments may be excessive given the need to provide for the replacement of the operating capability of the business. Even if the directors of the company appreciate the problem, their perception may not be shared by shareholders. The impact of inflation on accounting data also impacts on managerial decision making. Managerial decision making on pricing policy, production policy and performance evaluation should be based on realistic accounting data, suitably adjusted for the effects of inflation.

A similar problem arises in relation to corporation tax levied on corporate profits. Since corporation tax is based on historic profits (which overstate the net profit performance) the effective rate of tax is very high since profits are largely illusory. However, the problem is slightly alleviated by the system of capital allowances available to Irish industry. Starting in 1971, a system of accelerated capital allowances was introduced for expenditure incurred on new plant and machinery and was eventually extended to industrial buildings. The allowances were originally introduced to stimulate investment and to negate the effects of high inflation. This allowed a firm to write-off for tax purposes the entire cost of the new qualifying fixed assets in the year of acquisition. This resulted in firms, which invested in new fixed assets, postponing corporate tax liabilities to future years. However, the system of accelerated allowances has been recently curtailed by the Minister for Finance. The Finance Act, 1988 brought the ceiling down to 75 per cent for expenditure incurred between 1 April 1988 and 31 March 1989 and 50 per cent for expenditure incurred between 1 April 1989 and 31 March 1991. The intention is to eliminate the allowance entirely for expenditure after 1 April 1992 so that only the normal rates of capital allowances will then apply.

Accounting for inflation is not a new topic but its popularity is related to prevailing rates of inflation. As early as 1952 it was proposed that companies should consider setting amounts aside from profits to reserve. This recognises the effects which changes in the purchasing power of money have had upon the affairs of the business, particularly their effect on the amount of profit which, as a matter of policy, can be prudently regarded as being available for distribution by way of dividend. However, little notice was taken of this suggestion since the sudden and dramatic surge in inflation at that time quickly subsided. It was not until the late 1960s and early 1970s, when annual inflation at times exceeded 20 per cent, that the attention of the accountancy profession was focused, yet again, on the problem of accounting for changing price levels.

One of the dominant considerations in the inflation accounting debate is the measurement of profit during a period of changing prices. However, measurement of profit presupposes a definition and, perhaps, the most accepted definition of income is that suggested by the economist, J.R. Hicks (*Value and Capital*, Oxford University Press, 1946), who wrote:

> The purpose of income calculations in practical affairs is to give people an indication of the amount they can consume without impoverishing themselves. Following this idea it would seem that we ought to define a man's income as the maximum value which he can consume during the week and still be as well off at the end of the week as he was at the beginning.

This definition of income only applies to an individual but it can be adapted to a business context to define a firm's income as representing the maximum amount a company could distribute by way of dividend during an accounting period and still be as well off at the end of the accounting period as it was at the start. The problem that Hicks leaves us with is how to measure 'well-offness'. His definition does not view income as a matching process between revenue and expenses. Rather, according to Hicks, income is measured with reference to the valuation of assets at the end of an accounting period and the setting aside of a sufficient amount to ensure that the business is as 'well off' at the end as it was at the beginning. In a business context, this is called 'capital maintenance'. Thus income can only be measured with reference to the maintenance of capital. The concept of capital maintenance is fundamental to the measurement of income. To further complicate matters we shall see that there are *three* concepts of capital maintenance which can logically be applied to the measurement of business income.

One way to measure business income would be to compare valuations of a business at the start and end of an accounting period. This is the approach the economist would take. For example, two businesses purchased £1,000 of identical investments at the start of a period. On the last day, company A sold its investments for £1,300 whereas company B sold its investments on the first day of the second accounting period for the same amount. The economist would argue that the income of both companies for period 1 was identical. Company A had realised a gain of £300 and this compared to a capital appreciation of £300 applicable to company B.

However, accountants dislike valuations which in many cases are difficult to apply and are very subjective. For example, what is the value of a fixed asset with a remaining life of seven years? Because of difficulties associated with valuations, accountants prefer to measure income with reference to the *transactions* of the enterprise. There is less subjectivity associated with the transactions approach to income measurement and transactions are more easily verifiable. The surplus of revenue over expenses is deemed to be the profit figure, but even this simple approach creates its own problems, e.g. realisation of revenue, classification of capital and revenue expenditure, stock valuation required for cost of goods sold computation, etc.

Using the transactions approach to income measurement for the above example, company A would have generated an accounting profit of £300 during period 1, whereas company B would have generated no revenue (and no profit). The other interesting feature of this example is that the total transactions income of the two companies is identical if you expand the relevant accounting period to more than twelve months.

Capital maintenance concepts

There are three commonly accepted concepts of capital maintenance, namely, the maintenance of nominal money capital, the maintenance of purchasing power of the owners' investment and the maintenance of operating capital (capacity). All three concepts will be explained using the following simplified example.

Example:

At the start of a year an individual invests his entire capital in the acquisition of goods for £100 which were sold on the last day of the year for £150 cash. During the period the general price level, i.e. CPI, increased by 10 per cent. However, at the end of the year the replacement cost of these goods was estimated to be £130.

Requirement:

You are required to calculate:

(*a*) Historic cost profit (HC) corresponding to the maintenance of nominal money capital. This is the traditional approach to income measurement based on the transactions recorded.

(*b*) Current purchasing power profit (CPP) using the maintenance of current purchasing power of money capital.

(*c*) Replacement cost accounting profit (RCA) based on maintaining the operating capital/capacity, i.e. physical assets.

Maintenance of nominal money capital

The traditional capital maintenance concept adopted by accountants in the income measurement process is that of 'nominal money capital maintenance'. As long as revenues exceed expenses, the 'nominal money capital', i.e. the original capital invested, is being maintained. On the other hand if expenses exceed revenues then the money capital is being depleted and an accounting loss is being incurred.

Historic cost profit based on the maintenance of money capital:

	£
Sales	150
Less: cost of sales	(100)
Net Profit	50

Maintenance of current purchasing power of money capital

Under this concept of capital maintenance, income is measured in relation to maintaining the purchasing power of the owners' investment. One way to achieve this is to make a specific provision in the profit and loss account to maintain the purchasing power of the owners' investment with reference to the consumer price index. This method of accounting was referred to as Current Purchasing Power (CPP).

CPP profit based on maintaining purchasing power of money capital:

	£
Sales	150
Less: Cost of sales	(100)
	50
Less: Provision to maintain purchasing power of owners' investment (10% x £100)	(10)
CPP profit	40

At the start of the year the owner's investment was £100. At the end of the year, assuming £40 was distributed by way of dividend, total shareholders' funds would amount to £110. This £110 provides the exact same purchasing power to the owner as the £100 investment at the start of the year.

An alternative term for CPP accounting is that of General Price Level (GPL) accounting since the index used is that of general price levels.

Maintenance of operating capital, i.e. capacity

Under this concept of capital maintenance, the business is considered to be a separate entity and emphasis is placed on the physical structure and capability of the business. Thus, it is important to provide for the replacement of fixed assets and stock. Otherwise, the firm may not have sufficient resources when the assets need to be replaced and the operating capacity of the business may have to be curtailed. One way to apply the maintenance of operating capital in the profit and loss account is to make a specific provision for the replacement of assets.

A replacement cost accounting profit and loss account, based on the maintenance of operating capital is as follows:

	£
Sales	150
Less: Cost of sales	(100)
	50
Less: Provision for maintenance of operating capital (stocks)	(30)
RCA profit	20

Hence the maximum dividend which could be distributed under replacement cost accounting is £20. Such a dividend would leave total shareholders' funds at £130 by the end of the year which is sufficient to maintain the operating capacity, i.e. to replace the stock.

The various income alternatives are summarised below in Exhibit 13.1.

Exhibit 13.1

Capital Maintenance Concepts		
Concept Capital	To Be Maintained	Profit
Historic cost	Nominal money capital	£50
Current purchasing power	Capital adjusted by CPI	£40
Replacement cost	Operating capacity	£20

Each concept of capital maintenance has its advantages and disadvantages. However, the dominant consideration should be which system satisfies the information needs of users. The historic cost concept is simple to use and is more familiar to users. In addition, it is less subjective than the other two approaches. Also, for the purposes of strict accountability, it is more easily verifiable than other systems.

From the point of view of the owners it may be said that the effect of inflation on the spending power of owners' capital, is more relevant than the specific price changes of the business's assets. If this is the case, a current purchasing power system should be adopted for the benefit of shareholders. Its disadvantage is that it restates the historic cost accounts which are themselves subject to a number of limitations. However, it is common to view the business from an entity point of view rather than from the shareholders' viewpoint. The business is considered to be an entity separate from its shareholders and it is a fundamental accounting concept that the business is assumed to be a going concern. Therefore the business is expected to continue in operational existence for the foreseeable future and there is no intention to liquidate the assets and return capital to the shareholders. Thus, it is anticipated that the business will replace its assets with others of a similar productive potential. In such a case, the specific replacement cost of fixed assets is surely of greater relevance than their general purchasing power.

Replacement cost accounting takes into consideration specific price changes of productive assets rather than general price changes. However, ascertaining replacement costs can be difficult and very subjective.

THE CURRENT PURCHASING POWER (CPP) ALTERNATIVE

During the 1970s the accountancy profession accepted that inflation adversely affected the validity of traditional, historic cost accounts. The problem was in recognising the appropriate way forward. Basically two alternatives were proposed by way of an accounting standard. The first is referred to as current purchasing power (CPP) accounting and the second as current cost accounting (CCA). Current cost accounting is similar in many respects to replacement cost accounting but there are important differences which are beyond the scope of this book especially. Both CPP and CCA will provide different profit figures simply because they are based on two different concepts of capital maintenance. In turn, both of these profit figures will be significantly different from the historic cost profit figure. The accountancy profession initially adopted the CPP alternative.

CPP accounting was recommended by the accountancy profession in May 1974 as a provisional accounting standard (pSSAP 7). The objective of SSAP 7 was to show the affairs of the enterprise in terms of current purchasing power. The accounting procedure involved was to prepare historic accounts as normal and then restate them into current pounds of uniform purchasing power with reference to the closing consumer price index. Usually the base point is taken to be the end of the accounting period in question. Monetary items on the balance sheet are already stated in end of year pounds, but other balance sheet items need to be analysed by age and adjusted, using the CPI. In general the conversion factor can be expressed as:

$$\frac{\text{CPI at balance sheet date}}{\text{CPI when item was acquired}}$$

Hence, the historic cost accounts would be restated in terms of current purchasing power. This approach was literally accounting for inflation. The advantage of this system was its simplicity, since there was little subjectivity involved in its application. Likewise the index used, namely the CPI, was produced regularly and frequently by the Central Statistics Office and so would not delay the publication of accounts.

Its disadvantage was that the CPI indicates price changes of *general* consumer goods rather than goods and services purchased by the company. A second disadvantage was that CPP accounting was concerned solely with removing the distorting effects of changes in the general purchasing power of money on accounts prepared under the historic cost convention. What was really happening was the 'indexation' of financial statements for reporting purposes and, as such, no attempt was made to rectify some of the important limitations of financial statements. A third disadvantage was that users now had two profit figures which, in many cases, were significantly different. Naturally some users of financial statements were confused since they did not understand the underlying capital maintenance concepts. CPP accounting is illustrated using the following example:

Example: A company was incorporated on 1 January 19 . 1 with capital of £200. The only transactions during the year were the purchase of stock for £200 on the 30 June which was sold the same day for £300. Both transactions were for cash. The opening consumer price index was 120 and the closing price index was 144. Prices increased uniformly during the year.

The historic profit and loss account and closing balance sheet are restated in terms of current purchasing power. Both sales and cost of sales are restated by an index of the closing price index (144) divided by the average price index (132) for the year. The average point is used since the profit and loss transactions are assumed to take place evenly throughout the year. The difficult figure to calculate in the profit and loss account is the loss arising from holding monetary items—in this case, cash. By holding cash, a business loses purchasing power. The opening cash balance was £200, which was held throughout the year. Since the consumer price index has risen 24 points from the start of the year from 120, the loss of purchasing power is £40 (i.e. £200 x 24/120). In addition, cash of £100 was generated mid-way during the year as a result of the sales transactions. Since the surplus was retained in cash form it also lost purchasing power due to the rise of 12 points in the price level during the latter six months of the year. This provides a loss of purchasing power of £9.90 (i.e. £100 x 12/132).

PROFIT AND LOSS ACCOUNT FOR 19 . 1

	Historic cost £		CPP £
Sales	300	x 144/132 =	327.27
Cost of sales	200	x 144/132 =	218.18
Net profit	100		109.09
Loss on holding monetary assets (*note*)	—		49.09
Net profit	100		60.00

Note: The loss on holding monetary assets can be proved as follows:

Cash balance held for year	200 x 144/120 =	£240.00
Additional cash on sale transaction	100 x 144/132 =	109.09
Required purchasing power of cash assets		349.09
Actual purchasing power		300.00
Loss due to holding monetary assets		49.09

The above figures indicate that CPP profit equals the historic profit of £100 less a sum to provide for the purchasing power of owner's capital; in this case (200 x 144/120 – 200) = £40.

The balance sheet is also restated in terms of current purchasing power. Cash on hands, being a monetary item, is already stated in terms of current purchasing power so that no adjustment is necessary. Share capital is restated with respect to closing purchasing power relative to when the capital was subscribed.

BALANCE SHEET AT 31 DECEMBER 19 . 1

	HC £	CPP £
Assets:		
Cash on hands	300	300
Financed by:		
Share capital	200	x 144/120 = 240
Reserves	100	60
	300	300

The accounting treatment of the profit/loss on monetary items became a contentious issue although most favoured its inclusion in the profit and loss account. Thus CPP enhanced the profits of companies that were heavily borrowed, particularly those showing low profits on an historic cost basis.

CPP accounting never became standard practice because of the sudden and unanticipated intervention of the UK government who, in July 1973, appointed its own committee of inquiry under the chairmanship of F.E.P. Sandilands to enquire into the subject of accounting for inflation. It was possible that CPP accounting, which represented the 'indexation' of company accounts, could have ultimately led to a call to the UK government for the indexation of the income tax code by, for example, employees' representatives (including the trade union movement). At that time inflation averaged in excess of 20 per cent for a number of years. Proper indexation of the income tax code for inflation would have resulted in significantly reduced tax yields for the government. On the other hand, failure to index the tax code for inflation facilitates the phenomenon of fiscal drag or bracket creep. This results in rising money income, perhaps constant in real terms, being taxed at higher rates under a progressive income tax structure. Fiscal drag was certainly present in the UK and Irish economies during the 1970s.

The Sandilands Committee, consisting of twelve members but only three accountants, reported in September 1975. It suggested that 'of UK company accounts are to show more accurately than at present, the effect of changes in prices, it is accounting *practices* that must be changed, not the *unit of measurement*'. The recommendation was that instead of supplementary CPP accounts provisionally proposed by the accountancy profession, historic cost accounts should be replaced for all companies by a system of current cost accounting. This would involve the continued use of money as the unit of measurement, the expression of assets and liabilities in the balance sheet at a current valuation (broadly equivalent to replacement cost) and the measurement of profit after allowing for the replacement cost of the resources consumed. CPP accounting was no longer recommended. Rather a form of replacement cost accounting, known as current cost accounting, was recommended.

In addition to the UK government's intervention another major reason for the failure of CPP accounting was the doubt about whether the information that it provided was particularly useful to decision makers. Criticisms were made about the difficulty in understanding CPP accounts, about the lack of relevance of adjusting fixed assets, depreciation and stock by a general consumer price index rather than a specific price index.

THE CURRENT COST ACCOUNTING (CCA) ALTERNATIVE

The accounting profession as a result of the Sandilands Report, appointed an Inflation Accounting Steering Committee (IASC) in January 1976 under the chairmanship of Douglas Morpeth, whose terms of reference were to prepare an exposure draft on current cost accounting. The Morpeth Committee adopted the Sandilands proposals to a large extent and produced an exposure draft (ED 18) on current cost accounting in November 1976. CPP accounting and its provisional accounting standard (SSAP 7) was formally withdrawn.

The essence of CCA was that provision should generally be made for the replacement of fixed assets and stocks. In general assets were shown on the balance sheet at their replacement cost and the profit and loss account would contain current cost figures for cost of sales and depreciation. However, there would be no adjustment for monetary items. In addition, ED 18 proposed a new appropriation account, where directors' discretion would be used to sort out problem areas such as replacement reserves and profit available for distribution.

ED 18 was widely regarded as too complicated. A commonly held view was that the 94-page exposure draft and its accompanying guidance manual was too detailed. Many accountants felt that ED 18 was too subjective and some felt that the current cost accounts would be unauditable and would have disastrous effects on the profit figures. It would be a time-consuming exercise for companies (especially small companies), and therefore expensive. An intelligent minority of accountants questioned its relevance to the needs of users of financial statements.

Like all other accounting standards, it would be impossible to produce an accounting standard dealing with the effects of changing prices unless such proposals were acceptable to the rank and file members of the accountancy profession. In many ways, setting accounting standards is a political process, and any proposals contained in accounting standards would have to be acceptable to preparers and auditors of accounting statements. In other words, such an accounting standard would first have to satisfy the preparers of financial statements and then, subsequently, be assumed to be relevant and to satisfy the information needs of users of financial statements.

Because of the dissatisfaction with ED 18, the members of the Institute of Chartered Accountants in England and Wales voted at a specially convened extraordinary meeting in 1977 that current cost accounting should not be made compulsory. The motion was passed by a small majority. In some disarray, the ASC then set up the Hyde Committee with the task of providing guidance, as an interim measure, on how information on the effects of inflation should be provided in the accounts of quoted companies. It was obvious to all that any further proposals in the area of current cost accounting would have to be fairly simple and non-controversial if they were to gain general acceptance. Yet another accounting proposal was produced (ED 24) and published and subsequently formed the nucleus of SSAP 16— an accounting standard on current cost accounting as opposed to an accounting standard on current purchasing power accounting.

SSAP 16 was issued in March 1980. The purpose of this accounting standard was to establish what adjustments to the historic accounts are necessary to show:

1. The profit/loss for the period after maintaining the *operating capital/capacity* of the business. As a result, provision would have to be made for the replacement costs of assets consumed during the period.

2. The balance sheet of the firm would show all operating assets at their current value, broadly equivalent to their replacement cost.

The adjustments in the profit and loss account are necessary to set aside additional funds to provide for the replacement of the three categories of operating assets, i.e. (1) fixed assets, (2) stocks and (3) net working capital. These adjustments to the historic cost profit and loss account are made in two stages. The first stage is to establish the current cost operating profit which requires the deduction of the following three adjustments from the historic cost profit:

(*a*) Depreciation adjustment
(*b*) Cost of sales adjustment (COSA)
(*c*) Monetary working capital adjustment (MWCA)

Depreciation adjustment

This is the amount necessary to increase the historic cost depreciation expense to a charge based on the replacement cost of the fixed assets. For example, if a fixed asset with a *two*-year life originally cost £5,000 and had a replacement cost at the end of the first year of £7,000 the depreciation adjustment at the end of the first year is £1,000. Thus the total current cost depreciation (historic cost depreciation plus depreciation adjustment) represents the value to the business of those fixed assets consumed during the accounting period. It acknowledges the reality that as a firm consumes resources in order to continue in existence it must replace those resources.

Cost of sales adjustment

Similar to the above, this adjustment represents the difference between the historic cost of sales and the replacement cost of goods sold. Ideally, CCA would require the replacement cost to be ascertained every time a product was sold. This is impractical so that some way must be found to approximate the cost of sales adjustment. The most common method is that of averaging. This is done by looking at the money increase in stock during the period and then distinguishing the increase due to higher stock levels from the money increase due to rising prices. The averaging method converts both opening and closing stocks to *average* prices for the year and this allows one to differentiate between stock increases due to stock levels and increases due to rising prices.

Example:

	Units	£	Index
Sales		15,000	
Opening stock	20	1,800	90
Purchases	110	11,000	
Less: Closing stock	(30)	(3,300)	110
Cost of sales (HC)	100	9,500	

Total money increase in stocks		1,500
Closing stock restated at average	3,300 x 110/100 = 3,000	
Opening stock restated at average	1,800 x 90/100 = 2,000	
Physical increase in stock	1,000	i.e. (1,000)
Money increase due to inflation i.e. cost of sales adjustment		500

In this example, the cost of sales adjustment (COSA) can be proved accurate. The average replacement cost of goods sold during the year was £100. Thus cost of sales on a replacement cost basis must be 100 times £100 = £10,000. Therefore, an adjustment of £500 is needed.

It should be noted that the LIFO system of valuing stock will provide broadly similar figures to the current cost accounting system, i.e. you will get an historic cost of sales of £10,000. This is because LIFO prices stock issues at their latest price which approximates replacement cost.

Monetary working capital adjustment (MWCA)

The above two adjustments are based on the necessity to replace the firm's non-monetary assets, namely, stocks and fixed assets. However, we have ignored the need to hold large quantities of monetary assets, especially where extended trade credit is granted to customers. Every business has both debtors and creditors as a result of trading during the year. Both of these items will be inflated due to price increases during the period. The purpose of the monetary working capital adjustment (MWCA) is to allow for the additional (or reduced) finance needed to support the higher level of monetary working capital as a result of increased price levels. In computing this adjustment cash/bank balances are *excluded* from the definition of monetary working capital because it is difficult to determine how much of the cash balance is a necessary part of working capital and how much is merely being held in this form awaiting reinvestment or distribution, or indeed being held due to bad planning. However having excluded cash/bank balances from MWCA, SSAP 16 recognises that this could provide misleading answers. It therefore allows one to include as part of monetary working capital that portion of bank balances which fluctuate with the volume of stock. The reader will appreciate that the discretion regarding cash/bank balances increases the amount of judgment and discretion to be applied in the preparation of current cost accounts.

The method of calculation is the same as that for stocks and it is appropriate to use the same index.

Example:

	Opening £	Closing £
Debtors	800	1,200
Less: Profit margin	200	300
Debtors at cost	600	900
Less: Creditors	330	460
MWC as defined	270	440

Increase in MWC for year (price and volume)		170
Closing MWC restated: 440 x 100/110 =	400	
Opening MWC as restated: 330 x 100/90 =	300	
Increase due to volume	100	100
Increase due to price only		
i.e. monetary working capital adjustment		70

Using the three examples above, the adjustments can be summarised as follows:

	£
Depreciation	1,000
COSA	500
MWCA	70
	1,570

The sum of £1,570 will be deducted from the historic cost profit amount to give current cost operating profit. This amount provides for the maintenance of the operating capacity of the business.

The second stage in the CCA process is to calculate the current cost operating profit attributable to shareholders and this requires an adjustment for *gearing*.

Gearing adjustment

Where an enterprise is financed partly by borrowing, the three previous adjustments, from the point of view of shareholders, are too high. This is because part of the adjustments will be borne by lenders. The purpose of the gearing adjustment is to limit the burden of the other three adjustments accordingly. The basic argument to be stressed is that the maintenance of operating capacity is shared between shareholders' funds and debt and this fact should be reflected in the CCA profit and loss account.

The gearing adjustment is fundamentally different from the three other adjustments. The three operating adjustments *reduce* historic cost profits by the amount of the extra finance required. The gearing adjustment on the other hand *increases* the restated profit figure since a portion of these adjustments will be financed by borrowings. You will see that this gearing adjustment takes the 'string' out of the three operating adjustments and was much favoured by companies that were highly geared! In this regard the gearing adjustment is controversial in that it assumes that the extra finance for replacement will be obtained in the same proportion as in the existing capital structure. Assuming the capital structure of the company was:

	£
Share capital and reserves	200,000
Loan capital	100,000
	300,000

The gearing adjustment is based on the capital structure which currently has a debt proportion of one-third. The gearing adjustment is £1,570 x £100,000/£300,000 = £523 and it reduces the three operating adjustments from £1,570 to £1,047. The presentation of the CCA profit and loss account would be as follows:

CURRENT COST PROFIT AND LOSS ACCOUNT

Historic cost profit (say)		8,000
Less: Current cost operating adjustments		
Depreciation	(1,000)	
Cost of sales	(500)	
Monetary working capital	(70)	(1,570)
Current cost operating profit		6,430
Gearing adjustment		523
Current cost profit attributable to shareholders		6,953

The following are the main implications of CCA if it were adopted in preparing financial statements:

(*a*) It is inevitable that profits under CCA would be lower than under the historic cost system and consequently dividends would be significantly reduced in many instances. Indeed, some companies would probably generate a CCA loss and an historic cost profit. It remains an empirical issue whether stock market prices are affected and whether firms would have additional problems in raising additional capital under a CCA system with relatively lower profits.

(*b*) If CCA financial statements were accepted by the Revenue Commissioners in computing corporate tax liabilities, then lower profits should mean lower tax burdens. In many ways, the argument is academic, since companies in Ireland pay relatively little tax on business profits due to accelerated capital allowances and reduced rates of corporation tax which apply to manufacturing operations.

In any event, in a recent tax case in Ireland current cost accounts have been rejected as a basis for assessing corporation tax. The action was taken in 1987 by Carroll Industries plc, who argued that they should be assessed for corporation tax purposes on a current cost basis. They claimed that CCA was the most appropriate basis for the company which bought tobacco, since accounting based on historic costs produced a totally incorrect result when dealing with an agricultural product which was held in stock from fifteen to thirty months. CCA meant that costs could be related to current costs at the time of sale and not to the cost of tobacco purchased a considerable time previously. However, it was held by the High Court judge that CCA does not show the expenditure laid out to earn receipts during the accounting period. It substitutes current replacement cost for actual cost of stock against current sales, even though the stock has not yet been replaced and the expenditure has not yet been incurred. The fact that CCA was or was not the prevailing system of accounting was not relevant. The basic premise for corporation tax was that profit is the difference between receipts and expenditure laid out to earn those receipts (sic).

Recent developments

CCA is an attempt to provide a more realistic view of the profit performance of the business than either historic cost accounting or current purchasing power accounting method. But the system is not widely understood and causes a little confusion, especially when two profit figures are now available to readers of financial statements. However, the main criterion by which it should be evaluated is whether or not it is relevant to user needs.

SSAP 16 applied to listed companies and a relatively small number of large private companies. By June 1985, compliance with SSAP 16 quoted companies in the UK had fallen to below 30 per cent, forcing the suspension of its compulsory status. The standard was formally withdrawn in 1988. In relation to Irish companies Carroll Industries were the last to produce current cost accounts but then they were only supplementary to the historic cost accounts.

One can only speculate what the future holds for the inflation accounting debate. Much will depend on the future rates of inflation. If inflation rates rapidly increase in the future, then the topic is likely to receive fresh scrutiny and discussion. Whatever the future holds, it is likely that the new accounting standard in this area will contain minimum adjustments to the historic cost accounts: adjustments that are commonly understood and are reasonably easy to apply, such as the depreciation and cost of sales adjustments. The standard will probably apply only to large quoted companies. At present the issue of accounting for changing prices is no longer a serious issue—that is, until inflation beings to increase rapidly in the future!

Analysis
and Interpretation
of
Financial
Statements

14.

Ratio Analysis and Interpretation of Financial Statements

METHODS OF INTERPRETATION OF FINANCIAL STATEMENTS

For the most part, this discussion will be limited to the kind of analysis which can be made by 'outsiders' who do not have access to internal accounting records. This is particularly the case for shareholders who must rely to a considerable extent on financial statements in published annual and half-yearly reports.

The first point to note is that it is not, as a rule, useful to look at figures for a single period for the purpose of analysis. But the usefulness of comparative data covering two or more periods is well recognised. By observing the change in various items, period by period, the analyst may gain valuable clues as to growth and other important trends affecting the business.

Few figures in financial statements are highly significant in and of themselves. Rather, it is their relationship to other quantities or the direction and amount of change over a period that is important. However, one should realise that financial analysis should 'help' to indicate the areas and items which require more detailed examination and questioning. Five analytical techniques which can be used are:

—Horizontal analysis
—Trend analysis
—Common size statements
—Ratio analysis
—Cash funds flow statements (chapter 15)

Horizontal analysis

This is the simplest technique and involves comparing one year's figures with another on a line-by-line basis and identifying the percentage change as follows:

Example:	*19 . 1 £m.*	*19 . 2 £m.*	*% Change*
Sales	951	1156	+ 21.5%
Cost of sales	617	739	+ 19.7%
Gross profit	334	417	+ 24.8%
Interest	12	19	+ 58.3%
Other expenses	261	323	+ 23.7%
Net profit	61	75	+ 22.9%
Taxation	15	16	+ 6.6%
Profit after tax	46	59	+ 28.2%

This method is limited in that it compares the performance of only two years. It is usual to extend the analysis of several years to identify significant trends, if any.

Trend analysis

This involves using several years' data and giving the figure for an item in the first year of the series a value of 100 and restating subsequent years' figures to base 100.

The major limitation of this type of analysis of trends over several years is that the figures can be misleading, especially in periods of high inflation. Thus, the increase in money sales over a period could be declining in real terms. Some attempt should be made to take account of inflation by using an inflation index such as the Consumer Price Index (CPI). From the data below, one can see that the actual money value of sales have increased gradually. However, this increase in monetary amounts does not take account of inflation which occurred during the period. Prices had increased by 12 per cent during 19 . 2 and so the monetary trend is scaled to 'real' sales (109 x 100/112) = 97. The trend analysis in real terms indicates that sales have remained virtually static during the years.

	19 . 1	*19 . 2*	*19 . 3*
Sales (£m.)	630	688	750
Average CPI	100	112	120
Trend analysis (monetary)	100	109	119
Trend analysis (real)	100	97	99

Common size statements

This approach is sometimes referred to as 'vertical analysis' since one works vertically down the profit and loss account or balance sheet rather than working across over several years. For the profit and loss account, all items are expressed as a percentage of sales.

Likewise, the balance sheet items can be expressed as a percentage of total assets, capital employed, etc. Regardless of the method of presentation one can see how, for example, the major components of net profit are changing.

	19 . 1 (£m.)	%
Sales	500,000	100
Cost of sales	350,000	70
Gross profit	150,000	30
Expenses	100,000	20
Net profit	50,000	10

Ratio analysis

A ratio is a simple mathematical expression of the relationship of one item to another. In order to compute a meaningful financial ratio, there must be a significant relationship between the two figures. Thus, the relationship between, say, sales and wages has validity, but the relationship between wages and fixed assets has little significance. A ratio focuses attention on a relationship which is significant, but the interpretation of the ratio usually requires further investigation of the underlying data. Ratios are an aid to analysis and interpretation; they are not a substitute for sound thinking.

Ratios can be logically and conveniently divided into three main groups:

(*a*) *Financial structure*, i.e. balance sheet structure. It should be assessed whether the company is likely to experience cash flow problems and/or whether the business is adequately financed and from what sources. The two main areas are liquidity and gearing or leverage.

(*b*) *Operating performance*, i.e. profit generated in relation to sales and overall investment.

(*c*) *Investment ratios*. These are the ratios which will be primarily used by investors in deciding whether a share should be bought, sold or retained. They relate the number of ordinary shares in issue to the profits (earnings), dividends and assets of the company. The typical ratios calculated are:

- (*i*) PE ratio
- (*ii*) Earnings yield (inverse of P/E ratio)
- (*iii*) Dividend yield
- (*iv*) Dividend cover
- (*v*) Asset backing per share

These ratios are frequently used in the context of valuation of companies and are covered in the final chapter of this book.

LIQUIDITY RATIOS

As noted above, the two principal areas of concern regarding financial (balance sheet) structure are liquidity and leverage (gearing). Liquidity indicates the ability of the firm to pay its debts as and when they become due. Financial statement users are likely to be interested in liquidity ratios because a weak liquidity position entails an increased challenge to the achievement of long-term objectives (including the generation of future cash flows). Liquidity ratios provide information about the organisation's ability to generate *cash* and may suggest, by highlighting the inefficiencies, ways in which the cash position could be improved.

Two financial ratios are commonly used to assess the liquidity position of the firm, namely, (*a*) the current ratio and (*b*) the acid-test ratio. These are calculated as follows, based on the balance sheet of A Ltd:

A LTD
BALANCE SHEET AT 31 DECEMBER 199 .

		£		£
Fixed Assets		50	Capital and Reserves	45
			Long-Term Debt	25
Current assets:				—
Stock	25		Capital Employed	70
Debtors	15			
Cash	10	50	Current Liabilities	30
		100		100

The current ratio indicates the firm's ability to meet its short-term cash obligations (current liabilities) without having to raise finance by borrowing, issuing more shares, or selling assets, all of which might adversely affect the firm's ability to generate future net cash flows for the existing participants.

$$\text{Current ratio} \quad = \quad \frac{\text{Current assets}}{\text{Current liabilities}} \quad = \frac{50}{30} \quad = 1.67 \text{ times}$$

Since this ratio provides some indication of the firm's current financial position, one might expect that the higher the ratio the better it is. Generally, it is agreed that a current ratio of around 2:1 is appropriate for most businesses. The 2:1 rule of thumb is an arbitrary standard and is subject to numerous exceptions and qualifications. Much depends on the nature of the business. Many firms can and do survive with ratios considerably less than 2:1 and conversely, firms with ratios of 2 or more may have liquidity problems. Also, in interpreting this ratio it is important to bear in mind that the current ratio at the end of the year is not necessarily representative of that ratio throughout the year.

A very high current ratio can cause almost as much concern as a low ratio. A very low ratio might indicate that the firm is unable, at this point in time, to meet its short-term obligations as they become due. A very high ratio might be an indication of over-investment in current assets such as stock and debtors.

The current ratio is a rather crude measure of liquidity. For example, if the current assets comprise, say, £750 stock and £250 debtors, and when the debtors are requested to pay are they unable to do so, while the current liabilities comprise £500 creditors which are overdue for six months and who are now demanding payment, the firm is effectively unable to meet its short-term obligations. In such a case, the current ratio of 2:1 was a misleading measure of liquidity.

The current ratio, while crude, is considered to be a good measure of the adequacy of working capital in a going-concern context. Working capital is defined as the excess of current assets over current liabilities and indicates, subject to the reservations mentioned above, the ability of the business in gross money terms to meet its day-to-day obligations as they fall due. The comparison of current ratios in different accounting periods can be very useful in helping to detect trends.

$$\text{Acid-test ratio} = \frac{\text{Current assets less stock}}{\text{Current liabilities}} = \frac{25}{30} = 0.83 \text{ times}$$

While it is similar in form to the current ratio the acid-test ratio is considered to be a somewhat more severe test of liquidity as it excludes the least liquid portion of current assets—the stock. Stock is specifically excluded for two reasons. Firstly, stock is stated at historic cost in the balance sheet, yet its net realisable value would be a better measure of its potential contribution to the firm's liquidity. Secondly, and more importantly, if the firm sells its stock to pay its debts how is it to continue trading?

Once again there is no general optimal value for the acid-test ratio. To the extent that it measures a firm's ability to pay its debts during a crisis one might expect that it should normally not fall below 1:1. However as with the current ratio, it will be found that many firms can survive quite well with ratios considerably less than 1:1 and others can have liquidity problems with ratios in excess of this.

As with all ratios it is important to remember that these liquidity ratios are only indicators of position/trends and do not give a complete picture. The trends or position highlighted by these ratios should be investigated further and it is particularly important that, before drawing any conclusions from an assessment of liquidity ratios, a detailed examination of the quality and ageing of the current assets and the current liabilities should be undertaken. It is only after such examination that any meaningful interpretation can be made.

The similar ratio to the current ratio (CA:CL) is the relationship between long-term assets and long-term capital employed (i.e. FA:CE). People often fail to appreciate that liquidity problems in a company are frequently caused by the incorrect financing of fixed assets. As a general rule long-term assets should be financed by long-term finance as this would otherwise place liquidity strains on the company. In this respect it must be remembered that a basic level of working capital will also be present in all businesses. Such working capital will be permanent and should be financed by long-term funds.

GEARING (LEVERAGE) RATIOS

The second area of concern with any balance sheet is the composition of long-term capital, i.e. capital employed. It will be recalled that capital employed typically comprises of invested share capital, retained earnings and long-term borrowings. Some borrowings are usually beneficial to a company since interest payments are tax deductible, making it a cheap form of finance compared to ordinary share capital. Dividends are not deductible for tax purposes but there is no requirement to pay them (to ordinary shareholders) if the company cannot afford to. Nevertheless interest on borrowings must be paid regardless of the underlying profitability of the firm. Thus excessive 'gearing' or 'leverage' increases the risk for ordinary shareholders due to large interest payments, eventual repayment of loans and perhaps curtailing the borrowing potential in situations of emergency. If a business incurs so much debt so that it becomes unable to meet the required interest and capital repayments, lenders can appoint a receiver, often to the detriment of shareholders.

The importance of gearing ratios is that they provide information about one aspect of the firm's risk, its *financial risk*. If an organisation increases its gearing, the return expected by its owners should increase, as a result of acquiring 'cheaper' loan financing. In other words, the prior right to income (and eventual repayment) determines that the return attributable to lenders of loan capital is generally less than that required by the ordinary share-holders. On the other hand, the financial risk to ordinary shareholders is increased with the higher leverage because:

(*a*) the increased risk of the loss of control and (possibly) liquidation, if fixed interest payments cannot be met, and

(*b*) the increased variability of returns to owners, since in years of low profits only small dividends can be paid.

Two commonly used ratios to evaluate gearing are calculated as follows, based on the balance sheet of A Ltd:

$$\text{Debt/equity ratio} = \frac{\text{Long-term debt}}{\text{Shareholders' funds}} = \frac{25}{45} \times 100 = 55\%$$

$$\text{Debt/capital employed ratio} = \frac{\text{Long-term debt}}{\text{Capital employed}} = \frac{25}{70} \times 100 = 35\%$$

In calculating gearing ratios, preference shares create a definitional problem. Although preference shares are not regarded as debt in the normal sense of the word, they do carry a fixed rate of dividend that is payable ahead of ordinary dividends. If preference shares are redeemable by the company at some future date then they are more closely related to debt rather than equity. In such circumstances, redeemable preference shares would be classified as debt for the purpose of ascertaining gearing levels. However, if preference shares are not redeemable there is a strong argument for treating them as equity. Otherwise it would be misleading to ascribe the same debt/equity ratio to a company with, say, a 50% debt/50% equity as one with 50% preference shares/50% equity.

It should be noted that since capital employed is the aggregate of shareholders' funds and long-term debt, both these ratios provide the exact same message but in slightly different ways. As a result it is usual to calculate only one gearing ratio based on the balance sheet of a company. Care must also be taken in making inter-company comparisons that gearing ratios have been calculated in a similar manner for all companies. For example, it is not uncommon to include overdrafts as part of long-term finance in some calculations.

Like all financial ratios, there is no optimal level that is appropriate in relation to gearing levels. Much depends on the assets of the company and the expected volatility of future earnings. As a crude rule of thumb, if a company's debt/capital employed percentage exceeded 50 per cent this would indicate the presence of a substantial financial risk. However, it is important to remember that it is often the change in the ratio over time that is more informative than its actual level at a given point in time.

PROFITABILITY AND THE PYRAMID OF RATIOS

The final area to evaluate in any company is its overall profit performance. This is usually done by calculating a number of financial ratios relating the profit performance of the business to the overall capital invested. 'Investment' can be defined in a number of different ways and is commonly defined either in terms of capital employed, shareholders' funds or total assets. Thus, the overall measure of profitability relating to investment can be either (1) return on capital employed (ROCE), (2) return on shareholders' funds (ROSF) or (3) return on total assets (ROTA). In other words, the overall profitability is usually measured in relation to the funds invested in the business. It is a measure of the effectiveness (especially when viewed over a period) of the custodians of a business in managing the resources entrusted to them. Depending on the purpose for which this ratio is being used—and thus, determining the basis for both the calculation of 'profit' and 'investment'—the ratio enables comparisons to be made either with the expected return, the return generally obtained by other businesses in the same sector or other returns generally available in the market. A satisfactory return on investment is the long-run objective of any business. It is important that whatever measure is used it will be used consistently. The consistent application of a financial ratio allows profitability trends to be observed. They are calculated as follows:

(1) ROCE = Profit before interest and tax (PBIT)/capital employed.
(2) ROSF = Profit before tax (PBT)/shareholders' funds (although this ratio is sometimes calculated on an after-tax basis).
(3) ROTA = Profit before interest and tax.

The choice of profit figure for each of these ratios is important. Profit before tax (or after-tax) is related to shareholders' funds, since this is the residue from trading operations which is available for distribution by way of dividend to shareholders. (Interest expense is automatically deducted in arriving at profit before tax.) However, profit before interest and tax (PBIT) is used in relation to return on capital employed (ROCE). This is because the appropriate return to long-term capital employed is the profit available to the providers of all long-term capital. Since interest is part of that return, return should be defined in terms of profit before interest (and tax).

Likewise in relation to return on total assets (ROTA), the profit before interest and tax (PBIT) is also used. This is because we want to ascertain the return on investment in the form of total assets and so we exclude interest which is the result of a financing decision rather that an investment decision. Thus, the owner of a house which he rents to tenants will generate the same ROTA regardless of the method used to finance the investment.

Any of these three profitability ratios can be used to construct a pyramid of ratios. The pyramid of ratios can take many forms, depending on the nature of the company's activities and the preference of the user. One version, based on ROTA, is shown below:

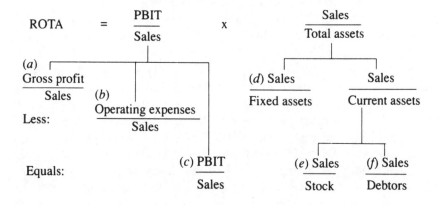

Hence, overall profitability performance of any enterprise can be determined by reference to the following areas:

(*a*) Gross profit ratio
(*b*) Operating expenses ratio
(*c*) Profit margin ratio
(*d*) Turnover of fixed assets
(*e*) Stock turnover ratio
(*f*) Debtor days ratio

Each of these ratios will be discussed in turn. It should be stressed that, in addition to the above ratios, many more can be specified. However the benefit of calculating additional ratios can only be evaluated in the context of providing additional information to the decision maker. Extracting a comprehensive set of accounting ratios may not be efficient as a means of evaluating financial statements. Because of the commonality between the financial data used, there will be a strong relationship between the various ratios which are computed from the same data. Consequently, beyond a limited set of ratios, there is very little information to be obtained in calculating additional ratios. Preliminary research conducted by the author in Ireland suggests that there is only a small number of ratios which need to be used in evaluating financial statements, although there is some ambiguity concerning which ratios comprise this small set.

Gross profit ratio
This ratio tells us the profitability of the business relative to sales after deducting the cost of producing the goods sold. In non-manufacturing businesses, the cost of goods sold is usually taken to be purchases adjusted for opening and closing stock. In a manufacturing business cost of goods sold will include all material, labour and overhead costs incurred in producing the goods which have been sold.

$$\text{Gross profit ratio} = \frac{\text{Gross profit}}{\text{Sales}} \times 100 = \%$$

The gross profit percentage, it should be noted, is always related to sales. However, gross profit ratio is sometimes interchanged with 'mark-up', which is the gross profit expressed as a percentage of costs. Thus, a gross margin (on sales) of 20 per cent is the same amount expressed as a mark-up (on costs) of 25 per cent.

The gross profit ratio is an indicator of the efficiency of the production operations and also of the appropriateness of the product pricing policy of the business. If for example the gross profit ratio has fallen in relation to the previous period we know that either increased costs have not been passed on by means of higher selling prices or that production inefficiencies have occurred which are not possible to recover through increased sales prices, or that the sales prices have been reduced. Alternatively, the change in the gross profit ratio may be due to an error or change in stock valuation methods.

In a situation where the gross profit ratio has changed either up or down from one period to another it can be very useful to examine each individual cost item contained in the cost of goods sold as a percentage of sales. If detailed information is available to do this it will be possible to pick out the specific area of improvement or deterioration. The precise reason for the change, however, can only be ascertained by asking the line manager for detailed explanations.

Operating expenses (to sales) ratio

Operating expenses (which exclude interest on borrowings) must, by definition, be the difference between gross profit and profit before interest and tax. It is usual that operating expenses would in turn be divided into appropriate classifications such as distribution costs/sales, administration expenses/sales etc. In this way dominant expense headings can be identified and their trend monitored over time. A typical sub-division of the operating expenses/sales ratio would be:

$$\frac{\text{Distribution costs}}{\text{Sales}} \times 100\% = \%$$

Profit margin (to sales) ratio

This ratio indicates the profitability of the business relative to sales after deducting all operating expenses excluding interest. It is a general indicator of the overall profitability and a measure of the ability of management to react to changes in the business environment and maintain the profitability of the firm. A study of this ratio gives the user an indication as to the quality of management, especially when the business in general, or the specific business sector, is in a recessionary state.

$$\text{Profit margin ratio} = \frac{\text{PBIT}}{\text{Sales}} \times 100 = \%$$

When calculating either return on capital employed (ROCE) or return on total assets (ROTA), the net profit figure used is that of profit before interest (and taxation). However, in calculating return on shareholders' funds (ROSF) the profit figure chosen is that of net profit after interest. Thus the ROSF ratio uses the net profit figure (profit before tax—PBT) which represents the residue available to shareholders. (This ratio can be calculated on an after-tax basis.)

A reduction in the profit margin to sales ratio may indicate that the costs are increasing at a faster rate than can be recovered through increased sales, e.g. the rent of a shop may have been increased but the sales volume did not increase, or the cost of materials may have increased but the full increase could not be passed on to the customer. Conversely, an increase in the percentage could indicate that a higher volume of goods was being sold from the same sales outlets at the same prices as those of the previous period, thereby spreading costs over a larger volume of sales.

Variations in this percentage are important since profit is the lifeblood of any business, and adverse variations may be warnings of future problems.

Turnover of fixed assets

This ratio indicates the relative efficiency with which the firm utilises its resources to generate sales. It is, again, a measure of overall efficiency. However, if the book value of fixed assets is used then this ratio should automatically improve over time as the same quantity of assets are depreciated.

$$\text{Fixed asset turnover} = \frac{\text{Sales}}{\text{Fixed assets}} = \text{£x}$$

Stock turnover ratio

The stock turnover ratio estimates the number of days' stock being carried by the business. It is an indicator of the liquidity of the stock as it tells the number of days taken to convert the stock into either cash or debtors. The ratio is only an estimate. The important thing to remember, however, is that, when calculated on a consistent basis, any comparison of the ratios between periods will be valid.

$$\text{Stock turnover} = \frac{\text{Average stock} \quad \text{x} \quad \text{no. of days in period}}{\text{Cost of goods sold}} = \text{days}$$

However, the ratio is sometimes calculated using closing stock rather than average stock and sales rather than cost of sales.

Where the accounting period is for twelve months' duration, the number of days in the period will be 365 (or 360 to simplify calculations). Care must always be taken to note the length of the period before calculating ratios such as this. The stock turnover ratio, based on monthly accounts, would use 30 days as opposed to 365 days.

The number of days' stock carried by a manufacturing business should relate closely with production and marketing requirements. Indeed, the level of stock maintained is subject to conflict between the various functional managers. The marketing manager may wish to see a high level of finished goods so that orders can be filled immediately. This is particularly important where competition is intense between products, and customers do not have brand loyalty. The production manager will have other priorities, especially regarding the supply of raw materials. The finance manager generally seeks to minimise stock levels in order to eliminate the costs of holding stocks, including potential obsolescence costs. On the other hand, incremental sales can be very profitable. Consider the financial impact on a small shop having a generous supply of raincoats during a particularly bad spell of weather during a typical Irish summer.

Generally, the lower the number of days' stock being held the greater the efficiency of the inventory management of a business, but it could also indicate, particularly if it is lower than the industry average, a deficiency in stock management resulting in too low a level of stock being carried which could lead to frequent interruptions of production and possible consequent inability to meet orders. However, in most cases a minimising of the inventory period, consistent with the production cycle, is desirable as it in turn minimises the financing required to carry stocks.

A deterioration in the stock turnover ratio could be an indicator of any or all of the following factors:

(*i*) Inefficiency may have arisen in production resulting in a slower through-put of stock or overproduction of finished goods.

(*ii*) Inefficiencies may have arisen in the control of stock resulting in excessive purchases.

(*iii*) Items of stock may have become slow moving or obsolete, resulting in a build-up of the overall stock level.

(*iv*) A fall-off in sales demand may have resulted in a build-up of finished goods in stock.

If there has been a change in the stock turnover period, further insight can be gained by examining the individual components of stock relative to the cost of goods sold. Stock is usually made up of raw materials, work in progress and finished goods, and if each of these is compared to the cost of goods sold it will help to pinpoint more closely where the change has arisen, e.g. if it is found that the raw material figure in relation to cost of goods sold has gone up then it indicates that it is probably in the stock control/ purchasing area that the problem has arisen or that possibly increased levels of purchases are being made.

Debtor days ratio

This ratio gives an estimate of the *average* number of days' credit taken by debtors and is therefore an indicator of the liquidity of the debtors.

$$\text{Debtor days} \; = \; \frac{\text{Debtors} \quad x \quad \text{no. of days in period}}{\text{Credit sales}} \; = \; \text{days}$$

It is unlikely that credit sales will be available from the financial statements. Consequently the total sales (turnover) figure will be used as a proxy measure for credit sales. Clearly, the resulting credit allowed period will be biased but, more often than not, it is the trend of the ratio that is important rather than its absolute value.

It is useful to compare the 'debtor days' with the actual credit terms being quoted as a measure of the efficiency of credit control in the business, especially when compared to industry norms, and as a guide to the quality of the debtors. The collection cycle can be reduced by reviewing all of the following:

—promptness of invoicing
—accuracy of sales invoices
—invoice frequency and timing
—accounts receivable monitoring procedures
—cash discounts
—cash lodgment procedures

The reasons for any changes in the collection period from one year to the next should be ascertained. For example, changes in credit terms may occur, such as more exports at 90 days' credit. In this context it is important to note that credit terms are an important element in the marketing mix. A firm offering lower credit terms than those available from competitors may find sales more difficult to obtain.

Any change in credit terms given is particularly important, not only when comparing accounts of past periods, but also in assessing the validity of projections for future periods. For every additional day's credit given an appropriate amount of finance will be needed to carry the additional debtors. Thus a lack of control in this area very often leads to excessive borrowing requirements.

As with all financial ratios the debtor days ratio can be distorted by abnormal year-end activities. Thus, abnormal year-end sales in a particular year would result in debtor days not being comparable to prior years. Likewise seasonal sales just before accounting year end will give a biased debtor days ratio. For example, a company selling central heating oil on credit will have a distorted debtor days ratio if significant sales are made on credit during December, the last month of of the accounting period.

If the collection period differs from the actual terms quoted the additional finance needed can be calculated as follows:

$$\text{Proposed debtors} = \frac{\text{Sales} \quad x \quad \text{credit period}}{\text{No. of days in period}}$$

Now this proposed debtors figure should be deducted from the actual debtors figure to give the extra finance needed to carry the additional debtors, e.g. if a business projects sales of £1,000 for a particular year and quotes credit terms of 90 days the debtor financing requirement will be calculated as follows:

$$\frac{£1,000}{365} \quad \text{x} \quad 90 \text{ days} \quad = \quad £246$$

If the debtors actually took 120 days to pay the figure would be:

$$\frac{£1,000}{365} \quad \text{x} \quad 120 \text{ days} \quad = \quad £329$$

Therefore the additional finance needed to extend credit from 90 days to 120 days, based on credit sales of £1,000, will be (329–246) = £83.

Credit period received

Although this ratio has not been specified in the above pyramid of ratios it should be mentioned since it measures the average period of credit received from suppliers.

$$\text{Credit days received} \ = \ \frac{\text{Creditors} \quad \text{x} \quad \text{no. of days in period}}{\text{Credit purchases}}$$

Like the figure for credit sales in the debtor days ratio, the figure for credit purchases will rarely be available. Consequently, the cost of sales figure or even the sales figure will be substituted. Clearly, the credit received period may be biased as a result. Nevertheless, the ratio provides a useful key in assessing the management of working capital. Moreover, what is important is the trend in this ratio rather than its absolute value.

In many ways it is complementary to the debtor days ratio. Ideally a business would like to receive as much credit from suppliers as it grants to its own customers. While credit from suppliers is a valuable course of finance there is always the possibility of extracting credit to an unacceptable level. Indeed, beyond certain limits interest penalties may be imposed by the supplier.

Example:

The various financial ratios outlined above can be calculated from the following profit and loss account and balance sheet:

PROFIT AND LOSS ACCOUNT FOR THE YEAR ENDED
31 DECEMBER 19 . 1

		£	£
Sales:	cash		64,000
	credit		360,000
			424,000
Less:	Cost of goods sold		
	Opening stock	16,000	
	Purchases	350,000	
	Deduct: closing stock	(22,000)	(344,000)
Gross profit			80,000
Less expenses:			
Administration			(30,000)
Distribution			(25,000)
Interest			(2,000)
Profit on ordinary activities before tax			23,000
Tax on profit on ordinary activities			(10,000)
Profit retained for year			13,000
Profit brought forward			17,000
Profit carried forward			30,000

BALANCE SHEET AS AT 31 DECEMBER 19 . 1

	£	£
Fixed assets		162,000
Current assets		
Stock	22,000	
Debtors	53,000	
Bank	12,000	87,000
		249,000
Financed by:		
Ordinary share capital		150,000
Profit and loss account		30,000
		180,000
10% Debentures		20,000
Current Liabilities—creditors		49,000
		249,000

The following represent some major calculations and figures:
—Shareholders' funds (Share capital + Reserves) = £180,000
—Capital employed (SC + R + LTD) = £200,000
—Net current assets or working capital (CA – CL) = £38,000
—Net assets (FA + CA – CL – LTD) = Shareholders' funds = £180,000
—PBIT (profit + interest) = £23,000 + £2,000 = £25,000
—PBT = £23,000
—Profit after tax = £13,000

Liquidity
—Current ratio (CA divided by CL) = 1.77 times
—Acid-test ratio ((CA – S) divided by CL) = 1.32 times

Gearing/Leverage
—L.T. debt equity ratio (LTD divide by SF) x 100 = 11.1%
—L.T. debt as % of capital employed (LTD divided by CE) x 100 = 10%

Profitability
—Return on shareholders' funds (ROSF) (PBT divide by SF) x 100 = 12.77%
—Return on capital employed (ROCE) (PBIT divide by CE) x 100 = 12.5%
—Return on total assets (ROTA (PBIT divide by TA) x 100 = 10.04%
—Return on sales (PBIT divided by sales) x 100 = 5.89%
—Gross profit (on sales) (GP divided by sales) x 100 = 18.86%
—Operating expenses to sales (operating expenses divided by sales) x 100 = 12.97%
—Turnover of fixed assets (Sales divided by FA) = 2.61 times
—Stock turnover (AV. stock divided by COGS) x 365 = 20 days
—Debtor days (Debtors divided by credit sales) x 365 = 54 days

LIMITATIONS OF RATIO ANALYSIS

A number of financial ratios have been discussed in the above section, (and many more could be added). Although ratio analysis may be a useful way of interpreting financial statements, it is important to note some limitations in their use and to keep them in perspective.

Ratios must be interpreted in the light of the individual circumstances. For example, a return on capital employed of, say, 10 per cent cannot be interpreted as being good or bad. With an inflation rate of 20 per cent, the return is inadequate. Alternatively, a rate of 10 per cent may be acceptable for a very low risk business.

Financial analysts constantly search for some standard of comparison against which to judge whether the relationships that they have found are favourable or unfavourable. One such standard is the performance of companies in the same industrial sector. For example, Allied Irish Banks will be frequently compared to the Bank of Ireland. The yardstick may be a comparable company or the average record of a number of companies in the industry. For instance, company A suffers a drop of 5 per cent in its return on total assets during an accounting period. However, if the return on total assets of other companies in the same industry fell by 20 per cent, then company A's performance was favourable rather than unfavourable. One difficulty, however, is in defining an industry within which companies may be compared. Thus, while the comparison of say, Jury's Hotels and Ryan Hotels may be valid, the comparison of say, Jury's and Xtravision's is not, even though both companies are classified in the 'leisure' sector. In addition, inter-company comparisons create their own problems, especially where companies do not employ similar accounting methods. Thus, a firm which uses the straight-line method of depreciation is not directly comparable with a firm that uses the reducing balance method. Likewise, different accounting treatments of, say, grants received on fixed assets (i.e. capitalisation or immediate write down against the relevant fixed asset) will also distort the comparative ratios.

As an alternative to making comparisons of firms within an industry, the analyst may make judgments about a company over a number of accounting periods. However, this approach may not be necessarily informative, especially where the environment in which the firm operates changes or the company enters a different line of business. Past performance is not necessarily the performance that *should* have been obtained. Thus, the fact the net margin on sales was 3 per cent last year and 5 per cent this year indicates improvement, but if there is evidence that the margin should have been 10 per cent, the return in both years was poor.

There a number of other limitations associated with using ratio analysis as a means of interpreting financial statements. Over a period of years, changes in the value of money and/or rising prices need to be adjusted for. For example, the ratio of sales to fixed assets will be automatically biased by changing price levels. Sales, by definition, will be stated in terms of current revenues whereas, more often than not, fixed assets will be shown at their historic cost (less accumulated depreciation).

Moreover, ratios reflect past performance which is not necessarily a reliable guide to what may happen in the future. There are many factors not contained in historic financial statements which are relevant to estimating the future financial performance of an enterprise. What are the future plans of the business? The quality of its workforce? Its distribution and marketing network? All such factors are highly relevant for a comprehensive analysis to be undertaken.

The principal benefit of ratio analysis is to suggest questions that need to be answered. Ratios never provide the answers but should lead to an investigation as to what may be right or wrong. In other words, ratios are a tool which should be used in a critical fashion and as an aid to judgment.

QUESTION 14.1 (SM)

A business may generate problems but simultaneously experience liquidity problems.

Requirement:
  (a) Define profitability and liquidity.
  (b) Explain the difference between them.

QUESTION 14.2 (A)

One common definition of working capital is, 'current assets minus current liabilities'. An analysis of a company's recent financial statements showed:

	£
Turnover for year (all credit sales)	240,000
Purchases for year (on credit)	140,000
Gross profit for year	70,000
Opening stock	90,000
Closing stock	60,000
Trade debtors at end of year	40,000
Trade creditors at end of year	45,000
Corporation tax payable on profits for year	20,000
Dividends proposed (but not paid)	15,000
Bank and cash balances	55,000

Requirement:

(*a*) Comment upon the definition of working capital.

(*b*) Calculate the net current assets from the above data.

(*c*) Calculate the time needed for goods purchased to be converted into cash assuming 360 working days in the year.

(The Chartered Association of Certified Accountants)

QUESTION 14.3 (SM)

The following are summarised balance sheets of TV Company Ltd, as at 31 December:

	19 . 7	19 . 8
	£	£
Fixed assets (Net)	25,000	30,000
Stock	60,000	70,000
Debtors	50,000	60,000
Bank	20,000	15,000
	155,000	175,000
Shareholders' funds	85,000	105,000
10% Debentures	20,000	20,000
Current liabilities	50,000	50,000
	155,000	175,000
Profit and loss account extracts		
Sales (all on credit)	250,000	288,000
Gross profit	67,000	76,000
Profit before interest and tax	22,000	24,000
Net profit (before tax)	20,000	22,000

Requirement:
Calculate the following ratios for 19 . 7 and 19 . 8:
(1) Current ratio and acid test ratios
(2) Return on shareholders' funds
(3) Return on capital employed
(4) Average period of credit allowed (assume 360 days)
(5) Stock turn ratio (assume 360 days)
(6) Gross profit ratio
(7) Turnover of fixed assets
(8) Profit margin ratio

QUESTION 14.4 (SM)

The following data relate to Modern Developments Ltd, a manufacturing company, at 31 March 199 . based on its first trading year ended on that date.

	£
Trade creditors	60,000
Closing stock	40,000
Debtors	90,000
Plant and machinery (net)	185,000
Land at cost	105,000
Buildings (net)	110,000
Share capital	250,000
Debentures	200,000
Cash and bank balance	45,000
Sales (all on credit)	350,000
Direct materials	80,000
Production wages	50,000
Production overheads	40,000
Interest paid	25,000
Administration costs	90,000

Note: Plant, machinery and buildings have been depreciated and are included in production overhead above.

Requirement:
(*a*) Calculate the amount of profit earned by the company during the year ended 31 March 199. and prepare a balance sheet as at that date.
(*b*) Calculate appropriate ratios which will help to explain the performance of the organisation.
(The Chartered Association of Certified Accountants)

QUESTION 14.5 (SM)

The accountant in your company has developed a computer spreadsheet to assist in the prediction of profits and closing balance sheets. The model has been prepared using important accounting ratios and relationships.

By entering the sales forecast and the values of various parameters, the model will print data about profit for the accounting period and a closing balance sheet. The parameters are as follows:

Gross profit % sales	60
Selling expense as % sales	15
Administration costs, excluding interest	£12,000
Tax rate on profits	40%
ROCE (PBIT/CE)	20%
Debt equity ratio	1:2
Interest rate % on debt	10
Ratio of fixed to net current assets	1:1
Current ratio	3
Ordinary dividend pay out %	25

The first trial of the model will use sales of £80,000. The only expenses to be deducted from gross profit are selling expenses, administration costs and interest payable on debt.

Requirement:

(*a*) Prepare a profit statement based on the above factors and using sales of £80,000 which shows:

(*i*) Net profit before interest and tax;

(*ii*) Profit available for distribution;

(*iii*) Dividends.

(*b*) Determine the book value of long-term debt and the current liabilities and prepare a closing balance sheet in as much detail as possible.

(The Chartered Association of Certified Accountants)

QUESTION 14.6 (A)

You are given summarised information about two sole traders in the same line of business; A and B, as follows:

BALANCE SHEETS AT 30 JUNE

	A			B		
	£000	£000	£000	£000	£000	£000
Land			80			260
Buildings		120			200	
Less: Depreciation		40	80		—	200
Plant		90			150	
Less: Depreciation		70	20		40	110
			180			570
Stocks		80			100	
Debtors		100			90	
Bank		—			10	
		180			200	

Creditors	110	120
Bank	50	—
	160	120
	20	80
	200	650
Capital	100	300
Profit for year	30	100
	130	400
Less: Drawings	30	40
	100	360
Land revaluation	—	160
Loan (10% p.a.)	100	130
	200	650
Sales	1,000	3,000
Cost of sales	400	2,000

Requirement:

(*a*) Produce a table of eight ratios calculated for both businesses.

(*b*) Write a report outlining the strengths and weaknesses of the two businesses. Include comment on any major areas where the simple use of the figures could be misleading.

(The Chartered Association of Certified Accountants)

QUESTION 14.7 (SM)

At the end of its first year of trading Bert plc has the following summarised balance sheet. The fixed assets were bought, and the debentures issued, at the beginning of the year.

	£
Fixed assets at cost	120,000
Current assets	130,000
	250,000
Share capital	100,000
Profit and loss account	65,000
Debentures (10%)	50,000
Creditors	30,000
Bank overdraft	5,000
	250,000

This balance sheet is after all adjustments except for depreciation of fixed assets. The bank overdraft is temporary.

Requirement:

(*a*) Prepare in columnar form five balance sheets, headed (i) to (v), incorporating the assumption that:

  (*i*) no depreciation is to be provided;

  (*ii*) depreciation of 10 per cent (straight-line basis) is to be provided;

  (*iii*) depreciation of 20 per cent (reducing balance basis) is to be provided;

  (*iv*) fixed assets are to be revalued by plus 20 per cent and no depreciation is to be provided;

  (*v*) fixed assets are to be revalued by plus 20 per cent and depreciation of 10 per cent (straight-line basis) is to be provided.

(*b*) For each of the five balance sheets, calculate: (showing workings clearly)

  (*i*) Return on closing owner's equity (ROOE);

  (*ii*) Return on closing capital employed (ROCE).

(*c*) Explain clearly but simply, in your own words, what these two ratios (ROOE and ROCE) are designed to show.

(*d*) Assuming that the estimated useful life of the fixed assets to the business is correct at ten years, which of the five balance sheets you prepared in (a) above is likely to be most useful for the calculation of these two ratios if the fixed assets are buildings? Why?

(*e*) Would your answer to (d) above be altered if the fixed assets were machines used in manufacturing? Why?

(The Chartered Association of Certified Accountants)

QUESTION 14.8 (A)

For a number of years Martin Smith has been employed as the works' manager of a company which manufactures cardboard cartons.

He has now decided to leave the company and to set up a similar business of his own on 1 January 19 . 6 but, before taking this step he wants to see what his financial results are likely to be for his first year of operations.

In order to do this, he has obtained certain 'average industry' ratios from his trade association, the Cardboard Carton Manufacturers' Association (CCMA), which he wants to use as his norm for predicting the first year's results.

	CCMA statistics 19 . 4 (based on year-end figures, 365 days)
Sales/net assets employed	2.8 times
Gross profit/sales	28.0%
Profit margin to sales	10.0%
Fixed assets/working capital	1.5:1
Current assets/current liabilities	2.25:1
Debtors collection period	36.5 days
Creditors payment period	58.4 days

At this stage he consults you, asks for your professional assistance and supplies the following information.

He informs you that he is able to contribute £40,000 as capital and has been promised a long term loan (interest free) of £6,000 from a relative.

Initially, he intends to acquire a stock of materials at a cost of £20,000 but his (simple) average stock for the first year will be £18,500. Purchases of materials for the year, excluding the initial purchase of stock, £20,000, will be £97,800. All purchases and sales will be on credit.

Sundry accruals at 31 December 19 . 6 are estimated at £350 and bank and cash balances at £5,000.

He proposes to withdraw £10,000 during the year for living expenses.

Requirement:
Prepare, in as much detail as can be elicited from the information supplied, a forecast trading and profit and loss account for Martin Smith's proposed business for the year ended 31 December 19 . 6, and a forecast balance sheet at that date.

All figures should be stated to the nearest £10.
(The Chartered Association of Certified Accountants)

15.

Flow of Funds Statements

FUNDS FLOW STATEMENTS AND SSAP 10

Traditionally, published accounts of companies have comprised of a profit and loss account showing, inter alia, the amount of profit generated in the business during the year, and a balance sheet showing the disposition of the company's resources at the beginning and end of the year. However, for a fuller understanding of the company's affairs it is also necessary to identify the movements in assets, liabilities and capital which have taken place during the year and the resultant effect on net liquid funds. The profit and loss account does not show why the amount of cash available to the organisation has increased or decreased during the accounting period. In other words, a company may be earning a large amount of profit but not generating a great deal of cash.

This information is not specifically disclosed by a profit and loss account and balance sheet but can be made available in the form of a statement of source and application of funds, which has different formats and titles. The funds flow statement is not a replacement for the profit and loss account and balance sheet, although the information which it contains is a selection, reclassification and summarisation of the information contained in those two statements.

There are, at least, two commonly used definitions of funds. The narrowest definition assumes that funds consist only of cash resources, i.e. the net liquid funds. The resulting statement, often called a cash funds flow statement, explains the movement in cash (and cash equivalent) funds between successive balance sheets. Thus, the cash funds flow statement explains the change in the 'net liquid funds'which is the firm's cash at bank and in hand less other borrowings repayable within one year of the accounting date.

A broader definition of funds is that of 'working capital funds'. The working capital cycle of a business is the length of time required for a company to transform cash into stock, stock into debtors and debtors into cash again. This cycle is continuous, and at various stages within the cycle the cash balance will fluctuate although the total amount of working capital will remain unchanged. Thus a cash receipt of £10,000 from a debtor will change the bank balance of the company but it does not change the amount of working capital. Likewise, the payment of cash to creditors represents a rearrangement of the balance within the working capital cycle, but it does not change the overall amount of working capital.

The choice of a cash-based or working capital-based funds flow statement depends on the potential use of the information. If users are interested in the liquidity position of the business they may be very interested to know that the cash balance has been maintained relative to the start of the year, but this has been achieved by slowing down the payment to creditors. Alternatively, they may be interested to know that the increased overdraft is due to excessive holding of stock and debtors. From the perspective of evaluating financial management decisions, the user may want to identify whether more or fewer funds have been tied up in working capital as a whole.

Because of the importance of funds flow to businesses in general, and to users of financial statements, the ASC produced an accounting standard in July 1975. The standard (SSAP 10) requires all reporting entities with an annual sales of £25,000 or more to produce a Statement of Source and Application of Funds as part of their audited financial statements. This was the first accounting standard to require an addition to the basic financial documents of the balance sheet and profit and loss account. However, the accounting standard does not specify a prescribed format. Instead it acknowledges that different methods of presentation may equally comply with the provisions of SSAP 10.

Basically, the funds flow statement moves attention away from profit and towards the cash flow. The objective of the funds flow statement is to show the manner in which the operations of the business have been financed as well as showing how its financial resources have been used, and the format selected should be designed to achieve this objective. It should clearly show the funds generated or absorbed by the operations of the business and the manner in which any resulting surplus of liquid assets has been applied or any deficiency of such assets has been financed, distinguishing the long term from the short term. The statement should distinguish the use of funds for the purchase of fixed assets from funds used in increasing the working capital of the business.

In other words, a funds flow statement will show the funds generated (absorbed) from operations during the period, in addition to providing information about all the investing and financing activities of the company during the period. Thus, a funds flow statement should assist shareholders, creditors and others in assessing such factors as:

—Reasons for the differences between the net profit reported and the increase/decrease in the bank balance.

—The company's ability to meet its obligations and pay dividends.
—The company's ability to generate positive cash flows in future periods.

Preparation of funds flow statements

Funds flow statements are prepared from successive balance sheets and the firm's profit and loss account. The following sequence is recommended with respect to their construction:

1. Funds flow statements start with the source of funds generated by the company during the year. One source of funds generated by a company is that of 'profitable trading'. If all trading transactions were transacted in cash, ignoring other transactions involving the purchase of fixed assets etc., then net profit earned would correspond to the increase in the cash resources of the firm and hence result in an increase in working capital. (A net loss would represent funds absorbed, i.e. would indicate that the firm, ignoring other transactions, was depleting its working capital funds.)

However, the net profit calculation will automatically include non-cash items of expenditure, of which depreciation is the most common. Depreciation is a charge against profits for a year, being an attempt to reflect the partial using-up of the life of the company's fixed assets; it is simply a book-keeping entry and cannot possibly of itself use or generate cash. Therefore, *funds from operations* can be determined by either of two methods to be illustrated using the following simplified example where the only asset of the business is cash and there are no liabilities. Thus, depreciation is the only item in the profit and loss account not involving cash. For example:

PROFIT AND LOSS ACCOUNT FOR YEAR ENDED . . .

		£
Sales		21,000
Less: Purchases		10,000
Gross Profit		11,000
Less: Wages	5,000	
Administration	2,000	
Depreciation	1,000	8,000
Net Profit		3,000

The simplest or most straightforward method would be to deduct from sales the outlays on cost of sales and operating expenses such as wages and administration. This surplus (£4,000) is, by definition, the cash funds generated from operations.

As an alternative, the 'add back' method is proposed and is used almost exclusively in preparing funds flow statements. Using this method, funds from operations can be determined by taking the net profit figure (given) and adding back the depreciation expense.

Unfortunately, this shortcut method of adding back depreciation to net profit may, at first sight, create the false impression that depreciation is a source of cash. Depreciation is purely a book-keeping entry and, as such, can never generate cash funds for the business. It is not a source of cash. In constructing cash funds flow statements we add back depreciation to the net profit figure simply because it provides a convenient short-cut in arriving at funds from operations.

However, to arrive at 'funds from operations', one further adjustment can be made to net profit in respect of profit (loss) on the sale of fixed assets. Consider the sale of land with a book value of £10,000 being sold for £12,000, thus generating a profit of £2,000. It is more meaningful to consider the entire £12,000 proceeds of sale as a distinct source of funds. Since the £2,000 gain has already been included in net profit, then the amount of the gain would be double counted, unless eliminated. Profits from the sale of fixed assets should be eliminated (deducted) from net profit. Likewise, losses on disposal must be ignored and are eliminated by adding them to our net profit figure.

In summary, we seek to initially determine net trading profit rather than net profit. Gains or losses on the sale of fixed assets do not constitute trading items and therefore, for cash funds flow purposes, should be eliminated from the net profit figure. However, the amount of cash involved will be included in total as a source.

2. Identify any other sources of funds, e.g. share issue. This information may need to be generated from the financial statements by, for example, comparing opening and closing figures relating to share capital, loans etc. in order to determine the amount of cash raised (or repaid).

3. Identify the application (uses) of cash, e.g. purchase of fixed assets, payment of tax and dividends. The purchase of fixed assets, if relevant, should be obvious from the note to financial statements relating to fixed assets. A separate reconciliation should be done for both taxation and dividends to identify the amount paid under both these headings during the year.

4. Prepare a schedule of changes in working capital items. Thus, for stocks, debtors, creditors and cash/bank balances identify whether the items have increased or decreased during the period. Increases in any current assets (or decreases in current liabilities) represent an increase in working capital. Increases in current liability items (or decrease in current assets) represent a decrease in working capital.

Example:
The following information has been presented to you and you are required to prepare a Statement of Source and Application of Funds for the year ended 31 December 19.2

BALANCE SHEET AT 31 DECEMBER　19.1　19.2

	£	£	£	£
Fixed assets (net)		23,500		26,000
Current assets				
Stock	10,500		12,800	
Debtors	11,000		13,000	
Bank	1,000		100	
	22,500		25,900	
Current liabilities				
Creditors	(13,900)		(15,500)	
Taxation	(2,000)	6,600	(1,000)	9,400
		30,100		35,400
Financed by:				
Share capital		10,000		12,000
Retained profits		10,100		13,600
14% debentures		10,000		9,800
		30,100		35,400

PROFIT AND LOSS ACCOUNT FOR YEAR ENDED 31 DECEMBER 19.2

	19.2
	£
Sales	85,000
Cost of sales	58,000
	27,000
Expenses (*Note 1*)	17,500
Net profit before tax	9,500
Taxation	3,000
Profit after tax	6,500
Dividends	3,000
	3,500

Note: Expenses for 19.2 includes £2,000 depreciation on fixed assets. There were no disposals of fixed assets during 19.2.

STATEMENT OF SOURCE AND APPLICATION OF FUNDS FOR YEAR ENDED 31 DECEMBER 19.2

		£
Sources of funds		
Net profit for year before tax		9,500
Add back: Depreciation		2,000
Funds from operations		11,500
Funds from other sources		
Issue of shares (*Note 5*)		2,000
		13,500
Application of funds		
Payment of tax (*Note 1*)	4,000	
Payment of dividends (*Note 1*)	3,000	
Purchase of fixed assets (*Note 2*)	4,500	
Repayment of debentures (*Note 3*)	200	11,700
		1,800
Increase/decrease in working capital		
Increase in stocks	2,300	
Increase in debtors	2,000	
Increase in creditors	(1,600)	
Movement in net liquid funds		
Decrease in bank balance	(900)	
	1,800	

Note 1. Reconciliation of tax and dividends

Taxation account				Dividends account			
		Bal.	2,000			Bal.	Nil
*Bank	4,000			*Bank	3,000		
Bal.	1,000	P/L	3,000	Bal.	Nil	P/L	3,000
	5,000		5,000		3,000		3,000
		Bal.	1,000				

* This must represent payments during the year. It is the only figure in this account that will not be directly evident from either the profit and loss account or balance sheet.

Note 2. Reconciliation of fixed assets

	£
Opening book value of fixed assets	23,500
Add: Additions during 19 . 2	4,500*
	28,000
Less: Disposals at book value	Nil
Depreciation for year	(2,000)
Closing book value per balance sheet	26,000

* Must represent the balancing figure, i.e. bank transaction.

Note 3. Opening liability re debentures	10,000
Closing liability re debentures	9,800
Amount repaid during 19 . 2	200

Note 4. Reconciliation of opening/closing retained profits

Opening retained profits	10,100
Add: retained profits for 19 . 2	3,500
Closing retained profits	13,600

Note 5. Opening share capital	10,000
Closing share capital	12,000
Share issue during year	2,000

A statement of source and application of funds is a record of historical fact. It will record payments in relation to dividends and purchase of fixed assets. It does not express an opinion whether the expenditure was necessary or whether it will provide long-term benefits for the company. Similarly, it may show an expansion of stock but it does not indicate whether this was due to:

(*a*) poor stock or production control.
(*b*) inability to sell the finished product.
(*c*) deliberate company policy to build up stocks.

Likewise, in the case of increased debtors it does not indicate whether the credit policy of the firm has changed or whether customers are taking additional credit, or indeed if the expansion in credit is due solely to the expansion of turnover. Thus, it is advisable to supplement the information contained in a statement of source and application of funds with basic financial ratios and information contained in the reports of the directors and the chairman.

CASH FUNDS FLOW STATEMENTS

For reference purposes, a funds flow statement in terms of cash funds is presented using the above data. The basic difference between the two statements concerns the definition of funds. A cash funds flow statement defines funds in terms of net liquid funds and thus explains the movement between the opening and closing cash (or cash equivalent) balances. All movements in balance sheet items are analysed in relation to their impact on cash funds. Thus the increase in stocks during the year, indicating a stock build-up, has a negative impact on cash funds. However, there are many different formats, of which the following represents one:

CASH FUNDS FLOW STATEMENT
FOR YEAR ENDED 31 DECEMBER 19 . 2

	£	£
Net profit for year		9,500
Add: Depreciation		2,000
Funds from operations		11,500
Changes in working capital		
Increase in stocks	(2,300)	
Increase in debtors	(2,000)	
Increase in creditors	+ 1,600	(2,700)
Funds internally generated		8,800
Long-term sources		
Share issue		2,000
		10,800
Applications		
Tax paid	(4,000)	
Dividends paid	(3,000)	
Purchase of fixed assets	(4,500)	
Repayment of debentures	(200)	(11,700)
Movement in net liquid funds		(900)
Proof:		
Opening bank balance		1,000
Closing bank balance		100
Decrease in bank balance		900

The above presentation highlights the need for a company to correctly finance its capital, i.e. long-term expenditure. In the above case, expenditure on fixed assets amounted to £4,500 and, in addition, the company repaid £200 debentures during the year. The total 'long-term' cash outflow amounted to £4,700. This was partly financed by the proceeds from a new share issue, £2,000. The shortfall, £2,700, must be financed therefore from internal cash flow. In general, when expenditure of a long-term nature, e.g. purchase of fixed assets, is not adequately financed by long-term sources, the firm's internal cash flow will be put under strain. However, it may well be that the firm is capable of generating sufficient funds from trading so that liquidity problems will not arise.

In brief, the above presentation focuses on the four main elements of cash flow, namely, profitable trading, management of working capital items, long-term sources of funds and long-term applications.

SOURCES OF FINANCE

A funds flow statement may indicate that additional finance is needed by the company. There are many sources of finance available in Ireland and a small number of important sources are now discussed.

Factoring

One short-term source increasing in popularity is that of factoring. This source of finance is extensively used in the US, England and, more recently, Ireland. Factoring operates in the following way: a firm sells its debtors to a factor for cash. It is then up to the factor to collect the money from the debtors. The factor may or may not accept the risk of bad debts, this depends on whether the factoring is with or without recourse. If it is factoring with recourse it means that the factor does not accept the risk of bad debts, in such a situation there is no risk involved in buying the debtors, so the firm selling them will receive more than if the 'bad debts' were also being sold. Before buying the debtors, the factor company must receive a list of who the debtors are so that they can assess their credibility and decide if there are some debtors they will not buy. Once the debtors have been sold it is usual to inform them that the debt has been transferred to the factor, and this is called 'Disclosed Factoring'. If it is the wish of the firm selling the debtors not to inform them this is called 'Undisclosed Factoring'. In such a case, the debtors pay their bills in the usual way and the money is immediately transferred to the factor. Factoring is suitable for a firm with a large amount of debtors which requires finance in a short time. However, it can be expensive.

The total factoring cost is made up of two elements; (1) interest charges which are are about 4 per cent above overdraft rates and, (2) a service charge to cover debt collection, accounting services etc. Normally this service charge will be about 2 per cent of the net sum factored.

The advantages of factoring are as follows:

(*a*) It releases money tied up in debtors. If the goods were sold, on say, six weeks credit, instead of having to wait six weeks for the money, the firm receives most of it now,

(*b*) If the factoring is without recourse it follows that the selling firm will not have to worry about bad debts.

(*c*) There is the elimination of sales ledger accounting.

(*d*) There is a saving in management time.

(*e*) No security has to be given to obtain the finance from the factor.

(*f*) Obtaining the required finance without having to resort to the bank means that the firm is less risky as it does not have to depend on one source for its finance.

(*g*) There is a saving in the discount allowed to customers.

(*h*) If the factoring is undisclosed the reputation and goodwill of a firm is not affected in any way.

The permanent needs of a firm cannot be properly financed from short-term sources, such as factoring. Such firms must be clearly aware of the medium- and especially the long-term sources of finance.

Sale and leaseback and leasing

This is a suitable source of finance for items who own valuable fixed assets such as land and premises. Using this method, the firm may sell its premises for cash to a financial institution who specialises in offering this service. The firm immediately takes out a long-term lease on the premises. In fact, what has happened is that the firm is now paying a rent for the use of the premises they formerly owned. They have forfeited the ownership of the premises but they still own and control the business. Alternatively, a company may simply lease assets whereby it gets the use of the asset but does not have to pay immediately its full market value. The duration of the lease agreements vary depending on what agreement is reached between both parties to the contract. The costs involved in using this source of finance are the yearly rent plus whatever reviews are built into the contract. The advantages of using this source of finance include the following:

(*a*) The finance required for expansion is obtained.

(*b*) Capital tied up in premises is released for immediate use.

(*c*) The business continues in the same premises.

(*d*) The control of the business remains intact.

(*e*) The lease payments are tax deductible.

There are, however, some disadvantages in using this source of finance.

(*a*) The firm loses out in the increasing market value of the premises.

(*b*) The firm will not be able to use the deeds of the premises as security for future loans.

(*c*) A fee must be constantly paid for the use of the premises. Contrast this situation with a bank term loan where the loan will eventually be repaid. In sale and leaseback, the firm must pay the lease fee for as long as the business continues.

Assets for leasing purposes can cost as little as £1,000. Many different types of assets can be leased. A company could consider leasing its office equipment such as typewriters instead of buying them. Telephone systems, computer systems, forklift trucks, manufacturing plant and cars can also be leased. One in four cars in Ireland are currently leased compared with one in ten a decade ago. The average value of leasing contracts written by members of the Irish Finance Houses Association (IFHA) during 1989 was £9,000.

As leasing became increasingly popular during the 1980s it became obvious that an accounting standard was needed to reflect the financial obligations arising under leases. SSAP 21 'Accounting for leases and hire purchase contracts' published in August 1984 divided leases into two types: financial leases and operating leases. A financial lease is a lease that transfers substantially all the risks and rewards of ownership of an asset to the lessee. All other leases are operating leases and are akin to the ordinary renting of an item. In brief, SSAP 21 requires that finance leases should be recorded in the balance sheet of the lessee, as an asset and an obligation to pay future rentals. Prior to this accounting standard a company which leased an asset would neither show the relevant asset on its balance sheet nor the financial obligations. This was known as 'off balance sheet financing'.

Retained profits

It is unusual for companies to pay out all their profits in the form of dividends. Directors usually prefer to declare a 'reasonable' dividend and hold on to the balance either for contingencies, expansion or investment purposes.

By ploughing some of the profit back into the business, the directors have decided that the shareholders will derive a greater return in the future by increasing their investment in the company. Some of the advantages in using this source of finance are as follows:

(*a*) There is no change in the control of the company.

(*b*) No security has to be given.

(*c*) There are no interest repayments.

(*d*) The money is available for use with no delays involved in negotiating loans or agreeing on security etc.

However, there are disadvantages associated with relying on retained profits as a source of funds and these include:

(*a*) If the profits are small the amount available for 'ploughing' back is automatically small.

(*b*) If the source of finance is continually used it could result in low dividend payments and some shareholders may wish to sell their shares and perhaps invest in deposit accounts where they are sure of a 'fixed interest return'. This could result in the share price falling (of a public quoted company) and make it difficult for the company to raise finance by issuing shares in the future.

Issuing ordinary shares

To raise the finance required the directors may decide to increase the issued equity by issuing ordinary shares. Before doing so the directors must realise its implications:

(*a*) Issuing more ordinary shares could possibly affect the 'control' of the company as they will carry voting rights.

(*b*) The 'new shareholders' will receive dividends from future profits so if future profits are not satisfactory it follows that the 'earnings per share' and 'dividend per share' will be reduced. It follows that existing shareholders will receive a smaller dividend in the future than at present. There are, however, certain benefits to the company by issuing ordinary shares:

(*a*) The capital base of the company is definitely improved.

(*b*) The creditworthiness of the company is improved.

(*c*) No security has to be provided.

(*d*) No fixed charges, i.e. no interest repayments are involved.

(*e*) The new capital raised is 'permanent', i.e. it does not have to be repaid since there is no maturity date.

Many ordinary share issues take the form of a rights issue. Existing shareholders can be offered extra shares in the company in proportion to the number already held by them. The existing shareholders are offered the shares at a preferential price which is lower than the current market price, in the case of a listed company. Existing shareholders who do not wish to increase their holding in the company can sell the 'option' on the stock market. Using this source of finance is cheaper than a normal share issue as the issuing costs are lower.

Convertible Loan Stock

A company may decide to raise the necessary finance by issuing convertible loan stock. To the investor, this brings the opportunity of exchanging it for a definite number of shares at a later date if he so wishes. From the outset he receives a fixed interest return on his 'loan', but if in the future the company is making big profits and paying large dividends he can exchange the stock for shares and then receive large dividends rather than fixed interest. The investor is under no obligation to convert the stock into shares. From the viewpoint of the stock investor he is hoping that investing in loan stock is a cheaper way of buying shares in the company than purchasing the shares on the open market.

QUESTION 15.1 (A)

The following summarised profit and loss account and balance sheet of Mr Wood are presented to you:

PROFIT AND LOSS ACCOUNTS	*19 . 1*	*19 . 2*
	£	£
Profit for year	50,000	45,000
Taxation	21,000	19,000
Profit after taxation	29,000	26,000
Brought forward	9,000	38,000
	38,000	64,000

BALANCE SHEETS		*19 . 1*		*19 . 2*
		£		£
Fixed assets (Net)		37,000		39,000
Current assets				
Stocks	231,000		281,000	
Debtors	294,000		408,000	
Cash	1,000		2,000	
	526,000		691,000	
Current liabilities				
Creditors	387,000		445,000	
Bank Overdraft	45,000		104,000	
Taxation	5,000		9,000	
	437,000		558,000	
Net Current assets		89,000		133,000
		126,000		172,000
Financed by:				
Share capital		73,000		83,000
Profit and loss account		38,000		64,000
Debentures		15,000		25,000
		126,000		172,000

Depreciation of fixed assets amounted to £6,000 during 19.2 and there were no disposals of fixed assets.

Requirement:
Prepare a cash funds flow statement for 19 . 2.

QUESTION 15.2 (SM)
The following profit and loss account and balance sheets have been prepared for Galway Ltd. (see next page)

During the year, fixed assets with a book value of £10,000 were sold. Some new fixed assets were purchased during the year. Depreciation on fixed assets amounted to £12,000.

PROFIT AND LOSS ACCOUNT FOR YEAR ENDED 31 DECEMBER 19 . 8

	£	£
Trading profit for year		21,000
Less: Loss on sale of fixed assets		6,000
		15,000
Taxation	4,000	
Dividends	6,000	10,000
		5,000
Add: Balance brought forward		10,000
Closing retained profits		15,000

BALANCE SHEETS AT 31 DECEMBER

	19 . 7	19 . 8
Fixed assets (Net)	102,000	124,000
Investments	20,000	23,000
Stock	16,000	14,000
Debtors	32,000	30,000
Bank	—	43,000
	170,000	234,000
Called-up share capital	100,000	150,000
Profit and loss account	10,000	15,000
Creditors	54,000	69,000
Bank Overdraft	6,000	—
	170,000	234,000

Requirement:

Prepare a funds flow statement for the year ended 31 December 19 . 8

QUESTION 15.3 (SM)

The following summary balance sheets have been prepared in respect of Munu Ltd at 30 June 19 . 7 and 30th June 19 . 8

BALANCE SHEETS AS AT 30 JUNE

	19 . 7	19 . 8		19 . 7	19 . 8
	£	£		£	£
Premises	50,000	76,000	Share capital	80,000	97,000
Plant	42,000	69,000	Share premium		
Stock	28,000	30,000	account	10,000	11,000
Debtors	10,000	9,000	Profit and		
Bank	5,000	2,000	loss account	23,000	52,000
			Creditors	17,000	16,000
			Dividends	5,000	10,000
	£135,000	£186,000		£135,000	£186,000

The following is a summarised profit and loss account for the year ended 30 June 19 . 8

		£
Net profit for the year		47,000
Less: Dividend paid	8,000	
Dividends proposed	10,000	18,000
Profit retained for year		29,000
Profit brought forward		23,000
Profit carried forward		52,000

Note:

(*i*) During the year, £70,000 was spent on acquiring new premises.

(*ii*) During the year, plant which has a written down value of £1,000 was sold for £1,200, while £40,000 was spent on acquiring new plant.

Requirement:

Prepare a funds flow statement for the year ended 30 June 19 . 8

QUESTION 15.4 (SM)

The following data has been prepared for the managing director of Package Ltd, a small company, as part of the planning process for the financial year which ends on 31 December 19 . 8

SUMMARISED FINANCIAL DATA RELATING TO PACKAGE LIMITED

Financial year	19 . 7	19 . 8
Year-end balance sheet data	£000	£000
	Actual	*Forecast*
Fixed assets (book value)	130	150
Stocks	124	170
Debtors	341	491
Bank loan	49	39
Creditors	203	150
Called-up share capital	200	200
Profit and loss account	158	?
Cash on hands	15	?
Other information for financial years	£000	£000
Fixed asset acquisitions	34	46
Sales	1,587	1,988

The company estimates to earn £80,000 profit during 19 . 8 and plans to pay a dividend of £32,000 in respect of the financial year, 19 . 8. The managing director has now asked for a preliminary appraisal of the forecast on the company's cash flow, and at the first stage will ignore the impact of taxation as it has been of negligible importance in the past. You may assume that bank overdraft facilities are available, if required.

Requirement:
(a) Prepare a forecast balance sheet at 31 December 19 . 8.
(b) Prepare a budgeted funds flow statement for the year ending 31 December 19 . 8, in a format suitable for presentation to the managing director.
(The Chartered Association of Certified Accountants)

QUESTION 15.5 (A)
The opening and closing balance sheets of a sports and leisure club, together with the linking income and expenditure account, have been summarised and are shown below:

	1/1/199 . £	31/12/199 . £
Tangible fixed assets at cost	18,000	27,000
Aggregate depreciation	(10,000)	(12,500)
	8,000	14,500
Current assets:		
Stock	4,000	6,000
Subscriptions due	3,500	5,000
Cash	2,500	500
	£18,000	£26,000
Retained surpluses	6,000	9,500
Creditors due after one year:		
Loan from bank	2,500	10,000
Creditors due within one year:		
Trade creditors	9,500	6,500
	£18,000	£26,000

INCOME AND EXPENDITURE ACCOUNT
FOR YEAR ENDED 31 DECEMBER 199 .

	£
Subscriptions	24,000
Sundry expenses	(18,000)
Depreciation	(2,500)
Surplus for year	£3,500

352 *Financial Accounting*

Requirement:

Prepare a funds flow statement for 199 ., showing clearly the reasons for the decline in the cash balance.

(The Chartered Association of Certified Accountants)

QUESTION 15.6 (SM)

You are given below, in summarised form, the accounts of Algernon Ltd for 19 . 6 and 19 . 7

	19 . 6 BALANCE SHEET			19 . 7 BALANCE SHEET		
	Cost £	Depn £	Net £	Cost £	Depn £	Net £
Plant	10,000	4,000	6,000	11,000	5,000	6,000
Building	50,000	10,000	40,000	90,000	11,000	79,000
			46,000			85,000
Investments at cost			50,000			80,000
Land			43,000			63,000
Stock			55,000			65,000
Debtors			40,000			50,000
Bank			3,000			—
			237,000			343,000
Ordinary shares £1 each			40,000			50,000
Share premium			12,000			14,000
Revaluation reserve			—			20,000
Profit and loss account			25,000			25,000
10% debentures			100,000			150,000
Creditors			40,000			60,000
Proposed dividend			20,000			20,000
Bank			—			4,000
			237,000			343,000

	19 . 6 PROFIT AND LOSS A/C £	19 . 7 PROFIT AND LOSS A/C £
Sales	200,000	200,000
Cost of sales	100,000	120,000
	100,000	80,000
Expenses	60,000	60,000
	40,000	20,000
Dividends	20,000	20,000
	20,000	—
Balance brought forward	5,000	25,000
Balance carried forward	25,000	25,000

Requirement:

(*a*) Prepare a source and application of funds statement for Algernon Ltd for 19 . 7, to explain as far as possible the movement in the bank balance.

(*b*) Using the summarised accounts given, and the statement you have just prepared, comment on the position, progress and direction of Algernon Ltd.

(*c*) Comment on the position, progress and direction of Algernon Ltd, using appropriate ratios.

(The Chartered Association of Certified Accountants)

QUESTION 15.7 (A)

The following summarised balance sheets and profit and loss account for Malt Ltd are presented to you.

BALANCE SHEETS AS AT 31 DECEMBER

	19 . 6		19 . 7	
	£	£	£	£
Fixed assets at cost		6,723		12,014
Less: aggregate depreciation		2,946		3,572
		3,777		8,442
Current assets				
Stock		6,012		8,219
Debtors		3,992		4,141
		10,004		12,360
Less: current liabilities				
Creditors	2,189		2,924	
Proposed dividends	622		622	
Bank overdraft	1,516	4,327	4,737	8,283
		5,677		4,077
		9,454		12,519
Financed by:				
Issued share capital		6,000		7,500
Profit and loss account		454		3,019
		6,454		10,519
Debentures		3,000		2,000
		9,454		12,519

PROFIT & LOSS ACCOUNT FOR THE YEAR ENDED 31 DECEMBER 19 . 7

	£
Net profit for year (*Note 1*)	3,187
Add: profit forward from previous year	454
	3,641
Dividend	622
Reserves carried forward	3,019

Note 1: The net profit for the year includes a loss on sale of fixed assets of £114. the items sold had cost £2,070 and had a written down value of £1,000 at date of sale.

Requirement:
Prepare a funds flow statement for the directors of Malt Ltd explaining how a net profit of £3,187 resulted in a significant increase in the company's bank overdraft position.
(The Institute of Chartered Accountants in Ireland)

QUESTION 15.8 (SM)
The following information relates to Stat Ltd, a manufacturing company, for the year ended 31 May 19 . 4:

(1) Debenture interest due and paid	£8,000
Sales	£780,000
Current ratio	2 times
Stock turnover (based on year-end stocks and cost of sales for year)	3.12 times
Credit period allowed to debtors (1 year = 52 weeks)	6 weeks
Gross profit as percentage of sales	20%
Net profit before interest and tax as a percentage of sales	10%
Taxation as a percentage of pre-tax profits Current (due 1 February 19 . 5)	40%

(2) All sales were on credit and accrued evenly during the year.

(3) Dividends proposed at 31 May 19 . 4 were £10,000 (19 . 3—£10,000 paid on 1 September 19 . 3).

(4) The debentures were issued in 19 . 2 and interest at 12.5% per annum is payable on 30 November and 31 May each year.

(5) Fixed assets movements during the year were as follows:

	£'000
Net book value at 1 June 19 . 3	104
Additions	27
Disposal proceeds	(5)
Loss on sale	(1)
Depreciation for year	(17)
Net book value at 31 May 19 . 4	108

(6) The following figures are taken from the balance sheet at 31 May 19 . 3:
£'000

Stocks	180
Debtors	80
Bank overdraft	10
Current taxation (paid 1 February 19 . 4)	18

(7) Trade creditors increased by £12,000 during the year ended 31 May 19 . 4.

(8) Retained profits at 31 May 19 . 3 were £88,000.

Requirement:
  Reconstruct:
(*a*) the profit and loss account and a cash funds flow statement for the year ended 31 May. 19 . 4, and
(*b*) the balance sheet as at that date.

16.

Valuation of Companies

RATIOS FOR VALUATION

Investors are primarily concerned with a return on their investment. This return can be generated by way of dividend and so investors are interested in the current and expected level of dividend. Return can also be generated through the disposal of shares at a profit and so investors will be concerned about the current price of the shares and possible future prices.

Investors therefore need to relate the price of the shares to the return to be generated from them, bearing in mind the level of risk involved and the rate of return available from other investment opportunities. In evaluating investment in shares, the investor will use the ratios concerned with the measurements of dividend, yield, price/earnings ratio, dividend cover and net assets per share. A newspaper showing financial intelligence for various quoted companies, such as the business pages of *The Irish Times* or the *Sunday Business Post*, would be useful. The student should read through the explanations which follow and, after selecting a number of companies, see how the measurements for the selected companies are displayed in the table of the newspaper. Although this area has been separated from the notes on the interpretation of accounting, the segregation is arbitrary, for the two chapters are closely related. The principal ratios used in the valuation process are:

1. Dividend yield
2. Price earnings (PE) ratio
3. Dividend cover
4. Net assets per share

Dividend yield

This is the amount of the dividend expressed as a percentage of the market price of the shares. The dividend yield values the company on the basis of its existing level of dividend payments. Thus, the dividend yield changes as the share price moves and/or the level of future dividend changes. The effect of an upward movement in share price will be to depress dividend yield.

Investors will only be prepared to accept a low dividend yield if they feel that future rewards (i.e. returns) will compensate them for the current shortfall. The reward could take the form of increased future dividends and/or increases in share price.

Example:

Assume that the market price of the company's ordinary shares is 37.5p each. Each share is entitled to 2.5p dividend. Therefore, an investment of 37.5p would buy one share which has an entitlement of 2.5p dividend. The return or dividend yield would be 6.67 per cent as follows:

Market price of share	37.5p
Dividend per share	2.5p
Dividend yield (2.5/37.5 x 100)	6.7%

There are two limitations associated with the dividend yield approach. First, some companies have a very conservative dividend policy, perhaps reflecting the need to retain profits for future expansion plans. In such cases, the dividend yield method will provide a conservative valuation. Second, some companies do not pay any dividends by way of policy but retain all profits within the business.

The principal application of the dividend yield method is in valuing minority shareholdings in an unquoted company. In this case, the shareholder may have difficulty in selling his shares and he may also be unable to influence dividend policy. His main motivation for holding the shares will therefore be to receive a steady stream of dividend income.

Price earnings ratio

This is the ratio between the price of an individual share and the earnings per share. It can be contrasted with the dividend yield, which is the ratio between share price and the dividend paid per share. The price earnings ratio values the shares on the basis of a multiple of existing earnings. Continuing the above example, the earnings (assumed to be after corporation tax) are £1,000; this is 5p per share if there are 20,000 shares in issue. Assuming the market price of the share is 37.5p then the price earnings ratio is 7.5 times as follows: market price of share 37.5p; eranings per share 5p; PE ratio 7.5. The price earnings ratio is an indication of the collective market expectations for the company. The higher the ratio, the more the future of the company is favoured in the market.

A company which is in a growth industry and which displays increasing profits each year may have a PE ratio in excess of 20 in buoyant Stock Market conditions. Conversely, a firm in a declining industry with a poor profit record might be valued on the basis of a PE ratio of 10. This means that the price of the individual share in the company was 20 times the earnings attributable to that share. The problem with using PE ratios as a basis for share valuations is that historic earnings may be an imprecise indictor of future earnings. The purchaser is likely to underestimate anticipated increases in future earnings, whereas the seller is likely to project optimistic future earnings patterns.

The PE ratio will often reflect differences between industries. For example, the electronics industry, a growth industry with expansion opportunities within this sector will have companies with a relatively high PE ratio. On the other hand, the tobacco industry, by comparison, is a mature industry whose days of growth are probably over. The price earnings ratio of companies will reflect this and the other peculiar features of their industries by means of a low PE ratio.

One of the problems of the price earnings method is that accounting earnings can be affected by a variety of acceptable accounting policies which may make comparisons between companies difficult. This is particularly the case in relation to the distinction between exceptional and extraordinary items. It will be recalled that extraordinary items, by definition in SSAP 3, do not effect earnings per share. On the other hand, exceptional items do effect EPS calculations. Accounting earnings have a further limitation in that they do no necessarily reflect the cash generation potential of each company.

Dividend cover

This ratio compares the dividend costs with the amount of profit generated and available to meet them. It is a measure of security, showing as it does the relationship between dividend, and earnings, and indicating the excess of earnings over interest or dividend. From this the financial analyst can see how much earnings could fall, and yet still cover claims of dividend by the current earnings of the company. For example:

	£000
Profit before interest	2,100
Interest	700
	1,400
Taxation	400
Profit after tax	1,000
Dividend	500
Profit retained	500

Dividend cover   1,000/500 = 2 times

Net assets per share

The net assets can be used in a variety of forms. In its simplest form, the book value of the net assets in the balance sheet is divided by the number of ordinary shares in issue, to give the net assets per share. However, it is not clear what value this is to the investor since fixed assets are stated at their historic cost less aggregate depreciation. If the company is to be liquidated it is the net realisable value of the assets which is relevant. Yet, in accordance with the going-concern concept, fixed assets are *not* stated at their net realisable value. If the company is to continue trading it is the earning power of those assets which is important to the investor. This is typically measured by the dividend yield, price earnings ratio or indeed, cash flow. Book values simply represent past expenditures and not future potential. Nevertheless, the net assets per share provides, in theory at least, a minimum price for the shares.

THE VALUATION OF SHARES

Where a company is quoted on the Stock Exchange the market price provides a ready guide to the price of the shares. However, the majority of companies do not have their shares quoted, though it is often necessary to value these shares for buyers and sellers. The price which is agreed between the purchaser and the seller will ultimately be a matter of bargaining and negotiation. There is no perfect theoretical model for predicting a price that will be acceptable to both parties. The final purchase price, if agreed, will depend not only on accounting numbers, accounting ratios and their inter-pretation but will also depend on how willing or determined the vendor is to sell and how willing and determined the purchaser is to buy.

The purpose of making an investment is to receive a future income. Income in this context means the total returns arising out of the investment. The rational investor is assumed to require income from the investment higher than the outlay necessary to obtain the income.

The valuation of the shares of a company for which there is no market quotation is a particularly difficult exercise, since there is normally no established market for dealing in the shares. In many cases the number of share sales is not large, and is infrequent. As a result, the prices at which such sales are made are either not known or have occurred too long ago to be a useful guide to present conditions. In any event, the sales may have been of quite different quantities of shares than are now being valued, and may also have occurred in quite a different economic and financial climate. Any approach to the valuation process must therefore be tentative, and with this in mind, three major strands running through the general valuation approach can be examined.

Example:
An investor is interested in calculating the value of the shares of the company shown below:

PROFIT AND LOSS ACCOUNT FOR YEAR ENDED 31 DECEMBER 19..

	£
Profit before taxation	40,000
Taxation	10,000
Profit after taxation	30,000
Dividends	18,000
Profit retained for year	12,000
Losses brought forward	(2,000)
Profit carried forward	10,000

BALANCE SHEET OF Z COMPANY AT 31 DECEMBER 19..

	£
Fixed assets (net)	13,000
Investments, government securities	
£20,000 5% loan stock at cost	20,000
Current assets	9,000
	42,000
Financed by:	
Issued share capital of £1 each	10,000
Profit and loss account	10,000
7% Debenture loan	14,000
Current liabilities	8,000
	42,000

1. *Net asset value*: In the above balance sheet, gross assets are £42,000. The current and long-term creditors are owed £22,000, which if met out of assets would leave £20,000 for the residual claim, i.e. that of the owners of the ordinary equity in the company. As there are 10,000 shares it follows that each share would be valued at £2 each. However, the net asset value of £42,000 is based on the historic costs and not the realisable value. The realisable value of most of the assets, especially investments, will only by chance match the figure (i.e. cost) shown for them in the balance sheet.

Fixed assets will be shown at historic cost or valuation, and depreciation will have been provided by one of the several methods mentioned earlier, e.g. straight-line or reducing balance. Thus, the book value of the fixed assets would only equate their net realisable value by pure coincidence.

This will almost certainly be true of most of the other assets shown in the balance sheet. The most obvious exceptions to this general rule are bank balances.

It is therefore necessary to attach realisable values to the assets as a step in determining the break-up value of the business. Assume that the realisable values for the assets shown in the example amount to £75,000, that expenses of realisation and liquidation would amount to £13,000 and that the creditors, short- and long-term, can be discharged for the sums shown in the balance sheet. Then the break-up value of the shares would be £4 each as per Exhibit 16.1:

Exhibit 16.1

	£	£
Realisation of assets		75,000
Less: Costs (say)	13,000	
Liabilities	22,000	
		35,000
Balance remaining		£40,000

£40,000 divided by 10,000 shares = £4 per share

However, it must be stated that a company acquiring another as a going concern is not only concerned with the net asset value of the business but with the earning potential on these assets. Thus the same asset will have different earnings potential for different interested purchasers.

2. *The dividend yield* approach assumes that a purchaser is solely concerned with income and he will be influenced by the alternative opportunities open to him. Dividends of £18,000 are declared and paid to shareholders this year. However, the profit and loss account reveals accumulated losses brought forward, suggesting that dividends have been passed in previous years. If the industry yields 10 per cent, then, because of the higher risks attached to Z company, investors would expect, perhaps, an additional 5 per cent yield. The value of Z company shares would then be £12 each as per Exhibit 16.2:

Exhibit 16.2

	£
Dividend payable	£18,000

Investors would want 15% dividend yield.
Dividend of £18,000 represents an overall valuation of £120,000.
Therefore, 10,000 shares each share is worth £12.

It is evident that the value of this company to a shareholder as a going concern (£12) is very different from its value on a break-up basis (£4).

3. *The price earnings ratio* values the shares on the basis of a multiple of existing earnings. The major problem is to decide on an appropriate PE ratio of earnings multiple. One approach is to examine PE ratios for quoted

companies in the same industry. For example, if a quoted food producer has a PE ratio of, say, 18, then a private food producing company might be valued on a PE ratio of 12. Almost without exception PE ratios in private companies will be less than those of similar but quoted companies because shares in quoted companies are more marketable. In deciding on the appropriate PE ratio (or earning multiple) the purchaser must take into consideration the earnings before and after the amalgamation as well as alternative opportunities. In addition, he will want to look at previous profit figures and estimate future profits. Using the above example, with profits of £30,000 and an industry PE ratio of 8 times, the valuation is:

$$PE\ ratio\ =\ \frac{Market\ price\ of\ share}{Earnings\ per\ share}$$

Market price	=	PE ratio	x	Earnings per share
	=	8	x	£3
Market price	=	£24 per share		

Paying for acquisitions

There are two principle ways of paying for acquisition: for cash or by paper. These two methods are summarised below.

1. *Cash purchase*: This is the simplest method and involves payment of the entire consideration by cash. While this arrangement may be attractive to the seller it forces the acquiring company to have sufficient cash resources at its disposal including, perhaps, a line of credit. It is attractive to the shareholders in the selling company since they can realise their investment and, perhaps, avail of other investment opportunities. The acquisition agreement may require immediate and full payment although it may specify payment by instalments. In many cases the instalments are linked to the future profitability of the company being acquired over a specified period. This arrangement is applied where the profits of the company being acquired are rapidly expanding so that valuation based on historic earnings is somewhat irrelevant. Conversely, the instalments to be paid and their amount may be reduced if certain profit projections are not met by the company being acquired. The advantage of the instalment method is that it allows the purchaser and seller to agree to a range of prices rather than one specific price. If projected earnings are met by the company being acquired then the higher price will prevail. If profit projections are not met, then a lower price will be paid.

If the acquisition is for a majority stake, e.g. 51 per cent, then the minority shareholders (49 per cent) have certain well-defined rights contained in the Companies Act, 1963. And, if the company being acquired is a quoted company, there are additional formalities to be complied with under an agreed takeover code which is policed by the Stock Exchange. In brief, the code requires that a bid for a majority percentage must be extended to all shareholders. This requirement effectively stops an acquiring company gaining a majority shareholding, while not making a similar offer to all shareholders. In addition, the code requires the acquiring company to make a full takeover bid if it purchases 30 per cent of the voting stock.

2. *Payment by share issue*: This method of payment is becoming increasingly common in Ireland and is sometimes referred to as a paper exchange because no cash changes hands. Rather, the acquiring company issues additional shares and exchanges these for the shares in the company being acquired. If the acquiring company is quoted, then a market price is available and this can be used to determine a reasonable share exchange. The receipt of marketable shares is attractive since shareholders can always realise their investment without undue difficulty. Moreover, they share in the good fortunes, if any, of the public company. However, if the acquiring company is a private company then no market price is available and this complicates the share exchange process.

In any event, payment by share exchange can be an expensive process. The additional shares will qualify for dividend and this may reduce dividends available to existing shareholders, especially if the acquired company's profit performance is less than expected. In addition, there will be a greater number of shareholders in the enlarged group so that some dilution of control will take place.

In many cases, acquisitions are paid for by a combination of both methods, part cash and part paper. The attraction of this joint approach is that it does not require the purchasing company to have a large amount of cash. From the sellers' point of view they receive a small amount of cash and a share interest in the new business. This investment may, consequently, grow as the acquiring company expands and develops in future years. The balance between cash and paper exchange is a matter for negotiation between the two parties. In some cases the balance will depend on the agreed price for the acquisition.

CONCLUSION

A company's valuation, based on any of the above methods, is not necessarily the price which the purchaser is prepared to pay or the seller willing to accept. In any share valuation situation there are many factors present which will influence the share price. For example, what are the objectives, if any, of the purchaser other than those of pure investment? Will the purchaser acquire a majority or a minority holding in the company? Is the seller a willing seller or has he displayed an unwillingness to sell?

The valuation of a company's shares, like many aspects of accounting, is an art rather than a science. The purchaser will want to pay the lowest possible price whereas the seller will want the highest possible price. The final, negotiated price will probably lie between these two extremes. In the context of share valuation there are no absolute truths. Rather, the truth is conditioned by judgment and the context in which the decision is being made. This may seem a little perplexing to readers but it does portray accounting as an exciting, challenging discipline and an evolving one. Accounting practice and the judgments that support it are inevitably flexible and will continue to be so. Accounting is an art and not a science, and any attempt to prove it otherwise is bound to end in disappointment.

QUESTION 16.1 (A)

The directors of Bolmin plc are anxious to purchase all the shares of Tooden Repairs Ltd and require your advice on the possible purchase price. They are aware that similar companies have an average dividend yield of 2 per cent and appropriate PE ratio for this type of company is between 10 and 15. The following information is available for Tooden:

PROFIT AND LOSS ACCOUNTS	£	19.1 £	£	19.2 £
Sales		250,000		290,000
Less: Cost of goods sold	161,000		181,000	
Directors' remuneration	20,000		24,000	
Other expenses	54,000		60,000	
		235,000		265,000
Net profit before tax		15,000		25,000
Taxation		6,000		10,000
Dividends		2,000		3,000
Retained profits for year		7,000		12,000

BALANCE SHEETS	£	19.1 £	£	19.2 £
Fixed assets				
Freehold property		80,000		80,000
Equipment (net book value)		35,000		30,000
		115,000		110,000
Current assets				
Stock	35,000		45,000	
Debtors	60,000		85,000	
	95,000		130,000	
Less: Current Liabilities	(28,000)	67,000	(34,000)	96,000
		182,000		206,000

Financed by:	£	£
Share capital (£1 Ord. shares)	50,000	50,000
Retained profits	132,000	144,000
Long-term loans	Nil	12,000
	182,000	206,000

In addition to the accounts the chief accountant of Bolmin has obtained the following information concerning Tooden:

(1) Equipment has been depreciated at an annual rate of 10 per cent on cost but no depreciation has been provided against the freehold property. At the end of 19 . 2 the estimated realisable values of the freehold property and equipment were £169,000 and £24,000 respectively. The freehold property was stated in the books at £80,000 and had a remaining life of 40 years.

(2) At the end of 19 . 2 it was estimated that the stock could be disposed of for £17,000 in a forced sale or closure.

(3) In addition to the regular provision against bad debts, an additional provision of 10 per cent would be appropriate on a closure basis.

(4) Directors' remuneration is considered to be excessive and a reduction of 50 per cent is to be made in the profit and loss account with respect to the figures shown for directors' remuneration.

Requirement:

In order to guide the directors of Bolmin plc:

(a) Calculate the value per share and the total value placed on Tooden Repairs Ltd on the basis of the range of PE ratios. Your calculations should be based on 19 . 2 results, having made whatever adjustments to the reported profit figure as deemed appropriate.

You should clearly specify what adjustments you have made to the reported annual profit figures.

(b) Calculate the company's valuation based on the dividend yield method.

(c) Calculate the break-up value per share on Tooden Repairs at the end of 19 . 2, and

(d) Comment on the different methods of valuation above.

(The Chartered Association of Certified Accountants)

QUESTION 16.2 (SM)

Extracts from the accounts of Astwood Beverages plc, a company not listed on the Stock Exchange, appear below:

ASTWOOD BEVERAGES PLC
PROFIT AND LOSS ACCOUNT YEAR ENDED 31 DECEMBER

	19.1 £000	19.2 £000	19.3 £000
Turnover	48,500	50,200	40,200
Profit before interest and taxation	4,700	5,000	3,200
Interest payable	2,100	2,200	2,300
Profit before taxation	2,600	2,800	900
Taxation	800	960	300
Profit after taxation	1,800	1,840	600
Extraordinary items	–	–	380
	1,800	1,840	220
Dividends	480	480	120
Profit retained for year	1,320	1,360	100

BALANCE SHEET AT 31 DECEMBER 19.3

	£000	£000
Fixed assets		
Cost	19,300	
Accumulated depreciation	6,800	12,500
Current assets		
Stock		5,200
Debtors		8,300
Cash		200
		13,700
Less: Creditors (amounts falling due within one year)		
Creditors		14,000
Total assets less current liabilities		12,200
Less: Creditors (amounts falling due after one year)		6,000
		6,200
CAPITAL AND RESERVES		
12m. ordinary shares of 25p		3,000
Profit and loss account		3,200
		6,200

Additional information:

(1) A competitor has offered to purchase Astwood's retail outlets and its current assets and assume responsibility for its current liabilities, but not its long-term loan, for £10m. If this deal goes ahead, Astwood's only remaining asset, its factory, will be closed, its staff made redundant and the site sold to developers. It is estimated that the sale of the site will give Astwood £8m.

after all costs including redundancy payments, and the company will be liquidated.

(2) Similar companies have price earnings ratios of 13 and dividend yields of about 4 per cent.

Requirement:
(*a*) Estimate the value of each share of the company by the following methods:

  (*i*) Assets valuation, assuming the competitor's offer is accepted. (This is the liquidation option.)
  (*ii*) Using the price earnings ratio of a similar company.
  (*iii*) Using the dividend yield of a similar company.
(*b*) Comment on the relative merits of each valuation.
(The Chartered Association of Certified Accountants)

QUESTION 16.3 (A)

Giant Holdings plc is about to make an offer of one ordinary share for every two shares in Minnow plc. If the offer was successful, Giant would use Minnow's distribution facilities to expand its sales and this would result in increased profits of £3m. per year after tax.

Extracts from the accounts of the two companies appear below:

BALANCE SHEET AT 30 JUNE 19 . 1

	Giant plc £m.	Minnow plc £m.
Fixed assets	250	120
Current assets	300	70
Less: creditors due in under one year	(200)	(70)
Total assets less current liabilities	350	120
Less: loans due in more than one year	(100)	(60)
	250	60
CAPITAL AND RESERVES		
Share capital (£1 shares)		50
(50p shares)	100	
Profit and loss account	150	10
	250	60

PROFIT AND LOSS ACCOUNT FOR YEAR ENDED 30 JUNE 19 . 1

	£m.	£m.
Profit after taxation	50	10
Dividends	20	7
Profit retained for year	30	3

Currently, the share price of Giant is 500p and that of Minnow 200p.

Requirement:

(*a*) Calculate the price earnings ratio of Giant and Minnow before the merger. What can you deduce from this information?

(*b*) What will the price earnings ratio of the group be if the value of Giant's shares increase by 50p after the merger?

(*c*) Calculate the net dividend income the holder of two shares in Minnow would receive before and after the merger, assuming that Giant maintains the same dividend per share as before the merger.

(*d*) If you were a shareholder in Minnow what would your reaction to be the merger? State your reasons by reference to financial accounting ratios and this data, if relevant.

(The Chartered Association of Certified Accountants)

QUESTION 16.4 (SM)

Alpha plc, a dynamic fast-growing company in micro-electronics has just made a bid of seventeen of its own shares for every twenty shares of Beta plc who manufactures a range of electric motors.

Balance sheets and profit and loss accounts for the two companies are as follows:

PROFIT AND LOSS ACCOUNTS YEAR ENDED 31 MARCH 19 . 6

	Alpha plc £000	Beta plc £000
Turnover	3,000	2,000
Profit before interest and taxation	300	140
Interest	100	10
Profit on ordinary activities before tax	200	130
Taxation on profit on ordinary activities	100	65
Profit on ordinary activities after tax	100	65
Dividends	20	30
Retained profit for the financial year	80	35
Number of issued shares (million)	1.0	0.5
Earnings per share	?	?
Price earnings ratio	?	?
Market price per share	200p	130p
Capitalisation of companies	?	?
Dividend per share	?	?

Historical share prices have been:

31 March	19.1	19.2	19.3	19.4	19.5
Alpha plc	60	90	150	160	200
Beta plc	90	80	120	140	130

BALANCE SHEETS AT 31 MARCH 19.6

	Alpha plc £000	Beta plc £000
Fixed assets	1,200	900
Current assets	900	700
Creditors (amounts falling due within 1 year)	300	600
Net current assets	600	100
Total assets less current liabilities	1,800	1,000
Less: long-term loans	800	120
	1,000	880
Financed by:		
Share capital (25p ordinary shares)	250	125
Profit and loss account	750	755
	1,000	880

The merger of the two companies will result in after-tax savings of £15,000 per annum to be made in the distribution system of Alpha. One of the shareholders of Beta has queried the bid and has raised the following points. Firstly he understands that Alpha normally only pays small dividends and that his dividends per share will decrease. Secondly, he is concerned that the bid undervalues Beta since the current value of the bid is less than the figure for equity in Beta's balance sheet.

Requirement:
   (a) Calculate EPS, PE ratio, dividend per share and total market capitalisation for both companies.
   (b) Calculate the bid consideration.
   (c) Calculate the earnings per share for the combined group.
   (d) Calculate the theoretical post acquisition price of Alpha shares, assuming that the PE ratio of Alpha remains the same.
(The Chartered Association of Certified Accountants)

Solutions
to
Selected
Problems

QUESTION 1.1

Note: This is not presented as a 'model' answer, more as a series of pointers towards possible answers.

(*a*) This question is worded in an extremely general way, and a number of quite different answers would be acceptable. All financial information is required for decision making of some sort, and different users face different decisions. Shareholders face investment decisions often with long-term implications; suppliers are much more likely to be concerned with short-run liquidity; the local community may be mainly interested in employment prospects and in pollution control. It is not obvious that the traditional statements based on the steward-ship principle will satisfy these needs. Cash flow accounting, alternative valuation bases, alternative reporting statements, social reporting, might all be considered here.

Various characteristics of useful information have been suggested, for example in the Corporate Report (1975). The information should perhaps be presented more rapidly and frequently, broken down in different ways, simplified and summarised. Alternative methods of presentation could be considered—a multicoloured pie chart may be much more useful to many readers than a profit and loss account and a balance sheet.

(*b*) This question tests an awareness of the different requirements of accounting infor-mation, and seeks evidence of *some* understanding of possible problems for the accountant.

Three possible classes to discuss would be:

(*i*) *Creditors/lenders*. Their primary interest is in whether or not they will get their money back. Short-term lenders will therefore be largely interested in current liquidity, but longer-term lenders will also be interested in long-term profitability and viability.

(*ii*) *Employees and employee organisations*. Their interest is perhaps on two levels: (*a*) Continuity of employment—clearly a long-term consideration of profitability, viability and management intention; (*b*) Scope for wage bargaining and improving working conditions—requiring short and medium-term information on both profitability and cash availability. This again implies some knowledge of management intention.

(*iii*) *Taxation authorities*. Their interest is primarily in a simple clear-cut and consistent basis of profit determination. This implies that there should be a minimum of scope for subjectivity and for manipulation. There are a number of differences arising here, concerned with objectivity v. intention, short-term v. long-term, cash emphasis v. profit emphasis, and so on. The requirements are therefore not closely compatible. Accountants accordingly have to consider how (or to what extent) they can satisfy these various requirements.

QUESTION 1.4

These regulatory influences are:

(*a*) Companies Acts
(*b*) Statements of Standard Accounting Practice (SSAPs)
(*c*) Stock Exchange regulations

Companies Acts provide the basic framework. They stipulate minimum requirements, but do not generally go into great detail. We could say, perhaps, that Companies Acts tell you what to do, but not how to do it. This is obviously something of an over-simplification.

However in general the point is valid, and it is the SSAPs which fill in the details. For example, a company must depreciate its fixed assets according to company law. An SSAP exists to provide the detailed ground rules. The penalties for failure to comply with SSAPs are generally investigation and possible disciplinary proceedings against the accountant in-volved by his professional body. The practical penalties are zero, although quoted companies have to be careful of Stock Exchange regulations. These are additional requirements, mainly of disclosure, required of companies before their shares can be quoted, or traded, on any particular stock exchange. They are created, and monitored, by the Stock Exchange itself.

It is not obvious, that this regulatory system is entirely effective. Stock Exchange regulations and SSAPs could be said to overlap in intention. The 'debate' over the role of SSAPs and their relationship with the law is an active one. Many of the issues are for consideration at higher levels. SSAPs are easier to change as circumstances require. On the other hand to have 'regulations' which can be ignored with impunity can be in no one's long-term interests. Accountants argue, defending the role of the SSAP as something distinct from government control, that they, as the expert professionals, should have control. If they wish to sustain this argument they will have to 'deliver the goods' more effectively than they have managed in recent years.

QUESTION 2.3

(a) Fixed asset
(b) Current asset
(c) Current liability
(d) Current asset
(e) Current asset
(f) Current liability
(g) Long-term liability
(h) Fixed asset
(i) Current asset
(j) Current liability
(k) Fixed asset
(l) Current asset
(m) Current asset

QUESTION 2.4

1. CAPITAL — £ 178
2. LIABILITIES — £ 8,746
3. ASSETS — £ 4,727
4. DEFICIENCY — £ 3,359
5. CAPITAL — £ 44,040
6. ASSETS — £ 7,966
7. CAPITAL — £ 6,782
8. ASSETS — £ 25,428

QUESTION 2.6

Explanation of transactions

(a) Sept. 1 Received £2,000 from debtors,
2 Bought £1,000 stock on credit,
3 Owner introduced £4,000 capital.
4 Received £2,500 from debtors.
5 Purchased stock for cash, £3,000.
8 Bought fixed assets £4,000 of which £2,000 was paid by cash and £2,000 was on credit.
9 Bought fixed assets for £2,000 cash.
10 Paid creditors £1,000.
11 Sold fixed assets at cost for £1,000.
12 Sold stock for £2,000. No profit was made on this transaction.
15 Purchased stock on credit £4,000.
16 Sold fixed assets at cost for £1,000, on credit.

(b) Current ratio

$$\frac{30,000}{12,000} = 2.5 \text{ times}$$

QUESTION 3.1

A. GREEN

Bank Account					Capital Account		
Capital	5,000	Equip	2,000			Bank	5,000
Sales	4,000	Fix's	1,500				
Sales	5,000	Purchs	3,000				
Sales	3,000	Wages	1,000		**Equipment account**		
Equip	1,000	Purchs	2,000				
		Staty	1,000		Bank 2,000	Bank	1,000
		M. exs	1,000			Bal.	1,000
		Purchs	2,000		2,000		2,000
		Wages	2,000				
		Tel.	200		Bal. 1,000		
		Bal	2,300		**Fixtures Account**		
	18,000		18,000				
Bal.	2,300				Bank 1,500	Bal.	1,500
					1,500		1,500
					Bal. 1,500		

Purchases (of Stock) Account					Sales (of Stock) Account		
Bank	3,000					Bank	4,000
Bank	2,000					Bank	5,000
Bank	2,000	Bal.	7,000		Bal. 12,000	Bank	3,000
	7,000		7,000		12,000		12,000
Bal.	7,000					Bal.	12,000

Wages Account					Stationery Account		
Bank	1,000				Bank 1,000	Bal.	1,000
Bank	2,000	Bal	3,000		1,000		1,000
	3,000		3,000		Bal. 1,000		
Bal.	3,000						

Motor Expenses Account					Telephone Account		
Bank	1,000	Bal	1,000		Bank 200	Bal.	200
	1,000		1,000		200		200
Bal.	1,000				Bal. 200		

Note: It is not usual to formally balance a ledger account that contains only one entry, e.g. capital or motor expenses accounts.

A. GREEN

TRIAL BALANCE	DEBIT	CREDIT
Bank	2,300	
Purchases	7,000	
Wages	3,000	
Motor expenses	1,000	
Capital		5,000
Equipment	1,000	
Fixtures	1,500	
Sales		12,000
Stationery	1,000	
Telephone	200	
	17,000	17,000

QUESTION 3.3

Bank

1/3	Capital	5,000	4/3	Cash	20
3/3	Sales	4,512	5/3	O'Sul	950
8/3	Bailey	400	9/3	Wages	479
18/3	Stapl.	1,200	10/3	S Ltd	2,500
29/3	Bailey	1,000	10/3	Purch	1,200
			12/3	O'Sul	2,000
			15/3	R&R	214
			16/3	W/S	526
			25/3	Adv.	373
			27/3	W/S	614
			27/3	Cash	50
			31/1	Bal	3,186
		12,112			12,112
1/4	Bal.	3,186			

Capital

			1/3	Bank	5,000

Cash

4/3	Bank	20	27/3	Sundry	12
28/3	Bank	50	31/3	Sundry	22
			31/3	Bal.	36
		70			70
1/4	Bal.	36			

Purchases

2/3	O'Sul	950			
10/3	Bank	1,200			
12/3	O'Sul	5,000	31/3 Bal.		7,150
		7,150			7,150
1/4	Bal.	7,150			

O'Sullivan

5/3	Bank	950	1/3	Purch.	950
12/3	Bank	2,000	12/3	Purch.	5,000
31/3	Bal.	3,000			
		5,950			5,950
			1/4	Bal.	3,000

Furniture

2/3	S.Ltd	2,500	

S Ltd

10/3	Bank	2,500	12/3	Furn.	2,500

Sales

				2/3	Bailey	475	
				3/3	Bank	4,512	
				15/3	Robson	425	
				17/3	Stapl.	1,500	
31/3	Bal.	8,212		17/3	Bailey	1,300	
		8,212				8,212	
				1/4	Bal	8,212	

Bailey

2/3	Sales	475	8/3	Bank	400
16/3	Sales	1,300	29/3	Bank	1,000
			31/3	Bal.	375
		1,775			1,775
1/4	Bal.	375			

Robson

5/3	Sales	425

Wages and Salaries

9/3	Bank	479	16/3	Bank	526
27/3	Bank	614	31/3	Bal.	1,619
		1,619			1,619
1/4Bal.		1,619			

Stapleton

11/3	Sales	1,500	18/3	Bank	1,200
			31/1	Bal.	300
		1,500			1,500
1/4	Bal	300			

Sundry Expenses

27/3	Cash	12			
31/3	Cash	22	1/4	Bal.	34
		34			34
1/4	Bal.	34			

Rent and Rates

15/3	Bank	214

Advertising

25/3	Bank	373

JOHN ARNOLD
TRIAL BALANCE AT 31 MARCH. 19 . 1

	DEBIT £	CREDIT £
Bank	3,186	
Capital		5,000
Cash	36	
Purchases	7,150	
O'Sullivan		3,000
Furniture	2,500	
Sales		8,212
Bailey	375	
Robson	425	
Wages and salaries	1,619	
Stapleton	300	
Rent and rates	214	
Advertising	373	
Sundry expenses	34	
	16,212	16,212

QUESTION 3.5
Analysis of transactions

(1)	Capital introduced by proprietor		£30,000
(2)	Purchased goods from Beta Ltd		£8,700
(3)	Paid rent by cheque		£1,200
(4)	Furniture (at valuation) introduced by proprietor		£1000
(5)	Furniture purchased by cheque		£15,000
(6)	Sales on credit to George Cranwell		£14,400
(7)	Pail advertising by cheque		£300
(8)	Received from George Cranwell	7,344	
	and allowed discount	56	
			£7,400
(9)	Paid salaries by cheque		£3,440
(10)	Returned goods to Beta Ltd		£600
(11)	Paid postage etc. by cheque		£170
(12)	Refund of advertising expenses		£30
(13)	Paid traveling expenses by cheque		£720

QUESTION 3.6

Jan. 1   Capital of £6,000 was introduced into the business in form of cash and this money was placed in the bank.

Jan. 2   Stock valued at £2,000 was sold for £4,000 cash thus increasing the capital by £2,000.

Jan. 3   Debtors pay £1,000 for goods previously sold to them and the owner withdraws this money thus reducing the capital by £1,000. Alternatively, a bad debt was written off.

Jan. 4   Creditors were paid for a £3,000 debt by means of a cheque for £1,500 which reduced the bank balance and also by introducing capital of £1,500.

Jan. 5   Purchased fixed assets for £4,000 on credit.

Jan 8   Sold fixed assets which cost £5,000 for £1,000 cash with a loss of £4,000.

Jan. 9   £1,000 was written off stock due to obsolescence, pilferage or drawings. This caused capital to be reduced by £1,000.

Jan. 10   The owner introduced a fixed asset worth £2,000 to the business.

Jan. 11   Debtors pay £1,500 cash in respect of a debt for £2,000 and are allowed a discount of £500 (or alternatively a bad debt of £500 is incurred).

Jan. 12   Stock is purchased on credit for £5,000.

Jan. 15   Fixed assets costing £4,000 are purchased by means of a cheque for £2,000 and the remaining £2,000 is on credit.

Jan. 16   Creditors are paid £1,500 in respect of a debt for £2,000 and discount received was £500.

QUESTION 4.1

J. O'NEILL

TRADING AND PROFIT AND LOSS ACCOUNT FOR YEAR 31 DECEMBER, 19 . 8.

	£	£
Sales		12,900
Less: Cost of goods sold		
Opening stock	1,600	
Add: Purchases	6,230	
Less: Closing stock	(1,800)	(6,030)
Gross Profit		6,870
Add: Miscellaneous revenue		
Deposit interest received		20
		6,890
Less: Expenses		
General expenses	360	
Telephone	240	
Advertising	130	
Interest	170	
Wages and salaries	2,100	
Rent and rates	630	
Administration expenses	510	4,140
Net profit for year		2,750

J. O'NEILL

BALANCE SHEET AS AT 31 DECEMBER 19 . 8

	£	£
Fixed Assets		
Premises		4,800
Plant and machinery		3,100
		7,900
Current assets		
Stock	1,800	
Debtors	4,100	
Investments	200	
Cash	40	6,140
		14,040
Financed by		
Invested capital		5,600
Add: Retained profit		2,750
		8,350
Long-term liabilities		
Long-term loan		2,000
Current liabilities		
Creditors	1,400	
Bank overdraft	2,290	3,690
		14,040

QUESTION 4.2

JOE HAYES
TRADING AND PROFIT AND LOSS ACCOUNT FOR YEAR ENDED
31 DECEMBER 19 . 0.

	£	£
Sales		44,900
Opening stock	4,100	
Purchases	26,419	
Less: Closing stock	(6,109)	(24,410)
Gross Profit		20,490
Less: Expenses:	6,555	
Advertising	4,063	
Rent and rates	3,886	
Postage and stationery	456	
Repairs	1,219	
Interest	700	
Commission	2,245	19,124
Net Profit		1,366

BALANCE SHEET AT 31 DECEMBER 19 . 0.

	£			£
Fixed assets		Capital invested		8,000
Premises	10,600	Add: Profit		1,366
Plant & Equipment	2,500			9,366
	13,100	10% Loan		7,000
Current assets:		Current liabilities:		
Stock	6,109	Creditors	2,936	
Debtors	3,800	Bank overdraft	1,493	
Prepayments (W1)	651	10,650	Accruals (W1)	2,865	7,294
	23,660			23,660

W.1 Schedule of accruals and prepayments at 31 December 19 . 0

	Accruals	Prepayments
Wages and salaries	268	
Advertising	914	
Postage and stationery	438	351
Rent (2/12 x £1,200)	200	
Rates (1/2 x £600)		300
Commission	745	
Interest	300	
Per balance sheet	2,865	651

QUESTION 4.6

JIM HUNT
Rent and Rates a/c

1 Jan.7	Balance	–	1 Jan.7	Bal.(3/6 x 720)	360
2 Jan.	Bank	1,200			
5 Jan.	"	720			
29 Jan.	"	1,200		* P/L account	6,420
3 Aug.	"	840			
2 Dec.	"	840			
5 Dec.	"	1,200			
31 Dec.	Balance	1,200	31 Dec.7	Bal. (3/6 x 840)	420
		7,200			7,200

*	Rent (4 x 1,200)	=	4,800
	Rates (3/6 x 720) =		360
	Rates (9/6 x 840) =		1,260
			6,420

QUESTION 4.7

RENT RECEIVABLE ACCOUNTS

1.1. 3.	Bal. (1=3x100) = 300		1.1. 3.	Bal. (2=3x150) 3 =	450
	(4=3x200) = 600				
		900			
P/L A/C (W1)		7,170		∴ Bank A/C (W2)	7,620
31.12. 3 Bal.		N/A	31.12. 3 Bal.		N/A
		8,070			8,070

(W1) Schedule of Rental Income for year ended 31.12.19 3

Flat	(Jan. - Jul. = 7 months)			(Aug. - Dec. = 5 Months)				Total per year
1	7 x 100	=	700	2 x 110	=	220	=	920
2	7 x 150	=	1,050	5 x 165	=	825	=	1,875
3	7 x 150	=	1,050	5 x 165	=	825	=	1,875
4	7 x 200	=	1,400	5 x 220	=	1,100	=	2,500
			4,200			2,970		£7,170

(W2) Computation of Cash Received

Flat	Arrears	Current rent			Total cash
1	300	700 +	220	=	1,220)
2	–	600 +	825	=	1,425)
3	–	1,050 +	825	=	1,875)
4	600	1,400 + 1,100		=	3,100)
					7,620

QUESTION 4.8

(*a*)

RENT RECEIVABLE ACCOUNT

1.7. 1 Bal c/d

A	3 x 200	=	600		
B	3 x 250	=	750	Bank A	3,940
C	3 x 150	=	450	" B	3,150
D	3 x 300	=	900	" C	2,385
			2,700	" D	3,780

P/L (W1)	11,370		
30.6. 2		30.6. 2 Bal. (arrears)	1,815
(Deposit on A)	1,000		
	15,070		15,070

Schedule of Cash Recd

A	600	+	600	+	660	+	1080	=	2,940	+ 1000 Dep.
B	750	+	750	+1,650	(6 mths)	=	3,150			
C	450	+	450	+1,485	(9 mths)	=	2,385			
D	900	+	900	+1,980	(6 mths)	=	3,780			

(arrears) + (Jul. – Sep.)

(W1) Schedule of rental Income

	Jul.–Sep.	Oct.–Dec.	Jan.–Jun.	Total
A	600	660	1,080	2,340
B	750	825	1,650	3,225
C	450	495	990	1,935
D	900	990	1,980	3,870
				11,370

(*b*) The accruals of matching concept requires that revenues arising during an accounting period be matched against the expenses incurred in earning the identified revenues.

The prudence convention would suggest that we include in our profit and loss accounts only those revenue items which have in fact been received or realised.

Note : Schedule of arrears

	£
A	Nil
B	825 (3 months)
C	Nil
D	990 (3 months)
	1,815

QUESTION 4.13
This question tests the ability to handle simple depreciation entries, and to explain the significance of what has been done.

(*a*) (*i*) Straight-line method

Fixed asset account

Yr 1 Cash	10,000	Disposal Yr 3	10,000

Provision for Depreciation Account

Bal. c/d	2,000	P/L Yr 1	
	2,000		2,000
		Bal. b/d	
Bal. c/d	4,000	P/L Yr 2	
	4,000		4,000
Disposal	4,000	Bal. b/d	4,000

Disposal Account

F.A	10,000	Depr.	4,000
		Cash	5,000
		P.L (loss)	1,000
	10,000		10,000

(*ii*) Reducing balance method

Fixed asset

Yr 1 Cash	10,000	Disposal Yr 3	10,000

Provision for Depreciation Account

Bal. c/d	4,000	P/L Yr 1	4,000
		Bal. b/d	4,000
c/d	6,400	P/L Yr 2	2,400
		(i.e. 40% £6,000)	
	6,400		6,400
Disposal	6,400	Bal. b/d	6,400

Disposal Account

F.A	10,000	Depr.	6,400
P/L (profit)	1,400	Cash	5,000
	11,400		11,400

(*b*) (*i*) The purpose of depreciation is to spread the total cost of having the asset available for use (i.e. its cost or other basic value less expected sales proceeds if any) over the accounting periods which will benefit from that use. It is an application of the matching convention, spreading the total cost over the useful life in proportion to the benefit.

The method chosen should be the one which most nearly spreads the cost in proportion to the benefit. Greater usefulness in early years would imply using the reducing balance method.)

Another argument for using the reducing balance method is that maintenance costs will rise over time, and therefore the annual depreciation charge should fall, to compensate and to give a (more or less) constant total charge.

(*ii*)   The net figure in the balance sheet at the end of year 2 is that amount of the original cost not yet expensed, or matched against revenue. It could therefore be alternatively described as the cost of the remaining benefits.

(*c*) The appropriate charge in year 1 would be zero, whichever method is being used. This is in accordance with the matching principle—no benefit, therefore no expense. Prudence might be felt to over-ride this argument, but the firm 'confidently anticipates' so prudence should not be given priority here.

SOLUTION QUESTION 4.16
(All figures in £000)

Creditors

Bank	560	Opening Balance	65
Closing Balance	130	Purchases	625 *
	690		690

Cost of Sales

Purchases	625	P/L a/c	600
Opening stock	75 *	Closing stock	100
	700		700

Debtors

Sales	1,000	Bad debt	2
Opening balance	52 *	bank	950
		Closing balance	100
	1,052		1,052

Bank

Receipts	950	Payments	560
		Payments	90
		Payments	150
		Closing balance	53
		Opening balance	97 *
	950		950

Plant and Machinery Cost

Bank	90	Closing balance	200
Opening balance	110*		
	200		200

Aggregate depreciation of plant and machinery

Closing balance	80	Profit and loss	20
		Opening balance	60 *
	80		80

Operating expenses

Bank	150	Profit and loss	120
Closing balance	5	Opening balance	35 *
	155		155

*Indicates the calculated figure.

SUMMARY BALANCE SHEET 1 JANUARY 199 .

	£000	£000		£000
Land and buildings		320	Capital	300
Plant and machinery				
Cost	110			
Depreciation	60			
		50	Creditors	65
			Accruals	35
Stock		75	Bank overdraft	97
Debtors		52		
		497		497

QUESTION 4.18

This question tests elementary manipulation of accruals and prepayments, and of ledger accounts generally.

SNODGRASS TRADING AND PROFIT AND LOSS ACCOUNT YEAR TO 31 DECEMBER 19 . 8

	£000	£000
Sales (W1)		1,061
Opening stock	200	
Purchases (W2)	680	
	880	
Closing stock	(230)	
		650
Gross profit		411
Discount allowed	8	
Bad debts	3	
Rent	28	
Insurance	38	
Electricity	23	
Telephone	7	
Wages	100	
Depreciation	50	
		257
Net profit		154

SUMMARISED BALANCE SHEET AT 31 DECEMBER 19 . 8

	£000		£000	£000
Fixed assets (net)	300	Capital	600	
Debtors and prepayments	262	Profit	154	754
Stock	230			
Bank (W3)	135	Creditors and Accruals		173
	927			927

Workings:

1.   Debtors

Opening balance	200	Bank	1,000
* Sales	1,061	Disc. Allowed	8
		Bad debts	3
		Closing balance	250
	1,261		1,261

2.   Creditors

Bank	700	Opening balance	180
Closing balance	160	* Purchases	680
	860		860

3.   Bank

Opening balance	20	Creditors	700
Debtors	1,000	Rent	30
		Insurance	20
		Telephone	10
		Wages	100
		Electricity	25
		* Closing balance	135
	1,020		1,020

QUESTION 4.20

(*a*) The figure should be the total cost of making the fixed asset usable, excluding all costs of actually using it.

Therefore 11,000 + 100 + 200 + 400 = £11,700

The additional component is part of the cost of the machine as it enhances the revenue earning capacity of the asset but the replacement parts are a cost of using the machine—hence the difference in treatment beween the two. Maintenance is obviously a cost of usage.

(*b*) Depreciation spreads the cost (or value) of an item over its useful life, in appropriate proportion to the benefit (usefulness). It is necessary in accordance with the matching convention—allocating expense against corresponding benefit, as part of the profit calculation.

(*c*) The straight-line method charges a constant percentage of the net beek value (cost less accumulated depreciation brought forward). Thus the straight-line method has a constant charge but the reducing balance method has a charge reducing each year of the asset life. The two methods therefore make different assumptions about the usefulness, the trend or pattern of benfit, of the fixed asset concerned.

(*d*) Objectivity implies lack of bias. It removes the need for, and the possibility of, subjectivity of personal opinion. For an accounting figure to be objective, it must be expected that all accounants would arrive at the same figure. Clearly the figure stated on an invoice has a high degree of objectivity. However, the calculation of depreciation is based on esti-mates of future life and future usefulness and is therefore highly subjective.

(*e*) This practice can claim the advantage of greater prudence, as the expense is always the higher of the two possibilities. However, it seems to lack consistency. Perhaps more importantly, it obviously fails to attempt to follow the matching convention. It makes no attempt to make the trend of expenses consistent with the trend of benefit or usefulness. If the profit figure, or profit trend, is regarded as important, then it seems an unsatisfactory practice.

QUESTION 5.1

Creditors control account

		Opening balance	4,600	
Purchases returns	6,000	Credit purchases	54,000	
Bank (cheques)	39,000			
Closing balance	13,600			
	58,600		58,600	
		Balance b/d	13,600	

QUESTION 5.3

The posting to the nominal ledger is:

Debit wages account with £60 and debit creditors control account with £90: credit discount received account with £10 and credit bank account with £140.

Nominal dedger:

Debit	Wages account	£60	
Debit	Creditors control account	£90	
Credit	Bank account		£140
Credit	Discount received		£10
		£150	£150

Subsidiary (Creditors) Ledger

Debit	Individual creditors with individual debit entries amounting to	£90

QUESTION 5.6

This question tests an understanding of the mechanics and the purposes of control accounts.

(*a*) the essential idea is to impose an automatic check on the records. The purchase ledger control account balance, which should agree with the sum of the individual balances on the purchases ledger, is arrived at in a different way. If the two do agree, then the figures are to some extent automatically confirmed. If the two elements are operated by independent personnel, some check on both their accuracy and their honesty is imposed. If incorporated in the nominal ledger, the control accounts can facilitate the production of the final accounts.

(b) (i)   Increase £198
     (ii) Decrese   £100
     (iii) No effect
     (iv) Decrease £400
     (v)   Decrease £120

QUESTION 5.9

(A)   BANK RECONCILIATION STATEMENT: 1 FEBRUARY

		£
Balance per bank statement		1,971
Add: O/S lodgment		129
		2,100
Less: O/S cheques – 15		100
Cash book		2,000

(B)   ADJUSTMENTS TO CASH BOOK

Balance per cash book (28 February)		2,949
Add: Dividend		15
		2,964
Less: Bank charges	2	
S/O – loan	120	
Error – lodgment (22nd)	1	
Error – cheque no. 25	10	133
		2,831

(C)   BANK RECONCILIATION STATEMENT: 28 FEBRUARY

			£
Balance per bank statement:			3,160
Add: O/S lodgments		364	
O/S lodgments		291	655
			3,815
Less: O/S cheques – 21		265	
23		234	
24		459	
26		26	984
Adjusted Cash book balance			2,831

QUESTION 5.11

(W1) Opening bank reconciliation – 1 June	£	£
Balance per bank statement		1,200
Add: Outstanding lodgment		260
		1,460
Less: Outstanding cheques:-		
No. 49	371	
No. 58	792	1,163
Balance per Nominal Ledger		297

(W2) Adjusted Cash Book for June

Opening Balance (given)			297
Lodgments		8,273	
		1,923	
		2,495	
		3,042	
	(corrected)	1,948	
		462	
		48	
	(bank given)	192	18,383
			18,680
Cheques	60	1,117	
	61	438	
	62	8,778	
	63	3,000	
	64	590	
	65	711	
	66	522	
	S/O	275	15,431
			3,249

BANK RECONCILIATION STATEMENT – 30 JUNE

Balance per bank statemnt		15,501
Add: Outstanding lodgment		48
		15,549
Less: Oustanding cheques:		
62	8,778	
63	3,000	
66	522	12,300
Balance per Nominal Ledger		3,249

Items requiring further investigation:
1. Why was there a £20 error in lodgment on 21 June?
2. Is the standing order (S/O) of the correct amount?
3. From what source is the Bank Giro lodgment of £192?

QUESTION 6.3

The basic problem with the draft profit and loss account of Stamp Company is that the closing stock of widgets are valued at selling price rather than the cost of production.

ANALYSIS OF COSTS	*Manufacturing*
Direct materials, labour	£100,000
production overheads	70,000
	£170,000

No. of units manufactured	100	
Cost per unit manufactured	£1,700	
Closing stock valuation	£17,000	

REDRAFTED PROFIT AND LOSS ACCOUNT:	£	£
Sales (of goods manufactured)		270,000
Cost of production incurred	170,000	
Less: Closing stock	(17,000)	153,000
Gross Profit on manufacturing		117,000
Administration costs		100,000
Revised profit		17,000

Note: The revised profit is explained entirely by the change in valuation of closing stock.

	£
Reconciliation:	
Profit per draft accounts	30,000
Revised profit (above)	<17,000>
	13,000
Original closing stock valuation	30,000
Revised closing stock valuation	17,000
	13,000

QUESTION 6.4

D.MURPHY LTD.
MANUFACTURING, TRADING AND PROFIT AND LOSS ACCOUNT
FOR YEAR 30 JUNE. 19 . 2

Opening stock of raw materials:		4,700
Purchases of raw materials		27,400
Duty on raw materials		2,040
		34,160
Closing stock of raw materials		5,100
Cost of raw materials consumed		29,060
Direct wages		21,900
		50,960
Factory overheads:		
Depr. - machinery (£10,000 @ 10%)	1,000	
Factory power (2,400 - 130)	2,270	
Factory light	1,200	
Rent and rates (3/4 x 1360)	1,020	5,490
		56,450
Sales		81,950

Opening stock	10,940	
Cost of manufacturing	56,450	
	67,390	
Closing stock	(7,200)	60,190
Gross profit		21,760
Depr. - m/vehicle	800	
Bad debts	700	
Rent and rates (1/4 x 1360)	340	
Office salaries (3,800 + 100)	3,900	
Office expenses	5,000	
Bank charges	100	
	10,840	
Bad debt provision (5,800 x 2.5%) - 500)	(355)	10,485
Net profit		11,275

BALANCE SHEET - 30 JUNE 19 . 2

Fixed assets	Cost	Depr.	£
Property	9,200	–	9,200
Plant	10,000	6,300	3,700
Vehicles	8,000	7,300	700
	27,200	13,600	13,600
Currents assets			
Stock of raw materials		5,100	
Stock of fin. goods		7,200	
Debtors	5,800		
Less: Provision	145		
		5,655	
Prepayments		130	
		18,085	
Current liabilities			
Creditor	4,900		
Accruals (W3)	660		
Overdraft	9,600	(15,160)	2,925
			16,525
Represented by:			
Capital account			8,150
Add: Net profit			11,275
			19,425
Less: drawings			(2,900)
			16,525

QUESTION 6.5

SNAG MANUFACTURING CO. (W1)

MANUFACTURING AND TRADING ACCOUNT FOR YEAR ENDED 31 DEC. 19 . 4

	£	£
Opening stock of raw materials	75,000	
Purchases (net)	195,000	
Less: Closing stock of raw materials	*(83,000)	187,000
Direct labour		125,000

Factory overhead:

Indirect labour	40,000	
Light and heat	35,000	
Insurance	6,000	
Maintenance	8,000	
Miscellaneous overheads	6,000	
Depr. - buildings	9,000	
Depr. - equipment	39,000	
Rates	3,600	*146,600
		458,600
Add : Opening work in progress		21,200
Less : Closing work in progress		*(39,800)
Cost of goods manufactured (given)		440,000
Add : Opening stock of fin. goods		50,000
Less : Closing stock of fin. goods		*(60,000)
Cost of goods sold (given)		430,000

	200,000 Units	100,000 Units
Direct materials	93.5p per unit	187p per unit
Depr. equipment	19.5p per unit	39p per unit

* Requirements of question.

QUESTION 6.7

(*a*) CALCULATION OF CLOSING STOCK UNDER FIFO

X:	200 Units @ £7	=	1,400
Y:	100 Units @ £11	=	1,100
	Total closing stock value		£2,500

(*b*) TRADING AND PROFIT AND LOSS ACCOUNT

	£	£
Sales (W1)		11,900
Cost of Goods Sold		
Purchases (W2)	10,200	
Less: Closing stock	(2,500)	7,700
Gross Profit		4,200
Less: Bad debt (11,900 x 5%)		(595)
Net Profit		3,605

Workings:
1. *Sales Computation*

X :	400 Units x £11	=	4,400
Y :	500 Units x £15	=	7,500
	Total Sales		£11,900

2. Purchases

X:	100 Units	x £5	=	500	
	200 "	x £6	=	1,200	
	300 "	x £7	=	2,100	
Y:	200 "	x £10	=	2,000	
	400 "	x £11	=	4,400	
				£10,200	

QUESTION 6.8
(*a*)

· Debtor control account

(W1) Jan.-Mar. 19 2	Sales	8,000	Bank	142,000
Apr. -Jun. "	"	20,500	Discount allowed	2,400
Jul. - Sep. "	"	56,700	Balance c/d	5,500
Oct.-Dec. "	"	64,700		
		149,900		149,900

Creditors control account

Bank	95,000	(W2) Jan.- Mar. ' 2	Purchases	12,500
Discount received	1,800	Apr. - Jun. "	"	22,750
		Jul. - Sep. "	"	39,500
Balance c/d	31,950	Oct. - Dec. "	"	54,000
	128,750			128,750

Workings

1. *Credit Sales*

	A		B		£
Jan. - Mr. 19 2	(400 x £10)	+	(200 x £20)	=	8,000
Apr. - Jun.	(1,100 x £11)	+	(400 x £21)	=	20,500
Jul.- Sep.	(2,500 x £13)	+	(1,100 x £22)	=	56,700
Oct. - Dec.	(2,500 x £13)	+	(1,400 x £23)	=	64,700
					£149,900

2. *Purchases on Credit*

	A		B		C
Jan. - Mar 19 2	(1,500 x £5)	+	(500 x £10)	=	12,500
Apr. - Jun.	(1,500 x £6)	+	(1,250 x £11)	=	22,750
Jul. - Sep.	(3,500 x £7)	+	(1,250 x £12)	=	39,500
Oct. - Dec.	(3,500 x £8)	+	(2,000 x £13)	=	54,000
					£128,750

3. *Cash Sales*

					£
Jan-Mar 19 2	(200 x £10)	+	(200 x £19)	=	5,800
Apr -Jun	(500 x £10)	+	(400 x £20)	=	13,000
Jul-Sept	(500 x £12)	+	(100 x £21)	=	8,100
Oct-Dec	(600 x £12)	+	(300 x £22)	=	13,800
					£40,700

(*b*) CLOSING STOCK COMPUTATION

A:	Units purchased	10,000
	Units sold	(8,300)
	Units of stock (A)	1,700
	Cost p.u.	x £8
	Value of stock A	£13,600
B:	Units purchased	5,000
	Sold	4,100
	Units of stock B	900
	Cost p.u.	x £13
	Value of stock B	£11,700

Therefore, total closing stock value = £13,600 + £11,700
= £25,300

(*c*) TRADING AND PROFIT AND LOSS ACCOUNT FOR THE YEAR ENDED
31 DECEMBER, 19 . 2

	£	£
Sales – Credit (W1)	149,900	
Cash (W3)	40,700	190,600
Cost of Sales		
Purchases	128,750	
Closing stock	(21,800)	(106,950)
Gross profit		83,650
Less: Discount allowed	2,400	
Bad debts	550	(2,950)
		80,700
Add: Discount received		1,800
Net profit		£82,500

QUESTION 6.9
Fixed production costs per tonne:
Units produced –

Purchase of raw material (tonnes) 52 x 100 =	5,200
Deduct: quantity unused	400
Production (tonnes)	4,800

Fixed cost for year   £196, 000
Cost per tonne   £196,000/4,800   =   £40.84
Fixed Selling Costs per tonne

Sales (tonnes) = Production less stock   =   4,800 - 600   =   4,200

Selling costs for year   £25,000
Cost per tonne   £25,000/£4,200   =   £5.95
Costs (per tonne)

Raw material

Material	120
Customs duty	5
Carriage	15
	140

Finished product

Raw material as above	140.00	
Labour	10.00 ⎫	
Production overheads	20.00 ⎬	Conversion costs £70.84
Fixed production o'heads	40.84 ⎭	
	210.84	

Net realisable value (per tonne)
• Finished product

Sale price	215.0
Less delivery costs	(8.00)
Selling costs	(5.95)
NRV	201.05

• Raw material

NRV of finished product	201.05
Less: Costs of conversion to finish product	(70.84)
NRV of raw material	130.21

Basis of valuation of stocks
Lower of cost or net realisable value
Raw material

Cost –	140.00
NRV	130.21
Therefore valuation per tonne	130.21

Finished product

Cost	210.84
NRV	201.05
Therefore valuation per tonne	201.05

Aggregate value of stocks at 31 December 19 . 6

Raw material – 400 x 130.21 =	£52,084
Finished Product – 600 x 201.05 =	£120,630
	£172,714

QUESTION 7.1

BALANCE SHEET AT 30 APRIL 19 . 7

Fixed Assets	Cost	Aggregate Depreciation	£
Lease	3,000	1,000	2,000
Equipment	3,000	500	2,500
	6,000	1,500	4,500

Current Assets		
Stocks (£2,100 x 100/125)	1,680	
Prepaid rates (1/3 x 900)	300	
Debtors (1,900 x 68)	1,968	
Bank (W1)	117	4,065
		8,565

Financed by:	
Capital	5,000
Less: Drawings (52 x £40)	(2,080)
Profit for period	2,967*
	5,887

Current liabilities		
Creditors (W2)	1,453	
Accruals (150 + 55)	205	
Term loan (2,000 - 980)	1,020	2,678
		8,565

(WI) Bank reconciliation statement at 30 April 19x7	
Balance per bank statement	(414) overdrawn
Add: Outstanding lodgment	800
Less: Outstanding cheque	(269)
	117

(W2) Computation of closing creditors	
Balance per suppliers' statements (given)	1,750
Less: Error in invoice	(54)
Cheque in transit	(243)
	1,453

Points relevant to profit calculation
1. Depends entirely on the accuracy of valuation of assets and liabilities in closing balance sheet.
2. Not acceptable for computing tax liabilities on an on-going basis.
3. Does not provide detailed information in relation to revenues and especially costs. Thus we have an inadequate accounting system for managerial decision-making.

QUESTION 7.4

D. BRADY

TRADING AND PROFIT AND LOSS A/C FOR YEAR ENDED 31.12.19 . 2

Sales		55,000
Opening stock	1,900	
Purchases	22,000	
	23,900	
Less: Closing stock	2,400	21,500
Gross profit		33,500
Depreciation of motor vehicle	560	
Loss on sales of vehicle	200	
Wages	12,040	
Rent and rates	1,550	
General expenses	17,520	
Discount allowed	1,255	33,125
		375
Add: Discount received		1,980
Deposit interest		45
Staff loan interest		45
Net profit		2,445

BALANCE SHEET AT 31.12.19 . 2

Fixed assets			Capital (W1)	5,940
			Add: net profit	2,445
Motor vehicle		5,040	Less: drawings	(4,215)
				4,170
Current assets:			Current liabilities:	
Stock		2,400	Creditors	2,900
Debtors		5,000	Accruals (270 + 450)	720
Sundry receivable		45	Bank overdraft	5,295
Staff loan		600		
		13,085		13,085

Debtors control

Balance (opening)	4,000	Discount allowed	1,255
Sales	55,000	Cash	52,745
		Balance (closing)	5,000
	59,000		59,000

Creditors

Bank	17,820	Balance (opening)	700
Discount received	1,980	Purchases	22,000
Balance (closing)	2,900		
	22,700		22,700

Motor vehicle

Balance (opening)	1,000	Disposal	1,000
Bank	4,800		
Disposal (trade-in)	800	Balance (closing)	5,600

Wages

Bank	8,980	Balance (opening)	400
Bank	2,960	Balance (opening)	220
Balance	450		
Balance	270	Profit and loss	12,040

Cash

		Bank	49,855
Debtors	52,745	Drawings	2,250
		Expenses	640

Deposit

Bank	1,000	Bank	1,045
Profit and loss account	45		

Loan interest receivable (10%)

Profit and loss account	45	Balance (9/12)	45
Balance	45		

Rents and rates

Bank	1,550	Profit and loss account	1,550

General expenses

Bank	14,480	Profit and loss account	17,520
Bank	2,400		
Cash	640		

Disposal

Motor vehicle	1,000	Trade-in value	800
		Loss on sale	200

Drawings

Bank	1,965		
Cash	2,250	Capital	4,215

(W1) Opening capital

	£ Assets	£ Liabilities
Bank	360	
Creditors		700
Debtors	4,000	
Motor vehicle	1,000	
Stock	1,900	
PAYE etc.		220
Wages		400
	7,260	1,320

Capital = (Assets - Liabilities) £5,940

QUESTION 7.7

B O'HARA
(WI) TRADING ACCOUNT FOR YEAR ENDED 31 DECEMBER 19 . 1

	£	£
Sales		45,420
Opening stock	9,369	
Purchases	36,592	
	45,961	
Closing stock	(9,625)	36,336
Gross profit (20%)		9,084

COMPUTATION OF CLOSING STOCK, 30 APRIL 19 . 2

	£	£
Sales		11,612
Less sales returns		37
Net sales		11,575
Opening stock	9,625	
Purchases	9,216	
	18,841	
Gross profit (20% x 11,575)	2,315	
	21,156	11,575
∴ Closing stock (21,156 - 11,575) =		9,581

COMPUTATION OF STOCK DESTROYED

Closing stock (computed above)	9,581
Less: Salvaged (given)	308
Stock destroyed	9,273

QUESTION 9.1

RODGERS LIMITED
PROFIT AND LOSS ACCOUNT FOR YEAR ENDED 31 JANUARY 198 .

	£	£
Turnover		2,750
Less: Cost of Sales		
Opening stock	400	
Purchases	1,188	
Less: Closing stock (WI)	(522)	1,066
Gross Profit		1,684
Expenses:		
Depreciation: Buildings	400	
Depreciation: Fixtures	96	
Rents and rates	220	
Salaries and Wages	70	
Advertising	170	
Bad Debts	200	
Light and heat	65	(1,221)
Operating Profit		463
Interest payable		(60)
Net Profit before taxation		403
Tax		(100)
Net Profit after		303
Less: Dividends		
Ordinary – paid	30	
– proposed	80	
Preference – proposed	20	(130)
Profit of the financial year		173
Profit brought forward		1,006
Profit carried forward		1,179

(W1) Units sold during year   =   95 units

Opening stock	40	
Purchases	89	= 129
Closing stock (units)		34

Valued as follows: (23 @ £16) + (11 @ £14) = £522

QUESTION 9.3

STANTON CONCRETE LTD
BALANCE SHEET AT 31.12.19 . 8

	£	£
Fixed assets		
Tangible assets (W1)		138,800
Current Assets		
Stock		55,800
Debtors		79,600
Investments (Market value £..)		9,300
Cash		1,000
		145,700
Creditors (amounts falling due within one year) (W2)		88,100
Net Current Assets		57,600
Total assets less current liabilities		196,400
Financed by:		
Creditors (amounts falling due after more than one year)		68,700
Capital and Reserves		
Ordinary share capital		77,000
Revaluation reserve		7,200
Profit and loss account		43,500
		127,700
		196,400

(W1) Schedule of tangible assets	Cost	Agg.Depr	£
Freehold land and buildings	85,800	11,300	74,500
Plant and machinery	92,900	47,100	45,800
Motor vehicles	34,500	16,000	18,500
	213,200	74,400	138,800

(W2) Creditors (amounts fallling due within one year)

Creditors	59,700
Bank overdraft	8,900
Tax due	15,700
Proposed dividends	3,800
	88,100

QUESTION 9.6

This question tests the ability to handle accounting adjustments and to present final accounts in good order.

	£000	£000	£000
Sales		750	
Less: Returns inwards		3	
			747
Opening stock	200		
Purchases	350		
Less: Returns outwards	1		
	349		
Carriage inwards	1		
	550		
Less: Closing stock	(180)		
Cost of sales			(370)
Gross profit			377
Discounts (allowed 3 less received 1)	2		
Carriage outwards	1		
General expenses (200 less 2 less 1)	197		
Advertising	10		
Debenture interest	10		
Depreciation – vehicles	20		
– machinery	10		
Bad debt expenses (20 + 3)	23		
Accountancy	1		
Total expenses			274
Net profit			103
Dividend			10
Profit retained for year			93
Profit and loss account brought forward			100
Profit and loss account carried forward			193

BALANCE SHEET AS AT 31 DECEMBER 19 . 7

Fixed assets	Cost/Valuation £000	Depr. £000	NBV £000
Buildings	260		260
Motor vehicles	100	80	20
Machinery	120	60	60
	480	140	340
Currents assets			
Stock		180	
Debtors	180		
Less: Provision	9		
		171	
Sundry		3	
		354	

Less: Creditors (amounts falling due with in one year)		
Creditors	200	
Debenture interest	5	
Accounancy fees	1	
Dividends	10	
Bank balance	5	
	221	
Net current assets		133
Total assets less current liablities		473
Creditors (amounts falling due after more than one year)		100
Net assets		373

Financed by:

	£000
Called-up share capital (200,000 @ 50p shares)	100
Share premium	50
Revaluation reserve	30
Profit and loss account	193
	373

QUESTION 9.10

R.JONES LTD
(a)   BALANCE SHEET AT 31 DECEMBER, 19 . 6

Fixed assets	*Cost*	*Agg.Depr.*	*£*
Equipment	25,000	5,000	20,000
Motor vehicles	11,000	2,750	8,250
	36,000	7,750	28,250
Current assets			
Stock		9,000	
Debtors (9000 – 1600)	7,400		
Less: Provision	(740)		
		6,660	
Prepayments (1,200 x 3/15)		240	
Bank		10,000	
Cash		290	26,190
			54,440
Financed by:			
Share capital			50,000
Loss for year			(8,010)
Long-term loan			5,000
Current liabilities:			
Creditors		7,000	
Accruals (£5,000 x 12% x 9/12)		450	7,450
			54,440

Reconciliation of Opening and Closing Reserves

Original Profit figure		3,400
Less: Depreciation	7,750	
Bad debts	1,600	
Bad debts provision	740	
Stock w/o	1,000	
Cash discrepancy	110	
Interest arrears	450	(11,650)
		(8,250)
Add: Prepaid rates		240
		(8,010)

(b)   Limitations of Depreciation under Historic Cost

1. Does not take into consideration replacement cost of the fixed asset.
2. Subjectivity involved in estimating useful life and residual value.
3. Choice between fixed instalment and reducing balance may distort profit performance.
4. Depreciation is in accordance with the accruals convention to write-off historic cost of asset over estimated useful life.

QUESTION 10.3

No, I do not agree with the managing director's analysis in these circumstances. Whilst I fully accept the two points that he has made, and also agree that his sentiments have substance, I believe that he had not used all the information available to him and that his actions have distorted the accounts of Contract Contracting Ltd so much that they do not represent a true and fair view. The materiality of the contract requires consideration.

The position on the contact with metal tools is:

	Per the Accounts	In reality
Profit and Loss:		
Sales	600,000	300,000
Costs	(560,000)	280,000
	40,000	20,000
Balance Sheet:		
Debtors	390,000	90,000
Stock	Nil	280,000*
	390,000	370,000
Profit	40,000	20,000

* Half of contract.

Thus, the net profit should be reduced by £20,000, being the reduction in the above contribution. Appropriate adjustments should be made to the balance sheet.

The argument that the managing director used has failed to account for two circumstances, namely:

(a) Metal Tools Ltd may not take all the goods they contract for.
(b) Some of the goods may be returned as faulty.

QUESTION 10.6

The Accounting Standards Committee issued in November 1971 a statement of standard accounting practice *Disclosure of Accounting Policies* which required all companies to disclose their accounting policies in financial accounts on or after 1 January 1972. Accounting policies were defined as the specific accounting bases judged by business enterprises to be most appropriate to their circumstances and adopted by them for the purposes of preparing their financial accounts.

Five possible sub-headings that might be included in the annual report and accounts, together with the type of information that might be disclosed, would include:

(a) Depreciation of fixed assets—details of the assets which are depreciated and the basis used for calculating depreciation.

(b) Stock Valuation—basis of calculation. In a manufacturing company information about the inclusion of overheads would be appropriate.

(c) Research and Development—whether any element of this item had been capitalised.

(d) Goodwill—basis of calculation of any item included in the balance sheet

(e) Conversion of foreign currencies—state rates of exchange used in converting assets and liabilities at year end.

QUESTION 10.9

(a) SSAP 6 *Extraordinary Items and Prior Year Adjustment* defines extraordinary items as material items which derive from events or transactions that fall outside the ordinary activities of a company and which are therefore not expected to recur frequently or regularly.

An exceptional item is a material item which derives from events or transactions that fall within the ordinary activities of a company, and which needs to be disclosed separately by virtue of its size or incidence if the financial statements are to give a true and fair view.

(b) (i) The profit on the sale of shares in a subsidiary would be an extraordinary item because the shares would not have been purchased with the intention of re-sale (otherwise it would have been a trade investment) and is thus outside the normal activities of the company. Such an amount will probably be material and would not occur frequently or regularly.

(ii) Insurance claims for loss of profits would be part of the ordinary activities of the company, because the amount received is in lieu of profits lost on ordinary activities. Such a claim would probably be material and should be separately disclosed as an exceptional item if the financial statements are to give a true and fair view.

(iii) A change in the basis of taxation would give rise to an extraordinary item. Such changes would probably be material, infrequent and unrelated to the ordinary activities of the company.

(iv) Material redundancy costs may either be extraordinary or exceptional and additional information would be necessary to make a decision. Where they relate to a continuing business segment then they would be exceptional; where they relate to the discontinuance of a segment then the cost would be extraordinary. It is part of the ordinary activities of a business which is a going concern to make changes to the size of the labour force; it is not part of the normal activities to discontinue part of its business.

(v) A material loss on the sale of a fixed asset may be either extraordinary or exceptional and additional information would be necessary on the nature of the event which gave rise to the disposal. A disposal as part of terminating activities within a company would be extraordinary; a disposal as part of the normal replacement of assets would be part of ordinary activities and would only be exceptional because of size, for example, where computer hardware is sold at a substantial loss because of accelerated obsolescence.

QUESTION 11.10

The matters outlined in this question are covered by the requirements of SSAP 17 *Accounting for Post-Balance Sheet Events* as well as the specific SSAPs mentioned in each answer.

(1) This event requires adjustment to the balance sheet as it provides additional evidence as to the true value of the debt of £400,000. The debt of £400,000 will be written-off. Because of its size and incidence in relation to the company, the write-off will be disclosed in the profit and loss account as an exceptional item (SSAP 6). The adjustment is necessary as the event has taken place before the proposed date on which the directors will sign the accounts.

(2) This is an event outside the ordinary activities of the company. It is therefore of an extraordinary nature. In relation to the company, £75,000 is a material item and will be disclosed as an extraordinary item in the profit and loss account after deduction of corporation tax (SSAP 6).

(3) Normally this type of expense is treated as an exceptional item. If, however, it is attributable to the factory closure mentioned in (2) then it has to be included as part of that extraordinary item. It falls to be disclosed (statutorily) as part of the directors' emoluments which must be disclosed in the notes to the accounts.

(4) As the claimant has not accepted the £17,000 offer, the figure of £20,000 is the liability. As this liability existed at the balance sheet date it is necessary to adjust the financial accounts. The claim is not a contingent claim as it is admitted that it is reasonable.

(5) This is an event which does not require the financial statements to be adjusted. However, this is a material event which would, if not disclosed, affect the ability of the user of the company's accounts to arrive at a proper understanding of the financial state of the company. Disclosure should be effected by means of a note indicating an after-tax proceeds of £570K and a net surplus over book value of £44K.

(6) This is a matter which , although material, is not an event which requires adjusting in the financial accounts. However, it must be disclosed by way of a note to the accounts indicating:

(a) the general nature of the claim
(b) the likely outcome—20% (or a statement to the effect that the company had received legal opinion indicating that the claim was unlikely to succeed).
(c) the financial effect (or a statement that it is not practicable to make such an estimate)
(d) the taxation implication (SSAP 18)

(7) Settlement of this claim provides evidence of the actual liability at Balance Sheet date. It is, therefore, no longer a contingent liability; the agreed liability needs to be provided for in the accounts. Consequently the excess of £10K should be written back as it is no longer necessary. This is not an exceptional item as it is not material; neither is it a prior year's adjustment because it is a normal adjustment of an accounting estimate made in a prior year. (SSAP 6)

QUESTION 12.1

H LTD
CONSOLIDATED BALANCE SHEET AT 31 DECEMBER 19 . 1

	£
Assets	
Goodwill arising on consolidation (W1)	10
Stock	150
Bank	40
	200
Financed by:	
Share capital (holding company)	200

W1. Goodwill arising on consolidation	£
Cost of investment in subsidiary by H Ltd	110
Less: Shares acquires in S Ltd	(100)
Goodwill arising on consolidation	10

QUESTION 12.3

H LTD
CONSOLIDATED BALANCE SHEET AT 31 DECEMBER 19 . 1

	£
Fixed assets	1,900
Goodwill arising on consolidation (W1)	200
Stock	1,300
Debtors	900
Bank	500
	4,800

	£
Financed by:	
Share capital (holding company)	4,000
Minority interests (40% x £2,000)	800
	4,800

(W1) Goodwill arising on consolidation	
Cost of investment in S Ltd	1,400
Shares acquired in S Ltd (2,400/4,000) = 60% x 2,000	1,200
Goodwill arising on consolidation	200

QUESTION 12.5

CONSOLIDATED PROFIT AND LOSS ACCOUNT
FOR YEAR ENDED 31 DECEMBER 19 . 1

	£
Turnover	200,000
Operating costs	90,000
Profit on ordinary activities before taxation	110,000
Tax on profit on ordinary activities	49,000
Profit on ordinary activities after tax	61,000
Minority interests (25% x £16,000)	4,000
Profit for the financial year attributable to group shareholders	57,000
Dividends	30,000
Profit retained for the year	27,000
Profit brought forward	10,000
Profit carried forward	37,000

QUESTION 12.7

(W1) BALANCE SHEET OF PREDATOR PLC AFTER TAKEOVER

	£000
Share capital	80
Revenue Reserves	60
	140
Net assets (cash)	92
Investment in Victim	48
	140

PREDATOR PLC
CONSOLIDATED BALANCE SHEET AT 1 JUNE 19 . 8

Goodwill arising on consolidation (W2)	22,400
Net assets (cash) (92 + 32)	124,000
	146,400
Financed by:	
Share capital	80,000
Revenue Reserve	60,000
Minority interest (20% x 32,000)	6,400
	146,400
(W2) Goodwill arising on consolidation	
Cost of acquisition	48,000
Net assets acquired (80% x 32,000)	(25,600)
	22,400

QUESTION 12.8

(*a*) An associated company is an company which is not a subsidiary of an investing company and in which:

  (*i*) the interest of the investing company is effectively that of a partner in a joint venture and the investing company can exercise a significant influence over the investee; or

  (*ii*) the interest of the investing company is for the long term and is substantial, and the investing company is in a position to exercise significant influence over the investee.

Significant influence over a company essentially involves participation in the financial decisions of the investee, for example by representation on the board of directors. Where the interest of the investor is not that of a partner in a joint venture then significant influence will be presumed to exist where the investor holds 20% or more of the equity voting rights of a company, unless circumstances suggest otherwise. These circumstances include the disposition of the other shares, particularly where there are a few substantial shareholdings. Where the investor holds less than 20% of the equity voting shares no significant influence over the investee will be presumed to exist, unless circumstances suggest otherwise, Evidence to support these circumstances would normally be obtained from the directors of the investee confirming that they accept that the investor can exercise significant influence over it.

(*b*)

	£000
Cost of investment	150
Post-acquisition profits	
(250 – 150) x 30%	30
	180

QUESTION 14.2

(*a*) Current assets include debtors,cash and bank balances and short-term investment. Current liabilities are all those items due for payment within twelve months of the balance sheet date. This is the most common definition but it may include, particularly amongst the liabilities, many special items e.g. taxation and dividends. Another definition which reflects the working capital cycle excludes the special items, but at the appropriate time funds must be available to meet the required payments.

	£	£
(*b*) Current assets		
Stock		60,000
Debtors		40,000
Bank and cash balance		55,000
		155,000
Deduct Current liabilities		
Trade creditors	45,000	
Taxation	20,000	
Dividend proposed	15,000	
		80,000
Net current assets i.e, working capital		£75,000

(*c*)   Cost of sales:

	£
Opening stock	90,000
Add: Purchases	140,000
Less: Closing stock	(60,000)
Cost of sales	170,000

Average stock (£90,000 + 60,000) divide by 2 = £75,000

Stock turnover rate	*Debtor days*
$\dfrac{75,000}{170,000}$ x 360 = 159 days	$\dfrac{40,000}{240,000}$ x 360 = 60 days

Thus, ignoring any trade credit received, the cash-to-cash cycle is 159 days plus 60 days = 219 days, i.e, the length of time taken for goods purchased to be converted back into cash form.

QUESTION 14.6
(a)

	A		B	
Gearing	$\dfrac{100}{200}$	= 50%	$\dfrac{130}{650}$	= 20%
Current ratio	$\dfrac{180}{160}$	= 1.12%	$\dfrac{200}{120}$	= 5.3
Acid test ratio	$\dfrac{100}{160}$	= .62%	$\dfrac{100}{120}$	= .83%
ROOE	$\dfrac{30}{100}$	= 30%	$\dfrac{100}{360}$	= 28%
ROCE	$\dfrac{30+10}{200}$	= 20%	$\dfrac{100+13}{650}$	= 17%
$\dfrac{\text{Gross profit}}{\text{Sales}}$	$\dfrac{600}{1,000}$	= 60%	$\dfrac{1,000}{3,000}$	= 33%
$\dfrac{\text{Net profit}}{\text{Sales}}$	$\dfrac{30}{1,000}$	= 3%	$\dfrac{100}{3,000}$	= 3%
$\dfrac{\text{Debtors x 365}}{\text{Sales}}$	$\dfrac{100 \times 365}{1,000}$	= 36 days	$\dfrac{90 \times 365}{3,000}$	= 11 days
$\dfrac{\text{Creditors x 365}}{\text{Cost of sales}}$	$\dfrac{110 \times 365}{400}$	= 100 days	$\dfrac{120 \times 365}{2,000}$	= 22 days

(*b*) Whilst A and B have very similar net profit to sales percentages, they reach this point in different ways. A has a high gross profit percentage (lower turnover, higher margin) and a higher ROCE. Its materially higher gearing ratio turns this slightly higher ROCE into a considerably higher ROOE. From a shareholder viewpoint most of this makes A preferable to B. But it should be remembered that B has more 'slack' in its structure. a lender might well feel happier granting further loans to B—lower gearing ratio, better liquidity ratios. A's debtors' payback and, particularly worryingly, creditors' payback, periods are much higher.

It must be noted that B's balance sheet includes a large revaluation of its land. This is a major inconsistency, and distorts the figures considerably. In terms of return on original investments, ROOE and ROCE for B are considerably understated. Perhaps more usefully to you, in terms of return on amount invested, ROOE and ROCE for A are overstated.

QUESTION 14.8

This is a test of ability to produce absolute figures from a given set of relationships in ration form.

M. SMITH
FORECAST TRADING AND PROFIT AND LOSS ACCOUNT
FOR YEAR ENDED 31 DECEMBER 19 . 6

	£	£
Sales (100/(100 − 28) x cost of sales)		140,000
Opening stock	20,000	
Purchases	97,800	
	117,800	
Closing stock ((18,500 x 2) - 20,000)	(17,000)	
Cost of sales (derived)		100,800
Gross profit (28% x sales)		39,200
Expenses (derived)		(25,200)
Net profit for the year (10% x sales)		£14,000

M. SMITH : FORECAST BALANCE SHEET AS AT 31 DECEMBER

	£	£
Fixed assets (1.5 + 1.0) x net assets employed		30,000
Current assets		
Stocks [per trading account]	17,000	
Debtors [(140,000 x 36.5)/365]	14,000	
Bank	5,000	
[equal to 2.25 x current liabilities]	36,000	
Current liabilities		
Creditors [(97,800 x 58.40)/365]	15,650	
Accruals	350	
	16,000	
Working capital		20,000
Net assets employed [(140,000/2.8]		£50,000
Financed by:		
Capital : opening	40,000	
: net profit of year	14,000	
	54,000	
: drawings	(10,000)	
: closing		44,000
Long-term loan		6,000
		£50,000

QUESTION 15.1
Note: Different formats are acceptable

MR. WOOD
FUNDS FLOW STATEMENT FOR 19 . 2

	£	£
Net profit for year		45,000
Add: Depreciation		6,000
Funds from operations		51,000
Changes in working capital		
Increased stocks	(50,000)	
Increased debtors	(114,000)	
Increased creditors	58,000	(106,000)
		(55,000)
Application of funds		
Purchase of fixed assets (W1)	(8,000)	
Taxation paid (W2)	(15,000)	
		(23,000)
Sources of funds		
Share issue	10,000	
Debentures issued	10,000	20,000
Net decrease in net liquid funds		(58,000)

Proof:	19 . 7	19 . 8
Bank overdraft	(45,000)	(104,000)
Cash	1,000	2,000
Net liquid balance	(44,000)	(102,000)

(58,000)

W.1. Reconciliation of fixed assets

Opening balance	37,000
Additions	8,000 (must be balancing figure)
	45,000
Disposals	Nil
Depreciation (given)	6,000
Closing balance	39,000
	45,000

(W2)   Taxation account

* Bank	15,000	Opening balance	5,000
Closing balance	9,000	P/L account	19,000
	24,000		24,000
		Balance	9,000

QUESTION 15.5

SPORTS AND LEISURE CLUB
FUNDS FLOW STATEMENT FOR YEAR ENDED 31 DECEMBER 199 .

	£	£
Surplus for year		3,500
Add: Depreciation		2,500
		6,000
Movement in Working Capital		
Increase in stocks	(2,000)	
Increase in debtors (subscriptions due)	(1,500)	
Decrease in creditors	(3,000)	(6,500)
		(500)
Sources of funds		
Increase in bank loan		7,500
		7,000
Application of funds		
Purchases of fixed assets		(9,000)
Decrease in cash resources during year		(2,000)
Proof:		
Opening cash balance	2,500	
Closing cash balance	500	
Total decrease in cash position	(2,000)	

QUESTION 15.7

MALT LTD
CASH FUNDS FLOW STATEMENT FOR YEAR ENDED 31 DECEMBER 19 . 7

	£	£
Net trading profit (3,187 + 114)		3,301
Add: Depreciation (W2)		1,696
		4,997
Changes in working capital		
Increase in stocks	(2,207)	
Increase in debtors	(149)	
Increase in creditors	+ 735	(1,621)
		3,376
Other Sources		
Share issue	1,500	
Sale of fixed asset (W3)	886	
		2,386
Payments:		
Purchase of fixed assets (W1)	(7,361)	
Dividends	(622)	
Repayments of debenture	(1,000)	(8,983)
		(3,221)

Overdraft	31/12/19 . 6		1,516
"	31/12/19 . 7		4,737
Total movement in cash resources			<3,221>

(W1)		Fixed Asset Account—Cost		
	Bal.	6,723	Disposal	2,070
	∴ Bank	7,361	Bal.	12,014

(W2)		Fixed Asset—Agg. Depr.		
	Disposal	1,070	Bal	2,946
	Bal.	3,572	Depreciation	1,696

(W3)		Disposal		
	Cost	2,070	Agg. Depr.	1,070
			∴ Bank	886
			Loss	114

QUESTION 16.1

(a)   Based on PE ratios

	19.2 £
Post-tax profits (reported)	25,000
Add: back 50% of director's remuneration	12,000
Less: Depreciation of property	(2,000)
	35,000
Less: Tax @ 40% (excluding depr.*)	14,800
After-tax profits	20,200

	PE RATIOS	10	15
Earnings (19 . 2 = £20,200)		£202,000	£303,000
Share value (50,000 shares in issue)		4.04	6.06

(b)   *Dividend Yield Method*

Current dividend = £3,000

Dividend yield = 2%

Company valuation (£3,000 x 100/2) = £150,000

Share value = £3

* Depreciation is not allowable in computing taxation liabilities in Ireland.

(*c*) *Break-up value, based on balance sheet at 19 . 2*

	£
Property	169,000
Equipment	24,000
Stock	17,000
Debtors	76,500
	286,500
Less: Trade creditors	(34,000)
Long-term loan	(10,000)
	£242,500

$$\frac{£242,500}{50,000} = \underline{\underline{£4.85 \text{ per share}}}$$

(*d*) The method of valuation suggested by Bolmin's directors is arbritrary. There is no indication of the basis for the calculation. Its result is less than the value placed on Tooden Repairs through an analysis of break-up values, but it is excessive when compared to the earning power of similar companies.

All methods identified have their weaknesses. This is particularly so in the case of the balance sheet approach. These figures are found on historical costs and completely ignore questions of goodwill, current values, potential synergy and the earning power of similar companies.

In a going-concern situation, the break-up value is not usually a significant method but the relatively high valuation in this case does suggest that the director's method of valuation would produce a potential gain even if it were decied to close Tooden Repairs immediately.

Earning yield in comparison with other companies depends on the similarities between the two companies. The amount of available information may be limited and the judgment of the person making the comparison may be defective. In any case, it is the prospect of maintaining earnings and dividends into the future which is critical. In view of the high valuation resulting from the directors'approach when compared with similar companies' earnings a further look at the multiple or the method itself is probably called for.

QUESTION 16.3

(*a*) *Price earnings ratios before merger*

	Giant	Minnow
Profits after taxation—£ m.	50	10
Number of issued shares—millions	200	50
Earnings per share—pence	25	20
Share price—pence	500	200
Price earnings ratio—times	20	10

The earnings ratio of Giant is double that of Minnow. This indicates that the stock market is prepared to pay more for Giant's earnings per share than for Minnow's, in the expectation that Giant's earnings will grow at a faster rate than those of Minnow.

(b) Price earnings ratio of the group after merger

		£ Million
Earnings of Giant		50
Earnings of Minnow		10
Increased contribution from Minnow		3
	A	63
Number of shares in issue before the takeover		200
Giant shares issued for Minnow		25
Number of Giant shares after takeover	B	225
Earnings per share of Group A/B		28p

Price earnings ratio

$$\frac{\text{Share price of Giant}}{\text{Earnings per share of Giant}} = \frac{550p}{28p} = 19.6 \text{ times}$$

(c) Dividend income

Before the merger
Minnow — total dividend declared	£7 million
Number of issued shares	50 million
Dividend per share	14p

After the merger
Giant — total dividend declared before the merger	£20 million
Number of shares issued	200 million
Dividend per share	10p

If Giant continues to pay 10p net, then adjusting for the share issue Minnow shareholders will be receiving 1/2 x 10.00 = 5p dividend x 2 shares, i. e. 10p where they would have previously received 14p net per share i.e. 28p.

(d) Giant is a more profitable company than Minnow and is also more soundly financed. The ratios below summarise some of the key features:

	Giant	Minnow
Return on equity	$\frac{50}{250}$ x 100 = 20%	$\frac{10}{60}$ x 100 = 17%
Gearing	$\frac{100}{50 + 100}$ x 100 = 29%	$\frac{60}{60 + 60}$ x 100 = 50%
Acid-test	$\frac{300 - 100}{200}$ = 1.0	$\frac{70 - 50}{70}$ = 0.3

Although Minnow is profitable, its liquidity and gearing must give rise to some concern. Giant's price earings ratio at 20 is double that of Minnow's, indicating the market's greater confidence in Giant's earnings potential. The bid is worth 250p for each Minnow share which is currently standing at 200p and, therefore, Minnow's shareholders will have an immediate capital gain of approximately 25 per cent. However, as illustrated in the last part of the answer, they will have a reduced dividend income after the bid.

However, the Minnow shareholders, if they wished to restore their income to pre-bid levels, can sell their Giant shares and reinvest the proceeds in higher yielding securities.

Index